Reforming Fundamentalism

FULLER SEMINARY
AND THE NEW EVANGELICALISM

by
GEORGE MARSDEN

WILLIAM B. EERDMANS PUBLISHING COMPANY
GRAND RAPIDS, MICHIGAN

Copyright © 1987 by William B. Eerdmans Publishing Co.
255 Jefferson Ave. S.E., Grand Rapids, Michigan 49503

Library of Congress Cataloging-in-Publication Data

Marsden, George, 1939–
Reforming fundamentalism.

Includes bibliographical references.
1. Fundamentalism—History.
2. Evangelicalism—United States—History—20th century.
3. Fuller Theological Seminary.   I. Title.
BT82.2.M38 1987   207′.79493   87-22243

ISBN 0-8028-3642-9

Illustrations on pages 283 and 284 from *The Wittenburg Door*. Used by permission.

Illustration on page 295 used by permission of Creation House, Altamonte Springs, Fla., from *Signs and Wonders Today* by C. Peter Wagner, © July 1985.

Contents

To My Family,
Lucie, Greg, and Brynne:
God's Gift of Wonderful Companions

The Shaping of a History

I N the early 1980s, as the author of a book on early twentieth-century fundamentalism, I suddenly found myself involved in current events.[1] Until then I had usually followed the conventions of the historical profession and worked on topics that only other historians were likely to learn about. Indeed, when I began working on fundamentalism in the early 1970s, most Americans were only dimly aware even of what that term might mean. By 1980, though, when my history appeared, Ronald Reagan had just been elected, and fundamentalists seemed everywhere. Once again, H. L. Mencken's quip seemed apt: "Heave an egg out a Pullman window, and you will hit a Fundamentalist almost anywhere in the United States today."[2]

The sudden and unforeseen popularity of my subject forced me to abandon plans to work on a topic truly buried in the past and to attempt a sequel instead. So I set out to write *Son of Fundamentalism*, a volume that would trace what had happened to fundamentalism since its heyday in the 1920s. Much of the discussion would focus on the sharp contests after World War II between two sets of fundamentalist heirs: neo-evangelicals and strict separatist fundamentalists. But the book would also have surveyed the recent re-emergence of broader evangelicalism, the new political fundamentalism, and the transforming impact of the charismatic revival.

Even an overview of these subjects would be a massive undertaking, however, especially since one of the chief features of these movements is their fragmentation. Each of the almost countless subgroups has its own emphases, institutions, and personalities, making responsible generalization extremely difficult. Moreover, as an outsider I could not hope to reconstruct the histories of these disparate groups and match an insider's knowledge except with the most careful historical research.

While I was still gathering material and looking for themes with which to tie together this remarkably complex subject, David Hubbard, president of Fuller Theological Seminary, asked me whether I would be willing to write the history of that institution. I immediately told him that I might be interested—not in writing an institutional history but rather in using Fuller as

1. See my *Fundamentalism and American Culture: The Shaping of Twentieth Century Evangelicalism, 1870–1925* (New York: Oxford, 1980).
2. H. L. Mencken, "Prejudices: Fifth Series" (first published New York, 1926) in *The Discontent of the Intellectuals: A Problem of the Twenties*, ed. Henry May (Chicago: Rand McNally, 1963), 30.

a window through which to focus my study of recent evangelicalism and fundamentalism. As it turned out, this was not far from Hubbard's own conception. Indeed, he seemed little interested in a conventional institutional history. Already in 1979 he had told his board that the history should "make a contribution to the larger evangelical history" with which the seminary's story was "so interwoven."[3] Although the seminary was willing to fund the project generously, Hubbard insisted that the history was not to serve as a seminary promotional piece. Clearly he was concerned most that the seminary's remarkable early history be recorded while many of the first generation were still available to provide first-hand accounts. Other than that, the chief value of the history for the seminary should be to help it better understand both itself and the evangelical movement of which it was a part.

I was impressed also that Hubbard had determined from the start that the historian should have had no previous connections with Fuller. This book, accordingly, is entirely my responsibility. I have had complete control over its content, themes, and selection of publisher. As to the latter, William B. Eerdmans was the obvious choice. Not only are they a publisher of distinguished books; they have also had a long and mutually beneficial relationship with Fuller Theological Seminary that deserves to be honored.

In the course of my research I talked to almost all the surviving faculty members from the seminary's early decades, including some no longer connected with the institution or sympathetic to its current tendencies. With two exceptions, one on each side of the major controversies of the seminary, everyone was cooperative. I also interviewed a number of past and present members of the board of trustees as well as the cofounder and former president, the late Harold John Ockenga. I wish to thank each who contributed to this history through interviews. Former Fuller students also added considerable insight, both in conversations and in their responses to a survey asking for recollections.

In the process of all this, I learned something of the strengths and weaknesses of oral and recollected history. There is no substitute for meeting the people directly involved. Even in an interview of an hour or two, and even long after the events, one will learn much about the personal dynamics that shaped activities and relationships. Such encounters also provide invaluable clues for further inquiry. A few people, especially some of the relatively young, have excellent memories, so good that they can recall events of thirty years ago in their proper sequence. Most, on the other hand, run events together and provide more by way of general insights and isolated anecdotes.

This sort of oral history is especially advantageous when it can be done in the context of investigating written sources. Such sources, often recounting events within days after they happened, are usually far more reliable than recollection. They also provide a solid gauge of who has a reliable memory, thus indirectly lending credibility to some recollections of events not recorded in the written documents.

3. Fuller Theological Seminary, Annual Board Report, October 19-20, 1979, vi.

Fuller Seminary was entirely cooperative in opening up its records for my historical inquiry. I was never refused permission to see anything. The secretarial staff were especially helpful in trying to find what I was looking for, and they also provided some insights of their own on the seminary's history. Delores Loeding, Wilbur Smith's secretary in the earliest days of the seminary and then faculty secretary at the School of Theology, was an especially astute source of informal opinion.

The written sources available include most of the seminary's records and publications from its early days. These have not been preserved systematically, but searches, including digging through some very dusty basement rooms, turned up enough to answer most questions. In addition a few collections of letters were available. Daniel Fuller provided many papers from his parents, and the seminary has preserved much of the correspondence of its deans. The Billy Graham Center in Wheaton, Illinois, also holds some useful materials in the papers of Harold Lindsell and Donald McGavran, and more in those of Herbert J. Taylor. Also of immense value were the papers of Harold Ockenga, which include considerable correspondence with the principals in the seminary's history. For the use of these I am indebted to the kindness and hospitality of Mrs. Ockenga. I am also indebted to Professor Rudolph Nelson of the State University of New York at Albany for copying for me from the Ockenga papers the entire correspondence with Edward J. Carnell. These letters, as will be apparent, were an invaluable resource. Professor Nelson, whose work on his biography of Carnell[4] paralleled this study, has assisted me in many ways—in sharing sources, and in providing invaluable critiques and insights on my work.

Another rich source of letters I came across by accident. Buried in a storage closet at Fuller were two file drawers of correspondence of Wilbur Smith dating from the 1920s to the 1970s. These were far more informative about Fuller's history than were the letters in the otherwise broad collection of Smith materials at Trinity Evangelical Seminary in Deerfield, Illinois. Though Smith's surviving correspondence is far from complete, it contains many items to and from well-known American religious leaders and also vivid comments on most of the religious questions of the era.

No doubt other letters, not available for this study, could fill in details of the seminary history. Nonetheless, the oral and written sources provided enough points of view on most of the major developments to give some confidence in reconstructing the outlines of the history.

To help eliminate errors arising from some inevitable speculation in such reconstruction, I submitted a draft of this volume to a number of the participants. I am grateful for the thorough reading and comments from Carl F. H. Henry, David Hubbard, and Harold Lindsell. Richard Mouw, Jack Rogers, Lewis B. Smedes, and Russell P. Spittler also read and commented on the later chapters. Other friends and colleagues, including Joel Carpenter,

---

4. Rudolph L. Nelson, *The Making and Unmaking of an Evangelical Mind: The Case of Edward Carnell* (New York: Cambridge University Press, 1987).

X   REFORMING FUNDAMENTALISM

Mark Noll, Jon Pott, and Grant Wacker, have also read the early draft and provided valuable comments.

My greatest debt is to Daniel P. Fuller, who went beyond the call of duty to provide me with an extremely detailed critique of the early draft. His lengthy commentary, based on his outstanding memory and his own checking of some of the details, constitutes an important historical document in itself, and I often refer to his comments in the notes. He has saved me from a number of embarrassments, and I have benefited in many other ways from the high standards of scholarship and integrity for which he has long been known. His biography of his father, *Give the Winds a Mighty Voice: The Story of Charles E. Fuller*,[5] is a thoroughly researched volume on which I have often relied. It is a model of the genre of sympathetic biography.

The present work is not a conventional institutional history that attempts to "cover" whatever happened during a certain time. Rather, it is a narrative built around the theme of Fuller Seminary's leading role in the the original new evangelical (or neo-evangelical) attempt to reform fundamentalism. This story, which I hope will be as engaging to read as it was to write, carries us from before the founding of the seminary in 1947 to about 1967 or 1968. Just about that time a number of the principal characters passed from the stage and the original new evangelicalism began both to seem old and to fragment.

Fuller's more recent history, however, is of interest to many people and illustrates impressively one of the directions that neo-evangelicalism could eventually lead. So at the risk of making this book end like a Beethoven symphony that "is never over until it is over," I have included both an Epilogue and a Sequel. Though based on more impressionistic evidence than the rest of the book, these comprise substantial parts of the story. The Epilogue summarizes Fuller's history into the 1980s. The Sequel reflects on the impact of the much-heralded "battle for the Bible," which first gave "the strange case of Fuller Seminary"[6] national prominence. Finally, an Appendix more modestly summarizes survey material based on questionnaires sent to alumni in 1985 and then compares these results with some survey data on Fuller and other evangelical seminaries from James Davison Hunter's 1982 study, "The Evangelical Academy Project." I am deeply grateful to Professor Hunter for providing materials from his work and for encouraging this research into how evangelicalism has changed. His larger study, *Evangelicalism: The Coming Generation*, offers useful information and observations that illuminate the wider evangelical context.[7]

Since the story told here is thematically selective and is especially concerned with how Fuller's history relates to larger trends in American religious and cultural history, it does not give equal time to everything or men-

5. (Waco, Tex.: Word, 1972).
6. See Harold Lindsell, *The Battle for the Bible* (Grand Rapids: Zondervan, 1976), 106-21.
7. James Davison Hunter, *Evangelicalism: The Coming Generation* (Chicago: University of Chicago Press, 1987).

tion everyone. This is a disadvantage of not doing a wholly conventional institutional history. Some may feel slighted that they, or their program, or their school, were not given more prominence. No doubt there are injustices and some omissions, but these reflect more on me than on those omitted.

Inevitably one's point of view will shape one's work. Since it is impossible to be objective, it is imperative to be fair. One way of being fair is to say something about one's point of view so that others can take it into account and discount it if they wish. Though I have tried to write this book with a detachment that will make it as palatable to secularists as to various partisan evangelicals, I work from a particular Christian commitment that makes me generally sympathetic to what Fuller Seminary has been trying to do since its inception. At the same time, I have also tried to step aside from my sympathies. I think the primary justification for having historians these days is that they can provide critical perspectives, especially on traditions that they take seriously. Partisanship, then, although to some degree inevitable, is to be suppressed for the purposes of such historical understanding.

This approach will not entirely please those who see Christian history as adequately understood only as a battle in which it is perfectly clear who stands with the forces of light and who with the forces of darkness. I do not have any difficulty with the concept of the Christian life as a battle; I do not believe, however, that we can identify the forces of light and darkness so easily. My world is filled with ambiguities. Even with the light of Scripture we are very limited humans who see as through a glass darkly.

With respect to the celebrated contest for control of Fuller Seminary, then, my aim has been to avoid partisanship, though to reject a simplistic partisan interpretation is in a sense to take sides. I hope that my account displays enough sympathies with each side in the Fuller controversies that it pleases neither entirely. That would be consistent with the tone set by Charles Fuller, who in the late 1950s, when the seminary was under fire from several sides, reportedly remarked resignedly to a group of students, "Well, when you're damned from the right and from the left you're probably doing what you're supposed to."[8]

By far my greatest debts in the production of this book, aside from the obvious ones to Fuller Seminary, are to Calvin College. Calvin has developed a remarkable balance between being a fine liberal arts teaching college and a center for Christian scholarship. Calvin funded reduced teaching loads for me as a sabbatical leave in 1981–82 and a Calvin Research Fellowship in 1982–83. From 1983 to 1986 Calvin was also extraordinarily cooperative in allowing me time off for research whenever I asked for it. During those years I worked on various projects in fundamentalism and evangelicalism and their relationship to modern America. In addition to editing a volume on that subject and writing a number of articles, I also spent time during these leaves for what

---

8. Alumni comments from 1985 survey. Most alumni comments were furnished anonymously and almost all will be reported here simply as "alumni comments."

proved to be valuable background research for the Fuller history. I also feel deeply in debt to many of my colleagues at Calvin who have helped shape so much of my intellectual pilgrimage. During my early years at Calvin I once remarked, with its dominant Dutch ethnicity in mind, "I am not one of us." Now that I have left, I realize that in the meantime I have developed bonds with them that make me permanently one of them.

I am also grateful to the history department of the University of California at Berkeley, where I taught in the spring of 1986, and to the Divinity School of Duke University, my present academic home, for opportunites to work on this project in its latter stages.

Two research assistants have helped considerably on this project. Dwight Maliepaard collected much useful material during the early stages, and James Whisenant did a great deal of efficient work for me at Fuller. Steven Patti, assistant to the president at Fuller, provided adminstrative assistance there. Susan Huizenga at Calvin typed part of the manuscript; and Cindy Boender, secretary to the Calvin History Department, assisted in innumerable ways. Professor Steven Wykstra of the Calvin Philosophy Department donated the better part of a day to helping me transfer my work from the Calvin computer to portable disks. And Hugh James and Richard Mouw of Fuller Seminary also gave me much help in finding pictures.

My inestimable personal debt is to my wife Lucie. In addition to being a delightful companion and at the same time always her own person, she has countless times gone out of her way to make my work go more smoothly. Our teenagers, Greg and Brynne have also provided much joy and good humor and have adjusted with good will to all the changes in locale and friends that my recent scholarly ventures have involved for them. All three family members have been equally supportive in encouraging me to stay in history rather than taking up a full-time career playing the violin.

ABBREVIATIONS USED IN THE NOTES

Names

BG Billy Graham
CF Charles E. Fuller
CH Carl F. H. Henry
CDW C. Davis Weyerhaeuser
DF Daniel P. Fuller
DH David Allan Hubbard
EJC Edward J. Carnell
FTS Fuller Theological Seminary
GA Gleason Archer
HJO Harold John Ockenga
HJT Herbert J. Taylor
HL Harold Lindsell
PKJ Paul King Jewett
WS Wilbur M. Smith

Location of Documents, Abbreviations in ( ).

Unless otherwise indicated, documents can be found in the Fuller Theological Seminary Archives.

(L) Harold Lindsell papers, Billy Graham Center, Wheaton, Illinois
(O) Harold John Ockenga Papers, Gordon-Conwell Theological Seminary, Hamilton, Massachusetts
(LA) Los Angeles Presbytery File, Presidential Archives, FTS (P)Presidential Archives, FTS
(S) Wilbur Smith Papers, FTS Archives
(SS) Slessor storage basement, FTS
(T) Herbert J. Taylor Papers, Billy Graham Center, Wheaton, Illinois
(V) Béla Vassady papers, Grand Rapids, Michigan
(WS) Wilbur M. Smith Papers, Trinity Evangelical Divinity School, Deerfield, Illinois

INTRODUCTION

Fundamentalists, Evangelicals, and New Evangelicals

AN INSTITUTIONAL LIFE AND TIMES

THE best telling of the story of the past relies on balance of the general and the particular. Histories that dwell on generalities lose the vividness of specific human experience. Textbooks make dull reading. Too much of the particular, on the other hand, can swamp historical understanding. The past becomes, in the inadvertently hyper-Calvinist words of Henry Ford, "one damned thing after another."

The concern to relate the general to the particular is behind the attractive suggestion that all history is biography. Through looking at an individual, one has the possibility both of retaining the crucial ingredient of a good story and of finding a lens through which to focus understanding of the broader issues of the day.

Though I hope that no one has claimed that all history is institutional history, the story of an institution does have some of the same potential that good biography does. This may not seem readily apparent, since institutions are usually a lot duller than individuals are. Nonetheless, institutions stand midway between the people who run them and the larger movements and cultural trends in which they participate. So, as well as being important in themselves, institutions can be means through which to look at both the more particular and the more general.

The early history of Fuller Theological Seminary is extraordinarily well suited to this three-way approach in which the stories of individuals, institutions, and movements all illuminate each other. First, in its early years Fuller Seminary was shaped by a striking number of remarkable individuals. Those of the greatest national prominence include Charles and Grace Fuller, Harold Ockenga, Wilbur Smith, Everett Harrison, Carl F. H. Henry, Harold Lindsell, Edward J. Carnell, William LaSor, Gleason Archer, Béla Vassady, Charles Woodbridge, George Eldon Ladd, Paul K. Jewett, and Daniel P. Fuller. All were strong personalities, and their combination gave rise to speculation from the earliest days as to whether so many "stars" could ever form a team. Besides these, one other luminary whose orbit was always close to Fuller's was Billy Graham. Most of the founders of the school were friends of Graham, and some were important to his career. So his vast success, beginning

1

in 1949, had a major, though usually indirect, impact on the school. The history of the institution was thus never far from the stories of individual personalities.

EVANGELICAL EMPIRES

At the same time, the institution has to be understood as an instance of a larger type. Fuller Seminary, as an American *evangelical* institution, is in the tradition marked first by a zeal to proclaim the biblically revealed gospel of salvation from sin through the atoning work of Christ. Two types of institutions have typically expressed this zeal. First are the Protestant denominations, most of which were, in America, at least at one time, evangelical. Second, evangelicalism has also always been a transdenominational movement. Since the nineteenth century it has worked increasingly through independent agencies— what are now called "parachurch" institutions. Modern individualism has only encouraged this trend. Though offering warm fellowship in local congregations, evangelicals emphasized that the church was made up of individual converts. Often these individuals would be so filled with zeal to proclaim the gospel that they felt compelled to move beyond ponderous denominational structures. They did not usually repudiate their denominations but simply set up their own extradenominational agencies in order to promote the cause more efficiently. Individualism, then, combined with the spirit of American free enterprise, has shaped transdenominational evangelicalism's distinctive institutions.

The most distinctive institutions of American evangelicalism have often have been parts of the personal empires of successful evangelists. Usually these institutions have been run autocratically or by an oligarchy; in any case, they have typically been regarded virtually as private property. They were designed for a special purpose, which could be defined by the people in immediate command, with no need to answer to ecclesiastical authority. These institutions were thus extraordinarily shaped by the personalities of the individuals who founded and controlled them. Fuller Seminary was such an institution. Its history also illustrates how an institution bound neither by any formal precedents nor by ties to an organized church is shaped by the individuals who control it.

The key question in such institutions is the question of authority: To what authorities or traditions can individuals appeal? Such questions become especially pressing when there is a crisis in personal authority—when the succession to power and control is contested, for example. Not suprisingly, then, much of the intrigue in the early Fuller history centers on the question of authority, which was intimately connected to a dramatic struggle for control.

THE AUTHORITY OF TRADITIONS

The individuals involved in such an institutional power struggle are not as free as they might appear to be. While the institution may be independent in name, it and the individuals in it are still part of movements that have histories that define individual and institutional identities. These identities can be slowly modified, but they cannot be truly revolutionized without both personal pain and the risk of losing one's constituency. So the heritages themselves exercise implicit authority by providing accepted traditions of interpreting experience and recognizing authorities. Thus the history of institutions and of the people in them must always be considered in the context of the movements and traditions to which they are remarkably bound.

Those who founded Fuller Seminary were consciously bound by allegiances to three major religious movements, although they did not usually see the three as distinct. They were loyal to a version of classical Protestant Christianity, they were loyal to the American evangelical heritage, and they were loyal to fundamentalism. These religious traditions are crucial for understanding both Fuller Seminary and the people who shaped it. The conflicts at Fuller often took the form of struggles among these three allegiances, and sometimes such struggles were dramatically internalized in an individual.

Of these three major religious heritages, the fundamentalist connection is the one most likely to be minimized in recollections of Fuller's past. Histories are typically written by victors, who inevitably emphasize those parts of the past that were the roots of later and lasting developments. Other roots, whose branches later withered or were cut off, are easily forgotten. Specifically, perceptions of Fuller's origins are shaped by the fact that by the late 1950s it had become so thoroughly identified with what then was widely called the "new evangelicalism" that the role of the seminary's fundamentalist roots had been discounted. By that time the new evangelicalism (or "neo-evangelicalism" or sometimes just "evangelicalism") already marked a break with fundamentalism.

Harold Ockenga popularized the term *new evangelicalism* in 1957, though he had earlier been using it in connection with Fuller Seminary— perhaps as early as the previous decade. Historians, in turn, have traced the beginnings of neo-evangelicalism still further back to the formation in 1942 of the National Association of Evangelicals, of which Ockenga was a founder. This organization rivaled a more separatist fundamentalist organization, the American Council of Christian Churches, founded just previously by Carl McIntire. In this picture, the founding of Fuller Seminary in 1947 looks simply like part of the "evangelical" or "new evangelical" break with fundamentalism that had already begun to take place in the early 1940s.

If we go back to the earliest days of Fuller Seminary in the late 1940s, however, we find that we are entering an era before all these categories were clear. To enter that lost world, one must put aside the distinctions of later days and realize that "evangelical" and "fundamentalist" were not then separate entities. Even though the early Fuller was a major part of a concerted attempt to reform fundamentalism, the unmistakable intention was, not a break with fundamentalism, but a reform from within. The early Fuller was in striking ways a fundamentalist institution with a thoroughly fundamentalist constituency. Though *evangelical* may have been the more respectable word to use, few would have questioned the fundamentalist identification.

FUNDAMENTALISM

To understand Fuller Seminary, then, we must first know something about fundamentalism. Fundamentalism arose out of the decline in influence of traditional revivalist evangelicalism in America during the first half of the twentieth century. In nineteenth-century America evangelical Protestantism had been the dominant religious ideology in a nation noted for its religion. Indeed, evangelical Protestantism constituted an unoffical religious establishment. American schools and colleges taught broadly evangelical doctrine, and even most of the early universities required chapel attendance. By the end of the century, evangelical piety in the White House, although not required, was expected.

Yet within the span of one generation, between the 1890s and the 1930s, this extraordinary influence of evangelicalism in the public sphere of American culture collapsed. Not only did the cultural opinion makers desert evangelicalism, even many leaders of major Protestant denominations attempted to tone down the offenses to modern sensibilities of a Bible filled with miracles and a gospel that proclaimed human salvation from eternal damnation only through Christ's atoning works on the cross. Fundamentalism was the response of traditionalist evangelicals who declared war on these modernizing trends.

In fundamentalist eyes the war had to be all-out and fought on several fronts. At stake was nothing less than the gospel of Jesus' blood and righteousness. On one front the fundamentalists emphasized the fundamental doctrines of the faith: dogmas that liberal Protestants, or "modernists," typically denied. Such denials always involved substituting natural or vaguely spiritual explanations for the traditional affirmations of the supernatural or miraculous origins of Christianity. So the fundamental doctrines for which they fought included the virgin birth of Christ, his miracles, his bodily resurrection, his substitutionary atonement for sin, and his second coming. Of particular importance was the nature of the authority of Scripture. Modernists, influenced by higher criticism, emphasized the Bible's human origins; fundamentalists countered by affirming its inerrancy in history and science as well as in faith and doctrine.

The battles over these issues were fought primarily in America's major denominations, especially in the Northern (later American) Baptist Convention and the (northern) Presbyterian Church in the U.S.A. During the 1920s, fundamentalists in each of these groups launched all-out campaigns for the recovery of traditional evangelical fidelity and for strict doctrinal control. Ultimately, however, moderates prevailed in each case, and modernism was tolerated. It became especially prevalent in denominational theological seminaries. By the 1920s few respected educational institutions of any sort in the northern United States would even tolerate fundamentalist teaching.

Despite such setbacks, fundamentalism was moving on a number of other major fronts. Most important was its influence in the parts of American evangelicalism that operated outside of the denominations, especially in free-enterprising revivalism. Antimodernism had long been an effective revival motif. As secularization accelerated in America by the early twentieth century, the fundamentalist style of antimodernism also spread. Sometimes this involved innovations: rather than being strictly conservative, fundamentalism generated both new doctrines and new institutions.

The most influential antimodernist doctrine, eventually spreading through most of intradenominational fundamentalism, was dispensationalism. Dispensationalism was a version of premillennialism, the doctrine that Christ will return personally to found a kingdom in Jerusalem where he will reign for one thousand years. This doctrine also provided a general theory of history, proclaiming that the present "church age," the sixth dispensation in the world's history, was marked by apostasy in the churches and the moral collapse of so-called "Christian civilization." Thus dispensationalism predicted the rise of modernism and emphasized the necessity of fighting to preserve the true faith and personal purity. These emphases also led dispensationalists to an antimodernist way of interpreting the Bible. They insisted on the inerrancy of Scripture and argued that each word was the perfect word of God. Confident that they could rely on even the details of Scripture, dispensationalists became fascinated by specific predictions of the cataclysmic events ushering in the millennial age, based on literal interpretations of biblical prophecies.

The chief institutional expressions of fundamentalist antimodernism were the evangelistic empires, for which Dwight L. Moody set the pattern in the late 1800s. In addition to his evangelistic agencies, he supported other means of fostering the gospel cause, especially publications and schools. Most important of these was the "Bible institute," of which Moody Bible Institute founded in Chicago in 1886 was the prototype. During the early decades of the twentieth century, as denominational colleges and seminaries cut themselves loose from their evangelical moorings, Bible institutes sprang up as alternatives, usually emphasizing evangelism, missions, and dispensationalist Bible study.

Yet another front in fundamentalism's campaign was the battle for America—the battle to save the nation as an evangelical civilization. While in theory this agenda conflicted with dispensationalism's pessimism about Christian civilization, in practice the two managed to coexist. Fundamentalism was thus a coalition of cobelligerents fighting against their common enemies, modernism and secularism. Yet fundamentalists themselves had not really agreed on what form the response to anti-Christian secularism should take. Many of them instinctively looked back to the recent evangelical heyday and proclaimed that the best way to fight secularism was to bring back the Bible-based civilization that they pictured in their grandparents' time. William Jennings Bryan's campaigns against evolution and strong drink were conspicuous expressions of fundamentalism of this stripe. So were fundamentalist superpatriotism, anticommunism, and anti-Catholicism. Dispensationalism, on the other hand, was suited more for people who saw themselves as becoming cultural outsiders, which white Protestants easily might in those changing times. It proclaimed that true believers were a holy remnant, that they should maintain personal purity while waiting for the Lord to return, and that they should concentrate on rescuing the perishing. All these dispensationalist emphases could dampen efforts to reform civilization either through politics or education.

NEO-EVANGELICALS AND THE DILEMMA OF SEPARATISM

This unresolved tension was crucial for understanding the movement that a generation later became known as the "new evangelicalism." Most simply understood, the "new evangelical" reformers repudiated both the doctrinal and the cultural implications of a thoroughgoing dispensationalism while they remained loyal to the fundamentals of fundamentalism. Put another way, their version of fundamentalism was defined primarily by the culturally centrist tradition of nineteenth-century American evangelicalism. Theologically, they stood for a moderate form of classic Calvinist Protestantism as opposed to some of the innovations of dispensationalist Bible teachers. Though they were influenced heavily by the conservative Presbyterian theology that had been closely associated with Princeton Theological Seminary, they were neither rigid "Old School" Calvinists nor champions of strict confessional and denominational orthodoxy. Rather, they were much more like the broadly Calvinist interdenominational evangelicalism that had wide influence in nineteenth-century American culture. In the nineteenth century, this outlook had often been designated "New School," especially among Presbyterians.[1] In the eighteenth century, such revivalist Calvinism had been called "New Light" and was central to America's first Great Awakening. Drawing on this venerable heritage with its deep cultural roots, they could find among their fellow fundamentalists a substantial constituency, including especially northern Baptists and Presbyterians with evangelical Calvinist heritages as well as some of the more moderate dispensationalists.

The most explosive issue facing these post–World War II reformers of fundamentalism was the same one that had plagued Protestant reformers in America since the first Puritans set foot on Plymouth Rock: Must they separate from corrupted denominations? Not only were the new evangelicals attempting to reform fundamentalism, they at the same time remained loyal fundamentalists who viewed their more basic mission as the reform of degenerating Protestantism. But they had to wrestle with the problem that faced each generation of reforming Protestants. Were those who witnessed against the grave apostasy of the comfortable, culturally respected churches obliged to separate themselves from that apostasy? Or could they still give loyalty to such contaminated institutions as representatives of the very church of Christ?

1. See George M. Marsden, *The Evangelical Mind and the New School Presbyterian Experience* (New Haven: Yale University Press, 1970).

Must they get out and become plaintive voices in the wilderness, or could they stay on and work for reform from their more influential positions within?

By the 1930s, when it became painfully clear that reform from within could not prevent the spread of modernism in major northern denominations, more and more fundamentalists began to make separation from America's major denominations an article of faith. Although most who supported fundamentalism in the 1920s still remained in their denominations, many Baptist dispensationalists and a few influential Presbyterians were demanding separatism. Yet the question was far from settled in the 1930s and 1940s. Some fundamentalists were making separatism into a high principle. Others happened to be in generally antimodernist denominations—such as many of the smaller northern bodies or the Southern Baptist or southern Presbyterian groups—but did not insist on total ecclesiastical separation from modernism as a test of purity. Still other fundamentalists were in denominations that tolerated modernists. During this era representatives from all three of these broad groupings might well attend the same fundamentalist schools or work together in nondenominational fundamentalist, or evangelical, enterprises.

The new evangelical fundamentalists were often de facto separatists for one reason or another. Working through their own nondenominational schools and evangelistic agencies automatically made them such. New evangelical reformers thus did not repudiate all separatism. On the other hand, they did reject making separatism a high principle. This was a fine distinction, however, exceedingly difficult to maintain consistently. The fact was that their heritage pointed in two conflicting directions. Part of it, most clearly anticipated in the New School tradition, was open and expansive, emphasizing positive evangelism. Another part, shaped by fundamentalist wars against modernism, was closed, cautious, and defensive. The problems of combining these two had always been present in American evangelicalism. Now, with the fundamentalist-modernist controversies still current, they were especially troubling.

TRANSFORMING CULTURE

The new evangelicals' rejection of separatism as an article of faith was related to their conception of the cultural role of fundamentalism or evangelicalism. They were closer to the heritage of the first Puritan governor of Massachusetts, John Winthrop, who aspired to build a Christian civilization, than they were to the dissident Roger Williams, who demanded a pure separatist church and saw the state as hopelessly secular. Like the New School evangelicals of the nineteenth century (and unlike both the strict Old School and the dispensationalists) these fundamentalists saw Christians as having a duty to transform culture in addition to their primary duty to evangelize. In early twentieth-century fundamentalism, such calls to cultural duties were often muted. Yet this heritage also included William Jennings Bryan, always an ardent champion of political reform, who turned out to be a sort of George Custer of fundamentalism. At the Scopes "monkey trial" in 1925, Bryan went down with guns blazing as he unflinchingly defended the Bible as the proper basis for the law of the land.[2]

By the 1940s hopes for political action to promote an evangelical America were far more dim than they had been in the 1920s; prohibition, after all, had been a recently enacted manifestation of "Christian civilization" in the earlier decade. The new evangelical reformers put more emphasis, therefore, on the other primary means of cultural transformation: intellectual reform. They were intellectuals with immense confidence in the powers of argument. In their emphasis on intellect and higher education they were drawing particularly on the Calvinist legacy in their heritage. They were rejecting the types of revivalism and dispensationalism that were so culturally pessimistic and so preoccupied with saving souls that they had virtually withdrawn from the Western cultural and intellectual heritage. The reformers were turning away in particular from the chief institutional sign of that withdrawal, the Bible institute. They were not interested simply in narrow Bible training. Rather, they were determined to produce a body of Christian writing that by force of argument would gain an audience even in the greatest intellectual centers of the civilization.

Since the 1920s, however, fundamentalists had had almost no entrees to such centers. In American colleges and universities the fires from the days of New Light and New School glory had burned low and then had been doused. In only a very few institutions left over from those days did the New Light intellectual ideals still glow. Wheaton College in Illinois was among those few, and in the 1930s it became the leading fundamentalist college and the principal place where visions of evangelical glory were revived for a younger generation. Park Street Congregational Church, next to the Boston Common, was another stronghold, somehow left from earlier times. There also, the ideal of an educated evangelical leadership survived. Bright young men connected with such institutions aspired to doctorates from the best universities possible so as to be prepared to lead America back to the doctrinal fundamentals and to its evangelical cultural heritage.

FULLER THEOLOGICAL SEMINARY

In the history of Fuller Theological Seminary, founded in 1947 by such new evangelical reformers, we can trace the renewal of America's nineteenth-century evangelical heritage as it developed from a reform within fundamentalism into a separate movement. By the late 1950s, the movement's advocates, strengthened by the popularity of Billy Graham, broke with the dispensationalist-separatist right wing of fundamentalism. This momentous schism immediately raised the question as to what the "new evangelicalism" stood

2. See the chapter "Christianity and Culture" in my book *Fundamentalism and American Culture: The Shaping of Twentieth Century Evangelicalism, 1870–1925* (New York: Oxford, 1980).

for. Nowhere was this question contested more dramatically than at Fuller Seminary, the intellectual center of the movement. What was essential to the "new evangelicalism"? Specifically, to what extent should it still be shaped by its fundamentalist heritage? Was it to be a simple return to the broader spirit of prefundamentalist evangelicalism, or should it also give continuing allegiance to the essential defensive and militantly antimodernist concerns of fundamentalism, of which the doctrine of scriptural inerrancy became the chief symbol? Despite this unresolved tension, it seemed (from the late 1950s until the late 1960s) as though the new evangelicalism, buoyed by the influence of Graham, might be a viable new movement forming the center of a wider coalition of transdenominational and denominationalist evangelicals. At the same time, however, the new evangelicalism itself was breaking apart over the unresolved issue of the degree of its loyalty to the militant fundamentalist agenda. Fuller Seminary was a focal point of this battle.

By the late 1960s, the rapid changes in American religion accompanying the cultural and political upheavals submerged neo-evangelicalism as a distinct movement. In addition, by the early 1970s "evangelicalism" in a much broader sense had become a major cultural phenomenon. Evangelicalism included a bewildering variety of denominational traditions, and some of these, such as black evangelical churches and some ethnic and regional groups, had been little touched by the heritage of interdenominational fundamentalism. Moreover, by this time the heirs to neo-evangelicalism were divided into contending parties, and none of these fundamentalist progeny could effectively speak for evangelicalism as a whole.[3] Rather, despite their continuing disproportionate influence in interdenominational evangelicalism, they were just one among many diverse voices.

Since neo-evangelicalism provides the organizing principle of this volume, the story is skewed in several ways that it would not be were it simply a history of Fuller Seminary. First, it is weighted heavily toward the seminary's first twenty years, 1947 to 1967, when the new evangelicalism was a major national phenomenon. Second, because the drama in the story is found in the struggles of reformers to change a movement and yet still remain loyal to it, the tone of the history is considerably more negative than would be a straight history of the seminary. From this account, one might conclude that Fuller was constantly fraught with conflicts both within and without. In reality there were many more harmonies, much more warm fellowship among the faculty, and more cordial relations with the surrounding religious communities than appears here. Finally, this emphasis on conflicts among champions of contending movements obscures what in another sense is the "real" history of Fuller—its often successful fulfillment of its primary mission as a center for training young men and women for ministry. The most important history of Fuller may indeed be found in the biographies of the men and women whose enthusiasm for the gospel was significantly challenged by their experiences at

---

3. See the discussion in the introduction to *Evangelicalism and Modern America*, ed. George Marsden (Grand Rapids: Eerdmans, 1984).

Fuller and then carried into pastorates, the mission field, classrooms, counselling centers, and many other professions.

"FUNDAMENTALISTS" AND "EVANGELICALS"

Because of its centrality to the title, thesis, and theme of this study, it is appropriate to conclude these introductory remarks by making sure that readers are clear about how I use the word *fundamentalism* in this book. As should be apparent from the preceding historical summary, fundamentalism was originally a broad coalition of antimodernists. From the 1920s to the 1940s, to be a fundamentalist meant only to be theologically traditional, a believer in the fundamentals of evangelical Christianity, and willing to take a militant stand against modernism. *Conservative* was sometimes a synonym. So to call oneself a fundamentalist did not necessarily imply, as it virtually does today, that one was either a dispensationalist or a separatist. Neither did it necessarily imply, despite efforts to the contrary by its detractors, that one was obscurantist, anti-intellectual, or a political extremist. So when I speak of fundamentalism here, I do not use the word in such pejorative senses.

On the other hand, original fundamentalism did include certain elements, including *tendencies* toward all the traits mentioned above, that separated it from the mainstream of traditional evangelical Protestantism. As we have seen, much of the plot that shaped the Fuller heritage centered around efforts to get rid of these more recent aspects of fundamentalism and yet retain its essential commitment to evangelical orthodoxy and antimodernism. Those at Fuller were not breaking away entirely from original fundamentalism since original fundamentalism included the defense of the very orthodoxy they were attempting to recover. As Carl Henry put it in retrospect, "In the 1930s we were all fundamentalists. . . . The term 'evangelical' became a significant option when the NAE was organized (1942). . . . In the context of the debate with modernism, fundamentalist was an appropriate alternative; in other contexts (of the debate within the fundamentalist movement), the term evangelical was preferable."[4] My own solution in dealing with this era when the two terms were interchangeable is to refer to the movement then as fundamentalist-evangelical.

Once the debates within fundamentalism led to a split, the "new evangelicals" or "evangelicals" came together as a party of former fundamentalists. Although they successfully reappropriated "evangelical" as the primary designation for biblicist American Protestantism, by no means all "evangelicals" had shared their struggles with fundamentalism. On the other hand, a substantial number of American Protestants had experienced something like this conflict, even if they may have only vaguely articulated it. After World War II, many people whose religious upbringing had been shaped by funda-

---

4. CH, letter to the author, 2-24-86. In another part of this letter Henry writes: "Nobody wanted the term 'evangelical' when NAE was formed in 1942; in social context and in ecumenical context it implied what was religiously passe."

mentalism were becoming more affluent and better educated and began moving from stricter fundamentalism to broader evangelicalism.[5] For some of these, probably for more than is usually recognized, the struggle with fundamentalism was a central event in their lives.[6] At Fuller Seminary from the late 1940s to the late 1960s, we can get a glimpse of these struggles in their classic form.

5. One evidence for this is the growth of well-staffed evangelical colleges and seminaries after the 1960s. George W. Dollar, *Facts for Fundamentalists*, rev. ed. (Sarasota, Fla.: privately published, 1983) lists forty-eight "Modified (New Evangelical) Fundamentalist" educational institutions including Fuller Seminary. See also Dollar's *Fight for Fundamentalism: American Fundamentalism, 1973–1983* (Sarasota, Fla.: privately published, 1983), which elaborates on recent transitions.

6. Garrison Keillor of Lake Wobegon fame is one well-known example.

CHAPTER I

Fundamentalist Stars

I agree with you perfectly that if this school is to be, it should be the best of its kind in the world. It should stand out first, as being absolutely true to the fundamentals of the faith and second, as a school of high scholarship. I note the four suggestions you mention which should dominate—particularly the study of the atoning work of Christ. I agree with you perfectly. Oh, brother, God has laid so heavily on my heart the need of this type of school for training men for the preaching of the Gospel in these terrible days but I am not qualified to plan such a curriculum. I see this great need but I am not an educator. I must have the help of men of like vision.
Charles E. Fuller to Wilbur M. Smith, October 7, 1946.

EVANGELISM IN A SECULAR AGE

BY 1947 fundamentalism seemed a cultural and intellectual wasteland. American opinion makers typically portrayed Bible-believing evangelicalism as a stifling vestige of the small-town past. Old-time religion, in the popular public image, supported the prejudices of overstuffed small-town Victorian busybodies, such as those who might look askance at the bibulousness of the hero of a W. C. Fields film. National prohibition, still a vivid memory, showed what can go wrong if religion gets out of hand. Revivalism, once the dominant religious motif of the respectable middle class, was now identified with memories of various fringe figures. The mention of fundamentalism sparked memories of Billy Sunday's antics, of William Jennings Bryan looking foolish at Dayton, Tennessee, of the rumors of scandal that had surrounded the enticing Aimee Semple McPherson, or of the vivid depictions of the chicanery of America's best-known fictional evangelist, Elmer Gantry. The cultured elite saw current fundamentalist evangelists as the denizens of tent meetings on the edge of town, hucksters of the air waves, or the impresarios at high-pressured youth rallies, corrupting the young and exploiting the impressionable.

Religion might be back in style, but even simple folk ought to know that those literal Bible beliefs the fundamentalists fought so fervently for "ain't necessarily so."

Fundamentalist leaders, despite far larger constituencies than America's secular self-image would admit to, felt keenly their lack of respect at the centers of culture. Academia was especially tightly closed. Only rarely did a bona fide conservative Bible believer gain a significant university position. The South was an exception, but then the South was also by definition culturally marginal. Universities were crucial to the future of the nation, and fundamentalist evangelicals could point to no nationally recognized scholar who spoke clearly for their cause.[1] Most of their own scholars could gain little recognition outside the Bible conference circuit.

Meaningful media access was equally difficult. In Hollywood's view of America in 1947, Bible-believing Protestantism almost did not exist. If it did, it was an aberration. The radio—at least the radio that received press coverage—was much the same: Jack and Bing did not talk about religion. Nor was religion a serious topic on "One Man's Family" or "The Romance of Helen Trent." On the national networks, NBC, CBS, and ABC, the only place for religion was during the free Sunday-morning time provided to both Catholics and Protestants. This arrangement was especially galling to fundamentalist-evangelicals, since the Protestant time was controlled by the major Protestant ecumenical group, the Federal Council of Churches, which had a strongly antifundamentalist bias. To increase the irritation, the most prominent Protestant beneficiary of the network's policy was Harry Emerson Fosdick, who had been on nationwide broadcasts since 1929.[2] In 1922 Fosdick's sermonic question, "Shall the fundamentalists win?" had been been the shot heard around the nation in the modernist-fundamentalist wars. Twenty-five years later, American public policy seemed be be proving correct Fosdick's resounding no to fundamentalism.

The founding of Fuller Theological Seminary in 1947 was a step toward demonstrating that the fundamentalists might still win. The heirs to fundamentalism were not giving up on America without a fight. They were also proving to be more resourceful than their liberal critics might have supposed. Even if they were often ridiculed, they had the multitudes behind them. Radio evangelist Charles E. Fuller had demonstrated this more dramatically than anyone else. In 1942 and 1943 his nationwide radio broadcasts "The Pilgrim Hour" and especially "The Old Fashioned Revival Hour" on the Mutual Broadcasting System had audiences surpassing in size those of the most popular secular shows, including Bob Hope and Charlie McCarthy.[3] When Mutual, following the patterns established by the other networks, limited Fuller's prime-time access in 1944, the evangelist successfully sustained a

1. Kenneth Scott Latourette at Yale Divinity School was perhaps the closest, but even he kept some distance from the fundamentalist-evangelical subculture. Philosophers William Harry Jellema and O. K. Bouwsma of the conservative Christian Reformed Church held university positions, however, and were respected in their fields.

2. On Fosdick see Robert Moats Miller, *Harry Emerson Fosdick: Preacher, Pastor, Prophet* (New York: Oxford, 1985).

3. See Daniel Fuller, *Give the Winds a Mighty Voice: The Story of Charles E. Fuller* (Waco, Tex.: Word, 1972), 149-52. Most of the information in this chapter on Charles Fuller and his broadcast is from this well-researched study.

Radio evangelist Charles Fuller

huge audience, estimated at twenty million worldwide,[4] by enlisting his own
network of independent stations which would air his hour-long broadcasts on
Sunday afternoons or evenings.

Charles Fuller's appeal was disarmingly simple. With the haunting
power of transparent sincerity, he pleaded with sinners to come to Jesus. The
ringing chorus of "We have heard the joyful sound, Jesus saves, Jesus saves"
opened "The Old Fashioned Revival Hour" on an upbeat. "Heavenly Sunshine," the theme song, tempered serious messages with sentimental enthusiasm. Mrs. Fuller, "Honey," as "Dr. Fuller" affectionately called her, provided
a down-home touch as she read letters of testimony from listeners, often from
simple folk. Though Mrs. Fuller's clear accents betrayed a sophisticated background, the atmosphere created was frankly "old fashioned," designed to
evoke nostalgia for the revival style of one's youth. Charles Fuller focused his
sermons on the marvels of what God has done for us in Jesus, the dangers of

4. The estimate is found in *Newsweek,* January 1, 1945, 74.

hell and God's wrath, the sinfulness of humanity, and the necessity of accepting Jesus before it is too late.[5]

> I want the choir to sing that third verse. Listen my friend, out in radio land tonight. You have tried a thousand ways to find peace and comfort. Perhaps your heart is breaking tonight with a load, with trouble, you are in despair and disheartened. I want you to know that in all the eternal realm there is only One throughout eternity that you can trust. You can trust Him right now, and He is willing to come in and be a friend, an advocate, a paraclete, one who stands by—a friend in Jesus. He's the one.[6]

Or, broadcasting from the packed Long Beach Municipal Center, he concluded characteristically: "If you want the joy of being a child of God simply by exercising faith in Jesus Christ, raise your hand. God bless you down there. I see you, and God bless you. Oh, to have the blessed knowledge that your past sins are washed away. How about those in the first balcony. . . . Yes I see you. Thank God."[7]

On first impression, Harold John Ockenga, cofounder with Fuller of the new seminary, would seem of a different stripe. Pastor of the Park Street Congregational Church next to the Boston Common, Ockenga was keenly aware of status and played the role of the nineteenth-century New England gentleman clergyman. Moreover, his style was as intellectualist as the Fullers' was folksy. Though known as an effective preacher, there was nothing "popular" in his New England style. He had earned a Ph.D., and on occasion he would go right over the heads of his largely nonacademic congregation, perhaps to impress the Harvard students in the crowd:

> Just as Greek history may be divided by the Persian wars, Greek thought may be divided into what is called the ontological and the anthropological period. The first period was marked with monistic philosophies which placed air, water, fire and other substances at the center of the universe and culminated in the glorious philosophy which came after the Persian wars, but was the fruitage of the first period, namely the Socratic and Platonic thought and so forth through the history of Greek philosophy and its present-day ramifications.[8]

5. "The Old Fashioned Revival Hour" is analyzed in Everett C. Parker, David W. Barry, and Dallas W. Smythe, *The Television-Radio Audience and Religion* (New York: Harper and Row, 1955). Their 1952 study showed that almost two-thirds of the Fuller audience were over forty-five years old and one-fourth were over sixty-five. Two-thirds of the heads of households were semiskilled or unskilled laborers. One-third of the audience had no church affiliation.

6. Charles Fuller, sermon manuscript, December 22, 1935, FTS archives.

7. From a 1938 sermon, quoted in Daniel Fuller, *Give the Winds a Mighty Voice*, 144-45.

8. Ockenga, "The Everlasting Gospel," sermon preached at Park Street Church, Boston, Massachusetts, October 14, 1945, 6.

Ockenga and Fuller actually had far more in common than these contrasts might suggest. Each was a self-made man from middling origins, though Ockenga's roots in Chicago were actually more modest than Fuller's in southern California; each impressed his associates as a natural leader; and each worked best on his own and was used to taking charge. Charles Fuller, though he did not publicly display his education, was a graduate cum laude from Pomona College and was married to the college-educated daughter of a doctor. He had even taught some Bible classes at Los Angeles Baptist Seminary in the late 1920s. But the most important commonality between Fuller and Ockenga was their passions, which for the two men were nearly identical.

Each focused his ministry on the urgency of massive efforts to win sinners to Jesus. The world was in crisis, the ultimate root of which was unbelief. The best way to combat the modernists and secularists who had undermined the civilization was to preach the gospel message simply and effectively. This message was found in the Bible alone. The certainty of the truth of the Bible, that every word was the word of God, was the only hope for a world in turmoil and uncertainty. Nothing else that the preacher or the Christian layperson could do was as important as convincing others of the truth of this message. Fuller and Ockenga accordingly had an unflagging passion for evangelism and missions. Park Street Church was in fact renowned for its missionary program. In the first ten years under Ockenga's ministry, beginning in 1936, Park Street's yearly missionary budget rose from less than $2,500 to close to $90,000, far surpassing the church's expenditures for everything else. Although Ockenga and Fuller had not been close friends before 1947, they were both fundamentalists and part of the transdenominational network of fundamentalist leaders. They had occasionally helped each other at evangelistic rallies, and each admired the other's abilities and influence.[9]

THE NEXT GENERATION

As Charles Fuller approached the age of sixty in 1947, he was troubled by the question of succession. How could he perpetuate his ministry? This question inevitably plagued American evangelists, in part because ever since the days of Dwight L. Moody most of them had operated with little regard for denominations. They depended on no institutions they themselves had not built. The fundamentalist divisions of the 1920s had only increased this propensity for independence. Fuller himself had split from a Presbyterian church in 1925 to found an independent congregration. Later, he built his radio ministry entirely on a free-enterprise basis. Now he faced the sobering question of whether his empire and the evangelistic good it was doing would outlive him.

Fuller had been thinking about founding a school since before the war, a school for training missionaries and evangelists. When he thought about a school, he thought, as most fundamentalists did, about something like

9. See Harold Lindsell, *Park Street Prophet: A Life of Harold John Ockenga* (Wheaton: Van Kampen, 1951), 99-103, 128.

a Bible institute. He himself had studied at the Bible Institute of Los Angeles (Biola) in the early 1920s and had served as president of Biola's board of trustees from 1928 to 1932. But he also hoped to go beyond that now-traditional format toward an academically stronger school focused on missionary and evangelistic training. In 1941 he had even talked about such a project with Harold Ockenga, though nothing more had come of the discussion.

In 1943, however, as his radio ministry was approaching its peak during the midst of the war, Fuller provided a financial base for a school by establishing the Fuller Evangelistic Foundation "for the purpose of training, or assisting in the training, of men and women for the Christian ministry and for evangelistic work."[10] Fuller's father, Henry, a prosperous orange grower and zealous Christian, had in 1918 set up the Immanuel Missionary Fund with initial assets of about $100,000 to support missionary work over the years. The new Fuller Evangelistic Foundation had goals sufficiently similar, including the support and training of missionaries and evangelists, that it could absorb the assets of the Immanuel Missionary Fund. Moreover, the radio ministry, now prospering, could also help raise funds for the missionary-evangelistic foundation. With the financial base laid, establishing a school required only the right initiatives.

In 1944 Charles Fuller used the foundation to purchase property in Pasadena as the site for his school. Acquiring five acres near the civic center and city library, he hoped to open the Fuller Seminary of Missions and Evangelism by the fall of 1945. Lake Avenue Congregational Church, a virtually independent Bible-oriented downtown Pasadena congregation in which the Fullers held membership, agreed to let the school use its educational facilities until Fuller could build.

The role of Lake Avenue Church in the story illustrates again the dual heritage of this wing of fundamentalism. Like Park Street Congregational in Boston, Lake Avenue was an anomaly in the history of American Congregationalism, a leftover from the days when Congregationalists were among America's most influential evangelicals. Founded in the late nineteenth century, Lake Avenue had been a typical Congregational church until 1921, when James Henry Hutchins began a lengthy pastorate. A graduate of both Xenia Theological Seminary and Moody Bible Institute, Hutchins had kept the church from the modernism that had become so pervasive in Congregationalism. Lake Avenue was definitely on the fundamentalist side, but its relatively staid style reflected its Congregational heritage. When the Fullers moved to Pasadena in 1933 they joined Lake Avenue and became very close friends with Hutchins, who eventually served on a number of their evangelistic boards. Though Fuller preferred the catchy choruses of less formal fundamentalism to Lake Avenue's anthems, his respect for intellect going back to his Pomona College days also fit with the older New England evangelical heritage.[11]

10. Daniel Fuller, *Give the Winds a Mighty Voice*, 190.
11. Ibid., 193. Note also the comments of Daniel Fuller on an earlier draft of this volume; hereafter these comments will be referred to as DF, on draft.

By 1945 Charles Fuller had decided to establish a "College of Missions and Evangelism" rather than a seminary. Now, however, the continuation of the war necessitated postponing plans to open the school until 1946. In the meantime Fuller petitioned his old Biola teacher and popular Bible conference lecturer, William Evans, to set up the new school and serve as its dean. Evans in turn recruited several other faculty members. Meanwhile Fuller secured an architect to draw up plans for six buildings on the lot in downtown Pasadena; he also purchased other buildings nearby for dormitories and parking space. The school printed brochures and application forms. The college would offer a two-year B.A. program for students who already had at least two years elsewhere. A one-year course beyond the B.A. would lead to a Master of Theology degree. The program would thus be something between that of a Bible institute and that of a seminary. The opening was scheduled for September 24, 1946.[12]

By late spring 1946, however, these plans had to be scrapped. Postwar building costs were three times what Fuller had anticipated, and some essential building materials simply were not available. In addition, William Evans suffered an apparent heart attack and had to withdraw. Commitments from other potential faculty had apparently not been entirely firm, and Fuller was finding that some of the better prospects were not sure that the oddly designed school would not be a fly-by-night affair.[13]

In the meantime Fuller was already searching for some younger men to give leadership and academic credibility to his project. He contacted Harold Ockenga, asking him if he knew anyone in the forty to fifty age category to recommend. Fuller added that frankly he had hoped that someday Ockenga himself might head the college, although he feared the suggestion might "sound absurd" to him. Ockenga responded that such a college was "the greatest need of our day" and said that if in five years "God abundantly blesses your school," he might come to Pasadena. "It would have to be a leading from him."[14]

By the fall, with the plans languishing, Fuller turned to his friend Wilbur Smith of Moody Bible Institute and invited him to head the new school. Smith, a prolific writer and editor of the widely used *Peloubet's Select Notes on the International Sunday School Lessons,* was probably the best-known Bible teacher of the day. He said he was flattered by the invitation and attracted by the prospect of "a beautiful home in a California climate, with fruit trees all around and three times the salary I am currently getting." He wondered, however, whether the evangelist's school would be a "one-man show." It must, he urged, have a proper board and so be assured of continuity after Fuller himself was gone.

Fuller assured Smith that he himself was "not an educator," and that

---

12. Preliminary bulletin announcement, Fuller College of Missions and Evangelism, 1946.
13. CF to WS, 10-7-46.
14. CF to HJO, 4-6-46; HJO to CF, 4-10-46.

"I should practically take my hands off as to choice of a faculty and curriculum." Smith replied that he had some enthusiasm for Fuller's new school, especially if it were the best of its kind. Still, he did not feel led at this time to cast his lot with it. On the other hand, he was uneasy with some of the developments at Moody Bible Institute and he was not sure what 1947 would bring.[15]

Grace Fuller, as it turns out, was ghostwriting her husband's correspondence with Smith. With considerable delight she later wrote to her son Dan, who in the fall of 1946 had just entered Princeton Theological Seminary:

> I feel quite set up by the fact that Smith said this letter, which he supposed Dad wrote, was the best and clearest he had received in ten years! He said the questions were answered "magnificently." Queer adjective. You will see how he feels about the school. As yet he feels no leading to leave Moody, but you will notice that he does not *close* the door. . . . We do not want him to come unless that is God's plan and we have put out the fleece and shall simply wait for God's further leading.[16]

Daniel Fuller himself was central to the picture. Charles and Grace Fuller's thoughts about succession focused on him, their only child. "The Old Fashioned Revival Hour," like the businesses that Fullers had conducted for decades, was a family business. That his son should succeed him was the evangelist's fondest dream. Dan was personally rather reserved, which might have made one wonder how he would be as an evangelist; but he was academically precocious and had graduated from Berkeley in a special wartime program at age nineteen.

The classic fundamentalist heritage had also been shaping the plans for the school. At the heart of much of fundamentalism was dispensationalist theology, and this is what shaped much of Charles Fuller's thought as well. Fuller had learned dispensationalism at the Bible Institute of Los Angeles, directly from one of the greatest early fundamentalist Bible teachers, Reuben A. Torrey. In his radio ministry, Fuller sometimes sent out dispensational charts detailing God's plan for each of the biblically revealed dispensations and pointing out prophecies that showed that our own era was in the last days.[17] Jesus might return at any moment. When Charles Fuller thought of seminaries, he thought of the dispensationalist stronghold, Dallas Theological Seminary. Accordingly, in March 1946, at around the same time he was writing to Ockenga for recommendations, Fuller wrote to Dallas president Lewis Sperry Chafer, asking for suggestions for a younger man, "preferably a graduate of Dallas Seminary," to help head his new institute. He added that his son Dan wished to prepare very thoroughly for Christian service and was

15. WS to CF, 9-26-46; CF to WS, 10-7-46; WS to CF, 10-14- 46.
16. Grace Payton Fuller to DF, 10-17-46.
17. "The Prophet Bible Correspondence Course," issued by the Gospel Broadcasting Association, Charles Fuller director, undated.

Charles, Grace, and Dan Fuller, about 1940

considering Dallas. Fuller hoped there would be a place for him there in the fall.[18]

THE PERILS OF PRINCETON

Dan decided to go to Princeton Theological Seminary instead. Attending Princeton continued to be an important option for evangelical students; it was the only seminary with real prestige where some sympathy for conservative faith survived. Dan also chose Princeton in part because Ralph Winter, his best friend from high school and Lake Avenue Church, was going there.

18. CF to Lewis Sperry Chafer, 3-27-46.

Winter, who later became a major force at the Fuller School of World Mission and then founded his own U.S. Center for World Missions in Pasadena, already had a consuming passion for world evangelism and deplored doctrinal controversies that might detract from that primary task. Daniel Fuller later described him as "the most influential person in my life (apart, perhaps, from my parents)."[19]

Princeton was of immense symbolic significance in the fundamentalist community. When all the other major northern educational institutions had turned away from evangelicalism, Princeton Seminary was left the last bastion of orthodoxy with any prestige. Finally in 1929 conservative or "fundamentalist" Presbyterians led by the famed New Testament scholar J. Gresham Machen split with Princeton to found their own school, Westminster Theological Seminary in Philadelphia. Later, in 1936, Machen was forced out of the Presbyterian Church in the U.S.A. itself, placing his new seminary in a strictly separatist position. By this time fundamentalism was dividing over the separatist question and Princeton Seminary provided a leading case in point. Was it acceptable for fundamentalists to continue to send their young men to Princeton where they could get a moderately conservative education mixed with some questionable teachings? Or should they take a stand against the seminary and its denomination, the Presbyterian Church in the U.S.A., because they tolerated apostasy? Was Princeton as liberal as some of its fundamentalist critics claimed? Was it safe to expose young people to sophisticated teaching that might undermine their strict fundamentalist faith?

No one watched for apostasy at Princeton more closely than Wilbur Smith did. Smith had become close friends of the Fullers at a Bible conference in 1946 and was now their informant about the dangers facing a young fundamentalist at the controversial seminary. During the fall of 1946 they interspersed discussions of this subject with talk of whether Smith could be enlisted at the new Fuller school. Always ready with hyperbole, Smith said he was "horrified" at a recent development at Princeton. John W. Bowman, a professor at the Presbyterian San Francisco Theological Seminary in San Anselmo, California, and an old college friend of Smith, had delivered the prestigious L. P. Stone Lectures at Princeton in 1946. In Smith's view, which he had published, Bowman was simply an out-and-out modernist "who denies the great verities of the faith." Along with many other moderate fundamentalists, Smith hoped that the remaining conservative faculty at Princeton could hold the line against modernism. Now, however, he wrote to Charles Fuller a second time that he was "horrified" at the further revelation that none of the faculty had opposed Bowman's appearance.

> Now, when the entire faculty of Princeton Theological Seminary unanimously approves of extending an invitation to one like Dr. Bowman who denies the great fundamentals of our faith, this same Dr.

19. DF, on draft.

Bowman to give the L. P. Stone Lectures, then I can no longer with hearty approval recommend Princeton Theological Seminary to young men. I am going to write Dr. Ockenga at Boston, and my friend, T. R. Phillips of Baltimore about this matter at once. I am going to let my voice be heard on this, though I will probably lose some dear friends in doing so.[20]

Grace Fuller forwarded this correspondence to her son and added a classic statement of fundamentalist ("conservative" is the term she uses) misgivings about his studying at an institution that had reputedly lost its moorings.

We are praying so earnestly for you that God will give you a crystal clear vision to detect the error and also to see and cling to the truth. Satan is a liar from the beginning, deceptive and *so* subtle! He is wiley, and so extremely clever and would deceive the very elect. May none of these heresies find any lodgement in your heart, and I pray the same for the other students. I pray that you may be able to help other men there who may be taken in by these subtle lies. Do you feel that you should leave Princeton? Do you feel by being there that you are endorsing the college for other young men? Dad has felt that if you could come through Princeton, which is good in many ways, a strong conservative like Ockenga and Munger [Robert Munger, an outstanding young west coast Presbyterian preacher who had graduated from Princeton] and many, many others, it would widen your field of influence and open many doors to you. . . . It may be God's plan to have this large group of ultra conservative students there to raise their voices and "fight like wild cats" if necessary for the truth and it may check Princeton and open [President John] McKay's [Mackay's] eyes and act as a purge.

Later in the school year Charles Fuller wrote to another friend that Dan was learning "a good deal about the subtle teaching of Barthianism and Liberalism today."[21]

In Grace Fuller's letter, which was immensely revealing of the dynamics behind the founding of Fuller Seminary, she also reiterated the hope that Dan would eventually play a leading role at his father's new college. "Dad feels," she wrote, "that you would have his vision and carry on in his way to mold the school, possibly to teach there, and to keep it in the middle of the road, though we did not say all this to Smith." Apparently elaborating on "the middle of the road," Grace Fuller observed that Charles was "very much disturbed by the division in the conservative ranks. Certainly in unity there is strength, but there is little unity today." She then added, "Dad has been wise in keeping clear of many entanglements."

20. WS to CF, 9-25-46 and 9-26-46.
21. Grace Payton Fuller to DF, 9-17-46; CF to HJT, 4-22-47 (T).

THE NEW PRINCETON

All these factors loomed large, then, when the Fullers finally met with Harold and Audrey Ockenga in February 1947 at the Fullers' resort home in Palm Springs to talk seriously about the new school. On the same trip Harold Ockenga had lectured at Dallas Seminary and had turned down an informal offer of the presidency of Westmont College in Santa Barbara.[22] Evangelical higher education was much on his mind, and he had concluded that now was the time to take a bold step. Collegiate education, however, was not the answer. Most of the best evangelical scholars were at seminaries. But the existing seminaries that spoke unequivocally for the fundamentalist-evangelical movement—notably Faith Seminary in Wilmington, Delaware, Westminster in Philadelphia, and Dallas Seminary—were tied too narrowly to their various party lines. Outside these schools, however, evangelical scholarship was scattered and languishing.

Ockenga saw scholarship as pivotal to the success of the whole evangelical movement and was distressed by its paltry scholarly achievements to that point. He was an organizer, though, and so in the summers of 1944 and 1945 he convened "scholar's conferences" of theologians at Manomet Point, Massachusetts, to talk about the need for first-rate evangelical scholarship.[23] Now he told the Fullers that what was needed was a true scholarly center to produce serious books that all the world would have to notice. In addition, the center should train the next generation of evangelical ministerial and missionary leaders. Ockenga was, in effect, proposing a new Princeton: the new west coast seminary would recapture the glory and academic standing of the old Princeton. Charles Fuller's practical vision could thus be combined with a strategic enterprise that might rearm the entire movement at one of its weakest points.

The Fullers quickly saw this new vision as an amplification of their own. In answer to Grace Fuller's question about whether there were enough truly qualified scholars to found such an institution, Ockenga quickly listed a dozen possibilities.[24] Within a few years, he thought, the ten best evangelical scholars in the country could be assembled in Pasadena. They would, of course, have to be paid well and given time to write. That was no problem, Charles Fuller assured him. The group caught the excitment as they contemplated the possibilities. They would open the seminary in the fall of 1948; in the meantime they would immediately begin assembling a board and a first-class faculty.

For the board, they agreed, the crucial figure was Herbert J. Taylor, president of Club Aluminum Company. In recent years Taylor had been a board member and backer of many of the most sucessful extradenominational evangelical enterprises. His support would be a "fleece," that is, his accep-

22. Lindsell, *Park Street Prophet*, 128-29.
23. Ockenga, foreword, in Harold Lindsell, *The Battle for the Bible* (Grand Rapids: Zondervan, 1976), 12.
24. Daniel Fuller, *Give the Winds a Mighty Voice*, 198.

tance would be interpreted as a sign that God approved the project.[25] "Since Dan is at Princeton," Charles Fuller wrote to Taylor after the philanthropist joined the effort, "we realize forcefully the tremendous need for such a training school." Princeton had its strengths, but it was not spiritually strong or theologically sound. "The communists and the Catholics have well-trained leaders," wrote Fuller, "but Protestantism keeps so divided and so poor, and especially do the conservative forces need to be unified to do effective work. . . ."[26]

A FOUNDING FACULTY

As to the faculty, Wilbur Smith was another fleece.[27] He was an effective popularizer and probably the best-known evangelical scholar. Many of the other prospects, though outstanding, were young and less well-known. With the vision for the school now of grand proportions, Smith quickly enlisted. When he wrote to a wealthy friend in March 1947 asking for money for a library, he stated that he had hopes that this would be "the most important theological seminary in American Protestantism for this strange day." Smith had the impression that the project had about one million dollars from the Fuller Foundation behind it as well as several other well-to-do backers. He was no doubt thinking of Herbert J. Taylor and the two other trustees, Dr. Rudolph Logefeil, a Minneapolis surgeon, and Mr. Arnold Grunigen, an investment banker from San Francisco. Adding to Smith's willingness to move was some frustration with what he considered a lack of vision at Moody Bible Institute. Moody's president, Will Houghton, was incapacitated and dying. And though the school was "big, rich and famous," it was "not meeting the opportunities of this age, and it is discouraging."[28] Fuller Seminary, on the other hand, offered exciting prospects for the future. Once Smith had made his decision, he was eager to get on with his new work, and so he wrote to Charles Fuller that he wished the seminary could open in the fall of 1947, instead of 1948.[29]

By this time Charles Fuller was already in high gear. Acting on his own in early April, he had the Fuller Evangelistic Foundation bid on a beautiful five-acre estate in one of the most luxurious sections of Pasadena for the site of the seminary. The thirty-two room mansion, built by one of the Cravens tobacco family, was reputed to be the most expensive home ever built in Pasadena, having cost about a half million dollars in 1929.[30] Fuller bid only the assessed value of $145,000 but was confident that he could afford to go higher. In the meantime, with high hopes that the building problem was about to be solved, and no doubt thinking about the dangers for Dan of another year at Princeton, Fuller pressed for opening in the fall.

25. HJO interview, 11-6-83.
26. CF to HJT, 4-22-47 (T).
27. HJO interview, 11-6-83; Dean Stephan interview, 11-4-83.
28. WS to Douglas Ober, 3-25-47 (S).
29. Daniel Fuller, *Give the Winds a Mighty Voice*, 199-201, is the basis for much of the succeeding account.
30. *Los Angles Times*, February 6, 1955, sec. 6, pp. 1, 13.

On April 17, 1947, Fuller, Ockenga, and Smith met at the Union League Club in Chicago. With Fuller pushing hard, they agreed to try for the early date. Ockenga would be the president, but would for the time being hold the position in absentia, making the formidable commute from Boston only when the occasion required. He would also recruit the faculty. If he could find four scholars willing to come on such short notice, they would forge ahead. They would just trust God that announcements on "The Old Fashioned Revival Hour" would bring sufficient students.

Of the younger men, Carl F. H. Henry was a key figure. Henry was as much a dreamer of big dreams as Ockenga and Smith were. A New Yorker converted to fundamental Christianity as a young adult, Henry had studied at Wheaton College and had completed both B.D. and Th.D. degrees at Northern Baptist Seminary in Chicago. Now, at age thirty-four, he was close to a Ph.D. in Philosophy from Boston University. With a background in journalism, he was known for his practical skills and effective writing. Already he had authored two major books, one an erudite analysis of modern thought and the other a manifesto for fundamentalist social action.

Henry enthusiastically joined the ambitious Fuller enterprise. He was enough of a realist, however, to wonder whether a school planned in the spring could open in the fall. For one thing, it would need students. Far more than four or five months seemed necessary for advertising and recruiting. Henry apparently convinced Wilbur Smith of this point, and the two wired Charles Fuller from Chicago suggesting that a year's delay would not be wasteful. Fuller, however, was reluctant to countenance any postponement. He also understood the powers of radio for recruiting better than his print-oriented cohorts did. The matter would have to be decided when the founders and faculty met together.

Everett F. Harrison of Dallas Theological Seminary was the third likely prospect for the initial faculty. The son of a well-known Presbyterian fundamentalist author and Bible teacher, Norman B. Harrison, Everett had studied New Testament at Princeton Seminary during the height of the fundamentalist controversies in the mid 1920s. At that time he had been a close follower of J. Gresham Machen; but, like Smith and Ockenga, he eventually proved to be a moderate when in the mid 1930s Machen urged his supporters to separate from the alleged apostasy of the Presbyterian Church in the U.S.A. Harrison was a dispensationalist, but only mildly so. At Dallas Seminary, where he had been on and off since its early days in 1928, he was a popular teacher. While at first he thought that Lewis Sperry Chafer, president of Dallas, was grooming him for leadership, by 1947 he realized that he had some serious disagreements with Chafer's hard-line dispensationalism. He now felt outside the inner circle and was ready to look elsewhere.[31]

On May 13 and 14, the prospective faculty members, Smith, Henry, and Harrison, met with Ockenga and Fuller at the Palmer House in Chicago for prayer and planning. They still had only three of the four they needed to

31. Everett Harrison interview, 11-23-83.

begin. Henry, however, suggested including his younger colleague, Harold Lindsell, who had administrative abilities and could serve as registrar as well as teach church history and missions. Lindsell was another New Yorker and Wheaton graduate. At Wheaton he had intended to major in business but soon developed strong interests in both missions and academics. A minor health problem kept him from the foreign field, so, instead, he completed a Ph.D. in history at New York University, specializing in U.S. relations with Latin America. He then taught at Columbia Bible College in South Carolina before going to Northern Baptist. Lindsell was eager to be part of the new project. Though he was not an established scholar, he fit in with the project in enough ways to be invited to join the others the next day.[32]

WHAT MIGHT HAVE BEEN

The composition of the founding faculty had not nearly the inevitability about it that was sometimes suggested in later years. Though Smith, Henry, and Harrison had been on Ockenga's original Palm Springs list, others on that list had been hoped for. One of the first people contacted was Charles J. Wood-bridge, a former missionary, a Southern Presbyterian pastor, and a popular Bible conference speaker. He was reputed to be learned, having studied at Princeton College and Seminary and several European universities, and he held a doctorate from Duke. Significantly, Woodbridge was another of the close student admirers of J. Gresham Machen at the old Princeton Seminary of the 1920s. In the 1930s he was the secretary of Machen's controversial Independent Board for Presbyterian Foreign Missions and, along with Machen, was suspended from the Presbyterian ministry for that association. Ockenga offered the church history post to him. Woodbridge was noncommittal, but Ockenga thought he would come to Fuller by 1948. In the meantime, however, he contacted another church historian of almost the same vintage, Paul Woolley of Westminster Theological Seminary. Woolley had also studied with Machen and had been suspended with him in 1936. Deep loyalties to Westminster, however, precluded long consideration of Ockenga's proposal.[33]

For the important position of dean, Ockenga hoped to enlist another widely respected gentleman of the movement, Frank C. Gaebelein, long the headmaster of Stony Brook Academy. Gaebelein, however, after initially expressing some interest, turned down the offer, though leaving the door open enough to allow renewals of the invitation in later years.[34] Ockenga also contacted Merrill Tenney of Wheaton about the deanship, but Tenney was not interested. Nor did anything come of the possibility of persuading Terrelle Crum of Providence Bible Institute to accept a position in biblical theology.[35]

32. Daniel Fuller, *Give the Winds a Mighty Voice*, 201-2. Carl Henry places this meeting at the Palmer House; see his *Confessions of a Theologian: An Autobiography* (Waco, Tex.: Word, 1986), 114.
33. HJO to CF, 5-20-47.
34. HJO to CF, 5-20-47; Frank Gaebelein to WS, 3-25-48 (S); HJO to Frank Gaebelein, 11-17-48.
35. HJO to CF, 5-2-47.

Later in the summer Ockenga contacted Herbert Mekeel, a Presbyterian pastor in New York state, for that position, though commenting to Fuller that Mekeel should not teach church history, since that would close off the position to Woodbridge. But Mekeel was not yet ready to leave his pastorate either.

Old Testament was the other key post. At Park Street Church, Ockenga had a young assistant named Gleason Archer who had a B.A., M.A., and Ph.D. from Harvard, a B.D. from Princeton, and a law degree. Ockenga considered him "the most outstanding young man in America," and he was a leading prospect for an eventual seminary appointment.[36] Ockenga, however, was not yet ready to give him up from the Boston church.

In the meantime, Ockenga was after bigger game. For the senior appointment in Old Testament he thought he might be able to get Allan A. MacRae, president of Faith Theological Seminary. MacRae, another Machenite, was one of the most highly respected Old Testament scholars in the fundamentalist-conservative movement. Faith Seminary was run by Carl McIntire, however, and McIntire and Ockenga were fast becoming bitter opponents. They had been students together at Princeton Seminary and had been part of the loyal group that left with Machen to found Westminster Seminary. By now, however, the former good friends had become rivals for leadership in the fundamentalist movement. McIntire built strictly separatist organizations while Ockenga built inclusivistic ones. The lines between the two types of fundamentalism were not yet entirely clear, though, so Ockenga could still hope to enlist separatists from Faith or Westminster. To get MacRae, the academic centerpiece of McIntire's seminary, would have been a momentous coup, and Ockenga thought he had a chance. After an initial contact, MacRae was "rather enthused," and Ockenga believed he would "be with us in '48."[37] When the first faculty members met together in May, MacRae remained high on their list for possible future additions.

A war was brewing.

STARS OR A TEAM?

A striking feature of the group that gathered in May was the number of strong individualists. Their rivals at Westminster Seminary immediately accused them of being a collection of "stars" and questioned whether they would be a real team.[38] Indeed, with the exception of Harrison, who was a model teacher-scholar without strong aspirations to power, the men who gathered to plan the new seminary were highly independent individuals. They were all in on the ground floor and each knew he could have a shaping role. Fuller and Ockenga

36. HJO to CF, 4-10-46. Ockenga also had extensive conversations with Edwin H. Rian, who, after a controversy with the faculty, had just resigned as executive secretary of Westminster Seminary. Their conversations presumably concerned a similar post at Fuller. See HJO to CF, 3-15-47.
37. HJO to CF, 5-2-47.
38. Ned B. Stonehouse, editorial, "Stars or a Team?" *Presbyterian Guardian,* July 10, 1947, 199.

clearly held the power. Smith, truly a character, was endearingly opinionated, used to commanding his own literary empire, and impatient with administration. He was, however, the senior faculty member and had the ear of the Fullers. Carl Henry had administrative talents but would offer them only sparingly, lest he squander the opportunities for intellectual leadership. Ockenga asked him to be the dean, but he turned him down. Lindsell, though as independently spirited as the rest, was clearly the junior member who had to prove his merit. For the time being he was ready to fall into line as the all-purpose administrator, teacher, and writer, intensely loyal in his service to Ockenga. For the immediate future this group, despite strong individual aspirations, was bound together by spiritual enthusiasm for a common cause. They shared the excitement of a new enterprise, and dreamed of turning around the whole fundamentalist-conservative community.

These individualists were remarkably free from external controls. None of them had a taste for strong denominational authority, and all were thus attracted to a situation free from such restraints. An independent seminary, they were convinced, could serve the whole church. When they thought of the church, however, they did not think first of institutions but rather of the "invisible" body of all evangelical believers. The church was essentially a collection of converted individuals. So the planners of Fuller Seminary could act freely without being subject to any formal ecclesiastical authority. Free enterprise was at work.

America's leading evangelists were almost always models of such American free enterprise. Charles Fuller, the most successful revivalist of his generation, had built a radio empire on his own, combining native talents with business skills learned in his earlier years. Individualistic principles for successful evangelism and similar principles for successful business went hand in hand.

All the men who gathered at the planning meeting in May shared this classic American, rugged individualist outlook. All, for instance, were conservative Republicans. They represented a mostly upper lower-class or lower middle-class aspiring white constituency: those who characteristically had struggled through the depression but who had maintained their pride and firm attachments to the traditional Protestant American values of hard work and self-help. They believed that freedom from external control was a chief social virtue and that rugged individualism was the key to success. Not surprisingly, these respectable fundamentalists got along especially well with a number of pious members of the conservative business community. Both Charles Fuller and Wilbur Smith came from wealthy business families. Ockenga and Smith each had wealthy patrons who supported many of their projects. Such valuable connections meant that, though they were poor fundamentists with little base for national influence, they had some reason to dream large dreams. Even more encouraging, the Fuller Seminary project had behind it both the popularity of Charles Fuller and the capital of the Fuller Evangelistic Foundation inherited from his businessman father.

The freedom and the resources seemed to be there to create whatever they wanted. So was the vision, even if neither the business community nor popular fundamentalism typically put much stock in higher education. The leadership of a few who had the vision could bring a new beginning, a rebuilding of evangelical seminary education from the ground up. All they needed to do was seize the opportunity.

CHAPTER II

The History before the History

We may preach with all the fervor of a reformer and yet succeed only in winning a straggler here and there, if we permit the whole collective thought of the nation or of the world to be controlled by ideas which, by the relentless force of logic, prevent Christianity from being regarded as anything more than a harmless delusion.

J. Gresham Machen, "The Scientific Preparation of the Minister,"
address at the opening of Princeton Theological Seminary,
September 20, 1912.

A COMMON HERITAGE

WHILE the men who met to plan the new seminary seemed free to design any sort of school they wished, they were not operating in a total ecclesiastical or historical vacuum. Rather, their outlooks and assumptions were formed primarily by the traditions of which they were a part, traditions that shaped their interpretations of the great needs of the day.

They belonged, of course, to many different and overlapping traditions. They were Christians, they were Protestants, they were evangelicals, they were Presbyterians, Baptists, or Congregationalist-independents, and they were fundamentalists. They were also American, white, middle class, politically conservative, and male. Moreover, they were shaped by certain traditions of education. Each of these heritages and others besides helped determine how they looked at their task. Each could provide a story in itself.

Nonetheless, when we look around the room at the men who gathered in Chicago in May 1947 (as well as at those they hoped would join their enterprise), one specific tradition strikingly emerges as a tie binding them all together. Each one's outlook was deeply influenced by one dramatic part of the American fundamentalist experience: the struggle within the Presbyterian Church in the U.S.A. Because the conservative wing of Presbyterianism was one of the rare parts of fundamentalism where high-level intellectual life had been greatly valued, it was natural that heirs to this tradition would be gathering to revive the evangelical intellectual enterprise. Though far from the only source of their fundamentalist heritage, this tradition provides the clearest window through which to see the history that shaped their conception of what Fuller Theological Seminary should be.

31

Still fresh in the memories of everyone present was the disappointment of the collapse, only a decade earlier, of the conservative Presbyterian renewal movement. The hopes for that movement, especially the hopes of those who saw education as the key to a national recovery of conservative Protestantism, had been focused largely on J. Gresham Machen. Machen, however, died suddenly in early 1937, when he was only fifty-five years old. His death was, in the view of many sympathetic observers, the last painful blow to a movement already irreparably divided and in ruin.

To understand the high hopes that Machen had kindled, we must go back one decade more, to around 1927, when he stood at the center of a fundamentalist-conservative movement that was still a formidable factor in American life. Machen then taught at Princeton Theological Seminary, the oldest seminary of the Presbyterian Church in the U.S.A. and long a distinguished academic center for conservative evangelical Christians, especially for those with Calvinist heritages. The dominant theological tradition at Princeton was known as "Old School" Presbyterianism, a nineteenth-century term for strict Presbyterian confessionalists. Old School Princeton emphasized the Westminster Confession of Faith and Catechisms, an inductive or scientific-rational defense of the faith, and a complete confidence in the authority of Scripture resting on its freedom from error in any part.

In the twentieth century the heirs to Old School Presbyterianism had become allied to fundamentalist revivalists whose more pietistic and less strictly Presbyterian emphases resembled those of the old nineteenth-century "New School" Presbyterians. Princeton had become a haven for intellectually aspiring fundamentalists. Militant conservatives on the faculty, despite some reservations, had developed cordial relations with dispensationalists and with the closely related advocates of "Keswick" holiness doctrines. Keswick teachings, developed among revivalist Calvinists in nineteenth-century England, emphasized a "victorious life" of suppression of known sin.[1] These various groups were closely united in their common resolve to concede nothing to the inroads of modernism. While differing on some details, they agreed that they must defend uncompromisingly the inerrancy of Scripture and the other fundamentals of supernaturalist Christian doctrines.

Machen, already a truly accomplished New Testament scholar, had risen to national prominence as a defender of fundamentalism (a term he did not like) with the publication of his *Christianity and Liberalism* in 1923. Even secular observers gave it notable acclaim. As the title suggested, Machen argued that the issues rending the largest American Protestant denominations were clear cut. Theological liberalism was not another variation of Christian theology, he claimed, but the basis of an essentially new religion. This modernist religion denied the supernatural elements that were central to Christianity and, while appropriating traditional language, promoted the worship of humanity. The honest solution would be for the liberals to withdraw peacefully

---

1. On Keswick see George M. Marsden, *Fundamentalism and American Culture: The Shaping of Twentieth-Century Evangelicalism, 1870–1925* (New York: Oxford, 1980), 72-101.

from the denominations and to start their own organizations. "A Separation between the two parties in the Church," Machen proclaimed, "is the crying need of the hour."[2]

Perhaps because of the logical force of Machen's account of the chasm between the conservative and the liberal extremes, he oversimplified the actual situation in his own denomination. Most northern Presbyterians were closer to traditional orthodoxy than to radical liberalism or "modernism." As late as the early 1920s approximately half the ministers and elders who made up the General Assembly of the denomination were ready to affirm the nonnegotiable importance of the "fundamentals," including the inerrancy of Scripture and the supernatural character of the person and work of Christ. Of the other half, most simply believed that the church should and could tolerate some theological variety, including modernism. To Machen, however, toleration of modernist unbelief in a Christian church was outrageous. Machen and other conservative leaders, most notably the Rev. Clarence Macartney of Pittsburgh and William Jennings Bryan worked assiduously to end such toleration.

Although unable to control the denomination, Presbyterian conservatives in the mid-1920s were riding a wave of profundamentalist sentiment and were able to hold their own. One of the first signs that the wave was beginning to falter was a crisis and then a serious defeat for Machen at Princeton. Keeping control of this prestigious seminary was central to the conservative strategy. Already, however, the seminary faculty was deeply divided, not so much on the question of doctrine as on that of tolerance. In 1926, in the midst of this acrimonious situation, the conservative board of directors elected Machen to the pivotal chair of apologetics. The moderates at the seminary mobilized their opposition to Machen's appointment and in 1927 the Presbyterian General Assembly, rather than approving the appointment, set up a committee to investigate the internal divisions at the seminary. This committee recommended a reorganization of the seminary's boards, a move that would wrest control from the militant conservative faction. When efforts at the General Assembly of 1929 failed to stop the reorganization, Machen and a number of colleagues launched plans in mid-summer to open in the fall a new school, Westminster Theological Seminary.

Machen saw in the Princeton situation a historical pattern repeated time and again during the preceding fifty years. As he told the 1929 General Assembly, here was "the same old story, so often repeated, of an institution formerly evangelical that is being made to drift away by insensible degrees from the gospel it was founded by godly donors to maintain."[3]

During these years of intense internal crisis at Princeton, Machen had cultivated deep loyalties within the student body. A fine teacher, both a natural showman and a southern gentleman, Machen won the hearts of many of his

2. J. Gresham Machen, *Christianity and Liberalism* (New York: Macmillan, 1923), 160.

3. Quoted in Ned B. Stonehouse, *J. Gresham Machen: A Biographical Memoir* (Grand Rapids: Eerdmans, 1954), 440.

students. Among those dedicated students were, as we have already seen, two of the group that gathered in 1947 to plan Fuller Seminary. Everett Harrison had studied New Testament with Machen and with his close associate William Park Armstrong from 1924 to 1927. He was also one of the organizers and early leaders of the League of Evangelical Students, an interseminary organization designed to strengthen a student base for combating modernism in theological education. Among his student associates were Charles Woodbridge and Paul Woolley, both of whom were later asked to be on the original Fuller faculty.

The Machen admirer of most central significance for the founding of Fuller was Harold Ockenga, who arrived at Princeton in 1927. Ockenga had been a Methodist; but he was so impressed by Machen that he soon adopted his brand of intellectually rigorous Presbyterian theology. The real test of loyalty came in 1929. Ockenga was approaching his senior year when Machen and a few others suddenly pulled up stakes to found Westminster. Could he give up the prestige of a Princeton degree to pursue the vision of renewal under Machen? With some agony, Ockenga made the sacrifice.

Under Machen's leadership, Westminster Seminary during the first years of the 1930s appeared as a beacon of hope for a conservative evangelical comeback. Unlike other movements associated with fundamentalism, this movement had a respected intellectual base and so offered some prospects for halting the steady slide of American churches toward liberalism. Scholarship as well as piety, Machen and his followers were convinced, was absolutely necessary for establishing a solid foundation for long-term evangelical survival and resurgence.

This basic conviction, central to the Presbyterian, Puritan, and Reformed heritages, grew in fundamentalism largely from Machen's own experience and influence. When he was a graduate student in Germany, Machen's own faith had been nearly totally undermined by the assumptions of modern scholarship. This soul-shaking encounter with the powers of secular thought convinced him that the most fervent proclamations of the gospel could prove largely fruitless in a civilization in which the most revered scholarship proclaimed that the traditional gospel was "a harmless delusion." In America, direct opposition to the gospel was augmented by relativistic anti-intellectualism, as exemplified in the social sciences and in modern theories of education. Fundamentalism was equally anti-intellectual in its own way and so provided little answer to the immense challenge of the prevailing thought forms of the era. Pious preaching without a firm scholarly base was, moreover, unbiblical, contradicting the New Testament pattern in which the leading evangelist was a classically educated intellectual.[4] In the intellectually barren realms of militant fundamentalism, Machen was a lonely prophet. Nonetheless, the vision he proclaimed at Princeton and carried to Westminster was inspiring a new generation of fundamentalist leaders.

4. J. Gresham Machen, *What Is Christianity? and Other Addresses* (Grand Rapids: Eerdmans, 1951), 162, 118-19 (cf. 231 and passim), 121.

Wilbur Smith, who during this era was a Presbyterian pastor in Baltimore, was just the sort of fundamentalist to be attracted by the magnetic excitement of Machen's scholarly vision. Smith was a purebred fundamentalist and so had somewhat different loyalties than did the strict confessionalist Presbyterians. Smith's father had been converted by Dwight L. Moody and his mother's father had been assistant to Moody's most influential fundamentalist successor, Reuben A. Torrey. Smith was reared practically in the shadow of Moody Bible Institute, where his father had long served on the board. So Smith grew up with a personal acquaintance with virtually every fundamentalist leader. Fundamentalist scholars, few as they were, were revered at Moody, and Smith early on developed an intense love of learning. He was impatient, however, with conventional molds and in fact never earned a degree of any sort, not even from high school.[5] This was a sign of precocity, not sloth. Before finishing high school, he entered Moody Bible Institute. Then he transferred to the College of Wooster where he spent three years before taking the opportunity to fill in as a pastor of a Presbyterian church. After a few years of such work, his presbytery recognized his talents and ordained him in 1921, even though he had never spent a day in seminary. He had become a loyal Presbyterian, but his primary spiritual community was interdenominational fundamentalism. Smith was an ardent dispensationalist premillennialist and by the end of the 1920s was a regular contributor to the leading fundamentalist journal, the *Sunday School Times*. He was also a good friend of its editor, Charles G. Trumbull, champion of the "Keswick" holiness teaching of the victorious life.

Militant Presbyterian conservatives of the Princeton ilk sometimes frowned on these fundamentalist doctrinal innovations. By the late 1920s, however, such differences had been put aside for the time being in the effort to solidify a common front against modernism. So, for instance, Trumbull supported Westminster Seminary in the pages of the *Sunday School Times*.

Smith was close to Trumbull, and he also had cordial contacts with Machen, whom he admired immensely. When Smith accepted a call to a Presbyterian church in Coatesville near Philadelphia in 1930, none other than Machen preached his installation sermon. Smith's first loyalties, though, still lay with the dispensationalist movement, of which Westminster Seminary took a dim view. So, when it came to seminaries, he recommended to prospective students the Evangelical Theological College in Dallas (Dallas Theological Seminary), founded in 1924 and prospering even in the depression years. The strengths of Dallas, he wrote in 1931, included its three-year course in

5. When Ockenga met Smith in Chicago in 1947, Smith immediately told him: "I have a confession to make to you. I can have no part in this great undertaking [the founding of Fuller Seminary]. I have led you wrongly. I do not have a single earned degree." Ockenga replied that at Fuller they wanted a practical application of the truths of Evangelical Christianity. "The idea is to train young men to be able to preach, to emphasize the great verities of the word of God, to lead people to Christ. You are best able to be a model to such a new breed of preachers and to inspire them." Ockenga recalled the conversation in his foreword to the Shepherd Illustrated Classics edition of Wilbur Smith's book *Therefore Stand* (New Canaan, Conn.: Keats Publishing, 1981), xi.

exposition of the English Bible (in addition to Greek and Hebrew) and its doctrinal orientations. Unlike even those seminaries that used Charles Hodge's text (clearly a reference to Westminster) Dallas "approaches theology from a distinct premillennial viewpoint, giving Scriptures their proper dispensational interpretation."[6] In 1932 the Evangelical Theological College honored Smith with a Doctor of Divinity degree.

What so closely united dispensationalists like Smith with the non-dispensationalists of the Princeton tradition in the early 1930s was their common conviction that, as Smith put it, "the most awful scourge in the Church of Christ today is unbelief, in the form of modernism."[7] Modernist unbelief was a consuming concern, the overriding force of which must be appreciated if one is to understand the dynamics of the fundamentalist movement in the middle decades of the century. Wilbur Smith was never bashful in presenting his views, nor in addressing famous people. In a private letter to the renowned modernist radio preacher Harry Emerson Fosdick, Smith summarized poignantly why the fundamentalist opposition to modernism was so passionate. "It was nothing less than heartbreaking," he wrote, to hear Fosdick plead with his audience "to follow their instinct for beauty, to cultivate a sense of honour, that these things would lead them into a religious life or experience." Oscar Wilde, Frank Harris, and Anatole France, the young fundamentalist pointed out, had cultivated a sense of beauty. But they had lived "utterly godless and abandoned lives." Smith yearned to hear, rather than such empty humanism, a message in which the coming of Jesus Christ meant something distinctive. Not wanting to let slip the chance to witness to Fosdick himself, he wondered if there was not a "hidden grief" behind Fosdick's words.[8]

REFORM OR WITHDRAW?

During the 1920s, fundamentalists discovered that they could not destroy the pernicious influence of leaders like Fosdick through traditional denominational means. The slide toward modernism, morever, seemed to be steady and progressive. Almost entire denominations, most notably the Congregationalists, had turned from evangelicalism to an empty liberalism. How was the trend to be reversed? Could conservatives bring reform within the denominational structures that remained? Or did they need a new institutional base?

The early success of institutions like the Evangelical Theological College in Dallas suggested that new academic centers would more and more be the answer. Among Northern Baptists, more moderate traditionalists had established two new seminaries, Northern Baptist in Chicago (1913) and Eastern Baptist in Philadelphia (1925). The foundation of Westminster Seminary was part of this trend. Where it stood in relation to independence or denomina-

---

6. Wilbur Smith, "They Teach the Gospel in Dallas," *Revelation* 2 (December 1931): 487, 514-15.

7. Ibid., 487.

8. WS to Harry Emerson Fosdick, 2-15-32 (S).

tionalism was, however, particularly ambiguous. Westminster professors remained in good standing in the Presbyterian church and were working for reform from within. Nonetheless, the seminary itself was free from denominational control. The Presbyterian church had long accepted pastors from independent as well as denominational seminaries, and so Westminster graduates were finding Presbyterian positions. Harold Ockenga was a notable example. Shortly after graduating from Westminster in 1930 he went to First Presbyterian Church in Pittsburgh to assist Clarence Macartney, Machen's coleader in the Presbyterian struggle. After that Ockenga accepted a call to another nearby Presbyterian congregation.

The relationship of the new independent institutions to the older denominational bodies was, however, tenuous and potentially explosive. Moreover, ominous signs of internal strife were also appearing. The fundamentalist movement, which was actually a coalition of submovements from various traditions, was already beginning to experience a series of implosions that were shattering it internally. The unresolved issue was the two-sided question of theological purity and ecclesiastical separatism. How tightly must church agencies, such as those for education or missions for example, be sealed off, not only from modernism itself, but also from tendencies that might lead to modernism? If they could not be tightly sealed, must one establish independent agencies in the hopes that they would remain free from modernist influences?

Even the establishment of independent agencies resolved only half the question. If one established such agencies to maintain theological purity, what was their ultimate purpose? Was it to reform existing denominations? Or was it perhaps a step toward total separation from apostasy, part of the effort to keep oneself pure? This dilemma remained far from resolved in fundamentalism.

The situation was complicated by the pervasive influence of dispensationalist premillennialists in the fundamentalist coalition. Dispensationalists taught that the present dispensation, or the "church age," would experience the "ruin of the church," or the apostasy of the major denominations. John Nelson Darby, who in the nineteenth century had brought dispensationalism to America, had urged separation from existing denominations; but until the controversies of the 1920s, relatively few of his American followers paid much attention to his separatist doctrine. In the meantime, however, dispensationalists were developing a major infrastructure of institutions, especially Bible institutes, Bible conferences, evangelistic agencies, missions societies, and publication agencies. These institutions formed the base for what was in effect an informal dispensationalist denomination, superimposed on various traditional denominations but usually not entirely separate from them. The new dispensationalist seminary in Dallas, for instance, did not demand ecclesiastical separation of its staff, a point important to the career of Everett Harrison, who maintained cordial relations with the Presbyterian Church in the U.S.A. Some dispensationalists were thus able to maintain the best of both denominationalism and independence. They had the support of a substantial subcommunity, but they also retained some of the respectability of the traditional denominations.

Independent agencies, however, almost automatically leaned toward sectarianism. To win constituents, they had to proclaim themselves superior to their denominational counterparts. Typically this meant saying that they were truer to the Bible than full-fledged denominationalists were. Such agencies thus became virtual subsects within the denominations, usually developing their own strict creeds to insulate themselves from any contamination of modernism. At the same time, because of their immense zeal for effective evangelistic outreach, they cultivated coalitions with other like-minded fundamentalists across denominational lines. So, as neither denomination nor sect, fundamentalists and their institutions sent out conflicting signals to their adherents.

CHARLES FULLER AND CONTROVERSIALISM

Two controversial episodes in Charles Fuller's early career in the 1920s illustrate the dynamics of fundamentalism centering around the unresolved questions of purity and independence. The first, leading to the establishment of an independent congregation, permanently scarred Fuller's reputation among loyal denominationalists. The second, an effort to purge the Bible Institute of Los Angeles (Biola) of alleged apostasy, closely paralleled the campaigns of Machen at Princeton at about the same time, although with a different result.

Charles Fuller in the 1920s was as archetypical a fundamentalist as could be found. His views of Christianity had been shaped by his studies at the Bible Institute of Los Angeles, especially those under the famed dispensationalist Bible teacher Reuben A. Torrey. A New Englander and a Yale graduate, Torrey was another of fundamentalism's direct links to the New School or New Divinity tradition of Congregationalism. Though a successful popular evangelist, he was also (as Ockenga was later) something of an intellectual who retained the dignified style of a Victorian clergyman.

In the early 1920s, fresh from his Biola studies, Fuller took over an adult Sunday school class at the Presbyterian church of Placentia, California. By 1925 the class had grown so large and so fundamentalist as to cause a serious rift with the pastor of the church. As a result, Fuller led his class out of the Presbyterian church and reorganized it as the Calvary Church of Placentia. Such schisms were becoming increasingly frequent among dispensationalist fundamentalists at the time. Until the 1920s such fundamentalists had usually taken for granted traditional denominational affiliations. Now, however, they were breaking off into independent (often "Calvary") churches which were forming the base for a vigorous branch of evangelicalism outside of the major denominations. Charles Fuller seems not to have cared much about one denomination above another. Having separated from the Presbyterians, he secured ordination through the Baptist Bible Union, an organization of the strict dispensationalist fundamentalist Baptists who had attempted to reform the Northern Baptist Convention and who also had separatist tendencies.

Charles Fuller (upper right) in his fighting fundamentalist days

During this period the energetic young pastor-evangelist stayed in close touch with the dispensationalist fundamentalists of Biola, and in 1927 he was elected to its board of trustees. This position placed Fuller in the middle of a classic intrafundamentalist struggle that revealed the tensions within the movement with which he would have to contend throughout his later, more moderate, years.

When Reuben Torrey retired in 1924 he was succeeded by John MacInnis as dean at Biola. MacInnis was uneasy with the dogfight mentality and announced in the Biola publication, *The King's Business*, his policy of seeking the "triumph of God's truth rather than the downing of the enemy." To many militant fundamentalists, such irenic statements themselves put MacInnis under a cloud of suspicion. Calls for peace and positive outlooks were just the tactics of liberals and moderate compromisers. MacInnis made the situation far worse with the publication in 1927 of his book *Peter, the Fisherman Philosopher*. Proclaiming in the book's subtitle a "higher fundamentalism," MacInnis argued that Peter's insights into the gospel were based on the homespun philosophy of the common man in contrast to later theological elaborations. This was another sentimental liberal line. The fundamentalist world was startled. Here, in 1927, at the height of the nationwide controversies, the dean of the Bible Institute of Los Angeles sounded like a modernist!

Charles Trumbull of the powerful *Sunday School Times* fulminated against MacInnis on this point. Biola's dean, said the outraged Trumbull, reduced the apostle's message of unique divine relevation to a philosophy available to any spiritually guided human. This was the message of Fosdick and his crowd and a disastrous teaching for one of the nation's leading Bible institutes. Trumbull ended with the demand that the directors "cleanse the Institute of all false teaching."⁹

Until Trumbull's outburst in the *Sunday School Times*, it appeared that MacInnis might weather the storm. In fact he had said nothing strictly unorthodox and he affirmed the creed of the Institute. Among fundamentalists he had supporters as well as detractors. The Biola board initially supported him (Charles Fuller was absent at the time), wishing that their hiring and firing not be dictated by every wave of popular sentiment. The way the fundamentalist movement was structured, however, an all-out attack from a national journal such as the *Sunday School Times* could destroy an independent institution like Biola. Lacking formal church connections, such instutitions were directly dependent on the goodwill of their constituents. The constituents, in turn, lacking any concern for ecclesiastical authority, were dependent for their opinions on the informal authority of prominent Bible teachers. Indeed, such authority was often conflated with the authority of the Bible itself. Thus a revered Bible teacher like Charles Trumbull could ruin an institution. In the summer of 1928 Trumbull exercised his authority and dropped Biola from his list of "Bible Schools that are True to the Faith." Other fundamentalist leaders, in the meantime, joined the chorus of protest.

Under this pressure, Biola's board of directors, on which Charles Fuller was playing a major role, reversed its earlier stand and voted six to four to accept MacInnis's resignation. In protest, the four supporters of MacInnis resigned as did the institute's own famed Bible teacher, G. Campbell Morgan. The directors who remained named Charles Fuller as the new chairman of the board, and on him fell the major task of reorganizing the school after the housecleaning had reestablished its reputation as a "safe" fundamentalist institution. Soon after this, Fuller immersed himself in radio ministry and after a few years put aside his activities as a patron of education. He was well schooled, however, in the trials and dynamics of fundamentalist academia.

Some outside observers thought that such internecine struggles would destroy fundamentalism. The structures of the movement, however, prevented that result. Lacking any commitments to centralized authorities, fundamentalism was almost infinitely divisible. Moreover, its free enterprise character meant that internal competition could even augment growth. Charles Fuller's immense success as a radio evangelist illustrated the resilience of the movement as a whole, despite its internal controversies. Yet at

---

9. This account is based on the more complete account in Daniel Fuller, *Give the Winds a Mighty Voice: The Story of Charles E. Fuller* (Waco, Tex.: Word, 1972), 68-74.

the same time, he quickly realized that if he was to build and maintain a truly nationwide audience, he should avoid the controversialism that would limit his appeal to only a few subparties of fundamentalism. He accordingly moved toward the side of fundamentalism that stressed the positive presentation of the gospel more than controversy. In the meantime, however, some other fundamentalists were moving rapidly in the opposite direction. J. Gresham Machen was a notable case in point.

SEPARATISM

In the early 1930s Westminster Seminary promised to be a rallying point for conservatives and fundamentalists who valued intellect. Its supporters' hopes that it would lead a broad movement were, however, bound to Machen's continuing struggles with the Presbyterian church. The independent seminary was becoming not only a center for fundamentalist renewal but also the headquarters for a party of strict Machenites who were embroiled in intense controversy with the hierarchy of their denomination. The Westminster situation was finally beginning to strain the denomination's tolerance for independent agencies. The denomination had long recognized independent seminaries, allowed its clergy to teach at them, and accepted their graduates as ministerial candidates. Westminster, however, was becoming the center for a sort of independent subdenomination within the denomination.

The crisis reached monumental proportions when Machen extended his campaigns for purity to the foreign mission fields. Again he attempted to have all the benefits of both denominationalism and independence. Missions was a paramount concern for all evangelicals. Ever since World War I, a succession of conservative and fundamentalist travelers had been bringing back alarming tales from the mission fields. Modernist missionaries, they reported, did not preach the gospel of salvation through the atoning work of Christ alone. Rather, they merely harmonized Christianity with non-Christian faiths. From the evangelical viewpoint, millions of souls were in mortal danger.

In 1933 the issue boiled to a peak in the northern Presbyterian church. The denomination's Board of Foreign Missions had declined to take a strong stand against the view that Christianity only supplemented truths in other world religions. When the General Assembly of 1933 backed the board, Machen, who was ordained in the Presbyterian church, made the audacious move of organizing his own Independent Board for Presbyterian Foreign Missions, in direct competition with the denomination's board.

The organization of the Independent Board split the Presbyterian fundamentalist renewal effort down the middle. A number of the future Fuller leadership were deeply involved. Wilbur Smith sided with Machen and accepted a position on the executive committee of the Independent Board.[10]

10. In private correspondence, Smith argued vigorously with Robert E. Speer, Machen's most effective conservative opponent and a former contributor to *The Fundamentals*, who now defended the evangelical integrity of the denominational board; WS to Robert Speer, 11-1-35. A note to Charles Woodbridge mentions earlier correspondence (S).

More militant still was Charles Woodbridge, who was then a missionary in the French Cameroon and was uncompromisingly faithful to Machen's cause. Woodbridge accepted the leading post of General Secretary of the Independent Board.

On the other side, even some of the staunchest supporters of semi-independence at Westminster Seminary broke with Machen when he applied the same strategy to foreign missions. The stand of Clarence Macartney was immensely important. Macartney had long been the coleader with Machen of Presbyterian fundamentalism and, as Wilbur Smith put it in 1933, "the one man . . . who can really command the absolute loyalty of the entire conservative side of the church."[11] Macartney vigorously defended the right of Presbyterians to form an independent board, but he himself would not so divide his denomination. Harold Ockenga, who had served as Macartney's assistant at First Presbyterian Church in Pittsburgh, took a similar position. He was sympathetic to the protesters but would not break with the denominational board.

The Presbyterian leadership, in the meantime, was outraged that Presbyterian ministers should form an alternative "Presbyterian" mission board, explicitly designed to deflect funds from the denominational board. The General Assembly declared the competing board unconstitutional and ordered its members to be tried by local presbyteries. The purge began. Machen, Woodbridge, Woolley, Carl McIntire, and some other leaders of the Independent Board were defrocked by their presbyteries. As the 1936 General Assembly approached, they announced their intention to found a new denomination if the Assembly sustained these convictions, as it almost certainly would.

Under such circumstances, everyone had to choose sides. Disagreements among conservative allies now turned into sorrowful, sometimes bitter, partings of ways. Machen now saw the Presbyterian church as hopelessly apostate and demanded that his allies join him on his separatist course. Under the threat of denominational censure, some of Machen's staunchest supporters deserted him. During the 1935–36 school year, Westminster Seminary suffered a crippling loss of one senior faculty member and thirteen members of the board of trustees, including Macartney.[12] Undaunted, Machen went ahead in the summer of 1936 with his plan to found a new denomination, the Presbyterian Church of America (later the Orthodox Presbyterian Church); but by this time his followers were few.

Wilbur Smith apparently tried as hard as anyone to remain on good terms with both sides. He strongly opposed Machen's separatist course—largely because he thought it would not amount to much. He was, however, as independence-minded as anyone, arguing for remaining in the Presbyterian ministry on the anomalous grounds that in it he was as free as "if I were the

11. WS to Clarence E. Macartney, 5-16-33 (S).
12. Stonehouse, *J. Gresham Machen*, 496-97. Edwin H. Rian, *The Presbyterian Conflict* (Grand Rapids: Eerdmans, 1940), 97-99.

pastor of a church entirely independent of any ecclesiastical organization."
This independent spirit also meant that he was reluctant to resign from Machen's Independent Board under ecclesiastical pressure. Meanwhile, he escaped the purge since his presbytery, the Presbytery of Chester, was predominantly conservative and refused to take action. The 1936 General Assembly,
however, took notice of the presbytery's recalcitrance and ordered it to bring
Smith to trial.[13] The heat was now on Smith to make a choice. In the fall of
1936 he found a way out. In response to an inquiry from Smith, Machen said
that he personally thought that membership on the Independent Board and
membership in the Presbyterian Church in the U.S.A. were no longer compatible. Although Smith had just been reelected to the board, he took Machen's
comment as an invitation to resign, which he gratefully accepted.[14]

     The events that immediately followed are also pivotal for understand-
ing the developments of the next decade. Machen's movement, which after
several schisms was only a remnant of the original, now faced another division.
In fact, those who at one time or another had been associated with Machen's
efforts for conservative Presbyterian renewal made up at least four distinct
groups. First, they were divided between strict Calvinist Westminster confessionalists on the one hand and dispensationalists on the other. Each of these
groups was further subdivided between those who, like Macartney and
Ockenga from the first group and Wilbur Smith and Everett Harrison from the
second, chose to work within the Presbyterian church and those who followed
Machen to the bitter end of schism. These twice-compounded divisions meant
that when Machen finally did leave the Presbyterian church, two different
types of followers went with him. As with all revolutions, they agreed on what
they were against, but the unresolved differences among the cobelligerents
became apparent as soon as they attempted to define their own positive course.

     J. Oliver Buswell and Carl McIntire led the fundamentalist opposi-
tion to the strict confessionalism of Machen and his closest followers. Buswell
was president of burgeoning Wheaton College, the one collegiate intellectual
haven for promising young fundamentalists, and hence as important as Westminster was if the movement was to have any future intellectually. McIntire,
formerly with Ockenga in the close-knit group of students who left Princeton
Seminary for Westminster, was now making a move for national leadership in
the separatist movement. In early 1936 he established a new fundamentalist
weekly, the *Christian Beacon*. Buswell and McIntire hoped to build a fundamentalist separatist movement with a broader base than the strict Calvinism at
Westminster Seminary. In the fall of 1936 they fell into intense fighting with
Machen and his closest Old School confessionalist followers. These Old
School Presbyterian traditionalists differed with the new-style fundamentalists on a number of the distinctives of fundamentalism. Old School Presbyteri-

─────────────────────────

     13. *Minutes of the General Assembly of the Presbyterian Church in the U.S.A.*, 3rd Series,
vol. 15 (1936), part 1 (Philadelphia, 1936), 37-39.
     14. Wilbur Smith, *Before I Forget* (Chicago: Moody Press, 1971), 116-17; see the
corrections of several details in Paul Woolley's review, *Westminster Theological Journal* 35 (Fall
1972): 68-72.

ans believed in the "Christian liberty" to drink alcoholic beverages and, contrary to almost all other American evangelicals, would not condemn their use. A more substantial rift was the intensification of the Westminster faculty's opposition to dispensationalism.

These issues split the Independent Board. McIntire and his more purely fundamentalist group wrested control from Machen and his Westminster allies. In the midst of this painful internal struggle, Machen, only fifty-five, died suddenly on January 1, 1937. The more fundamentalistic group, though in control of the Independent Board, was in the minority in the new Presbyterian Church of America; so they soon split off to found the Bible Presbyterian Church. In the meantime, Allan MacRae, who had taught at Westminster since its beginning, had resigned shortly after Machen's death and in the fall of 1937 became president of the new Faith Theological Seminary organized by the McIntire group.[15]

How deep the chasm would be was not always immediately apparent to the participants who had struggled together so earnestly against apostasy. In the summer of 1937, for instance, Carl McIntire, having rid the Independent Board of the Westminster group, privately invited Wilbur Smith to rejoin it. Smith's response showed that it was too late for reconciliation. In Coatesville, two of the Independent Board members, including Smith's predecessor, Roy T. Brumbaugh, had recently been holding Bible classes and other services. They promoted these by proclaiming that the Presbyterian Church in the U.S.A., and hence Smith and his congregation, were now apostate. Brumbaugh, when asked to assist in the wedding of one of Smith's parishioners, refused to do so if Smith had anything to do with the service. Smith, who did not have great tolerance for personal indignities, did not see how he could possibly work in fellowship with such men. Moreover, he could now gracefully step out of the situation by accepting a "glorious" invitation that filled his life's ambition to teach at Moody Bible Institute.[16]

Everett Harrison became involved in the Presbyterian controversies in a similar, though less dramatic, way. In the early 1940s, while he was working on his doctorate at the University of Pennsylvania, he was pastor of a Presbyterian church in Chester, Pennsylvania. This church too had suffered a painful fundamentalist schism. Though he had impeccable fundamentalist credentials himself, he had remained loyal to the Presbyterian Church in the U.S.A. He thus had the job of picking up the pieces for the congregation and got a taste of the resentments generated by the separatists. The separating congregation became part of McIntire's Bible Presbyterian movement. One of its pastors while Harrison was there was Francis A. Schaeffer, an outspoken McIntire defender in these decades.[17]

15. See George M. Marsden, "Perspective on the Division of 1937," in *Pressing Toward the Mark: Essays Commemorating Fifty Years of the Orthodox Presbyterian Church,* ed. Charles G. Dennison and Richard C. Gamble (Philadelphia: Orthodox Presbyterian Church, 1986), 295-328.
16. Carl McIntire to WS, 7-1-37; WS to McIntire, 7-2-37.
17. Everett Harrison interview, 11-23-83.

THE WHEATON CONNECTION

In the years immediately following the Presbyterian schism, much of the impact of the Presbyterian controversies (which would later hit Fuller Seminary) was channeled through events at Wheaton College. Under President Buswell, Wheaton had become the fastest growing college in the country. By the late 1930s, it had also attracted one of the most remarkably talented student bodies. Many of the evangelical leaders of the next generation were students at Wheaton at the same time. Just those who had a major impact on Fuller included Carl Henry, Harold Lindsell, Edward J. Carnell, Paul Jewett, Lars Granberg, Glenn Barker, and Billy Graham. In addition, Rebecca Price was teaching there. At Wheaton the atmosphere combined high commitment with the intellectual excitment that this generation could do great things for Christ and his kingdom.

Especially important in generating that excitement was Wheaton's impressive professor of philosophy, Gordon H. Clark, who had taught at the University of Pennsylvania until 1936. Buswell then brought him to Wheaton during the height of the Presbyterian controversies. Clark was intensely devoted to Machen and in 1936 had the honor of nominating him moderator of their new denomination. At Wheaton, Clark remained in the Orthodox Presbyterian Church and sometimes tried to guide his students to Westminster Seminary.[18] He inspired students to take seriously classical Reformed theology, to know equally well the history of Western thought, to be convinced that the Christian faith could be defended rationally, to be alert against modernism, and to regard ideas as the key to the future of civilization. Clark especially influenced a number of the students, including Henry, Lindsell, Carnell, Jewett, and Granberg, who later joined the Fuller faculty.[19]

In the meantime, Presbyterian controversialism was becoming a sore point at Wheaton. President Buswell, who had gone with McIntire into the tiny Bible Presbyterian denomination, guided some of Wheaton's best students to Faith Seminary. Wheaton, however, traditionally represented a broader interdenominational fundamentalism. Now, it was clear, fundamentalists everywhere had to face the question of separatism. In addition to the Presbyterian schism, a small Baptist group had already split from the Northern Baptist Convention in 1932 to form the General Association of Regular Baptists, and many other fundamentalists were actually or virtually independent of major denominations. The new separatists were attempting to make separatism an article of faith. This threatened to divide the movement even further. Reflecting such fears, the Wheaton College trustees in 1940 fired

18. Gordon H. Clark, letter to author, 9-9-80.
19. Interviews with CH, HL, and Lars Granberg. Granberg, who had a Lutheran and fundamentalist background, became Reformed through Clark's influence. William LaSor studied with Clark at the University of Pennsylvania, and Jewett and Henry showed their indebtedness by dedicating books to him.

Buswell as president. Gordon Clark lasted three more years; but then his insistence on strict Calvinism led to his dismissal as well.[20]

TOWARD MODERATION

Clark's Wheaton protégés who later went to Fuller proved to be more moderate ecclesiastically than their Orthodox Presbyterian mentor, though they shared most of his concerns. In 1943 fundamentalists in the Northern Baptist Convention organized the Conservative Baptist Foreign Mission Society as an alternative to the official mission board of the convention. This move paralleled Machen's organization of the Independent Board a decade earlier. Although Baptist traditions of decentralization made the split slightly less radical than Machen's, it was just as resented by the denomination's leadership. Carl Henry, then teaching at Northern Baptist Seminary, was sympathetic to independent missionary efforts. At the general meeting of the convention in 1946, when denominational pressures against the mission board were leading toward a showdown, he even allowed his name to be placed on the slate of fundamentalists nominated for convention offices. The slate was overwhelmingly defeated, however, as were other fundamentalist efforts at the 1946 meeting. With hope for alternative efforts within the convention structure shut off, dissatisfied fundamentalists formed both the Conservative Baptist Association, a secession group of about three hundred churches, and Denver Conservative Baptist Seminary. Henry regarded such separatism as premature and so stayed with the main Northern Baptist group. He estimated that about 85 percent of convention churches were evangelical, even if few approved of fundamentalist tactics.[21]

Harold Lindsell followed a path similar to Carl Henry's. Though Presbyterian in background, he became a Baptist while teaching at Columbia Bible College in the early 1940s. There he was ordained into the Southern Baptist Convention. His switch from Presbyterianism reflected not only his objections to infant baptism but also a preference for decentralized Baptist ecclesiology. In 1944 he joined Henry on the faculty of Northern Baptist Seminary, where, however, he felt unwelcome pressures for ecclesiastical conformity. Along with Henry, he too supported the Conservative Baptist Foreign Mission Society. The seminary administration, however, warned him that his speaking at a Conservative Baptist function was an embarrassment to the institution.[22] By 1946 or 1947, Henry and Lindsell were in a sort of ecclesiastical no-man's land. On the one hand, they sympathized deeply with the cause of the separatists; on the other, they rejected separatism itself.

20. See Paul M. Bechtel, *Wheaton College: A Heritage Remembered, 1860–1984* (Wheaton: Harold Shaw, 1984), 144-53, 207-9; see also Carl Henry, *Confessions of a Theologian: An Autobiography* (Waco, Tex.: Word, 1986), 66-68.

21. Henry, "Twenty Years a Baptist," *Foundations* 1 (January 1958): 50; and *Confessions of a Theologian*, 110-11. See also Bruce Shelley, *A History of Conservative Baptists* (Wheaton: Conservative Baptist Press, 1971).

22. HL interview, 10-27-83.

Their strongest loyalties were with the emerging renewal movement among nonseparating fundamentalists. Despite defeats in the denominations, the intrafundamentalist battles of the 1930s, and the impact of the depression, fundamentalist institutions had been growing. Everywhere the leadership talked of a coming nationwide revival.[23] Fundamentalists continually longed and prayed for such an awakening. Separatism, however, posed a dilemma. Although increasing numbers of fundamentalists favored ecclesiastical independence, often arguing that it was necessary if the gospel was to be freely proclaimed in its purity, most fundamentalists still remained in major denominations. Not only did traditional church loyalties prevail; many also felt that the constant controversialism of the separatists would distract from the positive presentation of the gospel.

Charles Fuller was one fundamentalist who moved away from controversialism toward concentrating on a positive message based on the word. The most recent great American revivalist, Billy Sunday, had mixed the gospel with a good measure of bombast. Yet his ministry had declined drastically in the decade before his death in 1935. Fuller, in the meantime, was presenting a warm, simple gospel, conspicuously free of rancor. While seldom getting the headlines, he used the radio to proclaim the gospel to the largest audiences in history. By the late 1930s he was the closest equivalent the fundamentalists had to a new Billy Sunday. Although not interested in sustained in-person campaigns, he sometimes appeared at "radio rallies," often drawing impressive audiences. In 1938 forty thousand Chicagoans got up at dawn to hear him at an Easter sunrise service at Soldier Field. In 1941 he preached to packed houses for two services at the Boston Garden. His greatest successes, however, were in his massive, though largely unheralded, radio ministry.

UNITY

Despite signs that promised wider revival, most fundamentalist leaders agreed that the anarchic nature of their movement dampened their collective impact. Certainly they were not getting the recognition that their numbers seemed to warrant. By the early 1940s, the need for united action was becoming apparent. The outstanding example of what could be done was the New England Fellowship, organized by J. Elwin Wright in 1929. Wright moved beyond the narrow party lines that characterized almost every fundamentalist association and proved that even in New England, where the cold winds of secularism seemed the strongest, more Bible-believers had survived than almost anyone had realized. During the fellowship's first five years, it garnered the affiliation of a thousand New England churches. It sponsored conferences, Bible camps, radio ministries, Bible teaching, and revival services—activities that helped people from small Bible churches avoid the discouragements of feeling "only I

23. Joel Carpenter, "The Fundamentalist Leaven and the Rise of an Evangelical United Front," in *The Evangelical Tradition in America,* ed. Leonard I. Sweet (Macon, Ga.: Mercer University Press, 1984), 257-88.

am left," in the words of Wright.[24] Such coordinated efforts could also bring in national leaders. Charles Fuller made several appearances in New England under the Fellowship's sponsorship; and Wright sealed the connection by publishing in 1940 a successful biography lauding Fuller's ministry.[25]

Wright, who was associated with Ockenga's Park Street Church in Boston, took the lead in exploring possibilities for a national counterpart to the New England Fellowship. Finding positive responses, he and other organizers formed a steering committee in 1941 and issued a call, signed by 147 evangelical leaders. Of the signers, those later connected with Fuller Seminary were Harold Ockenga, Charles Fuller, H. J. Taylor, William LaSor, Charles Woodbridge, Clarence Roddy, Robert Munger, and C. Davis Weyerhaeuser. These and others met again in the spring of 1942 and founded the National Association of Evangelicals (NAE), a fellowship of both individuals and denominations. They elected Ockenga its president.

In the meantime this new organization had already been upstaged by Ockenga's old seminary friend Carl McIntire, always a great showman. Despite the meager followers of the separatist groups he led, he never spoke of his projects in less than worldwide and indeed cosmic terms. In September 1941 he announced as part of his "twentieth-century Reformation" the establishment of the American Council of Christian Churches. In fact, McIntire's explorations for fundamentalist unity so far had brought together only two tiny denominations. Strict separatism clearly limited the ecumenical field. Undeterred, McIntire declared his council the true counterpart of the Federal Council of Churches, which had been organized in 1908 to promote cooperative efforts among the Protestant denominations.

At first, the founders of the National Association of Evangelicals thought this unfortunate duplication of their efforts and McIntire's might be remedied. Almost no one seems to have regarded the formation of the NAE as a sign that "evangelicals" were now breaking from "fundamentalists" over the principle of separatism. There was not a practical distinction between fundamentalist and evangelical: the words were interchangeable. All involved in the NAE were frankly fundamentalists, and among fundamentalism only a minority would make separatism a test of fellowship. Some of the most ardent fundamentalists, such as William B. Riley, the pope of Minnesota Baptist fundamentalism, were not separatists. And some of the most militant fundamentalists, such as Bob Jones, Sr., and John R. Rice of the influential *Sword of the Lord*, even joined the NAE. All were adamantly opposed to the Federal Council of Churches. They assumed that both the NAE and McIntire were basically on the same side. The NAE leadership accordingly invited McIntire to meet with them and to present his views to their organizing convention.

24. Wright, quoted in Joel Carpenter, "Tuning In on the Gospel" (unpublished paper, 1985), 9. Most of this account is drawn from Carpenter's work. His Ph.D. dissertation, "The Renewal of American Fundamentalism, 1930–1945" (Johns Hopkins University, 1984), is by far the most valuable work on the subject.
25. Wright, *The Old Fashioned Revival Hour and the Broadcasters* (Boston: Fellowship Press, 1940).

McIntire, however, was constitutionally unable to play any other role than chief. He also felt strongly about those who had rejected ecclesiastical separatism. The NAE allowed no denomination in the fellowship that also belonged to the Federal Council; but, unlike the American Council of Christian Churches, they did welcome individual members, such as Ockenga, Macartney, and many others, who retained ties with denominations affiliated with the Federal Council. Despite differing policies, negotiations between the American Council and the NAE continued for several years, but to no avail. The rivalry grew in bitterness. By the time of the founding of Fuller Seminary, McIntire was proclaiming that the compromises of the NAE were almost as dangerous as the outright subversion of the Federal Council.[26]

Ockenga meanwhile was plotting his own reformation. The new fellowship, he told the first assembly of the NAE, would be "the vanguard of a movement." It would bring together the "unvoiced multitudes," or those many Christians who, like himself, were "lone wolves," unrepresented in the other major organizations of the day. Ockenga observed that he had belonged to several denominations but could not give unreserved support to any organization except his independent church. "The division is no longer between the denominations," he proclaimed, in words that echoed Machen's *Christianity and Liberalism* of twenty years earlier; "the division is between those who believe in Christ and the Bible, and those who reject Christ—the Christ of the cross and the Bible."[27]

The remarkable feature of the NAE, in contrast with earlier fundamentalism, was that it was a movement that brought together a true variety of conservative evangelical groups. While the organizers were overwhelmingly from the core fundamentalist network of Presbyterians and Baptists, the NAE membership also included numerous small pentecostal, holiness, Methodist, and Mennonite groups. Pentecostalism, particularly, had been declared unacceptable by some of the militant fundamentalists. The predominantly Calvinistic leadership saw the possibility in the NAE of limited cooperation among conservative Protestants on matters of common interest without the necessity of sacrificing particular group distinctives.

The formation of the NAE pointed to a dimension of evangelicalism that is important for keeping the history of Fuller Seminary in perspective. As Ockenga was recognizing, evangelicalism was much more diverse than the movement represented by the heirs to the Presbyterian-Baptist fundamentalist network. Yet this group, having lost most of its denominationalist loyalties, was trying to take the lead in forging a new interdenominational alliance among conservative Protestants as diverse as pentecostals and Missouri Synod Lutherans. This predominantly Calvinistic core group continually at-

26. James DeForest Murch, *Cooperation without Compromise: A History of the National Association of Evangelicals* (Grand Rapids: Eerdmans, 1956), 32-71; see also J. Elwin Wright, "An Historical Statement of Events Leading up to the National Conference at St. Louis," in *Evangelical Action! A Report of the Organization of the National Association of Evangelicals for United Action* (Boston: Fellowship Press, 1942), 3-16.

27. Ockenga, "The Unvoiced Multitudes," in *Evangelical Action!* 35, 20-21, 33.

tempted to speak for evangelicalism as a whole. But because they themselves were a party within evangelicalism, they always had great difficulties getting other subgroups to follow their lead.

In fact, most American evangelicals had agendas set by their own denominational histories and were shaped only secondarily by their common experiences of opposition to modernism and modern secularism. This diversity of evangelicalism and priority of denominational loyalties immediately became a factor in efforts to organize the NAE. Delegates to its preliminary convention came from fifty denominations and represented a potential constituency of fifteen million. Most of the denominations, however—including the largest ones, such as the Southern Baptist Convention and the Missouri Synod Lutherans—decided to stay out of the formal organization. By 1945, the new organization had only a little more than a million members drawn from twenty-two denominations.[28]

The controversy surrounding religious broadcasting was one of the issues that brought the NAE into existence. The Federal Council of Churches, pointing out the dangers of religious racketeering, had persuaded CBS and NBC not to sell time to any religious broadcasters. Rather, the networks were allotting free time to Catholics, Jews, and Protestants, the only catch being that the Federal Council itself controlled the selection of the Protestants. In 1943 the Mutual Broadcasting Company, which carried "The Old Fashioned Revival Hour," also gave in to such pressures and virtually forced Charles Fuller to resort to an informal network for his broadcast. Both the NAE and the American Council of Christian Churches complained bitterly against this high-handed policy. Who made the Federal Council the representative of all Protestants? They saw the policy not as directed primarily against racketeers, but as part of the Federal Council's warfare against fundamentalism. A delegation from the NAE helped defeat a truly outrageous proposal that religious broadcasters address a "cross-section of the public" rather than present the specific beliefs of any one faith. More, however, was needed to break the emerging cultural monopoly of secularism in alliance with religion-in-general. Accordingly, the NAE sponsored the formation of the National Religious Broadcasters in 1944, an organization that eventually had substantial success in preserving evangelical broadcasting and providing some self-regulation.[29]

SUCCESS

Fundamentalism was rapidly building new institutions that were moving it away from preoccupation with negative protests toward organized enthusiasm for positive evangelism. The most exciting evidences that fundamentalism might have a bright future were the revivals among American youth during World War II. Three new youth organizations were flourishing by the mid-

28. Louis Gasper, *The Fundamentalist Movement* (The Hague: Mouton, 1962), 27-30.
29. Daniel Fuller, *Give the Winds a Mighty Voice*, 152-57; Murch, *Cooperation without Compromise*, 72-81.

war years. Young Life sponsored evangelistic clubs and rallies across the country and emphasized one-on-one evangelism in summer-camp ministries. Inter-Varsity Christian Fellowship was a British import that came to America in 1941 as a Christian ministry to college and university campuses. Most spectacular, however, was Youth for Christ.

Youth for Christ evolved out of impressive urban youth rallies during World War II. One key figure was Jack Wyrtzen, who preached on the radio to young people in the New York City area and by the late war years was holding mammoth youth rallies in the heart of secular America. Several times he drew more than twenty thousand to Madison Square Garden. The excitment of the much-sought revivals swept through fundamentalism as youth rallies became something of a national fad. In 1944, young people packed Orchestra Hall in Chicago for twenty weeks of rallies, ending with a "Victory Rally" bringing twenty-eight thousand to Chicago Stadium. On Memorial Day of 1945 Percy Crawford, Wyrtzen's mentor, preached to seventy thousand at Soldier Field. That same summer the various youth evangelists formally organized Youth for Christ International. Within a year, Youth for Christ was sponsoring nine hundred regular Saturday night rallies throughout the country with a total attendance of about a million.[30] The organization was soon able to hire its first full-time evangelist: an energetic Wheaton graduate named Billy Graham.

A leading promoter of all these movements was Herbert J. Taylor, the wealthy president of the Club Aluminum Products Company. Taylor helped organize the Chicago evangelistic rallies and was the chief financier of the Young Life movement as well as the chairman of the board of Inter-Varsity. His Christian Worker's Foundation was instrumental in building these and the burgeoning network of interdenominational parachurch agencies. When Ockenga and Fuller first conceived of their seminary project, they immediately recognized that Taylor's support would be of great strategic significance, even a "fleece."[31]

Exciting things were happening in fundamentalism, and all who met in Chicago in May 1947 to plan Fuller Seminary shared enthusiasm for the recent surge of evangelism and the new supporting organizations. These events shaped their most immediate past, and their clearest identity was as part of this burgeoning movement for positive evangelism. This was one side of their immediate history. What they added to it was a zeal for scholarship, which they regarded as crucial if Christianity was to have a lasting impact on civilization. They saw this tradition as extending back through Calvin to Augustine and the apostle Paul. While it had barely survived in popular fundamentalism, it had remained vigorous in Princeton Seminary and Machen's intellectual fundamentalism. This was the other side of their immediate

30. Joel Carpenter, "From Fundamentalism to the New Evangelical Coalition," in *Evangelicalism and Modern America*, ed. George Marsden (Grand Rapids: Eerdmans, 1984), 15.
31. This account of youth organizations and Taylor's role depends on the fine work of Bruce Shelley, "The Rise of Evangelical Youth Movements," *Fides et Historia* 18 (January 1986): 47-63.

history. The dual leadership of Charles Fuller and Ockenga well represented the the two-sided nature of this heritage in which everyone present shared.

Fuller Seminary was still just a conception. It was to be located in California, a land renowned for rootlessness. Nonetheless, the new seminary already had a history.

CHAPTER III

Rebuilding Western Civilization

Here we have the recrudescence of a culture. We have not only a recrudescence of what we call "western culture" but we have the birth of an American culture that is strictly indigenous to these parts. . . . Why, then should the west forever look to the east for its preachers? Why should it be, as it has been in part at least, a theological vacuum? Why has it not to date entered its maturity of Christian leaderhip so that it will in turn send forth those who may blaze the trail of theological and ecclesiastical and religious thinking in our own day? The hour for the west to enter its maturity theologically is come.

Harold J. Ockenga, "The Challenge to the Christian Culture of the
West," Convocation Address, Fuller Theological Seminary,
October 1, 1947.

"A CAL TECH OF THE EVANGELICAL WORLD"

WHEN the founders of Fuller met in Chicago on May 13, 1947, it was far from clear that the seminary could open as early as the coming fall. Carl Henry argued that a delay of a year would not be senseless. Wilbur Smith wavered. Yet, as Harold Ockenga later remarked, "Whatever Charlie Fuller said came to pass, in a way, because he saw that it came to pass."[1] Fuller viewed the question of opening the seminary in the fall of 1947 as a spiritual matter. The purchase of the Cravens estate, which he had undertaken without consulting Ockenga, seemed to him a clear leading from the Lord. On the day of the sale, other bidders known to be interested had not appeared. So, amazingly, he got the mansion for his low initial bid. Fuller was sure of divine intervention. With such a sign in hand, to say nothing of such an architectural gem, Fuller could see no point in delaying sending out the seminary's graduates for another year. With plenty of money, confidence in the power of radio to bring in students, and experience in managing one of the largest evangelical enterprises in the country, Fuller was convinced that he could make the seminary come to pass in short order.[2]

1. HJO interview, 11-6-83.
2. Daniel Fuller, *Give the Winds a Mighty Voice: The Story of Charles E. Fuller* (Waco, Tex.: Word, 1972), 201-2; Wilbur Smith, *A Voice for God: The Life of Charles E. Fuller* (Boston: W. A. Wilde, 1949), 189.

He eventually proved correct, after a brief scare. Because of delays in distributing radio transcriptions, the announcement of the seminary did not go out to all the stations carrying "The Old Fashioned Revival Hour" until June 22, and the first magazine advertising did not appear until July or August. As late as July 24 Fuller wrote to Ockenga with the news that there were "few applicants," and only Dan and a forty-nine-year-old Chinese man had been accepted. A week later Fuller observed that even some of the best friends of the seminary at key California Presbyterian churches, such as Robert Munger at First Church in Berkeley and Henrietta Mears at Hollywood Presbyterian, felt obliged to caution prospective Fuller students that they would be "guinea pigs."[3] Nonetheless, the response from prospective students was soon impressive. One of Miss Mears's converts, Bill Bright, who had attended Princeton Seminary the previous year, was among those to enroll at Fuller. Applications were picking up.

Despite the slow start, an early September advertisement in the NAE publication *United Evangelical Action* was already claiming that the entering class would be "limited to fifty graduates of accredited colleges," and that "they are being carefully selected from hundreds of applicants."[4] Though most of these "applicants" were likely only making inquiries, the initially grandiose description of the size of the student body turned out to be not far from the mark. By the time registration was complete on September 30, thirty-nine students were on hand. Many others had inquired or applied, but most had not graduated from accredited institutions. Those who came were generally solid, some with outstanding talent. More came from universities than from the Christian college circuit. Immediately the seminary began advertising that its "almost forty" students were from schools like Harvard, Dartmouth, Berkeley, and the University of Southern California.[5] The size of the entering class, assembled in so brief a time, made the faculty immediately confident that they could expand to one hundred students when they added a second year. Dallas Seminary, after all, had begun with only six students; Faith with only eight. Fuller's first-year enrollment was larger than Westminster Seminary's enrollment for all three classes and, as Wilbur Smith observed, was comparable to the entire enrollment of an established mainline school like the Pacific School of Religion at Berkeley.[6]

The literature of the new school explained its "purpose" largely in contrast to other seminary education available. First, "no interdenominational theological seminary of outstanding academic and evangelical qualifica-

3. CF to HJO, 8-2-47.
4. *United Evangelical Action*, September 1, 1947, 23.
5. See the official publication, the *Bulletin of Fuller Theological Seminary*, Fall 1947.
6. WS to Frank Gaebelein, 9-15-47; and WS to William Culbertson, 10-13-47 (S).

"A Center of Evangelical Scholarship." Advertisement for the opening of Fuller Seminary in United Evangelical Action, *September 1947.*

tions" existed in the rapidly expanding "budding culture" of the far west. Second, "naturalist modernism had invaded many old line seminaries." And third, other independent seminaries, (meaning Dallas, Westminster, and Faith,) were "too often associated with a particular doctrinal emphasis which limits their usefulness."[7]

This analysis corresponded with the perceptions of many prospective students. The great majority of those who responded to Fuller in the summer of 1947 (and for many years to come) heard about it through "The Old Fashioned Revival Hour." Many of the first class were war veterans, older students with some wide experience, often converts themselves, and dedicated to evangelism or missions. All these factors inclined them toward Fuller's less party-line approach compared to Dallas, Westminster, or Faith. Carl McIntire, concerned with the rivalry with Faith, tried to depict Fuller as a school of the NAE, a connection that the Fuller faculty attempted to play down.[8] Charles Fuller's attractiveness was enhanced precisely because he seemed to represent a warm evangelicalism, not part of any sect. The perception of this nonsectarian spirit, combined with the continuing wave of postwar zeal for evangelism, enhanced the immediate attractiveness of the suddenly announced seminary.

The prospect of academic excellence helped as well. Fuller's first news release described it as a "research center for evangelical scholarship,"[9] and the early advertising put this theme in bold letters. Scholarship had always been a top priority of the founders. Ockenga began his first approach to Carl Henry by saying, "You know I have been interested in writing a new theological literature of apologetic nature. . . ." Teaching loads, he continued, would be kept at eight to ten hours a week with summers free. Thus given the time, each faculty member would be expected to produce "a new book in his field every two or three years."[10]

Ockenga viewed apologetics based on impeccable scholarship as essential backing for effective evangelism. Ministers had to have the "best education" in order to answer rationalism, secularism, and evolutionary emphases. Most people, said Ockenga, "are acquainted with arguments against Christianity." So "if evangelists are to preach the gospel effectively, to produce the needed revival it must be after thorough training."[11] Charles Fuller was also persuaded of the importance of this dimension of evangelism. Referring to Pasadena's most prestigious school, he said he wanted his seminary to be "a Cal Tech of the evangelical world."[12] He was, moreover, willing to defer to the

7. FTS Catalog (undated [1947]); these statements appear in the first three catalogs.

8. Harold Lindsell, *Park Street Prophet: A Life of Harold John Ockenga* (Wheaton, Ill.: Van Kampen, 1951), 132.

9. As quoted in the *Presbyterian Guardian*, July 10, 1947.

10. HJO to CH, 4-9-47 (O).

11. Ockenga, "The Need for and Purpose of Fuller Theological Seminary," manuscript [convocation 1948?] (SS).

12. Daniel Fuller, *Give the Winds a Mighty Voice*, 211; much of the account of the seminary's early days follows DF's account.

technical experts when it came to education. He told Ockenga, in effect, "I'll handle the finances, you handle the academics."[13] They were both used to looking for quality. Though Fuller was not extravagant by radio-star standards, he lived well, drove expensive cars, owned several homes, and stayed in the best hotels. And Ockenga, though from a modest background, had acquired Eastern gentleman tastes. A determination to build a faculty of quality pervaded the early outlook at Fuller, and this no doubt was an attraction to prospective students who had reason to be suspicious of shoddy evangelical enterprises with great claims but little substance.

Ockenga worked out the curriculum and, with the assistance of Henry and Lindsell who were in New England in July, planned the catalog. The course of study, then for an entering class only, was designed on a provisional basis with the understanding that the details would be filled in as the faculty expanded to a total of ten by the third year. At the beginning, the students would take Greek and New Testament Introduction from Harrison but would have no Hebrew or Old Testament. Apart from that, the curriculum would be very heavy on apologetics. Wilbur Smith, because of his work in *Therefore Stand*, an important volume in that field, held the professorship in apologetics; and he would also offer a substantial required sequence in the study of the English Bible. Carl Henry's courses, listed under "Theology and Philosophy of Religion," would actually be a heavy dose of apologetics. Harold Lindsell, designated "Registrar and Acting Professor of Missions," would teach only the introductory sequence in church history.

The real work of the first summer was the formidable practical task of starting a sizable school in such a short time. Fortunately a number of talented people dedicated themselves to the task. Lindsell immediately demonstrated his skill at handling details, for which he became fabled at the institution. Although he had to spend the summer in New Hampshire, he handled the correspondence with prospective students routed through California. On the California side, Lindsell was assisted by Miss Mary Ashley (later Lansing), a secretary at the Fuller Evangelistic Foundation who became a key long-time administrator on the seminary staff. Charles Fuller, with help from Dan, oversaw the physical arrangements. The Cravens estate had thirty-two rooms and could house single students. When it soon became apparent that most of the prospective students were married, Fuller obliged by seeking out and purchasing a "court" of sixteen apartments. Although he spent the summer at the Mt. Hermon Bible Conference, the evangelist still felt the weight of the responsibilities for organizing practical details.

Particularly distressing was that what had seemed the clearest sign of God's blessing on the enterprise, the purchase of the Cravens property, was now apparently being countered by the strokes of Satan.[14] For all major decisions, Fuller and the other founders of the seminary spent much time in prayer and took seriously certain signs as messages from God as to whether to

13. HJO interview (paraphrased), 11-6-83.
14. Daniel Fuller, *Give the Winds a Mighty Voice*, 205.

proceed with a given course. The dominant immediate source of the twentieth-century fundamentalist version of this common Christian practice was the nineteenth-century holiness tradition, which emphasized particularly a personal walk with God and the leading of the Lord. These emphases were widespread in American revivalist Protestantism and had been reinforced in fundamentalism especially through the influences of Keswick piety. Even the practical-minded Carl Henry later wrote that "any statement of evangelical experience that does not include the possibility both of communion with God and the communication of the particularized divine will seems to me artifically restrictive."[15] Such divine communications came in varieties of indirect ways. Fundamentalists might look for verses of Scripture that were "given" to them. They would not arbitrarily take literally the first thing their eyes fell upon but might expect to find in their devotions a text that would suddenly illumine an issue. Or, as happened several times in the early days of Fuller, they would put out "fleeces" to find God's will, and they frequently spoke of his opening or shutting doors. These signs were not expected to be arbitrary but rather would usually appear in the form of remarkable successes or frustrations in the project in question. The problems arose in reading the signs.

This was just the case with the Cravens mansion. The disappearance of competitive bidders had seemed a clear sign of divine intervention and was Fuller's chief argument for opening the seminary in the fall. But now, in the summer, what was he to make of wholly unexpected setbacks in the zoning regulations for the building? It was set back from a palm-lined boulevard arrayed with great mansions from the golden age of the twenties. With the wealthy of the area now concentrated in the more secluded areas of the adjacent suburb of San Marino (where the Fullers themselves lived), expectations were high that the mansions could be turned to nonresidential uses. In fact, there had long been a girl's school across the street from the Cravens property. In June 1947, however, the zoning commission denied proposals for building a hotel and multiple units in the area. With those decisions went any realistic hope that a big-time operator, as the evangelist was considered locally, would be allowed to build a school there. Work in furnishing classrooms at the mansion continued as though there were going to be a dramatic reversal of the ruling; but realistically there was little hope.

By September the faculty members were arriving, filled with high spirits. The younger men with their families "camped out" in the extra rooms of the mansion. Wilbur Smith and his wife, Mary Jane, had already arrived and, with the aid of their friends the Fullers, had moved into a pleasant home in San Marino. Wilbur had solved one of the largest problems of opening the seminary with the shipment of his fourteen thousand-volume library. When his books were combined with the libraries of other faculty members and some purchases, the school had a respectable start for a theological collection. All the faculty had been promised substantial free time for research, a major

15. Henry, *Confessions of a Theologian: An Autobiography* (Waco, Tex.: Word, 1986), 53.

Harold Ockenga points the way for the founders (from left to right):
Harold Ockenga, Charles Fuller, Everett Harrison, Harold Lindsell,
Wilbur Smith, trustee Arnold Grunigen, and Carl Henry.

commitment of the early seminary. Carl Henry, who had special enthusiasm
for this opportunity, found out to his chagrin that he did he did not have a
blank check for time to devote to scholarship. When Ockenga had earlier
asked him to be dean, he had declined. Now he got a telegram announcing that
he was appointed "acting dean" anyway. He had little choice but to accept.[16]

16. Ibid., 115.

All the faculty were, however, situated handsomely in their offices. Wilbur Smith, as the distinguished senior member, was given particularly royal treatment. He was allowed to bring with him from Moody Bible Institute his talented private secretary, Delores Loeding (who long after Smith left remained an important background voice of wit and good sense). Moreover, he was surrounded with the vestiges of the tobacco merchant Cravens's opulence. Even Smith, who like the seminary's founders did not mind going first class, was a bit embarrassed by this luxury. The building was "as beautiful as one could ever conceive of, with gorgeous grounds that only a millionaire could have laid out." No doubt struck by the contrast to the stark halls of Moody Bible Institute, he wrote, "My office is about the most beautiful office, I suppose, occupied by any teacher in this country, and at times I am embarrassed with it. I often wonder if a man teaching the rugged realities of the Word of God ought to be housed in such luxury as this." No one talked about this, he added; they were to accept it without pride and be grateful to God.[17]

What Smith did not mention in his letter and what was not mentioned in the seminary's subsequent publicity was that the physical arrangements turned to near chaos when the students arrived. On Monday, September 29, the school held registration at the Cravens estate, and on Tuesday they gave some qualifying exams and even held some preliminary classes. But then the fire marshall arrived with orders that, while the property could be used for faculty offices and for housing and feeding students, class instruction would be illegal.

The next morning, for the first full day of classes, Dan Fuller was stationed at the estate driveway, diverting students to Lake Avenue Church, over two miles away across the city. The contingency of using the Lake Avenue facilities had been worked out between Charles Fuller and his good friend James Henry Hutchins, Lake Avenue's pastor. When Fuller first planned his mission school, Lake Avenue was to be the initial site, so this part of the plan was now revived. After some confusion, classes went on, although, as Dan Fuller remarked, "we members of that first class will never quite forget the incongruity of hearing Carl Henry's insights into the theory of religious knowledge while sitting on kindergarten chairs taking notes." Within a few days adult furnishings were brought to Lake Avenue, but the incongruities and inconvenience would remain for several years.[18]

THE ANSWER TO THE CULTURAL CRISIS

Such inconvenience did not dampen the enthusiasm and the fanfare accompanying the launching of the great new enterprise. The convocation was held on Wednesday, October 1, the same day as the move to Lake Avenue. True to the triumphalist spirit of the enterprise, the organizers presented the opening

17. WS to William Culbertson, 10-13-47.
18. D. Fuller, *Give the Winds a Mighty Voice*, 207-8.

as a truly epochal event, the beginning of a new age for evangelicalism. Twenty-five hundred people packed the Pasadena Civic auditorium. The leading attractions were a typical combination for high-brow fundamentalism: the chorus of "The Old Fashioned Revival Hour" sang, and President Ockenga delivered a New England style speech entitled "The Challenge to the Christian Culture of the West."

Along with accepting the task of training men to save souls, Ockenga proclaimed that the future of Western civilization was at stake. To a degree, this theme reflected the mood of 1947. World War II, even more than its awful predecessor, had raised serious questions as to whether Western civilization could survive. The seemingly demonic power of Hitler in a traditionally Christian land, the ruin of the war itself, the horror of the destruction unleashed on civilians, the subsequent use of atomic weaponry, and then the sudden appearance of a massive Russian-Marxist empire all presented a most disconcerting and bleak prospect for the future of what had been Christendom. Here indeed was one of the great questions of the hour that could make one forget about whether the right chairs would be at Lake Avenue in the morning. Many of the great minds of the age were asking the same question in one way or another. Given the awful horrors perpetrated in the name of saving Western civilization, what is there about it that is worth saving? Did Christianity still have a contribution to make to civilization? Or was the disintegration of both church and culture too advanced to be reversed?

The relationship of Christianity to Western civilization was a matter of much discussion. Emil Brunner, Herbert Butterfield, Christopher Dawson, T. S. Eliot, Kenneth Scott Latourette, Reinhold Niebuhr, and Arnold Toynbee were among those who expounded on this subject in the postwar years. Most argued that the genius of Western civilization, the values of "freedom and democracy" that they had suffered much for in the war, were grounded in a Christian heritage. Nonetheless, as Niebuhr argued forcefully, the relationship was ambiguous. For all, the crucial underlying question was whether it still made sense to talk about "Christian culture." In America the best wisdom of academia and public life had been dedicated for decades to a secular pragmatism that allowed little room for absolutes or for the glittering generalities of earlier eras. Was there any hope for recovery?

Harold Ockenga, just returned from a government-sponsored survey of the aftermath of the war in Europe, was acutely aware of the immense challenge of reconstructing Western civilization. As a former student of Machen, he had long thought of such massive social and political issues as being ideologically based. He saw them as ultimately tied to the whole fundamentalist-modernist battle over the place of the Bible in contemporary life. Machen, in *Christianity and Liberalism*, had attributed to the influence of the materialistic and utilitarian philosophies of the age a decline of Western culture manifested by the dominance of state-sponsored "experts" who would eliminate individuality and make of America "one huge 'Main Street.'" The rise of the socialist state, said Machen, had destroyed "the realm of freedom for the individual

man."[19] Ockenga and virtually all his evangelical associates shared this ab-
horrence of materialistic socialism, both in its Marxist form and in the more
benign American pragmatism that had revolutionized American government
during the past decade and a half. They were Republicans of the sort who
supported Robert A. Taft. They would add to the critique of other Republicans, however, the opinion that the real source of the ominous direction of
contemporary America was its forsaking of evangelical Christianity.

Ockenga and his cohorts had no doubt that the responsibility for the
reconstruction of the West lay primarily with America. In 1947 it would have
been difficult to think otherwise. Moreover, American evangelicals themselves
had a heritage, going back to the Puritans, of believing that the nation had a
special cultural mission as part of the history of redemption. The only hope to
refurbish this noble dream, so deeply ingrained in the American evangelical
psyche, was to refurbish American evangelicalism itself. Evangelical Christianity then was truly the last hope for the world since it was the only hope for
America.

Harold Ockenga carried this thought a step further. When he spoke of
"Christian culture in the West," he said in his Fuller convocation, he was using
west in two senses. He was referring not only to Western civilization but also to
the west coast, about which he proclaimed, "The hour for the west to enter its
maturity theologically is come." Such language was bound to rankle mainline
Protestants who had long had seminaries in California; but it made perfect
sense given the basic premise of the address—that *evangelical* theology was the
only adequate theology and therefore the only remaining hope for Western
(and western) culture. The mission of the theological seminary involved much
more than just training pastors and missionaries. It also involved a *cultural*
task, the task of saving Western civilization.

Ockenga expressed the vision of the entire faculty. The task to be done
in meeting the challenge of the age, he said, "is not going to be done by the
ordinary Christians alone." Rather it must be done by those who were "to
redefine Christian thinking" and who would be given the time to prepare the
"rethinking and the restating of the fundamental thesis and principles of a
western culture."

When Ockenga thought of Western civilization, he thought first in
terms of classic individualism in the context of responsibility to divine law.

> You might ask the question, "Well, what do you mean when you speak
> of western civilization?" Well, I mean those great Christian principles
> which have been infused into society over centuries, and which now
> are bearing their fruit. You all are aware of the concept of the infinite
> value of individual man, which concept is being battered about in
> these days by men who do not believe in its source nor believe in the
> principles which underlie it but will talk abut the infinite dignity of

19. J. Gresham Machen, *Christianity and Liberalism* (New York: Macmillan, 1923),
15, 10.

the individual; that concept, I say, is born out of the Hebrew-Christian tradition. Then, beyond that, comes the concept also of responsibility to God which has resulted in the moral fiber of our Christian thinking, the moral fiber of the masses of the people in which they have been responsible unto God and divine law. . . .

America's conservative evangelicals were the "heirs to Reformation culture," which was the key to the amazing rise to power of the West. This great cultural achievement was threatened on several fronts, however. Ockenga emphasized that he was "chagrined" that "we have allowed Romanism to step in with a social program that will make Romanism the challenging religious factor in western civilization, and in particular the United States." The even greater danger, however, was a return to heathenism and "rationalism, or the authority of the human mind above all else." This had already happened in Germany, which had fallen into moral relativism and barbarism. These, in turn, brought God's judgment. And the same thing could happen here.

What I have said about Germany in its intellectual development could be repeated out of the teachings of the leading educators of America in this day. Here comes the message to America—America, which is experiencing today that inner rupture of its character and culture, that inner division with vast multitudes of our people following that secularist, rationalist lie of "scientific naturalism" in the repudiation of God and God's law. I tell you on the authority of the Word of God and with the full sweep of history behind us that in the proportion that America does that, and the church has to withdraw itself to a separated community again, and there enters a time of hostility of the world and the persecution of the anti-Christian forces, in that percentage we will open ourselves up to the kind of judgement that God brought upon Europe from which we escaped almost unscathed in this nation.

"COME-OUT-ISM"

Ockenga's grand solution was undercut by the realities of the movement he hoped to lead. In his vision of Western culture, "the church" had to play an integral role. It must not withdraw itself to a separated community again, he said. This was a direct repudiation of the dispensationalist view of the church as a refuge in a ruined culture and a consequent affirmation of the Calvinist-Puritan view that the church must play a central civilization-building role. But where was this "church"? The recent history of the fundamentalist-evangelical movement was largely a history of schism. Though it repudiated the principial separatism of Carl McIntire's American Council of Christian Churches, what was in fact the National Association of Evangelicals but a repudiation of the very policies that united the mainline Protestant denominations. Fuller Seminary, and the rhetoric justifying it as the only theological hope for the West, was an even more direct affront to denominational agencies. Yet at the same time, Ockenga and the Fuller faculty wanted to retain the influence of being part of America's major denominations.

The Presbytery of Los Angeles of the Presbyterian Church in the U.S.A. had already declared war on the new seminary and was making things hot for Ockenga personally. In the spring Ockenga had written in his Park Street Church bulletin that Fuller Seminary was needed in California because "the testimony of most denominational seminaries has been vitiated by modernism" and "there is no outstanding seminary in the West." When this statement found its way to the west, Presbyterians there were duly offended. They had, in San Francisco Theological Seminary in San Anselmo, what they considered to be a fine seminary; and they well remembered that Wilbur Smith had labeled John Bowman of San Francisco Seminary an out-and-out heretic after Bowman delivered the Stone Lectures at Princeton.

Ockenga was still, technically, a Presbyterian minister. Exercising his practical independence of denominations, he had simply retained his membership in the Presbytery of Pittsburgh during the years since 1936 that he had been pastor at Park Street. So officials of the Presbytery of Los Angeles, sensing a sinister development in their own back yard, asked the Presbytery of Pittsburgh whether Ockenga had permission to labor within the bounds of the Presbytery of Los Angeles—knowing full well that he did not have it and could not get it.[20] This threatened Ockenga's Presbyterian ordination and forced him to meet with the executive council of the Los Angeles presbytery during convocation week. As far as that went, the presbytery could also refuse to accept Wilbur Smith and Everett Harrison when they attempted to transfer their Presbyterian ministerial papers to Los Angeles. Even more ominously, the Presbytery of Los Angeles had in September voted not to allow its candidates to the ministry to study at Fuller. Although this policy did not extend to the whole Presbyterian denomination, it meant that Presbyterian students from southern California who attended Fuller would pay the price of losing their presbytery's support as well as closing out future local prospects. It was a serious blow to Fuller.

With these threats to the seminary's influence explicitly in mind,[21] Ockenga attempted to pour oil on the waters. To do so, however, meant fueling a blaze on the seminary's right. Not surprisingly, then, what he said on this subject in his convocation address, almost as an aside, was remembered far longer than what he said about transforming the culture of the West. The seminary, he announced, would be "ecclesiastically positive." Although it would be free and interdenominational, "we do not believe and we repudiate the 'come-out-ism' movement." Here was a direct attack on the McIntire camp in its insistence that separatism was basic to fundamentalism. "Come out from among them, and be ye separate" was the Bible passage endlessly repeated by Carl McIntire. Ockenga, however, had clearly decided that it was

20. Lindsell, *Park Street Prophet*, 136-37.
21. HJO to HL, 10-23-47.

better to let that small band of fundamentalist separatists flail away at them than to risk entering a conflict with the left that might cut the seminary off from wider influences. He was ready to move to Congregationalism rather than fight with Presbyterians. In his convocation address he threw down the gauntlet with an unmistakable reference to his onetime friend. "Now there are those who exist in the world simply it seems to attack others, and to derogate others, and to drag them down, and to besmirch them. Our men will have no time for that kind of negativism."

OCKENGA VS. MCINTIRE

The coming conflagration on this front had been smoldering for months already. In the spring of 1947 Ockenga had attempted to enlist for the Fuller faculty Allan MacRae, the president and key Old Testament scholar at McIntire's Faith Theological Seminary. By the time that Ockenga presented MacRae with a formal offer in early June, however, MacRae had left on a trip to Europe.[22] In the meantime, someone at the Winona Lake Bible Conference was reporting that both MacRae and Wilbur Smith were going to Fuller in the fall and were going to receive the remarkable salaries of $8,500. McIntire was not to be upstaged. In early July he published news of the offer, including the salary, in his *Christian Beacon* and stated that MacRae had turned it down flat. McIntire added: "Faith Theological Seminary, under Dr. MacRae's presidency, has taught separation from apostasy and withdrawal from the Federal Council. Naturally, he could not consider an institution under the leadership of a man who attacks separation."[23] MacRae, still in Europe, knew nothing of all this until after the *Beacon* appeared and his wife's phone began ringing. Upon his return, he was introduced at a speaking engagement as the man who, rather than compromise, turned down an $8,500 job.[24]

In early August, as Charles Fuller reported to Ockenga, McIntire dropped in "to warn me most vehemently that I was making an irreparable mistake to line up with Ockenga." In the process, however, McIntire tipped his own hand. He argued for an hour "and then in a rather quavering voice asked sheepishly if MacRae *is* coming with us!"[25]

In the long run the ploy of preempting MacRae's decision worked for McIntire. MacRae remained at Faith, though the Fuller people continued to try to enlist him. They knew, however, that they had a battle on their hands. Ockenga's much-repeated words against the "come-outers" were, then, not the first shot but rather a sort of declaration of war amid already existing hostilities.

By the day after convocation these hostilities gave Fuller Seminary its first alumnus. A student who was also the pastor of a Bible Baptist church in a

22. HJO to CF, 6-14-47. CH suggested in an interview, 11-19-82, that McIntire intercepted the telegram to MacRae and publicly turned it down at a Bible conference.
23. *Christian Beacon,* July 8, 1947, 8.
24. CH to HJO, 8-19-47 (O).
25. CF to HJO, 8-2-47 (O).

nearby town wrote to Charles Fuller submitting his withdrawal from the seminary. He was, he said, a radio convert, but he was also a member of both the separatist fundamentalist General Association of Regular Baptist Churches and also McIntire's American Council of Christian Churches. He could not, therefore, accept a direct repudiation of his movement.

A carbon copy of this letter was also sent to registrar Lindsell, who suspected that the student had been "planted" by McIntire. But when Lindsell called him in for an interview, the student's sentiments seemed genuine. He professed deep love for Dr. Fuller, but repeatedly said, "The statement of Dr. Ockenga that he repudiated come-out-ism *nauseated* me."[26]

The expected larger assault from the *Christian Beacon* was not long in coming. McIntire knew where he had some leverage. Many of those who listened to Fuller and supported his radio ministry were also readers of the *Beacon*. Already, shortly after McIntire printed the report of the extravagant salaries at Fuller Seminary, Charles Fuller received some mail from ACCC people saying that if he had $8,500 for MacRae, he did not need any from them. Such reactions were still comparatively few, but a trickle of opposition might turn into a deluge.[27] The fundamentalist community was very susceptible to rumors. Unlike an organized church, it lacked common forums to adjudicate disputes; so it was always one person's word against another's. McIntire had already criticized Charles Fuller for his lack of consistent separatism, and now he suggested that Fuller was being led astray by his friends who sought worldly honors.

The October 9 issue of the *Christian Beacon* carried a story of the convocation address that featured a letter from a Bible church pastor, Peter F. Wall, to Charles Fuller. How could Fuller support such a repudiation of come-outer-ism? the letter asked. Wall, who had been a fellow student with Fuller at the Bible Institute of Los Angeles, knew what would sting the evangelist. Fuller, he argued, had betrayed the teachings of the revered Reuben A. Torrey and of "Daddy" Horton at the Institute. Jesus would have stood behind the "come-outers" and the "thrown-outers," Wall said; now many hundreds of thousands would have to look elsewhere for a seminary. To make sure no one missed the point, McIntire went so far as to have his American Council of Christian Churches, meeting in mid-October, include in its resolutions a condemnation of Ockenga's address and of Fuller Seminary for violating the commands of Scripture to separate from apostasy. The American Council further resolved that now it could not cooperate with the NAE "in Sunday school lessons, or in any matter which concerns a testimony for Jesus Christ."[28]

Such attacks hurt Charles Fuller. They hurt him financially because

26. HL to HJO, 10-11-47.
27. CF to HJO, 9-8-47.
28. "Ockenga Attacks 'Come-Outers' at Seminary Opening," *Christian Beacon*, October 9, 1947, 8; "American Council Resolutions from Sixth Annual Convention," *Christian Beacon*, October 30, 1947, 38.

every time there was a new attack a pile of mail would arrive announcing the end of support for the radio ministry.[29] Fuller nonetheless resolved to stay in the background as far as setting the policy of the seminary. That was the business of Ockenga and the other experts, he said. His own job was to manage the financial side. Even though that job was made harder when others stirred up controversy, and though he would sometimes complain about the losses of radio revenue, he seldom used such losses as a direct argument for modifying seminary policy. His willingness to defer to Ockenga and the faculty on seminary policy was the more remarkable in this first case given that his own instincts on separatism were somewhat different from Ockenga's. Fuller preferred to be irenic, not to discuss the issue. He would rather allow his long-standing fundamentalist credentials speak for themselves. Ockenga, on the other hand, specifically wanted to use the fundamentalist-evangelical power base to recapture influence in the powerful traditional American Protestant denominations. That required a thorough repudiation of the McIntire crowd, which was often thought by outsiders to be typical in its extremism of all fundamentalism.

THE CENTRAL MOTIF

A pattern was now set that would continue through Fuller Seminary's first several decades. The school would aspire to be a force for renewal and broadening of fundamentalism and evangelicalism. The seminary was, in a sense, like the original American Puritan experiment, meant to be a light on a hill (this time in the new world of California), a beacon signaling a new stage in world civilization. Yet the ideological hill on which the seminary was situated had long, steep slopes and deep valleys on each side. One of the valleys was inhabited by strict fundamentalists, the other by Protestant liberals. The seminary faced in two directions at once, but to residents of either valley it appeared somewhat alien.

Both the fundamentalists and the liberals who noticed the light on the hill were sure that its ultimate source was the camp in the valley on the other side. The question was, Could this movement establish an independent identity? Was it possible both to be a force for renewing fundamentalist-evangelicalism and simultaneously to reclaim the traditional power base of the denominations? Could the movement carve out its own identity and territory, or would the snipers from one side or the other eventually force it down the slope to the opposing valley? Student response always demonstrated that Fuller Seminary had a constituency that shared its vision; but if it was to have wide influence, it would have to resolve the question of to whom or what in this world it belonged. In the early days, hopes were high that it could carve out a large middle ground where a healthy third force in Protestantism could operate

---

29. "Proposed Draft of Dr. Archer's remarks . . . in LA Presbytery" (November 10, 1953), 7 (P), claims "large numbers" of people cut off their contributions to "The Old Fashioned Revival Hour" and even cut it out of their wills.

between the separatist fundamentalists and the modernists. There was always a considerable constituency who had sentiment for such a vision. Yet the problem was in getting the light to burn clearly when the middle ground was also a battlefield. The beacon light on the hill was too often obscured by the bombs bursting in air.

CHAPTER IV

Redefining the Fundamentalist Mission

Evangelical Christianity is once again, as in the early days of church history, a minority movement in a universally antagonistic environment— that much is certain. What is not so clear is whether the global crisis marks the terminus of western culture only . . . or whether . . . it presages also that "end of the age" when "the Lord Himself shall descend from heaven."

The answer to this question holds tremendous implications. Is it too late for Christianity to reintroduce into earthly history—before the advent of Christ—depths of meaning, as at the highest reaches of medieval culture and yet more at the Reformation, which can be found only in the message of a supernatural salvation? Is evangelicalism's only message today the proclamation of individual rescue from a fore-doomed generation? Or has this evangel implications also for the most pressing social problems of our day?

Carl F. H. Henry, "The Vigor of the New Evangelicalism,"
Christian Life, January 1948.

WILBUR SMITH: THE CLASSIC FUNDAMENTALIST

WHEN the seminary opened, Wilbur Smith was the centerpiece of the faculty. He was the senior man and had the largest office, his own secretary, a huge personal library, and by far the widest reputation. He and his wife, Mary Jane, had already become good friends of the Fullers. While Charles Fuller was not close to the younger faculty nor involved with their academic interests, in a Bible teacher like Smith he found a kindred spirit. With the other trustees far away, Fuller as the president of the board was used to acting freely on his own, and soon the Smiths and the Fullers became a sort of informal dining-room cabinet.[1]

Smith was a transitional figure between Charles Fuller's original vision of a missionary training school and the younger founders' vision of a great center for new evangelical thought. Smith had a foot firmly planted in each camp. Able to accomplish as much as two ordinary educators, he did an

1. R. Donald Weber interview, 10-25-83; CH interview, 11-19-82.

immense amount of practical work in compiling the widely used *Peloubet's Select Notes on the International Sunday School Lessons* each year and filling numerous speaking engagements. At the same time, he was a great proponent of scholarship. He had established his own reputation as something of a scholar with the publication in 1945 of *Therefore Stand,* a lengthy volume in apologetics that demonstrated his wide reading. The younger men at Fuller, who might have been put off by Smith's popular Bible-school style, all recognized that *Therefore Stand* was an important evangelical work on apologetics in a day when there was not much else. With the task and curriculum of the seminary defined with a heavy leaning toward defense of the faith, Smith was accordingly given the key position of professor of apologetics.

Smith was a voracious collector and lover of books and could rapidly skim through them and come away with some knowledge of their contents. *Therefore Stand* was impressive especially because of the wide use of apt quotations. Later, when Smith's scholarly star was fading, students called it "Therefore Quote." Nonetheless, in the mid-1940s, Smith commanded intellectual respect. Indeed, he played an important role during the dark age of fundamentalist scholarship after the death of Machen. He championed among fundamentalists something they did not much hear: the importance of the great tradition of Western literature. He thus helped keep fundamentalism from burning itself out entirely in a glorious blaze of practical enthusiasm. Moreover, he constantly exhorted fundamentalists about the importance of developing their own first-rate literature. One of the great revolutions of the past sixty years, he pointed out, was the vast increase in literacy. Yet there was still little first-rate Christian literature to counteract the "wave of soul-destroying, agnostic, God-denying books and periodicals." Smith was thus constantly thinking up suggestions for the production and distribution of beneficial reading materials—he thought that evangelicals should set up reading rooms, for instance. Despite the inroads of radio and film, the 1940s were still part of the age of print, and Smith remained very much a man of that age.

Smith's emphasis on developing a body of first-rate evangelical literature stemmed in part from one of evangelicalism's most difficult challenges: to witness to university-educated people. He had had a recent experience with a distinguished professor, long turned from Christ, who now wanted a recent Christian book both solid on apologetics and inspiring. Smith had nothing to offer, except presumably his own. He expressed these sentiments at the closing address of the NAE Convention in 1946; and *United Evangelical Action,* in conjunction with the publication of his address, announced a conference, "of evangelical educators, editors, authors, and publishers" to consider his proposals.[2] The vision that emerged the next fall of Fuller Seminary as a center for the production of evangelical literature fit Smith's program exactly.

While Smith championed solid Christian scholarship as the way to raise the level of fundamentalist communications, he himself directed most of

2. Wilbur Smith, "The Urgent Need for a New Evangelical Literature," *United Evangelical Action,* June 15, 1946, 3-5.

Wilbur Smith consults with a student

his insatiable zeal for writing toward producing semipopular Christian literature. When he came to Fuller, he was the editor of *His* magazine, the official
publication of the college-oriented Inter-Varsity Christian Fellowship. He
soon abandoned that post but remained a prodigious contributor to *Our Hope*,
to which in 1950 alone, for instance, he contributed nearly a hundred short
articles in his regular columns.[3]

    This sideline reflected Smith's real academic interests in the postwar
and early Fuller years. *Our Hope* was one of the oldest of the dispensationalist
fundamentalist journals, founded in 1894 by Arno C. Gaebelein. One of the
leaders of the old prophecy conference movement out of which had grown
much of organized fundamentalism, Gaebelein took a hard line against Christian efforts at social reform, viewing these as distractions from the main business of preparing people to meet the coming King. In the meantime, politics at
least provided grist for the mills of prophetic interpretation. Indeed, reading
the signs of the times was the main business of *Our Hope*. The widely informed
Gaebelein fit each historical event into the drama of the life-and-death conflict
between God and Satan. In perhaps the best-known of his many books, *The
Conflict of the Ages*, he outlined the satanic conspiracy of lawlessness through the
ages, transmitted to America first through the French Revolution and the
demonically inspired Illuminati.[4] Now Russia, which Gaebelein believed had

    3. The compilation "Titles of Articles in My Columns in *Our Hope*, 1950–51" (WS,
box 23) lists 96 titles for 1950. These are also collected in a scrapbook.
    4. Gaebelein, *The Conflict of the Ages* (New York: Our Hope, 1933).

been explicitly prophesied as a destructive power at the end of the age, had been advancing atheism throughout the world since 1917. The U.S.S.R. was even then spreading its evil influence in the United States through revolutionary propaganda, and its programs were naively supported by modernist church dupes in the Federal Council of Churches.[5]

Wilbur Smith did not share all of Gaebelein's extreme conspiratorial views, but he counted him as a "dear friend." When Gaebelein died in 1945, Smith preached a memorial service that was published in a booklet "Arno C. Gaebelein: A Memoir." Smith later called this "the most satisfying biographical work I have done."[6] When Smith was contributing heavily to *Our Hope*, Frank Gaebelein, Arno's cultured, well-educated, and more moderate son, was coeditor. Smith shared with both Gaebeleins a respect for scholarship and also carried on some of Arno's specific interests in prophecy. While he displayed greater restraint in prophetic speculations, he too focused his view of reality and history on "the conflict of the ages" between God and Satan and was also preoccupied with reading the signs of the times in the postwar crisis.[7]

While Smith's views were not dominant at Fuller, which contrasted itself to Dallas by not teaching dispensationalism as such,[8] they are important for understanding the point of departure in fundamentalist-evangelicals' views of the postwar cultural crisis. Whatever reformers like Ockenga or Henry were saying about transforming Western culture, Smith's interpretations were closer to the popular fundamentalist outlook. Not only were his views much like those of the Fullers, they were soon to have an immense influence through Billy Graham. In the fall of 1948 Smith spoke at Northwestern College in Minneapolis, where the youthful Graham was interim president. After Graham rose to fame the next year, he and Smith became regular correspondents and close friends. Graham, who spoke of Smith as the "greatest evangelical leader of our day," relied on the Bible teacher as a confidant and advisor, especially on interpreting world affairs through biblical prophecies.[9] The ideas that Smith was developing in the postwar era were, even if not typical of the entire seminary faculty, still being heard in his classes.[10] Moreover, they were as influential in the world of evangelicalism as anything being disseminated from Fuller in those early years.

Smith's reputation as an interpreter of prophecy had risen quickly with the publication just after the war of his thirty-page pamphlet "The Atom-

5. For a positive view of Gaebelein see David A. Rausch, *Arno C. Gaebelein, 1861–1945: Irenic Fundamentalist and Scholar* (New York: Edwin Mellen, 1983).
6. Wilbur Smith, *Before I Forget* (Chicago: Moody Press, 1971), 227, 148.
7. See, for instance, Smith's pamphlet "The Conflict of the Ages" (Grand Rapids: Zondervan, 1940), which has this theme.
8. The Presbytery of San Jose visiting committee, Oct. 11, 1949, reported of FTS, "There is nothing of either the Arminian or the Dispensationalist about its teaching" (LA).
9. BG to WS, 1-9-52. The correspondence between Graham and Smith indicates that Graham used Smith as a resource person for his books, especially in the area of prophecy (S). Graham also used Carl Henry as a resource person.
10. These themes are alluded to in the class notes of William Mull (class of 1950), e.g., Biblical Theology, 4-24-[49?].

ic Bomb and the Word of God."[11] Nearly every preacher in the country preached a sermon on the bomb in the years following Hiroshima, and Smith's facility at quickly mustering information and writing engagingly put him out in front. His pamphlet sold some fifty thousand copies and was excerpted in a number of magazines. By the summer of 1947 he had completed a full-scale book on the same subject, *This Atomic Age and the Word of God*,[12] and within three more years had produced a more general prophetic volume, *World Crises and the Prophetic Scriptures*.[13]

Smith was convinced that with the dropping of the atomic bomb the world had entered a new era. As was typical of his writings, he supported his conclusions with quotations from sophisticated current opinion, drawn from his wide reading. He cited Robert Hutchins, chancellor of the University of Chicago, for instance, who was one of many who predicted the doom of the race and who gave it only five more years unless there was a radical change in international relations. Civilization was now faced with the possibility of the destruction of the entire race, and there was no possibility of turning the clock back. In such times of crisis, Smith repeated urgently, Christians must turn to the Bible for guidance. Among the world's great religious books only the Bible prophesied such dark days. Smith warned, though, against "amateurish speculation." He was totally against setting any date for the end of the age and was thankful that he had been spared the embarrassment of many of his fellow fundamentalist interpreters of prophecy who had fallen into the error "of identifying Mussolini with Antichrist and claiming that we know whom the number 666 represents, etc."[14]

Nonetheless, Smith still found a remarkable number of prophetic statements that seemed to refer just to the present era. For instance, one of the key parts of his analysis regarding the atomic bomb was the passage in 2 Peter 3 that says "the elements shall be dissolved with fervent heat." This striking prediction of sudden judgment on the race, said Smith, at least refers to something *like* atomic destruction. Moreover, the dissolving of the "elements" suggests the exact principle of atomic energy. Smith's view of Scripture, characteristic of the fundamentalist outlook of the time, became apparent at this point. Peter did not know we would have a list of ninety-two elements in the mid-twentieth century—*"but God knew."* "I am sure," said Smith, "when the spirit of God guided the Apostle Peter to use this word, He was thinking of much more than the Apostle Peter understood when he put the word in this epistle."[15] Such a view of the overriding dominance of divine authorship in producing each word of Scripture entailed the widespread fundamentalist view of the Bible's inerrancy in every detail.

Smith found many other biblical phrases and predictions that in-

11. Smith, "The Atomic Bomb and the Word of God" (Chicago: Moody Press, 1945).
12. Smith, *This Atomic Age and the Word of God* (Boston: W. A. Wilde, 1948).
13. Smith, *World Crises and the Prophetic Scriptures* (Chicago: Moody Press, 1951).
14. Smith, *This Atomic Age*, 309, 15.
15. Smith, "The Atomic Bomb," 16.

creased his conviction that civilization was on the edge of the last days. These ranged from very general prophecies of "wars and rumors of wars" to more specific items, such as that "the prince of the power of the air" might refer to air power and to control of the radio air-waves. The founding of the state of Israel put the major piece in the prophetic puzzle, of course. Smith, despite his own warnings against being overly specific, argued that the Hebrew word *rosh* in Ezekiel 38:2-3 referred to Russia, which in the last days would ravage Israel.[16]

What were Christians to do about all this? Smith thought they should stay away from political answers. He would not even discuss arms control in his volumes on atomic war, arguing that experts disagreed and he saw no solution. He was equally apolitical on most other topics. Instead, his solutions were personal. The unprecedented world crisis should impel us to ask, "If you and I must live in such a world as this, how may we have victory over it, so that we may live for God, lives of righteousness and true holiness." Informed opinion about the state of the world, he wrote in the summer of 1948, was perhaps never before more gloomy. So young Christians should return to God's word, dwell in Christ, and witness for the Lord.[17] Here was fundamentalism in its classic form.

The one exception to this personalistic message was also consistent with the fundamentalist tradition. America, said Smith, was a Christian nation that had recently turned with alarming speed toward atheism. He sounded this warning in a substantial booklet that appeared the same year he went to Fuller. Above the picture of the U.S. Capitol was the title: "The Increasing Peril—Of Permitting the Dissemination of Atheistic Doctrines on the Part of Some Agencies of the United States Government." As was characteristic of him, Smith amassed quotations to support his "re-examination of the strong, undeniable Christian elements that gave such power, courage and nobleness of purpose" to America's founders. He hoped that these elements would "be once again acknowledged as the only faith which can maintain us as a great, powerful, undefeated Christian nation." He did not expect the government to promote Christianity; but he did think that freedom of speech was misunderstood if it allowed the dissemination of atheism, as in a recent FCC regulation permitting the broadcast of atheistic doctrines on the radio. Worse, the United States government was directly supporting the spread of atheism by financing UNESCO, which was headed by the atheist Julian Huxley. Any plans for one world government, moreover, would have to set aside specifically Christian traditions. Athough communism at home was not the main focus of Smith's alarm in this booklet, he concluded with a call to Congress to rid America—its educational institutions and labor unions particularly—from "atheistic communism."[18]

By his first year at Fuller, Smith seemed to be seeing the communist

16. Smith, *World Crises*, 241-91.
17. Smith, *This Atomic Age*, 17, 315; Smith, "The World Crisis and You," *HIS*, December 1948, 15.
18. Smith, "The Increasing Peril" (n.p., 1947), 15 and passim.

threat as the focus of the world crisis. This was hardly suprising given recent Soviet advances and the onset of the cold war. The emphasis on the domestic communist threat, though, was especially characteristic of the Republican business community and the traditionalist evangelical movement of which Fuller was a part. Smith typically emphasized the spiritual side of the threat: the communists who are now being exposed in the government, he wrote in 1948, are also "confirmed, determined enemies of the Christian religion." He was confident that "the influence of the anti-religious attitude of communism will grow in our western world, horizontally and vertically both, and we must prepare ourselves for such a conflict."[19]

Smith's combination of a generally apolitical stance with a celebration of the Christian basis of the American tradition and a priority on preserving traditional liberties against atheistic threats reflected a long-standing fundamentalist paradox. On the one hand, fundamentalism, especially in its dispensationalist version, tended to be sectarian and highly spiritualistic in its solutions. Civilization was beyond repair and Christians could only preach the gospel, hope to rescue the perishing, keep themselves pure, and wait for the coming King. With this emphasis, fundamentalism seemed a religion for cultural outsiders: a refuge for Anglo-Protestants who, as a group, felt a loss of status. On the other hand, though, fundamentalism simultaneously preserved another mentality, inherited from the Puritans and from the nineteenth-century era of evangelical dominance. When fundamentalists emphasized the Spirit they sounded more like establishmentarian insiders. They lamented the recent demise of Christian civilization and they still spoke as though concerted Christian action might turn things around.[20] Fundamentalists like Smith spoke far more often in the sectarian spiritualistic vein than in the vein that emphasized political involvement. In the 1930s and 1940s, the era when Smith rose to influence, this sectarian attitude prevailed in fundamentalism generally. Fundamentalists, then, despite seeing signs of revival, felt defeated in the battle to save American culture and the major American denominations. Consequently, their primary solutions were evangelistic and spiritualistic. Nonetheless, even in so characteristic a fundamentalist as Smith, the other mentality was perceptible, at least in vestigial form.

CARL HENRY: SKETCHES FOR A NEW EVANGELICALISM

If Wilbur Smith represented the old style of fundamentalism at Fuller, Carl Henry represented the new. He was just as convinced as Smith that spiritual revival was humanity's only real answer; yet he saw revival not simply as a spiritual rescue mission but also as the first step in the reversal of major cultural trends. He thus gave more emphasis than did Smith to the other, culturally involved, side of the fundamentalist-evangelical heritage.

19. Smith, "World Crisis and You," 15.
20. These themes are elaborated in my book *Fundamentalism and American Culture: The Shaping of Twentieth-Century Evangelicalism, 1870–1925* (New York: Oxford, 1980).

Fundamentalism as it emerged from the denominational controversies of the 1920s and 1930s was a coalition internally divided. The central core that had the strongest sense of being part of a movement had been shaped by the controversies in the northern Presbyterian and Northern Baptist denominations and was more or less Reformed in doctrinal emphasis. In addition to the traditional differences within this group (those between Presbyterian and Baptist, for example) and differences from other fundamentalists (from holiness groups, ethnic conservatives, black fundamentalists, southern denominationalists, and pentecostals, for instance), this core group itself had, as we have seen, suffered two internal splits that left it divided into four major types. The most serious of these splits, threatening the continued coherence of the core movement, was between separatists and nonseparatists. On this point, Henry and Smith were in the same camp. Cutting across the separatist issue, however, was dispensationalism. Some separatists were dispensationalists, a smaller group (such as those at Westminster Seminary) were not. Similarly, some nonseparatists (such as Smith) were dispensationalists and others (such as Henry and Ockenga) were not.

Smith's dispensationalism was sufficiently mild not to arouse doctrinal controversy with his colleages; nonetheless, it was significant in contributing to a different view of history. Conceptions of history were the key differences that separated the old fundamentalist mainstream, as represented by Smith, from the new evangelicalism. From their respective views of history grew their views of civilization, of the Christian mission to civilization, and even of ethical priorities. Henry, Ockenga, and some of the highly educated younger evangelical spokespersons, while remaining premillennialist in a general sense, abandoned the central dispensationalist preoccupation with reading the prophetic signs so as to indicate that the present was incontrovertibly the end time. In its place, they drew on a view of history more characteristic of the mainstream of the Reformed theological tradition. Modern culture, in this view, is not beyond hope, and Christians have the task of transforming culture to bring it more in conformity with God's law and will.

This Reformed vision had already had an immense impact on the American Protestant psyche through the influence of the Puritans. It continued to inform much of nineteenth century evangelicalism and had survived, though in a much attenuated form, in the Presbyterian fundamentalism of the old Princeton school that had touched so many of Fuller's founders. Though the young reformers of fundamentalism might differ with the old-style fundamentalists on only very few doctrinal or behavioral issues, they parted ways significantly in their views on history and hence in their views on the dimensions of the evangelistic task.

Carl Henry made such differences with old-style fundamentalism explicit in a series of popular articles published early in 1948, during Fuller's first school year. Writing in *Christian Life*, a sort of evangelical *Reader's Digest*, he discussed "The Vigor of the New Evangelicalism." This title suggested a new outlook among reforming fundamentalists, though "new evangelical" was

Carl and Helga Henry

not yet a common designation for a specific party. Perhaps with his well-known colleague in mind, Henry commented on the same world issues that were so alarming to Smith, but with a different message. He shared with Smith and their secular contemporaries alarm over the future of civilization in the wake of expanding testing of atomic weapons. Humanity, he observed, might be "on a tiny ledge above the abyss of annihilation," and the ledge could crumble in the next ten years. Henry, however, was more inclined to say that the current crisis was a sign of the end only of Western culture rather than of the entire world. Against the liberal Christians he wanted to emphasize that the world *would* end. "Fundamentalism," on the other hand, "was not wrong in assuming a final consummation of history, but rather in assuming that *this is it*."

Henry's alternative was that "while the Lord tarries, the gospel is still relevant to every problem that vexes the two billion inhabitants of an apprehensive globe." Fundamentalists, unfortunately, especially those in the generation that flourished in the 1930s, had, in his view, developed a disastrous isolation from the questions on which the future direction of civilization hung. They had virtually ignored the philosophical challenges that Christianity could bring against the prevailing cultural views, and they were ready to "fall all over each other in the rush to make it clear that they have no message which is relevant to modern political, sociological, economic and educational tensions."[21]

Henry's response to the cultural challenges was two-pronged. Not only did he call for fundamentalist social and political involvement; more basically he also saw it as crucial to reassess the entire ideological basis on which Western civilization rested. In his book *Remaking the Modern Mind* of 1946, he argued that philosophical-religious concerns were indeed the pivotal issues of the day. The past three decades, he wrote at the outset, "mark the end-time of an age." Modern Western culture had collapsed because the philosophical premises on which it was based had proved too flimsy to support the weight of civilization. These were the premises of humanism, or the "secular philosophy of humanism or naturalism," as Henry's mentor Gordon Clark put it in the foreword. The roots of this philosophy could be found in the Renaissance, and, according to Henry, its basic assumptions had dominated Western philosophy for the past 350 years, the same period during which the West rose to dominate world civilization. But now the presuppositions that were the ultimate outgrowth of humanism were all under fire: "the inevitability of human progress," "the inherent goodness of man," "the ultimate reality of nature," and "the ultimate animality of man." Christians, therefore, were not to despair at the crumbling foundations of Western culture or to act as though the entire world were at an end. Rather, they should seize the opportunity to build a new world mind for the forthcoming era.[22]

Drawing on his extensive philosophical training, Henry documented these points with the sorts of displays of erudition that soon became legendary at Fuller. Some of Charles Fuller's recent radio converts who were now studying for the ministry, with no philosophical background, were bedazzled and sometimes bewildered by the technical issues involved. It was difficult to miss, however, Henry's vision of the urgency of challenging Western thought on Christian grounds and then reorienting it spiritually and morally before civilization collapsed entirely.

Significantly, Henry dedicated *Remaking the Modern Mind* to three "Men of Athens." This trio suggests some of the influences on the new evangelical outlook that he was formulating. In addition to Gordon Clark, Henry's triumvirate included William Harry Jellema, professor of philosophy at the University of Indiana, and Cornelius Van Til of Westminster Theological Seminary, both graduates of Calvin College of the conservative Dutch immigrant Christian Reformed Church. By 1946 the threesome would not likely have appeared together anywhere except on Henry's dedication page, since they were deeply divided among themselves as only formerly close allies could be. Van Til had raised the Westminster Seminary principle of separatism to cosmic philosophical proportions. Drawing from an emphasis in the thought of Abraham Kuyper, the turn-of-the-century Dutch statesman-theologian, he

21. Henry, "The Vigor of the New Evangelicalism," *Christian Life*, January 1948, 30, 32; March 1948, 35; April 1948, 32.

22. Henry, *Remaking the Modern Mind* (Grand Rapids: Eerdmans, 1946), 19, 9, 26.

insisted on the "antithesis" between Christian and all non-Christian thought. Gordon Clark, just as much a polemicist, also emphasized the fundamental presuppositional antagonism between Christian and non-Christian thought, but he allowed a stronger place for human reason as a means for settling such controversies and hence as a way of testing Christian truth. Jellema was by far the most philosophically irenic of the three. He had a classicist's respect for the grand tradition of Western thought and hence found wide philosophical common ground between the believer and the nonbeliever. Nonetheless, he too was a follower of Abraham Kuyper both in recognizing the importance of the "mind" of the age in shaping its culture and also in seeing the Christian task as a broad one of transforming all of culture for God's glory.

Though Carl Henry did not follow his Dutch mentors closely, the very idea of remaking a "mind" was a concept that was far more developed in the Dutch Calvinist tradition than elsewhere in American evangelicalism or fundamentalism. The idea of a "mind" controlling an age was congenial with the personalism that Henry had studied at Boston University; but he applied it in ways that often reflected Dutch sources. They saw the thought of the modern world as controlled by the presuppositions of naturalistic or secular humanism. Henry cited Kuyper in tracing the roots of modern Western humanism back to Thomas Aquinas's concessions to human reason and followed Kuyper in insisting rather on an Augustinian position in which faith and revelation (Henry mentioned only revelation) were the necessary preconditions to a fully informed reason. To bring "harmony out of the modern cultural chaos," said Henry, more was needed "than a compromise position between theistic revelational truth and non-theistic philosophy." "The tremendous need today will appear only when men see, as Kuyper put it, that 'the radical difference between regenerate and unregenerate humanity *extends across the entire domain of the higher sciences.* . . .'"[23]

Henry, like Gordon Clark before him, resisted developing such principles to the point of asserting an absolute antithesis between Christian and non-Christian thought. Nonetheless, what Henry and the new evangelicals found in Kuyperian thought was a twentieth-century conservative Christian articulation of a point that had been part of the reformist side of the American evangelical heritage but which had diminished severely in fundamentalism since the 1930s. The point was the broadly Calvinistic vision that the Christian's mission involves not only evangelism but also a cultural task, both remaking the mind of an era and transforming society.

The importance of this general vision for fundamentalism became most apparent with the publication in 1947 of Henry's manifesto, *The Uneasy Conscience of Modern Fundamentalism*. This book, like *Remaking the Modern Mind*, was published by William B. Eerdmans, a Dutch-American promoter of the cause. *The Uneasy Conscience* complemented *Remaking the Modern Mind*, though it was much less elaborate, by presenting the second part of Henry's program—that dealing with social issues. In defining what Christians needed, both

23. Ibid., 227, 233.

Henry and Harold Ockenga, who wrote the introduction, used a phrase that was already a cliché in the Dutch-American community: a "world and life view."[24] By this they meant that transformation of thought and action should go hand in hand, that Christians should develop a comprehensive worldview that could be applied to all of life, including its social and political dimensions.

On this point Henry and Ockenga were zeroing in on what they saw as the major weakness in fundamentalism. The fundamentalist preoccupation with separation both ecclesiastically and in personal mores had cut the group off from any real social impact. Ockenga said quite frankly in an article in *Christian Life and Times* that fundamentalists could not win America without reconstituting their vision.[25] Henry underscored the same point in his book. Fundamentalists were so preoccupied with internal squabbles and trivialities that they lost sight of the world-shaking issues that surrounded them. He cited the recent controversy, apparently much discussed at Wheaton College, of whether the game of Rook fell under the prohibition against card games. He also noted the inconsistency in northern and southern fundamentalist attitudes to smoking and mixed swimming. Meanwhile Western culture was collapsing around them. Henry had no quarrel with the fundamentalist stress on evangelism or with the fundamentals themselves. The problem was that there was no recognition of the culture-transforming implications of these great Christian doctrines. "It is an application of, not a revolt against, fundamentals of the faith, for which I plead."[26]

Particularly, fundamentalism had abandoned any consistent Christian vision of social reform. "For the first protracted period in its history," Henry announced, "evangelical Christianity stands divorced from the great social reform movements." The fundamentalist repudiation of the social gospel seemed to have become also a "revolt against the Christian social imperative." Moreover, fundamentalists confused social reform with humanistic secularism and so abandoned drives for social reform. They thus confined themselves to the task of preaching personal salvation, which, crucial as it was, by itself made the gospel otherworldly. "If the evangelical answer is in terms of religious escapism, then the salt has lost its savor."[27]

Such statements sounded startling to fundamentalists, who by then routinely condemned any "social gospel" and in fact had been politically conservative, or antireformist, during the New Deal era as well. Harold Ockenga's introduction to the *Uneasy Conscience* may have reinforced the impression that these new-style fundamentalists were endorsing progressive politics. His language, however, seems carefully chosen to sound progressive and yet still allow a conservative Republican social agenda. Thus his strongest statement was a tautology: "If the Bible-believing Christian is on the wrong

24. Henry, *The Uneasy Conscience of Modern Fundamentalism* (Grand Rapids: Eerdmans, 1947), 14, and passim; Ockenga, introduction to *Uneasy Conscience*, 10.
25. Ockenga, "Can Christians Win America?" *Christian Life and Times*, June 1947, 13-15.
26. Henry, *Uneasy Conscience*, 20-21, 11 (quote).
27. Ibid., 36, 32, 37, 66.

side of social problems such as war, race, class, labor, liquor, imperialism, etc., it is time to get over the fence to the right side." While Ockenga called for a "progressive Fundamentalism with a social message,"[28] this was somewhat different from advocating a fundamentalism with a progressive social message. Henry was equally cautious in identifying the specific issues on which evangelicals should take a stance. His catalog included opposition to "aggressive warfare, racial hatred and intolerance, the liquor traffic, and exploitation of labor or management," and "political naturalism."[29] Yet even to discuss such issues seriously was for most fundamentalists a revolutionary step.

Henry's was no call for a social gospel in place of traditional evangelism. Regeneration, he made crystal clear, must come first. In his view, Jesus "shares the biblical conviction that redemption is the essential ingredient in the solution of economic problems." Jesus insisted that one must seek *first* the kingdom that is opened to sinners only by the vicarious atonement of Christ. Only after that "all these things shall be added." The kingdom itself could never be equated with "all these things," as nonevangelicals tended to do when they turned the gospel into a mere social message.[30]

Vitally important for understanding the agenda of the new evangelicals and its differences from both dispensationalist fundamentalism and modernism is their view of the kingdom—another central dimension in their view of history. Henry and Ockenga explicitly rejected both the "kingdom then" view of the dispensationalists[31] and the "kingdom now" view of the liberals. Rather, in agreement with some of the recent moderate biblical scholarship, they believed that the kingdom was partly realized in this age but would be completed upon Christ's personal return. Kingdom work today, then, should include not only preaching salvation but also exercising compassion in anticipation of the coming rule of Christ.

Henry worked out more clearly than did most of his evangelical colleagues the puzzling question of how social and political efforts could be kingdom work while the kingdom could never be equated with social, political, or national programs. His solution was essentially a version of Augustine's two cities conception, which sees a distinction between the city of God and the city, or civilization, of the earth. Kingdom principles can influence the earthly city but can never be fully realized there in this age. In the meantime, however, Christians owe some allegiance to both cities, although the allegiance to the civilization of the earth is always relativized by the higher loyalty. Still, though the absolute good is unattainable, our Christian duty toward civilization here is to work for the relatively better. Thus, although we must not identify the kingdom with the American experiment, we might still prefer Anglo-Saxon democracy to German totalitarianism. Similarly, a merely sub-Christian environment, as in the United States, is preferable to an anti-Christian one.

28. Ockenga, introduction to *Uneasy Conscience*, 13.
29. Henry, *Uneasy Conscience*, 17, 78.
30. Ibid., 42, 27-28.
31. Ibid., 50; Ockenga, introduction to *Uneasy Conscience*, 13-14.

Simple moral obligation ought to impel Christians to work for the relatively better in every sphere, including politics. Henry stressed, in contrast to Smith for instance, that Christians should support the United Nations' efforts for world justice, even while protesting the non-Christian frame of reference on which such efforts were based.[32] Such concerns, however, must always be subordinate to the Christian's allegiances to the higher, ultimate kingdom. So for Henry, evangelism remained the first task. Yet he and the other reformers revived another dimension of evangelicalism: that evangelism is the necessary first step toward a second task—the improvement of society.

In 1947 the call for more social involvement among fundamentalists was little more than that—a call. In reality, this theme received relatively little attention at the early Fuller. The two overwhelming priorities were remaking the modern mind and evangelism. The school was to be a great center for scholarship; and it was also Charles Fuller's school, a place for training a generation of missionaries and evangelists. For the moment, the preoccupying question was how the two tasks would fit together.

32. Henry, *Uneasy Conscience*, 84-89.

CHAPTER V
Evangelism

In Dr. Ockenga's last convocation message, "This is the Hour," this question kept coming to me as he so ably presented and marshalled the facts and told us of the need of this critical hour in the world's history. If this is the hour, I kept asking myself, what is the greatest need and how best to meet that need. And the answer came back, "the greatest need is to send out Holy Spirit empowered men, men in whom the Word of God dwells richly.
Charles E. Fuller, chapel address, Fuller Theological Seminary,
October 28, 1948.

THE ULTIMATE PRIORITY

EARLY in the second year, Charles Fuller, who had been staying in the background, spoke at the seminary chapel for the first time. His message rang with fundamentalist tones. We are, he said, "no doubt in the closing hours of the church age." The greatest need of the hour was to send out trained men, but not those "just with head knowledge." In "thirty-two years of field experience of lobbing gospel grenades into the enemy's territory," he observed in a revealing metaphor, he had learned that the key was to be sanctified, consecrated, and cleansed, to be "a spirit-filled, controlled, empowered true witness for Christ." Expanding on this theme of spiritual cleansing, all-important in the holiness tradition that had contributed much to fundamentalism, Fuller devoted the bulk of his address to an exposition of Leviticus 14, which describes the Old Testament regulations for cleansing those with infectious diseases.[1]

The tension between Fuller Seminary's two missions—being a center for apologetic scholarship and a training base for sending out spiritually empowered missionaries—dominated its quest for a self-image. The missionary themes in Charles Fuller's vision were more saleable and so dominated his representations of the school. For many years, most of the students first heard about the seminary through "The Old Fashioned Revival Hour"[2] and Charles Fuller took pride in the early years in pointing out that a remarkable propor-

---

1. Manuscript titled "First Chapel address given by Dr. Charles E. Fuller, founder, in the history of the Seminary," Thursday, Oct. 28, 1948.
2. "The President's Report," May 1959, 10; "Annual Report to the Board of Trustees," May 1960, 10.

tion (20 to 40 percent) of Fuller graduates went out to the mission field.[3] The missionary emphasis was indeed integral not only to Charles Fuller's vision for the school but also to the outlook of each faculty member.

Harold Lindsell was soon finding an academic niche for himself teaching the seminary's courses in missions. During his first years at Fuller he wrote *A Christian Philosophy of Missions,* published in 1949. Disclaiming originality, he articulated with logic and clarity the conventional evangelical views of the day. In line with the themes set by his colleagues, Lindsell placed the missions questions in the context of the world crisis. As the others would have agreed, Lindsell saw three massive world forces threatening Christianity: secularism-modernism, communism, and Catholicism. At the early Fuller, no one would have dissented from Lindsell's remark that Catholicism was among the "arch enemies of America and our way of life and of the true faith." Ockenga was renowned in Boston for his opposition to Catholic power, and Smith routinely listed Catholicism along with communism as a major threat. Anti-Catholicism was simply an unquestioned part of the fundamentalist-evangelicalism of the day. Lindsell's more direct concern, however, was with secularism and its inroads into the church in the form of modernism. Modernism in the church destroyed traditional missions because it questioned the uniqueness of Christianity. True missions, Lindsell countered, must be founded on a belief in the inerrant Bible as true in all its parts and on a message of salvation through the substitutionary atonement of Christ alone. In particular, Christians must not allow "weakened, watered down" evasions of the biblical teaching that without Christ every heathen will suffer eternal punishment in hell. This doctrine made missions the supreme effort of compassion. It could make them an overwhelming passion.[4]

THE CHURCH AS EVANGELISTIC AGENCY

This consuming vision of the urgency of evangelism shaped one of the peculiar traits of American evangelicalism: its doctrine of the church. Again, Lindsell did not propose anything new but stated with clarity what most others just took for granted. "The function of the church," he said flatly, "is to evangelize the world, and this evangelization is to be completed before the return of the Lord." This "primary aim" of the church—"to reach individuals with the gospel of Christ and to bring them together into churches"—ought not to be confused with the social or moral good the church might do. Doing good, individually or socially, is a Christian duty, but it is only "the fruit or product of conversion." The church is to be above all else an aggregate of saved individuals gathered together to evangelize others. The secondary task of

3. See Gleason Archer's testimony in the "Transcript of Proceedings of the Stated Adjourned Meeting of the Winter Session, Presbytery of Los Angeles, November 10, 1953," 45 (P).

4. Harold Lindsell, *A Christian Philosophy of Missions* (Wheaton: Van Kampen, 1949), 223, 54, 77.

Evidence of success. Harold Lindsell points out the location of Fuller graduates working in foreign mission fields around the world.

those gathered together is to build each other up in the faith, thus fulfilling the second part of Jesus' missionary command in the Great Commission (Matt. 28:19-20): "teaching them to observe all that I have commanded you." This is where "the social aspect of the gospel comes to the fore," as the secondary "fruit" of such teaching. Christians should certainly learn to do good at churches, and perhaps as a result even band together to do good. Nonetheless, as Lindsell repeatedly emphasized, it "is not to be confused with the function of the Church in the winning of men and women to Christ. . . ."[5]

Many of the churches that supported the early Fuller Seminary and that in turn fed on its message had this primary image of themselves. They were basically centers for missions and evangelism. Morning worship was not primarily for building up the saints; rather it was for evangelizing the unconverted. In such churches no public service without the invitation to accept Jesus into one's heart would be a proper service. Worship itself was secondary and subordinate to evangelism, so that catchy hymns and choruses or thrilling xylophone recitals to warm up the audience transformed or entirely crowded out the traditional American Protestant liturgy. Liturgy was, in fact, an alien word in many such churches. While some churches that supported Fuller, such as Park Street, Lake Avenue, or some of the big conservative Presbyterian

5. Ibid., 195, 133, 229.

churches of California, retained a more conventional Reformed style of worship, at the early Fuller itself worship in the sense of liturgy was only a minor concern. The subject does not appear in Fuller's early catalogs of course offerings, though in the fourth year the faculty did add a short course in hymnology. Even the word *worship* appears only once in the catalog course descriptions of that time, and that in the description of Everett Harrison's elective on the Psalms. For a sense of the majesty of worship, some classic hymns and Harrison's class-opening prayers, for which he was renowned, were the best that the Fuller low-church tradition had to offer.

THE HIGHEST CALLING

Since the overwhelmingly primary function of the church was to evangelize, this was also the first task of the individual believer. Americans in the revivalist tradition had come to think of the church as the simple sum of individual believers. One implication of such a view was that the same rules applied to the parts as to the whole. Therefore, each individual ought to be a missionary. Fundamentalists typically allowed little room for alternative occupations. "Individual believers," said Lindsell, "are the agents through whom God chooses to work in the accomplishment of the divine purpose," that is, "to take the gospel of Christ to all men everywhere." Hence every Christian must be a missionary in the sense of witnessing at every opportunity. Moreover, all Christians, except those with bona fide excuses, were called to "vocational Christian service," as pastors, missionaries, or the like. Working in medicine, law, or business might be justifiable if one used one's profession for witnessing and used one's wealth to multiply Christian ministries. But even then, justifying one's secular occupation by supporting missionaries might be only a rationalization to escape one's true duty.[6]

CONSECRATED FOR SERVICE

Lindsell's leave-no-way-out call for consecration to a life of missions was much like that repeatedly heard at young people's meetings, summer camps, and missionary rallies throughout the movement. The preachers at these rallies were calling for what in effect was a Protestant equivalent of an itinerant monastic preaching order. Indeed, they almost always tied the call to missionary service with God's call to "the victorious life" or a higher life of consecration and "yieldedness" to God's will. This yieldedness required strict spiritual discipline marked by regular and lengthy personal devotions of Bible reading and prayer as well as the renunciation of certain of the distracting temptations of the flesh. All Christians were called to this higher spiritual order, but many church members remained, in Lindsell's words, "carnal Christians . . . who still live in the flesh."[7] This was standard Keswick holiness teaching, central in the fundamentalist tradition of asceticism and evangelistic service.

6. Ibid., 161.
7. Ibid., 208.

This victorious life movement was organized in England in the 1870s and was often known by the name of its conference grounds at Keswick. The main tenets of its teaching were that Christians could attain a life of victory over known sins by yielding or giving up self to Christ and by being Spirit filled and thus consecrated for a life of service, especially the service of witnessing to others.[8] During the early twentieth century, Keswick teaching spread through the fundamentalist movement in America. Charles Trumbull, the editor of the *Sunday School Times* who had attacked MacInnis at Biola, was long its chief promoter. By the 1930s, Keswick doctrine had become more or less standard fundamentalist teaching on sanctification at places like Moody Bible Institute, Wheaton College, Dallas Theological Seminary, and Columbia Bible College (all of which were sources of Fuller faculty). Harold Ockenga was also one of its leading advocates. Victorious life teaching usually kept a low profile, so that many fundamentalists, including Charles Fuller himself, emphasized its method for holiness without knowing the details of Keswick doctrine as such.[9]

At Fuller Seminary there was no overtly party-line holiness doctrine, but the early faculty took for granted the typical fundamentalist views. "The Seminary," said the first instructions to students, "believes in a 'separated life' emphasis." Though they would impose no "legal code," they expected students to refrain from "habits which interfere with a vigorous Christian life and testimony." Prayer was expected. "Maintain your morning watch," the advice concluded.[10]

From the outset the faculty worried that in the high-powered intellectual atmosphere the spiritual life of their students might languish. Daily chapel attendance was required as essential to establishing a sense of spiritual community. The faculty also inaugurated days of prayer, ending with services of consecration. To emphasize the point further, they sponsored the first year a series of lectures on spirituality by Norman B. Harrison, father of Everett. Everett himself was widely regarded as a model of how scholarship and evangelical piety might be combined, and, while not as assertive as most of his colleagues, his calm and firm demeanor made a lasting impression on many students. In the words of one alumnus, "He was a man who beheld the face of God from close in."[11] Despite such influences from Harrison and others, the

8. Douglas W. Frank provides in a recent book (*Less than Conquerors: How Evangelicals Entered the Twentieth Century* [Grand Rapids: Eerdmans, 1986], 113-66) a useful history and a scathing critique of Keswick teaching, which he sees as an often self-serving technique—parallel to those taught by late nineteenth-century mind-cure movements or in twentieth-century self-help psychologies—for promoting a self-congratulatory, success-oriented spirituality. Such insightful observations should be balanced, however, by the recognition that the Keswick teaching also stood in a long tradition of techniques for Christian spirituality and that many of its advocates were energized by this sense of close dependence on God.

9. DF, on draft. At the Fuller Mt. Hermon Bible Conference in 1952, Fuller professor Clarence Roddy taught a course titled "The Victorious Life," announcement on "The Old Fashioned Revival Hour," 6-8-52 (tape).

10. *Bulletin of Fuller Theological Seminary*, September 29, 1947, mimeograph (with faculty minutes).

11. Alumni comments.

Students raise their voices in song in a Fuller chapel service in the early years

faculty remained uneasy about the heavily academic atmosphere. In the effort to establish more balance, they experimented with various minor courses and brought in other lecturers to address the topic "Evangelism and Christian Life."[12]

An early promotional film stressed the ties of the seminary to "The Old Fashioned Revival Hour" and its missionary emphases. The film, promising such attractions as the opportunity to "watch the fingers of world-famous Rudy Atwood at the piano console," was billed primarily as a film about the Revival Hour. The centerpiece, however, was the true story of a young man who during the war was remarkably converted through listening to the radio program and who later carried his zeal for evangelism to Fuller Seminary. After some shots of registration and of the faculty in their splendid offices in the Cravens mansion, the film turns to student field work, such as leading vacation Bible schools and other evangelism projects. Each student was indeed given a practical-work assignment in Sunday school teaching, youth work, choir di-

12. Faculty minutes, 11-17-49. The faculty voted to drop the class credit for this course and to hold it in the chapel hour once a week. During 1950–51 Arvid Carlson was at Fuller as Lecturer in Evangelism and Christian Life.

recting, visitation, or pastoral work.[13] In fact, however, the practical side, which was not yet highly organized, was the weak point of Fuller education.[14] Nonetheless, the ideal of training effective evangelists was held high. The film closes with a symbolization of this motif as the entire student body, dressed in coats and ties, parade two by two down the long elegant entrance walk outside the estate, presumably setting off to evangelize the world.

ENTHUSIASM

While some of the first students were enamored of the heady intellectual atmosphere, others presented the faculty with the opposite problem of impatience to get to their primary task of winning the world to Christ. The outstanding case, though not exactly typical, was Bill Bright, who had come to California a few years earlier as an aspiring young businessman. Once there, he was attracted to Louis Evans's Hollywood Presbyterian Church, first by the wealth and success of some of its members and then by the fact that they were more excited about Christ "than about their palatial homes and bulging bank accounts." He soon fell under the spell of the revered Henrietta Mears, director of Christian education at Hollywood Presbyterian and teacher of the remarkably successful "college department" class. In the days when the ordination of women was unthinkable among fundamentalist-evangelicals, Miss Mears, who in 1928 had come from the Minneapolis church of fundamentalist czar William B. Riley, had become one of the most influential evangelical leaders in southern California. Clarence Roddy, who came to teach homiletics at Fuller in 1951, remarked that she was the best preacher in southern California.

The connections between Fuller and Henrietta Mears and students such as Bright illustrate that the early success of the seminary was not a flash in the fundamentalist pan. Rather, the school was built on a solid network of fundamentalist-evangelical agencies and leaders, many of whom were, not so incidentally, well-heeled. Miss Mears, for instance, cultivated such Hollywood celebrities as Roy Rogers, Dale Evans, Tim Spencer, and Virginia Mayo in a Bible-study she held at her mansion. Her great work, however, was with college students. Just prior to Fuller's opening she had, at the urging of Bright and some other students, founded the Forest Home resort in the San Bernardino Mountains as a conference center for college students. Six hundred students attended the 1947 conference. Two years later it was at the Forest Home conference that Billy Graham had a profound religious experi-

---

13. Faculty minutes, 9-29-47.
14. Alumni survey respondents from the graduating classes of 1950 to 1952 rated courses in preaching as follows: Excellent 4, Good 13, OK 13, Fair 9, Poor 8. For courses in pastoral counselling or psychology: Excellent 2, Good 7, OK 8, Fair 15, Poor 14. Ratings of these areas improved markedly for alumni of 1957 to 1959 and 1965 to 1967. Alumni from 1950 to 1952 also rated quality of spiritual life at Fuller: Excellent 13, Good 29, OK 6, Fair 3, Poor 1. Respondents from the later eras gave comparably high ratings.

ence of rededication that immediately preceded his Los Angeles Campaign and rise to fame.[15]

During her career, Henrietta Mears was said to have guided five hundred men to the ministry;[16] and she may have had more to do with shaping west coast Presbyterianism than any other person. Many of her students went on to Princeton Seminary—Bright himself was there for part of the 1946–47 school year—but once Fuller Seminary was founded, some of her "boys" went there. Because of the opposition from the local presbytery, though, she herself had to exercise discretion about recommending the nondenominational school. Nonetheless, the natural affinities were sufficent to ensure that a flow of students from Mears's class to the local school would continue.

In the fall of 1947 Bill Bright enrolled at Fuller and was impatient to get on with the task of evangelizing the world. He and his friends thus maintained a heavy schedule of witnessing in addition to their seminary work. They were especially successful with campus leaders and had recently led the president of the UCLA student body to Christ. So eager were Bright and Gary Demarest, one of the most capable students in the entering class, to get on with their task that they announced in December their intention to pursue such work full time in the spring. Carl Henry had lunch with them and found "a happy alternative solution," convincing the two to stay on. While Demarest went on to graduate with the first class, Bright's seminary career remained more a part-time affair. Finally in 1951 he announced that he had learned his last Hebrew word, threw his vocabulary cards in the air, and left the seminary.[17] The needs of the world were too urgent. He devoted himself full time to his newly-founded campus ministry, which he named, at Wilbur Smith's suggestion, Campus Crusade for Christ. Dan Fuller, who had gotten to know him in their student years together, remained a close associate of Bright and aided him in early campus and Campus Crusade work. Though temperamentally much better suited to academics, Dan felt at the time immense pressures to follow his father in the reputedly higher calling of evangelism.[18]

EVERYONE'S TASK

The Fuller faculty wished to strike a balance between "the one extreme of overemphasis on evangelism and the other extreme of doing no evangelism at all."[19] The centrality of evangelism in the Christian life was essential to their message, so each of them had to be active on that front, even though they might aspire to maintain university standards of scholarship. Consequently, virtually everyone taught courses at Bible conferences each summer. Moreover, in the fall of the early years the entire faculty devoted the week of convocation

15. Richard Quebedeaux, *I Found It! The Story of Bill Bright and Campus Crusade* (San Francisco: Harper and Row, 1979), 7-10.
16. DF, on draft.
17. CH to HJO, 12-15-47; DF, on draft.
18. DF interview, 11-11-83.
19. HJO to CH, 12-11-47, re the Bright-Demarest case.

to a "Fuller Seminary Bible Conference" held at a half-dozen local churches with a different Fuller speaker each night. Charles Fuller also held an annual Fuller week at the Mt. Hermon conference grounds in northern California, where he also owned a home. These conferences were well attended by enthusiastic fans of Fuller's radio programs. Once the seminary began, Fuller faculty were among the regular speakers, thus helping the scholars and their constituencies keep more in touch.

Carl Henry provided the most striking example of the faculty's simultaneous deep commitment to evangelism and to scholarship. Though a leader in reforming fundamentalism, he always remained a true revivalist at heart. He retained the dedication of a new convert to his fundamentalist faith, including its mores. So on the one hand he could criticize fundamentalists for not keeping their priorites straight when they argued about the game of Rook; yet on the other his son Paul recalls being greatly impressed as a young boy by seeing his father, upon returning from a plane trip, lay on the table a pack of cigarettes and a deck of cards that he had confiscated from a convert to whom he had witnessed during the flight.

Many Fuller faculty took to heart the fundamentalist teaching that everyone should witness to others about Christ at every opportunity.[20] One former student recollects an early Saturday morning seminar to which Carl Henry often arrived looking bedraggled in an old baggy overcoat. Later the class learned that he would periodically spend half the night out in Los Angeles witnessing to derelicts and helping them find shelter.[21]

THE GRAHAM CONNECTION

In Pasadena Henry's most time-consuming evangelistic work was in organizing, together with Fuller business manager Richard Curley, the Mid-Century Rose Bowl Rally featuring Billy Graham. Graham's sudden rise to national fame in 1949 was a boon to the young seminary. A Wheaton graduate, a Youth for Christ evangelist, and the chosen heir to fundamentalist magnate William B. Riley in Minneapolis, Graham was already connected to the Fuller people by many of the strands of fundamentalist-evangelicalism. He also looked up to Charles Fuller as the leading evangelist of the day and admired Wilbur Smith.

When Graham launched his Christ for Greater Los Angeles campaign in 1949, the Fuller people expected nothing out of the ordinary. Some

20. DF recalls that later Lindsell regularly had lunch at the Pasadena University Club, next to the new seminary buildings; and once he remarked, "That University Club is the greatest mission field you could want." DF, on draft.

21. Henry had actively supported crusade evangelism in Chicago and published *A Doorway to Heaven* (Grand Rapids: Zondervan, 1942), a history of Chicago's Pacific Garden Mission. He had also been on the committee to promote the Soldier Field Easter sunrise services and in 1946 had handled publicity for the Life Begins campaign. An indication of the degree to which fundamentalism was still united is that the later separatists John R. Rice and Bob Jones, Sr., were among the speakers for the Life Begins rallies.

Fuller students were helping with the meetings and Graham spoke at a regular seminary chapel service. Wilbur Smith wrote a friend that after the first week, "Billy Graham's meetings . . . I think, were a little disappointing to him." Graham was preaching a compelling message of judgment on America for its sins, the impact of which was heightened by President Truman's announcement a few days earlier that the Russians had the A-bomb. Neither the Russians nor God, though for somewhat different reasons, were likely to spare a city like Los Angeles, according to Graham. Only repentance could save the city and individual souls from the impending judgment.[22]

While this message was bringing modest success to the crusade after several weeks, its impact was heightened by two developments. One was William Randolph Hearst's decision to give Graham major press coverage. The other, following the pattern set by Graham's older friend and adviser, Henrietta Mears, was the conversion of some Hollywood celebrities. Suddenly, Billy Graham was famous.

The Fuller connection, though never close, was sealed by the Los Angeles crusade's immediate sequel in the east. After Graham's triumph in Los Angeles, Harold Ockenga immediately invited him to campaign in Boston. Graham's meetings, at the turn of the year 1949 to 1950, were again an immense success. Ockenga and Graham gained wide support from Boston churches and received fine press coverage. Soon they decided to double their schedule, and finally they moved to the Boston Garden to accommodate the ever-expanding crowds. The triumph in Boston proved that Graham could be a major attraction anywhere he went. During the next year, Harold Lindsell wrote a biography of Ockenga in which Graham's remarkable Boston crusade was the crown of the Park Street pastor's career.[23]

Carl Henry, who because of his newspaper experience was the publicity man at Fuller Seminary, was enthusiastic about the school's connection with Graham. At first the school planned to invite Graham and his New England team for the Fuller convocation in the fall of 1950. The other organizations that had earlier sponsored Graham in Los Angeles, such as Youth for Christ, were extremely eager to support a return visit; but, as they told Ockenga, they did not want to be co-opted into a Fuller Seminary promotion. The seminary agreed, accordingly, to stay entirely in the background but to help organize a far more ambitious event. They would rent the nearby Rose Bowl for a giant "Mid-Century Rose Bowl Rally." The stadium could accommodate a crowd far surpassing those of the tent meetings in 1949 and truly worthy of headline news. The school had already helped sponsor, particularly with Henry's aid, annual Easter sunrise services in the Rose Bowl. Now the seminary gave Henry time and special help from business manager Curley to coordinate every detail for the great Graham rally. When the momentous day

22. William G. McLoughlin, *Billy Graham: Revivalist in a Secular Age* (New York: Ronald Press, 1960), 46-48.
23. Harold Lindsell, *Park Street Prophet: A Life of Harold John Ockenga* (Wheaton: Van Kampen, 1951), esp. 146-53.

arrived, fifty thousand people turned out. Yet Henry, as he recollected, was crushed. The immense stadium was still half empty. He had, however, ensured outstanding press coverage. The reporters were impressed and described the event as a grand success, the largest religious gathering ever in southern California.[24]

Even though Fuller Seminary had remained in the background in all the pre-event publicity, Harold Ockenga preceded Graham at the rally with an address entitled "The Answer to Communist Aggression." The Boston preacher stressed, as Graham himself often did, that a return to Christian theism was America's only hope for avoiding destructive judgment.[25]

Such messages had political connotations. The Korean War was underway and apprehension about communist aggression was intense. Nonetheless, despite occasional calls from Ockenga and Henry for evangelical social and political involvement, evangelization was overwhelmingly their top priority. When Ockenga or Graham spoke of the communist threat, it was almost always a prelude to the call for individuals, and thereby the nation, to turn to Christ. So the reformers of fundamentalism at Fuller Seminary remained faithful to what had been the central thrust of American evangelicalism at least since the days of Dwight L. Moody. While their agenda had expanded to include the rehabilitation of both scholarship and Christian social consciousness, evangelism remained the sine qua non.

24. CH interview, 11-19-82. Undated (ca. June 1950) document on Mid-Century Rose Bowl Rally.
    25. "Excerpts from Dr. Harold John Ockenga's address on 'The Answer to Communist Aggression,' The Rose Bowl, Thursday night, September 14 [1950]." Mimeograph.

CHAPTER VI
The Legacy of Fundamentalist Militancy

Some months later [in the spring of 1947] Smith invited me to lunch. "I have just received pictures of the new campus," he said, "and it is a veritable garden of Eden." "If so," I replied humorously, "there is a fall just around the corner."
Carl F. H. Henry, *Confessions of a Theologian: An Autobiography.*

When we first got to Pasadena, everything looked very bright, both literally and figuratively. No cloud appeared in the blue sky, and we were warmly received by the Fullers as well as the faculty. We yearned for a settled life, and under seemingly good auspices we looked for and then bought a darling little house surrounded by roses, azaleas, and palm trees.
Béla Vassady, *Limping Along: Confessions of a Pilgrim Theologian.*

THE STIGMA OF SEPARATISM

IF evangelism was to be effective in restoring the nation, reaching the people who led America and not just those on the fringes, fundamentalist-evangelicalism would have to regain influence in the mainstream Protestant denominations. This was a top concern for the reformers of fundamentalism. Separatism had plagued their movement for the past twenty years; and they increasingly viewed the rifts as destructive and embittering, narrowing the movement so that it was becoming sectarian, inward-looking, anti-intellectual, and antisocial. Worst of all, separatism hurt evangelism.

The return to mainstream influence, the reformers resolved, would be without compromise. Though these new evangelicals would abandon hardline dispensationalism and separatism, they were themselves still sufficiently fundamentalist to resolve not to yield an inch on any essential doctrine. Yet they did not reckon deeply with the fact that their movement, as a movement, was built around independent institutions, and that, from a denominationalist's point of view, the difference between independence and separatism was one of the mysteries of the fundamentalist faith. To the new generation of evangelicals, the distinction was clear enough. Some independent evangelical agencies, such as the American Council of Christian Churches, promoted separatism while others, such as the National Association of Evangelicals, did not. To the denominationalist, however, the point was not so clear. If some funda- mentalist-evangelicals were really nonseparatist, if they really thought, unlike their fellow fundamentalists, that the mainstream denominations were not apostate, why did they not work through the denominational agencies? Why did their rhetoric so clearly claim that transdenominational evangelical agen- cies must replace the inadequate institutions of the denominations?

Harold Ockenga, the leading promoter of the strategy to retain the respectability of fundamentalist-evangelicals in the major denominations, and also one of the most given to flying high the rhetorical flags proclaiming evangelical superiority, was the first to be forced to confront directly the mainline opposition to this anomalous stance. In the fall of 1947, the Presby- tery of Los Angeles began taking steps that could lead to his removal from the Presbyterian ministry if he contined his activities at Fuller. When he met with the executive council of the presbytery during the week of opening convoca- tion, he quickly discovered some of the reasons why the presbytery was launching such attacks against him and the new and untested seminary. Four of his interrogators had been on either the staff or the board of the Bible Institute of Los Angeles in the 1920s when Charles Fuller had helped organize the purge of John MacInnis. MacInnis, further, had been an ordained mem- ber of the Presbytery of Los Angeles. The majority of the presbytery, including many of those who now sat before Ockenga, had been outraged at the Biola action, and in a 1928 statement had declared that the majority of Biola's board (including Charles Fuller) had done "great wrong to a member of the Presby- tery, the late John Murdock MacInnis."[1] Moreover, there was now also a son of MacInnis in the presbytery. Perhaps most importantly, Charles Fuller's continuing legacy, as far as most of the presbytery members were concerned, was the independent church in Placentia that remained a center for anti- Presbyterian sentiment. Splitting a Presbyterian church was no small offense in the minds of most loyal Presbyterian clergy. In their view, Charles Fuller was a raving fundamentalist schismatic, long at war with proper Presby- terianism.

As the meeting with the presbyters wore on, Ockenga's mood changed perceptibly. Even if Charles Fuller had changed regarding separatism, the dominant party in the presbytery still had a formidable case against him, he thought. Moreover, they were bitter and unlikely to change their views. To them, the seminary was simply a new instance of church splitting and separa- tism. Ockenga's public and private assurances against "come-out-ism" could not convince them otherwise. As he left the meeting, he acknowledged that he faced a difficult decision about whether he would continue as a Presbyterian. He would advise them in two weeks.[2]

During the next days, Ockenga held long meetings with the Fuller

1. "Transcript of Proceedings . . . Presbytery of Los Angeles, November 10, 1953," 40, 38, 8 (P).
2. Ibid., 39-40.

faculty. Wilbur Smith remarked that these substantive discussions in a "faculty-controlled institution" were much preferable to those at Moody Bible Institute, "where faculty only met to waste time, to discuss railroad schedules, and excusing some girl from two hours of piano. . . ."[3] The Fuller faculty's eventual decision was not to take a stand on Ockenga's case. Rather than fight a losing battle, he would simply transfer his membership to the Congregational Conference.

While the seminary leadership thus side-stepped controversy with a key mainline denomination, their principal preoccupation on the public relations front during 1947–48 was to try to explain to critics on the right that Ockenga's attack on "come-out-ism" was not meant to condemn everybody who was outside the mainline churches. Though the seminary was in the unique position of not being immediately dependent financially on the whims of any considerable constituency, it could nonetheless not afford to alienate Charles Fuller's radio audience. Moreover, it had to establish what sort of church communities it would serve. Would it be the moderates outside the mainline denominations or the conservatives within those denominations? As long as all the students in 1947–48 were in their first year, addressing the problem was not critical. It could not be postponed for long, however.

Those California Presbyterians unhappy with Fuller's presence soon began turning the screw tighter on the Presbyterian students. San Francisco Seminary, where Wilbur Smith's adversary, John W. Bowman, was a leading figure, was understandably concerned about inroads Fuller might make with the Presbyterian constituency. In 1948 they declared that they would accept no transfer credits from students who had attended "divisive seminaries."[4] With the support of the San Francisco presbytery, the San Francisco Seminary informed all the presbyteries of California that Fuller Seminary was indeed divisive.[5] This category was created to explain a stance toward Fuller that went against Presbyterian precedents. Independent seminaries had long served the Presbyterian Church in the U.S.A., and Presbyterian seminaries customarily gave credit for equivalent work. Union Seminary in New York, for instance, though it had separated from the Presbyterian church, had long had most cordial relations with Presbyterians. With no investigation, however, Fuller Seminary was declared to be, by its very nature, divisive. In the fall of 1948 the Presbytery of Los Angeles sent a communication to southern California Presbyterian students at Fuller to remind them of this point. Theological training at Fuller was entirely unacceptable, the warning stated, and if any students wished to remain under the care of the presbytery, they would have to leave Fuller by January 1949.[6]

The seminary had already run into a similar stone wall when they attempted to place one of their students as a field worker in a Los Angeles

3. WS to Frank Gaebelein, 9-29-49.
4. "Policy on Divisive Seminaries," San Francisco Theological Seminary (n.d.) (LA). HL to HJO, 11-24-48.
5. Dwight W. Small to HL, 9-23-49 (LA).
6. Faculty minutes, 12-14-48.

Presbyterian church. The student, Lester Pontius, had been asked by the Korean Presbyterian Church in Los Angeles to be a youth director there. Pontius met a thoroughly hostile reception from the presbytery representative in charge of such work, however. Gleason Archer, Ockenga's protégé, who was just starting his career teaching Old Testament at Fuller, interceded in hopes of establishing more cordial relationships. Archer was an ordained Presbyterian clergyman himself and was hoping to transfer his membership to the Los Angeles presbytery. Yet his experience meeting with three members of the presbytery was similar to Ockenga's a year earlier. They were "fairly polite but also quite truculent." They thought that all the Presbyterian students that they knew of at Fuller were "of an intransigent temper and unusable as good Presbyterians."[7] Fuller Seminary was now being treated by the presbytery as though it were part of some sensational cult. Carl Henry (who had been cut off from the retirement program of the American Baptist Convention when he came to Fuller)[8] wrote to Ockenga that "as to denominations, it looks increasingly as if the major influence of the seminary will carry outside them." Presbyterians, he said, were making disparagement of Fuller a test of denominational loyalty. So were Methodists. And a similar pattern was emerging among Baptists, as some state secretaries were recommending that churches not take Fuller graduates. Our boys," wrote Henry, "are becoming jittery."[9]

A BOLD MOVE

As this crisis was unfolding in the fall of 1948, Ockenga was exploring with his faculty a remarkable step that, though not simply an attempt to cultivate an image and to gain an entree into the mainline denominations, had the conspicuous attraction of being a way to do just that. He was considering offering a faculty position to a highly accomplished Hungarian Reformed theologian, Béla Vassady (before 1952 spelled Vasady), who not long before had come from his homeland after the communist takeover.

Having Vassady on the faculty would surely be an extravagance. The fledgling seminary already had two theologians because Edward J. Carnell had just joined the staff in 1948. Carnell was a close associate of Carl Henry, had studied at Wheaton under Gordon Clark, had attended Westminster Seminary, had a Th.D. from Harvard Divinity School, and, like Henry, was completing a Ph.D. at Boston University. The two had talked of collaborating and Carnell had come to Fuller with the understanding that he would teach whatever aspects of systematics and apologetics that Henry did not.[10] Carnell was already indispensable to the seminary, a brilliant teacher and a prodigious writer. Still under thirty, he had worked out his own apologetics in *An Introduction to Christian Apologetics*, which had won the much-heralded Eerdmans Evan-

---

7. GA to HJO, 11-17-48.
8. Carl Henry, *Confessions of a Theologian: An Autobiography* (Waco, Tex.: Word, 1986), 118.
9. CH to HJO, 11-28-48.
10. EJC to HJO, 11-19-47 (O).

gelical Book Award Competition in 1948 with its prize of $5000 (virtually a year's salary).

Despite the promise of the seminary's young theologians, the possibility of adding Vassady, a man of internationally established credentials, was an immense attraction. Clearly the faculty thought it would be a shrewd triumph over their sophisticated critics were they to fit Vassady into the picture.

They knew, however, that Vassady already had two strikes against him when batting in the American evangelical league. First, he had some admiration for Karl Barth and neo-orthodoxy, rumored among many conservative evangelicals to be the wolf of modernism dressed in the clothes of the Lamb. Second, he was among the founders of the much-maligned World Council of Churches, feared by most evangelicals as part of a modernist effort both to homogenize and to dilute the faith. Dispensationalist fundamentalists went even further in their criticism of the WCC, typically describing it as the latest part of a satanic-Marxist conspiracy to form one church and one world under Antichrist. Though Ockenga and the Fuller faculty were well aware of these liabilities, Vassady was clearly an evangelical at heart, and nothing in his positions necessitated that he would incur the fatal third strike of denying some fundamental doctrine.

The resulting episode was both one of the most curious and one of the most illuminating in Fuller's history. In it the major themes of the history yet to come were anticipated in microcosm, even though the outcome was just the reverse of what happened later. The point tested in Vassady's appointment to Fuller was whether the fundamentalist movement could sustain the openness now being proclaimed by some of its younger leaders. Could the unity that seemed theoretically possible through emphasizing the positive aspects of the gospel transcend the heritage of division, suspiciousness, and theological caution fostered by the disputes of the 1920s and 1930s? In partial answer, this early experiment illustrated that the new evangelicalism, whatever its hopes and rhetoric, had not blossomed far from its fundamentalist roots.

EUROPEAN AND AMERICAN PERSPECTIVES

Béla Vassady had a number of credentials that fit with fundamentalist-evangelicalism as it was conceived of at Fuller Seminary. He was obviously a pious and deeply dedicated Christian and was thoroughly Reformed. He had published eight books, one of which was an exposition of John Calvin. This combination of Reformed piety and scholarship was just what Fuller was looking for. Perhaps most importantly as a symbol of compatibility with the seminary's heritage, Vassady had studied for a year at old Princeton Seminary, the very fountain from which flowed the Fuller ideal. In the early 1920s he had received a scholarship to study theology in America. After completing a B.D. at Central Theological Seminary (in Ohio) of the Reformed Church in America, he took in 1924–25 a Th.M. at Princeton, studying systematic theology with Caspar Wistar Hodge, the last scion of the famed family of Presbyterian orthodoxy. At Princeton Vassady was acquainted with Everett Harrison and got to know a number of the other of Machen's most dedicated students.

Back in Hungary after his studies in America, Vassady quickly became one of the outstanding theological leaders of the substantial Reformed church of that country. He served as professor of religious philosophy and education at the theological seminary at Papa, was professor of theology and ethics and, for two years, dean at the theological seminary at Sarospatak, and then held the chair in dogmatics in the Reformed Theological Faculty of the University of Debrecen, the center of Reformed strength in Hungary. He was also the editor of three church periodicals simultaneously. He was frequently his church's representative to ecumenical conferences and was a member of the Provisional Committee that planned the formation of the World Council of Churches, later consummated in Amsterdam in 1948.

In the meantime, after surviving painful hardships in Hungary during and after World War II, Vassady was sponsored by the American Committee of the World Council of Churches and the Federal Council of Churches on a sixteen-month speaking tour in the United States. Then in 1947 he received a two-year appointment as guest professor of theology at Princeton Seminary, where his wife Serena and family joined him. By mid-1948, with rapidly deteriorating relations between the United States and the Soviet Union, the Vassadys reluctantly concluded that their American connections would make it too dangerous for them to return to Hungary.[11]

In Amsterdam, when the World Council of Churches was meeting during the summer of 1948, Harold Ockenga heard from a fellow NAE observer, R. L. Decker, that Vassady was looking for a job for the following year. The Fuller president saw his chance for the great coup. Interviewing him shortly after they returned to the States, Ockenga was satisfied of Vassady's orthodoxy and piety and set the machinery rolling to add him to the Fuller faculty.[12]

While Vassady and the Fuller faculty had enough in common to convince both that they would be well matched, they were in fact facing cultural differences that neither appreciated fully in 1948. While a quarter of a century earlier Vassady and his theologically conservative student friends at Princeton may have found little to disagree about, much had happened since, especially in European Christianity.

The contrast points up the thoroughly American character of the new evangelicalism. Virtually all of Fuller's early faculty were educated entirely in America. At the time when they were in school, the fondest academic ambition of promising evangelical scholars was to study at Harvard[13] (as Archer and

11. The above material is from Vassady's biographical sketch to the Presbytery of Los Angeles, 9-6-49 (LA), from interviews with Vassady, 8-10-83, 12-12-84, 1-16-85, and a letter to the author, 1-17-86. For a more complete account see Vassady, *Limping Along: Confessions of a Pilgrim Theologian* (Grand Rapids: Eerdmans, 1985).
12. Vassady's account of the Fuller episode is found in *Limping Along*, 124-41.
13. Rudolph L. Nelson, "Fundamentalism at Harvard: The Case of Edward J. Carnell," *Quarterly Review* 2 (Summer 1982): 79-98.

Carnell did) or at least somewhere in Boston (as Henry did). This confinement of vision to Boston was necessitated by historical circumstances. From the 1820s through the 1920s, outstanding evangelical scholars had frequently studied in Germany, a trial by critical fire that could, if they survived, harden them for the defense of the conservative American faith.[14] During the 1930s and 1940s, however, this option was eliminated by the international crisis. Although Fuller Seminary soon encouraged its most promising early graduates to study abroad, the seminary had been founded by the generation of American fundamentalist-evangelicals that had been shaped most exclusively by their immediate American experience.[15]

In America, evangelicals had been relatively safe from external political threats and hence had the leisure to hone the fine points of their internal American Protestant disputes to razor-sharp quality. For many evangelical leaders these doctrinal battles were part of a greater spiritual war that overshadowed all politics, even the cataclysmic events leading to World War II. To them, as can be seen in the thought of Wilbur Smith, the international crisis was a revealing backdrop that added intensity to the consideration of the spiritual threats to civilization in the latter days.[16]

European Protestantism at the same time included some hard-shelled conservatives; but the political traumas also fostered among theological traditionalists a certain intra-Protestant generosity. At least Béla Vassady and the dominant party he spoke for in the Hungarian Reformed Church were ecumenically open, eager for allies. Vassady himself especially welcomed Karl Barth as the preeminent theologian of the age. Barth challenged the theological liberalism of the nineteenth century and called the church back to Reformed dogma, stressing the sovereignty of God, the centrality of grace through the work of Christ, personal encounter with the Savior, and the exclusive authority of Scripture. For Vassady, Barth signaled the return of European theology from destructive liberalism to Reformed and evangelical doctrines. Among the Hungarian theologian's publications were thus translations of two of Barth's books.

To American fundamentalist-evangelicals, European neo-orthodoxy looked considerably different. By the time neo-orthodoxy became influential in America, around 1930, the lines between fundamentalists and so-called inclusivists had already been drawn. Neo-orthodoxy was, in fundamentalist eyes, a theological movement on the inclusivist side. Its critique of modernism

---

14. One of the last to study in Germany in this era was Charles Woodbridge of the early Fuller faculty, who had studied there in 1928 and in France in 1932. Woodbridge, however, was so thoroughly hardened against European thought as to be seemingly untouched by it.

15. Even contacts with Britishers, always prominent before and since, were at their nadir in this era.

16. An example of this perspective is the later reminiscences of Francis A. Schaeffer that "a case could be made that the news about Machen (being expelled from the Presbyterian Church in 1936) was the most significant U.S. news in the first half of the twentieth century." Schaeffer, *The Great Evangelical Disaster* (Westchester, Ill.: Crossway, 1984), 35.

and return to orthodox doctrines did not much impress fundamentalists, for neo-orthodox theologians were no more orthodox than many moderate conservatives who had refused to join the fundamentalist cause. Moreover, the neo-orthodox were especially suspect on points that fundamentalists emphasized most: the historical accuracy of Scripture and the literal historicity of the miracles. To fundamentalist-evangelicals, then, neo-orthodoxy, far from being the needed antidote to modernism, was just a more subtle form of the modernist disease. The issue became a minor cause célèbre, when the European neo-orthodox leader Emil Brunner was offered a guest professorship at Princeton Seminary for the 1938–39 academic year.[17] Brunner, argued those who were already castigating Princeton, was no better than a modernist.

This characterization of European neo-orthodoxy gained scholarly status from Cornelius Van Til of Westminster Seminary, one of the few in the fundamentalist fold equipped philosophically and linguistically to deal with the complexities of European dialectic theologies. Van Til argued that while the crisis theologians Barth and Brunner were using the language of orthodoxy, their theologies were in fact controlled by the critical philosophical tradition of Kant and Kierkegaard, the same tradition that produced the old modernism. In either case, standards set by autonomous human philosophy were determining what theologians would accept from God's word.[18] Van Til encapsulated his thesis in the title of his 1946 treatise on Barth and Brunner, *The New Modernism.* Few fundamentalists read the book, but many repeated the title.

During Béla Vassady's lecture tour through America in 1946 and 1947, someone handed him a copy of Van Til's book. The two men, both born in European Reformed communities, had been friends at Princeton Seminary in the 1920s. Now Vassady was stunned to discover in his old friend's book that the "new modernists" were led by another friend of his, Karl Barth.[19]

Nonetheless, Vassady was sufficiently dedicated to the old-style theology of the Calvinist Reformation to have satisfied Ockenga as to his orthodoxy. To the Fuller faculty Ockenga reported that Vassady followed the classic Reformed confessions and that "he definitely believes in the objective inscripturated Word of God which is enclosed in the canon of Scripture." He judged that though he was an expert on Barth he was not a Barthian. When questioned on premillennialism, another special test for admission into American fundamentalist-evangelical circles, Vassady had to have the term explained to him. Once he heard what it was, Ockenga concluded, he allowed that it fit with his strong eschatological views.[20]

The Fuller faculty had been suspicious, however. In *Theology Today* Vassady had just published an essay on "the theology of hope" that, while not

17. Edwin H. Rian, *The Presbyterian Conflict* (Grand Rapids: Eerdmans, 1940), 265-70.
18. Cornelius Van Til, *The New Modernism* (Philadelphia: Presbyterian and Reformed, 1947), xii-xx.
19. Conversations with Vassady.
20. HJO to GA, 11-2-48.

unorthodox, stressed the "existential response to the Gospel." This raised some reservations for Carl Henry and Edward J. Carnell, who were Fuller's bright young experts on the nuances of modern theology and philosophy. Both had been influenced by Van Til, although they differed with him on important points. Carnell had studied with Van Til and, while he had sided on some philosophical points with Van Til's rival, his own former mentor Gordon Clark, he, Van Til, and Henry all shared the deep suspicion of neo-orthodoxy. Carnell had in fact made the subject one of his specialties, studying Kierkegaard and Reinhold Niebuhr in graduate school. In anticipation of the interview with Vassady, Carl Henry wrote to Ockenga that he and Carnell would "be most delighted to learn that he does not speak the dialectical tongue of Barth and Brunner."[21]

THE CLOSED DOOR

When Vassady visited Pasadena in December 1948 Henry and Carnell conducted the theological examination. They quizzed him carefully on his relation to Barth and noted with unease his "refusal to indict Barthianism."[22] They also wondered about his fondness for the terminology of paradox and dialectic. Vassady, for his part, found his examiners remarkably preoccupied with abstractions and far too concerned to avoid even the language of the encounter theologians.[23] Despite all this, they had much in common and the young Americans were highly impressed with Vassady on almost every count. Henry reported that Vassady regarded "the Bible as God's inscripturated revelation, and as infallible—as opposed to neo-supernaturalism. . . ."[24] Certainly they must have asked about his views on the historicity of Adam and Eve and of the biblical miracles. These questions were crucial ones for determining whether one believed in the unerring historicity of Scripture, a point that Carnell and Henry emphasized in opposition to neo-orthodox tendencies to put these events in a realm of "holy history," beyond the reach of ordinary historical investigation. Vassady did not use the American fundamentalist term *inerrancy,* but Henry and Carnell were satisfied that his affirmations of the actual historicity of biblical events was compatible with their own belief that the Bible could not err. Perhaps their eagerness caused them to see more commonality on this subject than was actually there.

In any case, they were eager. Henry saw ties to the four hundred-year-old institutions from which Vassady came as adding stature to the new seminary. Moreover, Vassady would be an asset for the planned initiation of graduate studies in 1950–51.[25] Carnell, whose zeal to put evangelicalism into the big time was unbounded, wrote that the Henry-Vassady-Carnell block

21. CH to HJO, 11-28-48 (O).
22. EJC to HJO, 12-15-48 (O).
23. Conversations with Vassady.
24. CH to HJO, 12-13-48 (O).
25. Faculty minutes, 9-28-48. In 1949 Ockenga appointed Vassady chairman of the graduate studies committee.

would give Fuller one of the strongest apologetic, systematic, and philosophical theology departments in the world.[26] To Vassady, he wrote that "being of Westminster vintage," he had wondered, "can anything good come out of Princeton." Now, he said, "I repent in sack cloth."[27]

When Vassady arrived the next fall as Professor of Biblical Theology and Ecumenics, the campaign to gain an entree into the Presbyterian church was in high gear. The Fuller leadership urged Vassady to transfer his ministerial membership from the Reformed Church of Hungary to the Presbytery of Los Angeles immediately. How could the presbytery turn down a founder of the World Council of Churches on the grounds that he was "divisive"? Gleason Archer consequently wrote a note to Vassady urging him to emphasize his role in the World Council of Churches in his application for transfer.[28]

Perhaps coincidentally, the seminary was strengthening the Presbyterian side of its faculty. In addition to Vassady, the latest additions to the faculty were a new dean and acting professor of practical theology, Herbert Mekeel, a Presbyterian pastor from New York State, and a professor of Old Testament, William LaSor, ordained a Presbyterian army chaplain during the war and most recently chairman of the religion department at Lafayette College, a school of the Presbyterian Church. LaSor was an admirer of Wilbur Smith, who first contacted him about the seminary post, and he possessed impeccable nonseparatist Presbyterian credentials. In the early 1930s he had studied at Princeton Seminary rather than at Machen's Westminster. And he had even participated as a member of the Special Judicial Commission of the Presbytery of West Jersey in suspending Carl McIntire from the Presbyterian ministry because of his participation on the Independent Board. The Fuller Seminary lineup of nonseparatists was thus dramatically strengthened.

Vassady, nonetheless, was the champion to be sent into the fray to calm the enemy. Shortly after his arrival in Pasadena in September 1949, the committee on new members of the presbytery met with him to review his application. Vassady was stunned by the result. After consulting privately, they came to him and said, in effect: "We don't know *how* to tell you this. . . . We would be honored to have you in our presbytery, but we are embarrassed to say that we will not be able to recommend it. For if you were allowed in the presbytery, these other men would come in on your coattails and we would be forced to condone the divisiveness of which we actually disapprove."[29]

Vassady had some reason to expect better from the Presbyterians. Even President John Mackay of Princeton had urged him to accept the Fuller position. Moreover, at an ecumenical gathering in 1948 the Vassadys had become friends with Eugene Carson Blake, pastor of the Pasadena Presbyterian Church and one of the most influential members of the presbytery. At Princeton's commencement in the spring of 1949 he too had encouraged Vas-

26. EJC to HJO, 12-15-48 (O).
27. EJC to Béla Vassady, 12-15-48 (V).
28. GA to Béla Vassady, 8-11-49 (V).
29. Conversations with Vassady and document (ca. November 1949) summarizing Vassady case (LA).

Béla Vassady

sady to apply to the Los Angeles presbytery. Blake, however, was caught in a dilemma, since he had sympathies both with Vassady and also with those who suspected that Vassady was being used by Fuller as a wedge to gain entry into the presbytery.[30] Immediately after the committee on new members recommended against Vassady, Blake called on him at his home and assured him he would still lobby to get him accepted. By mid-October, however, he determined that the doors were closed. Vassady then withdrew his application to avoid public embarrassment to the Hungarian Reformed Church.[31] He was, however, becoming extremely puzzled over the state of the American churches.

Many in the Presbyterian Church in the U.S.A. were also puzzled at the zeal of the Presbytery of Los Angeles to combat divisiveness by trying to cut Fuller Seminary out of contact with the church. Some parts of the church were of a different mind. So, for instance, when the Los Angeles presbytery requested in the fall of 1949 that all the eastern presbyteries that held the ministerial credentials of various Fuller faculty forbid them from laboring in the Los Angeles presbytery's bounds, Wilbur Smith's presbytery of Chester,

30. On September 11, 1949, the day before the Vassady interview, Blake argued the constitutional point that the Presbyterian professors at Fuller should all be banned by their eastern presbyteries from working in the Los Angeles area. From "Report to HJO concerning . . . presbytery . . . ," September 11, 1949 (LA).
31. Document summarizing Vassady case (ca. November 1949) (LA).

Pennsylvania, voted unanimously simply not to do anything. This stance was consistent with their earlier reluctance to prosecute Smith in the Independent Board case. Smith's loyalty to the Presbyterian church, on the other hand, was tenuous and highly selective.[32] He had not helped the case for Fuller's reputation in Presbyterianism when he called the latest Presbyterian church-school curriculum "blasphemous."[33]

Presbyterians were understandably sensitive about such remarks. Their denomination was, more than is usually acknowledged, deeply divided between conservatives and progressives. Especially in burgeoning areas like southern California, members were constantly transferring between Presbyterian and more fundamentalist churches. Tensions were often high. Soon after he came to Fuller in 1948, Gleason Archer walked innocently into one such ecclesiastical hornet's nest. The Presbyterian church in a nearby community was deeply divided because of a group who had transferred from a fundamentalistic church and taken control of the Sunday school. The pastor was pushing for adoption of the denomination's controversial new curriculum—what Smith had labeled blasphemous—but was meeting sharp opposition. After many requests from his fundamentalist Sunday school superintendent to invite a Fuller professor to speak, the pastor finally acceded. Archer, who came to speak, held to a style of Presbyterianism that was straight-laced and frankly traditional. He had won prizes at Princeton Seminary for his expertise in the Westminster Shorter Catechism, and in keeping with that he lectured the Sunday school class on the merits of the catechism. Though he did not speak directly of the new curriculum, he reportedly said, "There is only one curriculum . . . the catechism." The fundamentalist dissidents took this to be a stroke on their behalf and used the occasion to intensify their campaigns. According to the beleaguered pastor, one quarter of his daily phone calls were complaints from this faction, and this exacerbated the nervous condition of his wife. The pastor himself eventually became so distressed that he resigned his church.[34] While Archer's remark could hardly have precipitated this whole chain of events, the alleged connection was just of the sort that the majority of the Los Angeles presbytery suspected. The Reverend Glen Moore, the presbytery's counsellor to the pastor during his separation from his church in 1949, was probably the key figure in the presbytery's actions toward Fuller that same year.

The seminary also had Presbyterian friends. These included some important local pastors, such as Clarence Kerr of Glendale, Louis Evans of Hollywood Presbyterian, and Evans's assistant, Richard C. Halverson, as

32. According to Francis Schaeffer, Smith wrote to him on April 30, 1947, suggesting that the time might be ripe for leaving the Presbyterian Church in the U.S.A. Schaeffer, "A Look at the Future," *Christian Beacon*, February 2, 1950, 2. Smith advised Frank Gaebelein on October 26, 1949, against joining the PCUSA—"a vast ecclesiastical machine" (S).

33. CH (or posibly GA) to HJO, 12-15-48; WS to Frank Gaebelein, 10-26-49 (S).

34. "Transcript of Proceedings . . . Presbytery of Los Angeles, November 10, 1953," 90-91; GA to HJO, 11-17-48.

well as some conservatives elsewhere in California, such as Robert Munger in Berkeley. The small San Jose presbytery, hearing in September 1949 that the Los Angeles presbytery was tightening its anti-Fuller policy, decided to investigate for themselves before settling their own policy toward Fuller graduates. They sent a committee, composed of a conservative, a liberal, and a middle-of-the-roader to visit the seminary, a step not previously taken by any Presbyterian agency.

The committee found only three points of complaint. First, the seminary was deficient in field work. Second, at the fall convocation, Ockenga had pointedly referred to the recent moves of the Los Angeles presbytery against Fuller and suggested that "powerfully organized religious movements" might prove to be the enemy as much as secularism was. Alluding to the Vassady case, Ockenga suggested that such narrow attitudes of major denominations contradicted the true ecumenical spirit.[35] And third, the committee found that the seminary's provisional statement of faith was more specific—constrictingly so—than was the Westminster Confession on premillennialism and on the inspiration of Scripture. Positively, however, the committee agreed that the seminary had fine students, an impressive faculty, and as high academic standards as any seminary in the country. They were especially impressed by Béla Vassady and his perceptions of the compatibility of his ecumenism with Fuller's mission. Theologically, they found the seminary thoroughly Calvinistic, not at all Arminian or dispensationalist. They were pleased that the faculty, and not Dr. Fuller, ran the seminary. Most importantly, they judged unfounded the claim that it was "divisive." The San Jose presbytery thereupon adopted the committee's recommendation that, without actually approving of Fuller, they cease recommending against the seminary and discriminating against its graduates.[36]

Back in the Los Angeles presbytery, there was no crack in the ecclesiastical ice. When Gleason Archer tried to transfer his credentials to Los Angeles in November, he was turned down firmly by a vote of about two to one. While the minority initiated the long process of appeals to higher Presbyterian judicatories, the seminary in the meantime was ready to do almost anything to pacify the presbytery that dominated southern California. Herbert Mekeel, the new dean at Fuller, still a Presbyterian pastor in New York State and concerned about losing his Presbyterian ordination, took charge of a last set of negotiations with the presbytery.

Mekeel, Archer, and William LaSor met with an informal committee of the presbytery made up of Eugene Blake, Thomas Holden, and Glen Moore. Moore especially remained adamant in his opposition to Fuller, pointing out among other things that the divisiveness of the seminary was demonstrated by its intimate association with Lake Avenue Congregational Church, which long

35. *Los Angeles Times*, September 29, 1949, photographically reproduced in the *Christian Beacon*, October 6, 1949, 4.
36. "Report of Special Committee on FTS to the Presbytery of San Jose," 10-11-49 (LA). Dwight L. Small to HL, 9-23-49 (LA).

had been a refuge for malcontents from Blake's nearby Pasadena Presbyterian Church.[37] No progress was made.

Ockenga then apparently commissioned Mekeel to attempt one last desperate push. According to a report later publicized by an observer with close connections to both camps, Mekeel was authorized to meet any condition acceptable to the informal committee of the presbytery. The presbytery could offer its own course in church polity and would be granted the right to approve the occupants of Mekeel's own position in homiletics. It could even have some veto voice in Fuller policy. But even these concessions were not enough. According to the report, the informal committee decided after some lengthy and careful consideration not even to present the offer to the Los Angeles presbytery.[38] Mekeel, not wishing to give up his Presbyterian membership, was doubtless frustrated by these events. In addition, he often found his administrative tasks thankless and so eventually decided to return to his New York pastorate when the year was completed.

PANIC OVER ECUMENISM

While all this was happening, storm clouds had broken on another front. Already by late September, Béla Vassady's aspirations for Christian unity were dealt a second major blow. While his Presbyterian friends were telling him that his work at Fuller made him technically too "divisive" to be fit for the local Presbyterian ministry, his colleagues at Fuller now concluded that he was too ecumenical to remain long with them.

The Fall 1949 issue of the mainstream religious journal *Religion in Life* carried a short essay by Vassady, "Through Ecumenical Glasses," in which he lavishly praised ecumenism. The word *ecumenical*, he noted, was not well known in the United States; several times on his tour he had been introduced as being on a Hungarian "economical" committee. People needed, accordingly, to develop a "one-church-consciousness." They should "be seeing everything ecumenically," thinking always about "one world" and "one church," two ideas that "belong together organically."[39]

One world and one church were indeed concepts linked in the fundamentalist mind—but linked as signs of the approach of the empire of Antichrist and his allies. Charles Fuller himself held the dispensationalist view of

---

37. Report of meeting of 11-26-49 (LA).
38. John A. Hunter, "What about FTS?" (mimeograph). Hunter was pastor of the Pasadena United Presbyterian Church (not part of the PCUSA). This document is apparently based on conversations with Vassady and perhaps with Mekeel. GA, telephone conversation, 10-13-84, says he never heard of these offers of concessions, though he would not rule out that there might have been informal exploration of them. Hunter claims unanimous faculty approval for the motion granting the PCUSA the power to open "the chair of church polity . . . and . . . chair of homiletics to a faculty member of their choice, as well as offering the PCUSA the determining voice in the policies of Fuller Seminary." No such offer or discussion appears in the faculty minutes. It is possible, however, that Ockenga authorized such explorations.
39. Vassady, "Through Ecumenical Glasses," *Religion in Life*, Fall 1949, 1.

the matter and had as recently as that spring preached a radio sermon on the United Nations and the World Council as signs of the endtimes. Wilbur Smith had also been writing regularly on a milder version of this theme, warning that the United Nations was based on a materialistic philosophy aiming toward a "single world culture" and "an eclectic religion, stripped of everything supernatural."[40]

Though everyone at Fuller had known of Vassady's connection with the World Council, they now took his lavish praise of ecumenism as an uncritical endorsement of the organization. The stricter fundamentalists were also uneasy about the Vassadys violation of another of the unwritten rules of their community. As a matter of course, the Vassady family was attending Eugene Carson Blake's Pasadena Presbyterian Church. While nonseparatist fundamentalists remained within mainline denominations, they still drew clear distinctions between "true" and "apostate" local congregations. Pasadena Presbyterian, in their view, fit the latter category. One of the faculty wives from Fuller even later opined that the family had joined a "hell-hole" church and that such a "spiritual crime" would destroy Serena's otherwise impressive witness.[41]

Such a spirit, so common in fundamentalist circles, was a rude shock to the Vassadys. Béla first learned of it from a phone call in late September from Harold Lindsell, the acting dean until Herbert Mekeel arrived in that position. Lindsell said in no uncertain terms that it was not in the interest of the seminary for Vassady to write things that gave the impression that he was "sold on the World Council of Churches." The stunned Vassady replied that his article did not imply that he was "sold" on the council. He did think it was a useful, if imperfect, organization, though. To Ockenga he wrote in agony that he had understood that his connection with the World Council was one of the reasons for bringing him to Fuller. Now this unexpected hostility was making him wonder if he did not belong somewhere else.[42]

Whatever chance for reconciliation there might have been was soon demolished as Carl McIntire pounced on Vassady's article. McIntire's old rival Ockenga had already gone too far in hiring LaSor, who had endorsed apostasy by helping to drive McIntire out of the Presbyterian church. And now he had on his faculty an out-and-out champion of the perfidious World Council. McIntire had recently published his *Modern Tower of Babel*, a condemnation of one-world movements that had even received coverage in a *Time* magazine review. "One world, one church" indeed! This, McIntire fulminated in his *Christian Beacon*, was intended only to deceive, if possible, God's people and to pave the way for world domination by Antichrist. And what of Dr. Fuller? "How Dr. Charles E. Fuller could be a party to having a spokesman of the World Council on his staff is more than we can possibly under-

40. *The Increasing Peril—Of Permitting the Dissemination of Atheistic Doctrines on the Part of Some Agencies of the United States Government* (n.p., 1947), 12.
41. Vassady, *Limping Along*, 133-34; conversations with Vassady; see also letter of Vassady to John Mackay, 12-9-49 (V).
42. Vassady to HJO, 9-26-49 (V).

stand." Had he not, said McIntire with delight ill-disguised as dismay, recently preached on this very theme? Now Fuller should be able to see that McIntire was right all along. The evangelist could still save the day, though, by taking a courageous stand separating the seminary from Ockenga's "middle-of-the-road compromising position."[43]

The arrival in early October of the *Christian Beacon* containing McIntire's taunts, touching as they did an already sore point, caused consternation at the seminary. When Mekeel first rushed to Vassady's office with the *Beacon* he exclaimed, "We are all in trouble." Vassady skimmed the articles and then said calmly, "Hallelujah!" An attack from McIntire was as good as an endorsement by reasonable Christians.[44] The situation, however, was past the humorous stage. Charles Fuller was deeply embarrassed and knew that if he did not respond quickly he would face an avalanche of mail announcing cancellation of support for the radio ministry. The Smiths, who were the Fullers' closest advisors, were also dismayed by Vassady's stance. So Charles Fuller, contrary to his usual policy of staying clear of seminary affairs, let the faculty know that they had to do something fast about Vassady.[45]

Herbert Mekeel, the dean, called an emergency faculty meeting on a Friday afternoon, with instructions from Charles Fuller to have a statement concerning the World Council ready by Sunday, presumably for the Revival Hour broadcast. In the ensuing long discussion, the champions of a hard line prevailed.

The faculty stated that they "do not endorse the World Council of Churches, because of its present disregard of evangelical convictions." Moreover, in a binding directive, they declared that faculty members must "avoid approval" of the WCC. This ban, they explained, was not an abridgment of academic liberty or freedom of speech, "inasmuch as the defense and propagation of the historic Christian faith is a basic reason for the foundation of the Seminary." Vassady, of course, could hardly be expected to assent to these positions, which contradicted his World Council work and recent publications.

Vassady now stood firmly against an official seminary policy and faculty directive. The stage was set for his dismissal. He appealed to Ockenga, however, who apparently was chagrined over the sudden polarization and alarmed about the implications for Presbyterian relations (then still pending) of the anti-ecumenical, anti-Vassady moves. Ockenga flew back to Pasadena for a special meeting on October 20 to put together a compromise. Under his guidance, the faculty agreed to withhold their anti-ecumenical statement from publication indefinitely. Vassady would have to repudiate neither his former statements nor the World Council. But in the future he could endorse it only if he also provided evangelical criticism. He would also have to submit his books

43. *Christian Beacon*, October 6, 1949, 1, 8.
44. Vassady, *Limping Along*, 131.
45. William LaSor reports Fuller as saying, "I don't care how you do it, but get rid of Dr. Vassady." "Life Under Tension: Fuller Theological Seminary and 'The Battle for the Bible,'" *Theology News and Notes*, Special Issue, 1976, 7-8.

and articles on the subject for review. Other faculty members, for their part, would not officially condemn the World Council, though they might criticize it. The compromise position also declared that each professor must assent to any official decision of the faculty and that all new faculty members were on two-year probation before they could receive tenure. As a sort of symbolic purge (the actual and public purge having failed), the word *ecumenics* would be removed from the title of Vassady's professorship, and *ecumenics* and *ecumenical* were to be removed from catalog course descriptions.[46]

THE NEO-ORTHODOX MENACE

Vassady was far from in the clear. An important segment of the faculty shared a version of McIntire's critique. Though the Ockenga-imposed compromise put the World Council issue on the shelf, another question of equal import— one that Ockenga could not sidestep—was emerging. Was Vassady in fact neo-orthodox? Chester E. Tulga, another fiery fundamentalist publicist was pressing this issue. Tulga was a member of the Conservative Baptist Fellowship, the group that in 1947 had broken away from the Northern Baptist Convention in a dispute over missions. Moreover, the Conservative Baptists were also an important source of students for Fuller. Tulga was upset both about Vassady's praise of ecumenism and by a report that he had used neo-orthodox language in a recent speech. Carl Henry replied that their own suspicions of Vassady's neo-orthodoxy had been thoroughly allayed after two days of interviews the previous December. Tulga was far from satisfied, however. He had heard that Vassady had taught neo-orthodoxy openly at Princeton and was sure that, with several attacks on their way in Baptist publications, Fuller Seminary was in for difficult days.[47]

In the meantime, Wilbur Smith had also taken up investigating the neo-orthodoxy issue, an inquiry that may have been sparked in part by information from Professor Clarence Bouma of Calvin Theological Seminary in Grand Rapids, Michigan. Bouma was an ardent opponent of neo-orthodoxy and had in 1938 led attacks against the move to appoint Emil Brunner to Princeton Seminary. In October 1948 he wrote to Ockenga (and perhaps to Smith also), warning against Vassady. Bouma had letters from three Hungarians stating that Vassady was a leader of the Hungarian Barthians and a dangerous threat to orthodoxy.[48] When Ockenga traveled to Pasadena on October 20 to settle the World Council issue, he showed Vassady Bouma's letter. Smith, in the meantime had telephoned another Hungarian theologian living in New Jersey and had been told that Vassady was indeed a Barthian. When Vassady himself eventually found out about Smith's investiga-

46. Faculty minutes, 10-20-49.
47. Chester E. Tulga to HJO, 9-22-49 (O); CH to Tulga, 10- 27-49 (V); Tulga to CH, 11-14-49 (V); CH to Tulga, 11-21-49 (V). Prior to this the relations with the Conservative Baptist Fellowship seem to have been cordial; see, e.g., Robert Klingberg to HL, 4-21-48.
48. Clarence Bouma to HJO 10-8-49 (incorrectly dated 11-8-49 [?]) (O).

tion, he was greatly disturbed. In mid-November he wrote to Ockenga, point-ing out that Smith's informant had, years before, failed to get a key theological post in Hungary due to his, Vassady's, influence. More important for the moment, Vassady was much more concerned and agonized over the character of the community he had gotten into. Before he came to Fuller, people had warned him about fundamentalists there, but he thought he had no quarrel with those who emphasized fundamental Christian doctrine; now he was in the middle of what he viewed as spiritual totalitarianism. He consoled himself with the thought that if his family could survive the Nazis and the communists they could survive the fundamentalists as well. "In Europe," he wrote Ock-enga, "it is the method of totalitarian regimes to keep a secret about suspected individuals and to lay before them all the data at a time when their services are not any more needed. . . ." Now he was finding, instead of the open fellowship of believers, what looked alarmingly like "an ecclesiastical pattern of a police-state."[49] Though this sounds hyperbolic, it reveals how even moderate funda-mentalism could appear to other Christians who did not conform on a few key standards.

Attitudes toward neo-orthodoxy had become an increasingly impor-tant issue as the postwar fundamentalist community was struggling to define its boundaries. The separatists, such as Van Til and McIntire, were pressing anti-neoorthodoxy as a crucial litmus test. Francis A. Schaeffer, a Bible Pres-byterian missionary to Europe and one of McIntire's most vocal lieutenants, wrote an article in the *Christian Beacon* in the summer of 1948 claiming that Ockenga had counselled tolerance toward the World Council of Churches and that both he and the NAE had praised neo-orthodoxy, especially for its stand against religious liberalism in Europe. " 'Neo-orthodoxy' is not Christianity," said Schaeffer categorically. For evidence, people could write to the Indepen-dent Board for Presbyterian Foreign Missions and get several of Schaeffer's own pamphlets on the subject. The key difference between McIntire's Ameri-can Council of Christian Churches and the NAE, Schaeffer argued, was that the ACCC used the word *inerrant* in its statement, while the NAE used only *infallible*. To the Bible-believer, these terms might seem the same, but to the Barthian, said Schaeffer, they were not. "The Barthian will say that the Bible is infallible but he will *not* say that the Bible is inerrant."[50]

THE SAFEGUARD OF "INERRANCY"

The question of the "inerrancy" of Scripture, referring to its historical and scientific reliability, was a familiar one in the fundamentalist community. Some Protestants had been articulating this dogma as an important creedal test since at least the seventeenth century. Other Protestant groups did not

49. Vassady to HJO, 11-17-49 (V); *Limping Along*, 138; conversations with Vassady.
50. Schaeffer, "Should the Christian Tolerate the World Council? or Is Liberal-ism Dead?" *Christian Beacon*, July 29, 1948, 4-5.

address the question directly but remained content with broader statements of the Bible's authority, such as that of the influential American Presbyterian affirmation that the Bible is "the only infallible rule of faith and practice."[51]

With the rise of higher criticism in America in the late nineteenth century, however, interest in using the assent to "inerrancy" as a test for defining the community of true believers had been growing. Two groups of theologians had a particular impact on the fundamentalist concern about this point. Probably most influential in popularizing the concern were the dispensationalists. Dispensationalist readings of history depended in part on the exactness of numbers used in biblical prophecies. For instance, the millennial reign of Christ would be a literal one thousand-year reign, preceded by exactly seven years of cataclysmic events. Crucial to the dispensationalist system, then, was a hermeneutic that affirmed the reliability of every detail of Scripture. Such views coincided with tendencies in American folk piety to regard the Bible as simply and purely the words of God, as though the human component in its production were purely passive, incidental, or even nonexistent.

Among American fundamentalists, dispensationalist zeal for inerrancy was undergirded by the more sophisticated formulations of a second group, the Princeton theologians. In answer to the inroads of higher criticism in the Presbyterian Church, B. B. Warfield and A. A. Hodge had in 1881 formulated a classic defense of the long-standing Princeton view that the Bible, in its original manuscripts, was without error in historical or scientific detail. This view was sharply challenged by Charles A. Briggs, a professor at Union Seminary in New York City, who accepted what by twentieth-century standards would be a very mild version of the higher criticism of Scripture. But in the conservative religious atmosphere of the 1890s, Briggs was brought to trial and after considerable acrimony left the Presbyterian church—as, indeed, did his seminary.

The controversial energy invested in the conservative fight for a hard line during the Briggs controversy made a commitment to strict inerrancy an important test of the faith for conservative Presbyterians of the next generations. Three times during subsequent controversies (in 1910, 1916, and 1923) the conservatives prevailed in the General Assembly and forced it to declare that the inerrancy of the Bible was an "essential doctrine" of the church. This background was crucial to forming the conservative Presbyterian's strongly negative reactions to Barth's neo-orthodoxy. Barth might attack theological liberals, reassert old doctrines, and emphasize the authority of Scripture. But he made at least as many concessions to higher criticism as had Briggs. He was not an inerrantist.

---

51. The historical precedents are much debated. For opposing views see Jack B. Rogers and Donald K. McKim, *The Authority and Interpretation of the Bible: An Historical Approach* (San Francisco: Harper and Row, 1979); and John D. Woodbridge, *Biblical Authority: A Critique of the Rogers/McKim Proposal* (Grand Rapids: Zondervan, 1982). Ian Rennie, "'Mixed Metaphors. . . .' An Historical Response," paper presented at the Institute for Christian Studies, Toronto, March 22, 1981, suggests simply that there have long been two schools of thought among Protestants concerning Biblical inspiration.

Dispensationalist formulations of fundamental doctrines in the 1920s usually included an inerrancy clause. Nonetheless, the test was still not universal within the fundamentalist coalition. Even at Machen's Westminster Seminary, where there was, for conservative reasons, some uneasiness with formulating new sets of "essential" doctrines, inerrancy was not made a creedal test, even though it was greatly emphasized as a teaching. Harold Ockenga was among those who followed this precedent. As Francis Schaeffer pointed out, the NAE formula did not specify inerrancy. But Ockenga, unlike Schaeffer, did not view inerrancy and infallibility as substantially different concepts. At Fuller, his original proposed creed simply followed the classic Presbyterian statement that the Scriptures "are the Word of God, the only infallible rule of faith and practice."[52]

This early creed proposal, drawn up in the summer of 1947, had been minimal, based largely on the main headings of the Westminster Confession of Faith. The faculty eventually decided that its statement of faith should be more carefully framed and during the 1948–49 academic year put E. J. Carnell in charge of preparing the draft. Carnell was as alert as anyone to the subtleties of neo-orthodoxy and had brought from his Westminster Seminary training an arsenal of arguments for biblical inerrancy. He had also articulated his views earlier in 1948 in his prize-winning volume *An Introduction to Christian Apologetics*. Carnell's stance was thoroughly consistent with that of Warfield and Hodge. "The standing witness of the biblical text itself," he wrote in his apologetics volume, "is that in both part and the whole it is objectively and plenarily inspired." "Plenarily" in this context referred to the quality of the biblical revelation, so that the Scriptures could be said to be fully the word of God, even while fully human. "In both part and the whole" then referred to the *extent* of inspiration. No part was exempt. God's fully inspired word, as originally written, Carnell insisted, was therefore completely without error. Though he admitted, as the Fuller faculty typically did, that there were unexplained discrepancies, he pointed out, citing Charles Hodge as his authority, that these apparent errors were trivial compared with the evidence for the perfection of the whole. They reflected errors in our understanding of the Scriptures rather than imperfections in the original text. Even the most coherent system of thought, Carnell argued, has a few minor problems.[53]

Carnell's views on Scripture, which were shared by all his first colleagues, had already been incorporated into a draft of the statement of faith placed before the faculty in the spring of 1949. The key phrase was virtually identical to that in his apologetics book, that the original Scriptures "are plenarily inspired and free from error in the whole and in the part. . . ."[54]

52. Copy in FTS archives.
53. Carnell, *An Introduction to Christian Apologetics*, 3d ed. (1948; Grand Rapids: Eerdmans, 1950), 196-210. See Archibald A. Hodge and Benjamin B. Warfield, "Inspiration," *Presbyterian Review* 2 (April 1881): 225-50.
54. "Statement of Faith of Fuller," *Bulletin of Fuller Theological Seminary*, 1950–51, 6. This article on Scripture, except for peripheral stylistic changes, was already intact at the April 5, 1949, faculty meeting. The rest of the statement of faith follows roughly the headings

Contrary to later representations, the creedal statement was not drawn up in haste in response to the Vassady crisis. It was used, however, to resolve the crisis.

On October 11, in the midst of the consternation about Vassady's ecumenical statements, the faculty voted to move the final adoption of the statement of faith to the top of their agenda. Their intent was that every year each faculty member would have to sign the creed "without mental reservations." Vassady, however, pleaded that he had not had time to study the creed. LaSor said the same. The faculty then resolved to try to adopt the final revision of the creed by December and to hold a faculty forum on the subject of inspiration in the interim. Meanwhile, the World Council of Churches issue preoccupied their attention.

With the standoff on the World Council question, the failure to gain entry into the Los Angeles presbytery, and the rapidly spreading rumors about Vassady's neo-orthodoxy, the situation was deteriorating rapidly on all sides. Letters of complaint about the World Council question were "pouring into the seminary." Even Ockenga, Vassady's staunchest supporter, was worrying about the potential loss of the Conservative Baptist students.[55] Already by early December, Vassady had decided he would have to leave when his appointment expired. He had never experienced a seminary so evangelical in doctrine, he wrote privately, and so un-evangelical in practice.[56]

The fact of the matter was that Vassady could not in good conscience—"without mental reservations"—sign the seminary statement of faith. Inerrancy, he held, was a trait that could be applied to God alone and not to any production in which humans had a hand. The relevant question for him was whether the Scriptures were "an authentic source for our salvation."[57] Whether or not this was neo-orthodoxy, or the language of neo-orthodoxy, is a moot point. Back in December 1948, he had met for two days with Henry and Carnell, two of the most informed and alert of all evangelical critics of neo-orthodoxy and its view of Scripture. They had concluded that he only *sounded* neo-orthodox. Then, there had been goodwill all around. Now, in December 1949, that goodwill seemed to have evaporated. A last effort was made to resolve the difficulties over the creed as Henry, Carnell, Vassady, and Archer were appointed to a special committee. The questions were doubtless the same, but the old accord and desire to find commonality was gone. Vassady stood firmly against the inerrancy statement.[58]

---

of the Westminster Confession of Faith, though its statements of Reformed doctrine are less specific. The statement departs from Westminster in specifying that the return of Christ is premillennial.

55. Vassady to John Mackay, 2-4-50 (V); HJO to Vassady, 12-8-49 (V).

56. Vassady to John Mackay, 12-9-49 (V).

57. Conversations with Vassady; Vassady, *Limping Along*, 32.

58. Apparently the special committee made some effort to recast the article on Scripture. Whatever they proposed, however, proved unsatisfactory in light of faculty discussion. In the committee meetings, Carnell, seconded by Wilbur Smith, moved that the phrase, "free from all error in the original autographs," be inserted in the statement. Only

With some relief, the faculty could now declare him beyond the bounds of evangelical orthodoxy as they had defined it. They finally adopted the creed on January 31, 1950. William LaSor, a popular young teacher toward whom there was much goodwill, swallowed his uneasiness about the formulation of scriptural inerrancy and signed.[59] Vassady, who had already decided to leave, would not sign. The next day he agreed with Ockenga that he would immediately look for another position, though if nothing were available for the fall he would be allowed to stay peacefully through the second year of his appointment. Some students loyal to Vassady offered to circulate a petition protesting his dismissal, but true to his irenic convictions, he declined such public controversy. He served out his contract in relative peace, though occasionally he had to deal with conservative students, ever eager to catch him in a "liberal" error.[60]

The 1949–50 school year was pivotal in the early history of Fuller Seminary. By the time the first class graduated in May, the seminary had set on a course considerably different from what had been charted in early September. In September, the leading hope was for the seminary to gain an entry into American mainline Protestantism and thereby to establish a base for substantial evangelical influence. The school would be the west coast version of the old Princeton, conservative but respected within the Protestant establishment. It would thus help lead conservative evangelical forces back into the position in American life they had traditionally occupied.

By the spring of 1950, however, events had forced a considerably different definition of the movement. Fuller Seminary and the segment of fundamentalist-evangelicalism it represented would have to continue on a course whose boundaries were already fixed by previous controversies. While in principle the Fuller people might be nonseparatists sympathetic to conservatives in the mainline denominations, in fact they were institutionally separate and not entirely free to deviate from the patterns set by external fundamentalist forces. Any concessions in the direction of tolerance would be attacked unmercifully from the right. On issues such as dispensationalism that the Fuller people considered not a fundamental of the faith, they could weather the storm. The matter of the inerrancy of Scripture, by contrast, was too important both to them and to their constituency for them to be able to sustain even the appearance of uncertainty. The flag of inerrancy, signaling their exclusivist fundamentalist identity, had to be flown higher than ever.

Nonetheless, the new evangelicals were emerging as a distinct branch of fundamentalism. Billy Graham's rise to fame during this same eventful period from 1949 to 1950 gave the Fuller type of fundamentalism new viability as an independent force. Theologically, Graham was thoroughly a fundamen-

---

Vassady dissented. The recast proposal had apparently also included "certain historical references proposed by Dr. Vassady." When the statement of faith was next discussed by the faculty on January 31, 1950, the article on Scripture had reverted to Carnell's statement of the previous spring. Faculty minutes, 12-15-49 and 1-31-50.

59. LaSor, "Life Under Tension," 8.
60. Vassady, *Limping Along*, 134-37.

talist, the hand-picked successor to William B. Riley; but he sometimes looked to the Fuller-style evangelical intellectuals for guidance, and they in turn eagerly looked to him for visibility. Graham, however, was still essentially a tent evangelist and the Fuller Seminary events indicated that reconciliation between the fundamentalists and the mainline was still far away.

As far as the Presbyterian church's acceptance was concerned, the situation continued to appear dim, despite bright pockets of support. President John Mackay of Princeton Seminary encouraged the Presbyterian church to accept Fuller faculty and students, even though Fuller was probably drawing more students from Princeton than from any other seminary. On the other pole, Harold Lindsell met with the president and dean of Dubuque University and Seminary at the end of the academic year and found that these Presbyterians considered the rise of Fuller to be a direct affront to the entire Presbyterian church. Lindsell's own opinion was that students should be discouraged from working in the Presbyterian church and should even be encouraged to leave it, should a noncontroversial occasion arise to do so.[61]

A FITTING SEQUEL

The group at the seminary that inclined toward ecclesiastical independence (Lindsell, Smith, and Charles Fuller), was unexpectedly strengthened in the spring by a sudden turn of events. Charles Woodbridge, who had been on Ockenga's original list of faculty prospects but had declined the offer, wired Ockenga on April 6, 1950, with this message: "THE WAY IS FINALLY CLEAR FOR ME TO ACCEPT TEACHING POSITION THIS FALL. DECIDED TO NOTIFY YOU AS PRESIDENT OF FULLER SEMINARY FIRST. I HEREBY OFFER MY SERVICES TO THE SEMINARY. THIS IS DEFINITE AND FINAL. NO LOOKING BACK. PLEASE LET ME KNOW SOON WHETHER I AM NEEDED. CORDIAL GREETINGS."

Ockenga quickly wired back an invitation for the open position in homiletics, which would shortly be vacated by Mekeel. Woodbridge replied: "ACCEPT CHAIR OF HOMILETICS. DECISION IRREVOCABLE. VERY HAPPY." The next morning Ockenga wired Lindsell to put Woodbridge's name in the catalog.[62]

This startling chain of events was much discussed at the time and later. For one thing, it made clear how much the school was run by raw executive power, whatever its claims to be faculty controlled. For some of the faculty, the Woodbridge appointment came totally out of the blue. The background, however, made it more explicable. Woodbridge had been among the first to be recruited for a position at Fuller in 1947. Though he had turned down that initial offer, later in 1947 he had actually accepted a renewal of the offer, promising to come in either 1948 or 1949. Later he said he would defi-

61. HL to HJO, 6-29-50.
62. Telegrams in Ockenga papers; also HJO to HL, 4-13-50. F. D. Whitesell of Northern Baptist Seminary had just at the last minute declined the post in homiletics.

nitely come in 1949.[63] Now Ockenga was quick to close the deal before Woodbridge might change his mind again.

More to the story soon came out, however, much to the chagrin of
most of the Fuller faculty. Woodbridge was the pastor of the historic Independent Presbyterian Church of Savannah, Georgia, the church in which his
mother's first cousin, Woodrow Wilson, had been married. During the past
year Woodbridge and the church's deacons, who apparently represented older
families who had traditionally controlled the church, had fallen into a fierce
struggle. The conflict followed the classic pattern of the fundamentalist era.
Woodbridge launched a campaign to purge the church of modernism. The
active congregation of the church was fully behind Woodbridge. The deacons,
however, used to a more polite brand of Christianity, moved to oust the
militant pastor. Early in April Woodbridge offered his resignation and accepted the Fuller job. A week later the congregation met after the Sunday service
and unanimously rejected Woodbridge's resignation. They also moved
against the deacons, voting that a "code of standards" adopted a year before,
apparently having to do with the use of alcoholic beverages, would apply to the
deacons as well. Woodbridge promised to reconsider his move in the light of
this strong congregational support, but his "irrevocable" resolve to go to
Fuller prevailed.[64]

The schism in the congregation was characteristic of Woodbridge's
career. Central to determining his outlook was his service as secretary to the
Independent Board for Presbyterian Foreign Missions and his subsequent
deposition, along with Machen and McIntire, from the Presbyterian Church
in the U.S.A. Now he was on a faculty with William LaSor, who had voted to
oust Carl McIntire in a closely parallel case. Even the members of the faculty
more sympathetic to Woodbridge's strict conservatism were nervous that he
would bring to Fuller the image of fostering congregational schism—exactly
what they had been trying to dispel. According to LaSor's later recollection,
Wilbur Smith showed him a copy of a newspaper clipping from Savannah
reporting that Woodbridge had been asked to resign. "He didn't play fair with
us," Smith opined. Such sentiments are confirmed by remarks of Lindsell to
Ockenga at the time. "The faculty members, by and large," he wrote, "felt that
Dr. Woodbridge, upon offering his services to the institution, in fairness to us,
should have advised us regarding the internal situation in his church."[65] This,
Lindsell said, did not imply at all that they would have voted differently, but
they did see themselves open to criticism over the Savannah situation and

63. CH to HJO, 12-3-47 (O): ". . . glad to hear Charlie Woodbridge will come to
us in either 48 or 49"; HJO to CH, 12-2-47 (O): Woodbridge "has definitely accepted for 49."
The possibility of his coming in 1950–51 was discussed among the faculty as late as 3-1-49
(faculty minutes).
64. *Presbyterian Guardian*, May 1950, 99; Woodbridge, "Reaping the Whirlwind,"
Christian Beacon, May 5, 1977, 5, 7. Woodbridge's account mentions only the unanimous
endorsements of his congregation. GA, in a conversation of 10-13-84, mentioned Woodbridge's strong opposition to the use of alcohol as an issue.
65. HL to HJO, 6-29-50.

hoped that Ockenga would advise Woodbridge of the seminary policy to avoid such controversy. The faculty had discussed the same subject the previous day, concluding that the "official policy" of the seminary would be that "any pastor who finds himself in basic disagreement with the policies and program of his denomination, [is] to avoid at all costs, any schism in his church, and quietly withdraw to some other congenial denomination."[66]

During the year 1949–50 the new seminary touched both poles of its possible identity. Its course that year began with the arrival of a founder of the World Council of Churches. It ended with the hiring of the former secretary to the Independent Board for Presbyterian Foreign Missions. The turbulent year had proven that, despite grand rhetoric about returning to the unitive principles of the great evangelical tradition, the builders of Fuller Seminary had to contend with the divisive realities of the fundamentalist-modernist trauma. Like it or not, that dual heritage was an integral part of the seminary and, in varying degrees, part of the psyche of each individual associated with it.

66. Faculty minutes, 6-28-50.

CHAPTER VII

1950–1954: Amid the Fundamentalist Ethos

With the two great men coming to us this Fall and the possibility of Paul Rees and one other outstanding man in the Fall of 1951 we will probably then have the greatest evangelical faculty that has been assembled on the North American continent since the days of Princeton's glory.
Wilbur Smith to Mr. and Mrs. S. Kingsley Miner, May 12, 1950.

THE NEW SCHOOL

NO model was more commonplace in the minds of Fuller Seminary's supporters in the early years than that of Fuller as another Princeton. The phoenix, though displaced by three thousand miles, was arising.

One difference from the old Princeton, not much recognized in Pasadena, was that the New Jersey institution in its pristine days had been strictly "Old School" confessionalist Calvinist while Fuller Seminary was unmistakably "New School." That is, its supporters were broader interdenominational evangelicals. In nineteenth-century Presbyterianism, Old School and New School had split over the New School's emphasis on revivalism, interdenominational cooperation, extradenominational agencies, a broader interpretation of Calvinism, and zeal for social reform. The New School thus stood near the center of the massive evangelical consensus that dominated American Protestant culture. After the Civil War, the two schools of northern Presbyterianism reunited. New School tolerance, originally developed to promote revivalism, eventually revealed its legacy in fostering theological liberalism. Much less noticed was that the New School heritage survived in twentieth-century fundamentalism as well. Though broadly Calvinist, it was doctrinally tolerant and not exclusively denominationalist. It tended to work through extradenominatinal agencies, stressed evangelism, and still fostered some talk of evangelical cultural dominance.[1] Though those at Fuller frequently spoke of carrying on the Old Princeton heritage, they were in fact considerably closer to the spirit of the New School.

One small evidence of Fuller's difference from Old School Princeton

---

1. George M. Marsden, "The New School Heritage and Presbyterian Fundamentalism," *Westminster Theological Journal* 32 (May 1970): 129-47.

was Wilbur Smith's hopes that they could get an outstanding prospect to help complete the faculty, even though he was "not as Calvinistic as the rest of us."[2] Paul Rees, a well-known evangelist and writer, denied the Calvinist doctrine of the perseverance of the saints, or, as it was usually understood by modern evangelicals, "the eternal security of believers." Rees held the Arminian view that people who were once truly Christian could later fall from grace. It is significant that this was a major issue for the faculty. Though they were not strictly Calvinist themselves, they regarded Fuller as a definitely Calvinistic institution. True, their statement of faith was only minimally Calvinist—it did not talk about election, limited atonement, irresistable grace, or even the perseverance of the saints—and the faculty differed among themselves on a number of these points.[3] Yet some faculty members nonetheless insisted on a sub-rosa "Calvinist" standard that included "eternal security." Ockenga, in contrast, retained enough of his Methodist background not to make much of such issues and was eager to explore the prospects with Rees. For the time being, however, they did not have to face the issue, since Rees was not ready to move in any case.[4]

LADD AND WOODBRIDGE

The two men who did join the faculty in the fall of 1950 represented two opposing directions that Fuller might move from its moderate Calvinist, reforming fundamentalist starting point. Charles Woodbridge was one; George Ladd, the other. Converted in 1929 through the preaching of a Moody Bible Institute graduate, Ladd graduated from Gordon College in Boston and during the 1930s and early 1940s pastored Baptist churches in New England. During the same years he completed his studies at Gordon Divinity school and then earned a Ph.D from Harvard. He was thus one of a remarkable group of intellectually gifted fundamentalists who went to Harvard in the 1940s and became leaders of the neo-evangelical movement.[5] During the course of his studies Ladd had discovered in biblical theology one route away from dispensationalist fundamentalism. At Fuller, he found exactly what he was looking for: an opportunity to write on New Testament theology, especially on the kingdom of God, a subject he thought had suffered much from dispensationalist misinterpretations. A rigorous scholar himself, he inspired high standards among his students. Yet he also valued piety and lent a strong voice to the pervasive Fuller emphasis on missions.[6]

2. WS to Mr. and Mrs. S. Kingsley Miner, 5-12-50 (S).
3. DF, on draft.
4. WS to Mr. and Mrs. S. Kingsley Miner, 5-12-50. See HJO to CF, 4-9-52, indicating that HJO was even considering Rees a good possibility (as was Frank Gaebelein) for president of Fuller, though he feared Calvinism would be an issue.
5. See Rudolph L. Nelson, "Fundamentalism at Harvard: The Case of Edward John Carnell," *Quarterly Review* 2 (Summer 1982): 79-98.
6. David Allan Hubbard, "Biographical Sketch and Appreciation," in *Unity and Diversity in New Testament Theology: Essays in Honor of George E. Ladd*, ed. Robert A. Guelich (Grand Rapids: Eerdmans, 1978), xi-xv. See also George E. Ladd, "First Impression," *Bulletin of Fuller Theological Seminary* 1 (January-March 1951): 7.

Charles Woodbridge and the Fuller ideal   *George Ladd*

While Ladd was prepared to move away from the distinctives of classic fundamentalism, Charles Woodbridge hoped to make the school a bastion of the positions established in the previous decades. Even more than his colleagues, Woodbridge was prone to describe Fuller as a restoration of the old Princeton.[7] For him, old Princeton connoted simply militance against modernism. That he initially fit so well with the early faculty makes clear that the answer to the question of what direction the school would move, or whether it would move at all, was far less obvious in 1950 than it seems in retrospect.

Though impressive in both his piety and his breadth of knowledge, Woodbridge was not nearly the scholar that Ladd was. Personable, highly energetic, and versatile, Woodbridge was first appointed as professor of homiletics and practical theology but was immediately moved to church history. After a year he also became dean of students. His lectures were lucid and organized, but he was not thought of as a theological heavy hitter. One could find the substance of his lectures by looking in Philip Schaff's old *History of the Christian Church*. Thus students who asked hard questions were told to look it up and report the next day.[8] Woodbridge's real forte was as a popular Bible teacher, Bible conference speaker, Sunday school teacher, and preacher. Within a year and a half of his arrival, his prodigious activities in these areas, combined with his meager pursuit of scholarship, brought the disapproval even of Charles Fuller. The evangelist justified the faculty's large salaries as a means to free them for scholarship, something Woodbridge did not engage in. His acceptance of a position as the stated supply for Sunday evening and Wednesday evening services every week at Lake Avenue Congregational

7. Alumni comments.
8. Ibid.

Church was the last straw, and the faculty finally moved to limit such extended engagements.[9]

THE PRACTICAL AND THE THEORETICAL

Characteristic of the faculty's outlook in the early years was that filling positions in practical theology proved to be the lowest priority. Only after four years of makeshift measures did they permanently fill the homiletics position with the addition in 1951 of Clarence Roddy, an effective and experienced Baptist preacher from New England, recently of Eastern Baptist Seminary in Philadelphia.

Much as Roddy was appreciated, and as the building of a practical program was seen as a necessity, the strongest interests of the faculty were outside practical theology. The curriculum centered around biblical studies and responses to biblical critics, classical theology, and apologetics. Some two hundred questions and topics suggested for study for the senior comprehensive examinations in 1951 reveal these emphases. Excluding Woodbridge's church history questions, which ask simply about matters of fact, about 30 percent of the questions deal with biblical criticism (for example: "Name several inconsistencies of the critical theories. Tell how you would use these with college students who came to you with problems." "Give the chief arguments for the Mosaic authorship of the Pentateuch." "How would you reply to the statement that the nativity narrative of Luke is a late insertion?"). Another 30 percent or so deal with knowledge of biblical content. Another 25 percent have to do with theology (including questions such as "What is meant by 'forensic imputation'?" "Did God die on the cross?") And about 15 percent have to do with apologetics as such ("Explain the significance and ground for the neo-orthodox formula, 'Every man is Adam.'" "What is the instrumental cause of justification in (a) biblical theology, (b) Roman theology?").

The Fuller professors had high hopes of raising the levels of biblical, theological, and apologetic awareness in fundamentalist churches. Already in 1950 they began a graduate program leading to a Th.M. degree in biblical literature. Yet despite this emphasis on scholarship, they were working within a tradition that had long valued the practical. Moreover, they were working in southern California, a territory not renowned for enthusiasm for the fine points of classical theology. They further recognized that a first-rate seminary simply must develop a practical department. With this in mind, they added to the original ten faculty, who were now all assembled, a position in Christian Education.

In the process, they also took a small, and also equivocal, step away from their previous pattern of total male domination by appointing a woman to the post.

9. Faculty minutes, 3-27-52. See HJO to CF, 4-9-52, reflecting on CF's concern. Ladd had also been a regular pulpit supply in a church, but his case was not noticed until Woodbridge's became an issue.

WOMEN'S PLACE

When Fuller Seminary was started, it was assumed that it was strictly a men's school. Women were not allowed in the initial class. At first they were not even allowed to sit in on courses. During the first week of classes in 1947 the question of "opening classes to auditors and to women students" was brought to the faculty. "The consensus was that women should not be admitted to classes and that auditors should be discouraged."[10] Keeping women in their place, though honoring them there, had become part of the fundamentalist ethos. Progressive mainline denominations, by contrast, had since about the 1920s been cautiously reconsidering the role of women in the church. Some allowed ordination of women to the ministry or to other church offices, and most of the separate women's organizations had eventually merged with other denominational agencies.[11] Fundamentalists, on the other hand, had become even more strict about women's roles during the same period. Even evangelical churches in the holiness tradition, which had once been in the forefront of opening the church to women's leadership, sometimes drew back from such positions during the fundamentalist era from the 1920s to the 1950s.[12] The ideal for women that Fuller Seminary had inherited was that of the genteel helpmate dedicated to her husband's ministry. The reward for such selfless service might come only in the next life: "Eternity alone," said a typical statement in the women's *Auxiliary News*, "will reveal how much the unseen ministry of faithful women has helped Fuller Seminary."[13]

Grace Fuller was world famous as a radio personality, but she always played the role of her husband's homey helper, truly fitting this model of the "faithful helpmate." She took extensive interest in all her husband's work, including the seminary. Though she kept carefully to her supporting role, she clearly was a major partner in the family enterprises. At the seminary, she found tasks she considered appropriate to the woman's sphere. Every Fuller student felt something of a mother's touch when they noticed the skins in the dining hall mashed potatoes, an order from Mrs. Fuller to ensure that they got their vitamins. Administrators knew as well that early morning phone calls were likely to be from her, concerned over some detail of decorating the buildings.[14] "Playing on this [Dr. Fuller's] team has been pretty rugged at times," said a writeup about Mrs. Fuller's seminary work. "But at the Judgement Seat of Christ Mrs. Fuller's largest reward will be for her faithful behind-

10. Faculty minutes, 9-26-47. See also those of 10-2-47: "It was decided by consent that women should not be admitted to classes and that auditors should be discouraged."
11. Margaret L. Bendroth, "The Search for 'Women's Role' in American Evangelicalism, 1930–1980," in *Evangelicalism and Modern America*, ed. George Marsden (Grand Rapids: Eerdmans, 1984), 122-34.
12. An example of fundamentalist militance on this matter is the influential John R. Rice's *Bobbed Hair, Bossy Wives and Women Preachers* (Wheaton, Ill.: Sword of the Lord Publishers, 1941).
13. Harold Lindsell, "The Seminary Dean Writes—," *Fuller Seminary Auxiliary News* 1 (December 1951).
14. Interview with HL and Mrs. Marion Lindsell, 10-27-83.

the-scenes work in standing behind her husband in prayer and counsel and for her willingness to lend a helping hand in so many varied ways. . . ."[15] This was the ideal for Fuller wives to imitate.

Women in this tradition had their own auxiliary institutions. In 1948 the school founded two of these, the Fuller Seminary Auxiliary for support of the seminary generally and the Philothean Fellowship for seminary wives. The Auxiliary functioned to rally support, raise money, and distribute scholarships to needy students. Each fall they held an elegant tea at the seminary mansion, which they had named "Highgate," and each spring a Day of Prayer. The Philothean Fellowship, under the sponsorship of Wilbur Smith's wife Mary Jane, held regular meetings throughout the year for prayer, Bible Study, special speakers, and fellowship, as well as to organize helping hands for members in need.[16]

Mrs. Smith was unquestionably the leading force in women's activities at Fuller. She was a founder of the Auxiliary and devoted much of her boundless energy to it and to her Philothean work. Charles Fuller, observing that she devoted about four days per week to the seminary, suggested that she be paid something, at least to cover expenses for gasoline in going to speaking engagements and so forth. Mrs. Smith knew this would be too much for Wilbur's sense of decorum, though. He had been reared in a well-to-do home and would not stand for his wife working for pay. Charles Fuller decided to pay her something anyway and instructed the auditor to say nothing about it.

With such complete backing from the top, Mrs. Smith built her empire. Eventually, however, her preemptive style led to a major crisis. She personally oversaw much of the awarding of scholarships and student loans by the Auxiliary. In the fall of 1951 she awarded a student loan to a former Fuller student who had dropped out. This was the last straw for Lindsell, dean of the faculty, and Woodbridge, dean of students, who felt that the women's Auxiliary should not be controlling the entire scholarship and loan program in the first place. They also ferreted out that Mrs. Smith was receiving between $100 and $125 per month from the Fuller Foundation. Charles Fuller backed Mrs. Smith 100 percent and went over Lindsell's head to Ockenga, who supported the informal arrangements of his cofounder in opposition to his administrators. The deans both threatened to resign but did not. Nonetheless, the first real tensions had developed within the seminary's inner circle. Especially ominous was the beginning of a rift between Woodbridge and the Fullers (probably leading to the subsequent efforts to curb his outside activities). In the meantime, the faculty set up its own scholarship fund and made Mrs. Smith's continued sponsorship of the Philotheans an elected position rather than an appointment for life.[17]

The issue of women's proper role was still far from settled, as a sequel illustrated. One of the unannounced functions of the Philothean Fellowship

15. *Fuller Seminary Auxiliary News* 5 (February 1956).
16. *Bulletin of Fuller Theological Seminary* 4 (April-June 1954): 5.
17. Several letters from HL file, October and November 1951, FTS archives; faculty minutes, 2-19-52.

The Philothean Fellowship held regular meetings for fellowship, prayer, and Bible study

was to socialize student wives so that they might become properly genteel guardians of the parsonage. This sometimes meant honing down some rough edges since converts to Charles Fuller's radio ministry, who made up most of the student body, came from a wide variety of backgrounds. The ethos to which the Fuller faculty aspired, meanwhile, still reflected something of the Victorian upper middle-class standards set at Princeton.

The crisis over this style arose in 1951 with the arrival of Florence Roddy, the wife of Clarence. Mrs. Roddy was a woman similar to Mrs. Smith in her aspirations to lead, but with principles definitely her own. She was a plain country woman with hair pulled back and squared black shoes that announced that she was against fashion.[18] She was reported to have said, "I come from the country, I look countrified, and I am proud of it." Spiritually this attitude pointed her to a plain or puritan style. Accordingly, she was appalled by the putting on of airs, the fancy tea tables, refreshments, and long dresses at the Philothean Fellowship's high teas.[19] Moreover, she objected even to the serving of refreshments at the regular Philothean meetings every other Monday night. Prayerful spirituality and such indulgence and levity did not mix in her view.[20] Soon she organized her own seminary wives weekly prayer group, thus dividing the wives between those who followed her and

18. Conversation with Delores Loeding, fall 1983.
19. CF to HL, ca. 11-51.
20. Mrs. Marion Lindsell interview, 10-27-83.

Florence and Clarence Roddy

those who stayed with Mrs. Smith. In October 1952, at orders from the "trust-ee level" (meaning from Charles Fuller), Mrs. Roddy's class was told it must be integrated into the Philothean meetings on the Monday evenings alternate to the regular meetings. Thereupon Mrs. Roddy volunteered to withdraw from the situation entirely.[21] As an apparent compromise, the Philotheans organized several smaller Bible studies for the alternate Mondays, with the leadership divided among a number of faculty wives.[22]

Questions of women's leadership could not always be confined to such women's groups and to behind-the-scenes assistance of husbands, as had been the assumption thus far. One of the first things that the Philotheans did when they organized in the spring of 1948 was to request that classes be opened for credit to qualified student wives. The faculty accepted this arrangement with the proviso that it be only for introductory courses for transfer credit to other schools, not as a step toward a Bachelor of Divinity degree. The next year

21. HL to HJO, 10-21-52.
22. *Bulletin of Fuller Theological Seminary* 4 (April-June 1954): 5.

they apparently extended this permission to other women as occasional special students, inevitably observing that unmarried women who wished to attend seminary were really looking for a M.R.S. degree.[23]

During the eventful 1949–50 school year, however, the faculty found themselves with quite a different situation. Helen (Holly) Clark, a Wellesley graduate, was highly qualified and clearly serious in wanting to take a theology degree. The faculty at first considered simply opening the B.D. degree to women. In meeting with the American Association of Theological Schools, from which the seminary received associate membership (preliminary to possible accreditation) in June 1950, Harold Lindsell discussed a B.D. for women and found no particularly unfavorable attitude. Yet some Fuller faculty objected that this would be tantamount to approving women for the ministry. A solution they could all endorse, however, was the creation of a new degree, the "Bachelor of Sacred Theology," substituting some electives in Christian education for preaching and counselling courses.[24]

This move immediately led to the suggestion that the faculty appoint a full-time instructor in Christian Education. Many mainline seminaries offered a two-year Master of Religious Education degree, taken primarily by women who wished to work on the staff of a large church. Ockenga revolutionized the Christian Education proposal by suggesting that the faculty appoint Henrietta Mears. He wrote to Lindsell that he realized that presumably "the faculty will want nothing but men" but added that he thought it would be a "stroke of genius" to get Miss Mears on the faculty. No one had done more for Christian education—in young people's work, Sunday schools, publishing, and speaking—than she.[25] In fact, she had done as much as a woman could do within the limits set by the community and, in fact, had considerably expanded those limits.[26] The faculty did not object in principle to a woman professor for Christian Education, although they stated that this was "by way of exception,"[27] permitted by the anticipation that students in this field would be mostly women.

There was, however, some hesitancy concerning Henrietta Mears herself. Carl Henry and Harold Lindsell suggested, as an alternative, Rebecca

23. Faculty minutes, 3-5-48; William LaSor interview at faculty retreat, 9-83.
24. Faculty minutes, 6-28-50 and 9-13-50. Another equivocal step toward recognizing women's role was taken around this time when Mary Ashley was appointed registrar, relieving Harold Lindsell of such duties and freeing him to become dean of the faculty. Ashley, however, was listed as a member of the staff rather than as one of the "officers of administration."
25. HJO to HL, 12-8-50.
26. Charles Fuller argued that woman pentecostal preachers such as Aimee Semple McPherson provided evidence that the apostle Paul was verbally inspired to forbid women to teach on a regular church basis. Nonetheless, Fuller also said that next to Reuben A. Torrey, Mrs. A. L. Dennis had been his most influential teacher at Biola. Robert Munger reportedly once asked Henrietta Mears to preach at a morning service at First Presbyterian Church in Berkeley. She turned it down in deference to her understanding of the apostle Paul's command. She did speak informally at the pulpit in his evening services, however. DF, on draft.
27. Faculty minutes, 12-33-50.

Price, who had long taught Christian Education at Wheaton, was well-known to them, had superior academic credentials, and had even been sought by Princeton Seminary. The slight hesitancy about Mears was the result of the combination of her strong personality and her being a woman. Wilbur Smith was said to have remarked that if she came into the Monday morning faculty prayer meetings, she would soon take them over. As Lindsell perceptively summarized his colleagues' mood: "I gather they felt that the maleness of the faculty would be protected more by the addition of Dr. Price."[28]

Such reservations were not insurmountable, however. Though Price was initially extended the invitation, she declined, whereupon Mears was offered the position. Yet she too declined, and the faculty eventually renewed the invitation to Price. This time she accepted it for the fall of 1952. Unfortunately, she fell seriously ill shortly after arriving at Fuller. Nonetheless, though often confined to a wheelchair during the next decade, she successfully established a Christian Education program that was annually enrolling thirty to forty students, predominantly women. Fuller had taken an important step, though the fundamentalist assumptions about women's roles had not been altered.

STYLE, COMMUNITY, AND IDENTITY

The lives of the men students, or the "boys," as they were almost always called, seem typically to have been filled with study, with youth work and evangelism during weekends and summers, and with the cares of making a living and often of maintaining a family.

Throughout the 1950s the faculty seems to have kept up a running quarrel with the casual California lifestyle. Their Princetonian ideal for the pastor was that he should be a gentleman theologian. Students were thus expected to wear coats and ties to class. Occasionally, however, they would turn up in military fatigues or, even more intolerable, in Hawaiian sport shirts and sandals. A number of alumni recalled the "tirades" in chapel from various deans concerning the dress code. Dean Herbert Mekeel made a futile effort to enforce eastern standards in the dining hall as well. Ernie Buegler, the cook, had always placed milk cartons on the tables. When Mekeel arrived, he insisted that the milk be placed in pitchers—a touch of class that survived only about ten days. For years, however, some of the faculty, such as Carnell, Archer, and Ladd, continued to complain about the California casualness, especially in dress, and frankly wished they could "introduce New England culture."[29]

The Fuller professors were renowned for their hard work. They were trying to do everything at once. They were going to rise to the top of their professions, fill the Christian world with outstanding books and popular litera-

28. HL to HJO, 12-15-50, 1-12-51.
29. Alumni comments; Carnell, President's Report, April 1955; George E. Ladd, tape from student retreat, ca. 1961 (SS).

ture, be great teachers, be active in their churches, Sunday schools, and on the Bible conference trail, be models in their mostly young households, and maintain contacts with their admiring students. The norms they set for themselves combined all the usual expectations for faculties of graduate schools, liberal arts colleges, and Bible institutes and no doubt contributed to the striking number of psychological breakdowns, mostly temporary, among Fuller faculty during its history. Office lights would be on late at night and sometimes on Sundays. One of the more popular professors eventually began putting signs on his door with messages like "You have a very busy schedule. So do I. I don't want to make yours any worse. So don't come in."

Wilbur Smith, though often referred to as "beloved," was seemingly always preoccupied with his work and sometimes had a particularly gruff manner toward students. One new student hastened to hold the door for Smith, who, as often, was carrying a load of books piled to his chin. His bright "Good morning, Dr. Smith" was met with "Harrumph, harrumph, harrumph." The nonplussed student was reassured that these were friendly harrumphs. Smith was reputed never to call on a woman in class and to preface many of his remarks, in his famed Smithsonian tones, with a pointed "Now men. . . ." His most famous remark came most often in teaching his favorite subject, study of the English Bible. "Men," he would announce, "in preparing the lecture for today, I saw something I have never seen before." There was a joke going around that when Smith got to heaven he was dictating the last chapter of his book on Revelation to his secretary. When he finally looked up, he exclaimed, "Skip it, I've just seen something I've never seen before."[30]

Sharing his colleagues' gentlemanly standards, Smith was often both chagrined and amused by much of the fundamentalist style, especially the southern California variety. "Now and then you certainly strike some strange things out here among Christian people," he wrote back to a friend in Chicago shortly after moving west. The most bizarre of several instances, he thought, took place at the graduation of a nearby Bible institute. The dean of the school had done a lot of kidding with one of the student secretaries, who was now graduating. He had threatened that as he was handing out the diplomas he would pull the mortarboard off her head. "Well, this is pretty common," observed Smith, "but that is only the beginning." The young woman wired the tassel of her mortarboard to an electric battery, and when the dean "carried out his threat and grabbed the tassel, he got an electric shock that nearly knocked him off the platform, which threw the audience into convulsions." Smith then remarked: "I am going to talk to my men a little this fall on the simple word *sober*, with which the New Testament epistles are full, and I do not mean not to laugh and have a good time."[31] The truth of the matter was that Smith's fabled and essentially good-natured personality provided a lion's share of much-needed comic relief in the often serious Fuller atmosphere.

Close faculty-student relationships were difficult to sustain, although

30. Alumni comments.
31. WS to Mrs. S. Kingsley Miner, 7-11-49.

"Now men . . ."

the effort was constantly being made. Year after year, usually around February or March, the Student Council would come in with suggestions for improving contacts, the faculty would adopt these, and then the old pattern would be repeated.[32]

Part of the problem in sustaining the early sense of close community was that the number of students had grown to over 250, yet the seminary still had a divided campus. Hopes for a reversal of the zoning ordinance against building at the the Cravens estate continued for several years after 1947, only to be repeatedly frustrated. In the meantime, Charles Fuller and the faculty sought alternate sites. In the fall of 1950 the faculty even went on record favoring the acquisition of a campus site in Covina, a more rural setting some twenty miles east of Los Angeles toward Pomona. The reasons for recommending this move were revealing. One was that "a community life could be built up within the Seminary family, thus sequestered." Moreover, an urban location had no inherent advantage, save for attracting more part-time and commuter students. In fact, some noted that if the seminary moved, "the possible corrupting influence of a nearby large city with places of salacious entertainment would then be eliminated." The opportunity passed when the

---

32. In retrospect alumni saw the situation more favorably. Rating "approachability of professors," alumni from 1950–1952, rated it as follows: Excellent, 18; Good, 26; OK, 3; Fair, 2; Poor, 4. Their ratings (from Excellent to Poor) of "quality of community among students" were 7, 29, 3, 2, 4. Alumni for 1957– 1959 and 1965–1967 provided similar ratings, except that in the latter period "approachability of professors" dropped somewhat.

trustees decided to make no move until all hope for locating at the suburban location was eliminated.[33]

A year later, Ockenga proclaimed in the seminary *Bulletin* that "a theological seminary ought to be located in a city. . . . Ministerial training must be received in the midst of the throb and tumult of this teeming life."[34] Ockenga may have differed with most of the faculty on this point. In any case, the seminary had decided to build in downtown Pasadena. Charles Fuller was something of a financial speculator on behalf of the seminary and had been buying and selling city property for some time. In 1951, he obtained a pleasant site on Oakland Avenue near the center of the city and set plans for building. When the administrative and classroom building was completed two years later, the seminary had reached an important plateau of stability.

Determining the identity of the seminary remained the central question. One clue to the seminary's self-image was its choice of speakers for the Payton Lectures, founded in 1949 and named in honor of Grace Fuller's parents. These were envisioned as analogous to the Stone Lectures at Princeton or the Gifford Lectures in Scotland, with their later publication expected. The difficulty was that at mid-century distinguished conservative scholars were scarce. The first lecturer, William Childs Robinson of Columbia Theological Seminary in Georgia, a renowned southern Presbyterian scholar who had withstood liberalism, fit the bill perfectly. Most of those who followed during the early years, however, were from the seminary's own immediate circle of former Machen associates. Clarence Macartney, Gordon Clark, Oswald T. Allis, formerly of Westminster Seminary, and theologian John Murray, then of Westminster, were among the first lecturers, and all had known Machen. On the other hand, a plan to ask Joachim Jeremias of Germany to give the lectures was scuttled when it was pointed out that he did not exactly fit the Fuller position on Scripture.[35] After 1953 the lectures were held sporadically rather than yearly.

One bizarre example of the difficulties of finding distinguished scholars outside the immediate circle was the attempt to secure a well-known theologically conservative historian from a major American university for the 1954 lectures. After the agreement had been reached, the seminary faculty was startled to read in the newspapers that the prospective Payton lecturer was involved in a lawsuit against a spiritualist medium whom he accused of giving him faulty advice on financial investments. This became front-page wire service news and was soon picked up by *Life* magazine as well. The faculty concluded that their sponsorship of the historian would now be an "incalculable embarrassment" and that they must cancel the lectures. That was not so easy, however. The indignant historian pointed to the orthodoxy of his church affiliations, played down his connections with spiritualism, and denied as

33. Faculty minutes, 3-15-50, 9-28-50.
34. *Bulletin of Fuller Theological Seminary* 1 (July-September 1951): 2.
35. Faculty minutes, 2-1-55. The faculty did allow that he might be invited to lecture at Fuller under auspices other than the Payton Lectures. Paul Woolley and Ned Stonehouse of Westminster were also invited during this era.

Toward a new look. The new administration building rises as Harold Ockenga, Harold Lindsell, Charles Fuller, and the Rev. James Henry Hutchins of Lake Avenue Congregational Church look on.

"nonsense" the widespread rumors that he used a medium to help with his research on Luther and Erasmus. Harold Lindsell quite sensibly pointed out in reply, however, that "on the surface it would not appear that you could sue to recover monies lost by investments recommended by a medium unless, in point of fact, you had used the services of a medium and had followed the suggestions of said medium." The historian threatened to sue for the handsome $500 payment promised. The seminary settled out of court for $300. Ten years later, the historian, a Calvinist who apparently never gave up on a financial matter, ended the episode with a futile offer to deliver the lectures for the remaining $200.[36]

ACRIMONY ON THE LEFT

In establishing its own identity and that of the movement of which it was part, Fuller Seminary not only had to take into account what was acceptable to its own constituency, it also had to fend off perennial attacks from both left and right. During the years that it was establishing itself in downtown Pasadena, Fuller's relationship with southern California Presbyterians was actually getting worse. Gleason Archer's case—the test of his, Harrison's, and LaSor's efforts to gain admission to the presbytery—consumed hundreds of hours of the Presbyterian church's time as it wound its way through church courts for six years. Three times, in 1949, 1951, and 1953, the case came before the Presbytery of Los Angeles. Each time it was appealed to the Synod of California and then to the General Assembly of the Presbyterian church. The first two times, the national body was more favorable to Fuller than were the Californians, ordering the presbytery to reconsider the case. In the process, the General Assembly entirely reviewed and clarified its policy on its ordained clergy working for independent agencies. If a presbytery denied someone approval of work in such agencies, the new rules declared, it would at least have to give the applicant a full hearing.

This ruling brought a dramatic showdown on November 10, 1953. Eager to settle the issue once and for all, the presbytery scrupulously followed the Assembly's new directive, giving a full hearing not only to Archer, but to LaSor and Harrison as well. The tension of the scene was heightened when the stated clerk objected to Gleason Archer (who had a law degree) bringing in a court reporter to take down the proceedings. Archer was sustained, but the degree of distrust was indicated by the fact that (according to a later complaint) the leaders of the presbytery themselves had secretly attached a backroom tape recorder to the amplifying system.[37] The debate went on for six hours. The Fuller men could point to many graduates who had peacefully served the Presbyterian church outside southern California. But in the end the issues were just the same as they were four years earlier. Archer, Harrison, and LaSor were judged to be fine Christian gentlemen; but they could not be admitted to the presbytery. Of the three, only Archer had made a few remarks over the years that aroused any objection. The real issues in the case were not these three men and their actions but rather statements or actions, mostly long ago, by Charles Fuller, Harold Ockenga, Wilbur Smith, and, now, Charles Woodbridge. The seminary was inherently "divisive." The vote was 142 to 85.

36. File in archives.
37. "Complaint of the Rev. Clarence W. Kerr et al. against the action of the Presbytery of Los Angeles . . ." November 10, 1953, 14.

Everett Harrison

Gleason Archer

William LaSor

Since ultimately presbyteries control their own memberships and since proper procedures had been followed, the General Assembly of 1955 sustained the decision and the case was closed.[38]

ACRIMONY ON THE RIGHT

While Fuller Seminary had no room to move on the left, Carl McIntire was still blasting away on the right. Though McIntire had notoriety outside fundamentalist circles, he continued to have wide influence within. As a master of the media, both press and radio, McIntire knew how to turn the ordinary into the sensational and how to play on the fundamentalist community's prejudices and susceptibility to rumors of compromise. By 1951 Harold Ockenga was closely linked to Billy Graham and was thus McIntire's most formidable rival for influence in the fundamentalist world. McIntire accordingly took the first opportunity to try to discredit his more inclusivist counterpart.

In May 1951 McIntire published in the *Christian Beacon* a nearly nine thousand-word attack on Lindsell's *Park Street Prophet: A Life of Harold John Ockenga*, a volume that emphasized the Ockenga-Graham conection. In the midst of the polemics, Fuller Seminary got its usual jibes as a "N.A.E. citadel" and the place that hired ecclesiastical traitors such as LaSor. "The young men who go to Fuller Seminary are given the wrong impression concerning the position required by the Word of God in the great ecclesiastical struggle today. God's people cannot join in the Communion with unbelief and apostasy!"[39] This merely set things up for the real bombshell to be exploded a month later. In April Ockenga had attended a highly publicized "Communion breakfast" sponsored by a number of Protestant Churches in Boston. At the head table with Ockenga was a Unitarian pastor and a representative of the Masonic Knights Temple. Here was a separatist fundamentalist's worst (or best) dreams come true, and McIntire made the most of it. "PROTESTANTS IMITATING ROME: EVANGELICAL OCKENGA JOINS WITH UNITARIAN . . . IN MAMMOTH COMMUNION BREAKFAST" ran his banner headline. "It is indeed with heavy heart," wrote McIntire, that one reads the name of Dr. Harold John Ockenga among the head table guests listed with Dr. Dana McLean Greeley, Unitarian pastor of Boston."

> What possible justification could there be for an evangelical lending his presence and approval by participating in such a Communion breakfast? This, of course, is where the inclusivist position takes one. If we are going to be in the ecumenical movement and in the World Council of Churches, even though we are evangelicals, we are all

---

38. "Transcript of Proceedings of . . . the Presbytery of Los Angeles," November 10, 1953. *Minutes of the General Assembly of the Presbyterian Church in the United States of America*, 5th series, vol. 2, part 1 (Philadelphia, 1953), 110-33. The best summary of the case is in *Minutes of the General Assembly*, 5th series, vol. 4, part 1 (Philadelphia, 1955), 169-74. Other materials are found in L.A. Presbytery History file (LA).

39. *Christian Beacon*, May 10, 1951, 8.

wrapped up in participation in their programs and their leadership's emphasis.

In fact, Ockenga had not participated in the actual Communion services, which had taken place before the breakfast. Yet even his presence at the ecumenical breakfast offended the sensibilities of many fundamentalists, who typically stayed clear of their local ministerial associations. But McIntire's account, without actually saying it, insinuated that Ockenga had taken Communion with apostates. At least he had endorsed their Communion. "The apostasy is great!" said the *Beacon*.[40]

David Otis Fuller (no relation), a prominent pastor in the separatist General Association of Regular Baptists, wrote to the Fuller Seminary faculty saying that he had known Ockenga at Princeton but now had totally lost confidence in him upon hearing that he took Communion with a Unitarian. Lindsell wrote back that he too had been shaken upon first seeing the *Beacon* story, but that he now had the facts that Ockenga had not actually attended the Communion services. David Otis Fuller was glad to hear this, though he thought participating in the Communion breakfast was a mistake. The Baptist pastor was active in the American Council of Christian Churches and still had hopes that the ACCC and the NAE could join forces in fighting what he saw as the "lightning rapidity" of the trend toward "revolution and chaos." This continuing talk about merger was another sign of how close to the right wing of fundamentalism many thought Fuller Seminary to be. With reconciliation in mind, David Otis Fuller wrote to McIntire, informing him that Ockenga had not actually been at the Communion services and suggesting that he run a correction.

J. Elwin Wright of the NAE also pressured McIntire for a retraction and McIntire finally wrote to Ockenga directly. He defended his publication of the Communion story, but also offered to "print in full anything you say." The letter was a mixture of sentiment and prodding. McIntire recalled the days of their friendship and mentioned fondly that he still used the beautiful bookends Ockenga had sent as a wedding gift. On the other hand, he also hoped that Ockenga would "come absolutely clean" and admit his mistake.

Ockenga sent a stiff reply. He had been so often misrepresented in the *Beacon*, he told McIntire, that "I have lost confidence in your integrity." He would not write anything for the *Beacon* that would be subject to McIntire's reinterpretations. All hope of constructive communication was past. McIntire returned the bookends.[41]

The next episode hurt the seminary even more. In the fall of 1952 McIntire launched an all-out campaign against the new and much heralded Revised Standard Version of the Bible, published by the National Council of Churches. He was among the first to point out that, among other alleged shortcomings of its Old Testament translation, the RSV changed the famous

40. *Christian Beacon*, June 21, 1951, 2, 5.
41. Correspondence, 6-29-51 to 12-21-51, in David Otis Fuller file, FTS archives; HJO interview, 11-6-83

messianic passage of Isaiah 7:14 from "a virgin shall conceive" to "a young woman will conceive." Here, said McIntire, was a flagrant modernist attack on one of the classic fundamentals. Always a populist, he struck a chord that resonated with American folk reverence for the Bible. Fundamentalist and other conservative groups soon mounted a chorus of indignant response. The evangelist John R. Rice, who on the basis of the RSV New Testament (published in 1946) had allowed his name to be used in a *Sword of the Lord* advertisement endorsing the new translation, had to publish a retraction.[42] McIntire sponsored "Back to the Bible" rallies all over the country. Some pastors, he reported, had even publicly burned copies of the blasphemous translation. By the end of the year a Gallup poll showed that two-thirds of Americans knew about the new Bible. While 28 percent of those polled approved of the RSV, a startling 22 percent did not.[43]

Whether one accepted the RSV or not immediately became a symbol of loyalty either to the ecumenical movement or to its fundamentalist-conservative opposition. Predictably, Fuller Seminary stood precariously in the middle. The faculty, though mildly divided on the merits of the translation, took up the unpopular cause of defending it before a fundamentalist audience.

Even before the complete RSV appeared, E. J. Carnell had been urging its acceptance. The King James Version, overwhelmingly dominant in American Protestantism, had "outdated language" that fostered a "needless provincializing" of the gospel, according to Carnell. Protestants should thus welcome a clearer, more accurate translation.[44] When the new version appeared amid great fanfare, William LaSor also joined the fray, speaking widely on the appropriateness of using "young woman" rather than "virgin" in the translation of Isaiah 7:14. George Ladd and Dan Fuller, who became an instructor in English Bible in 1953, also vigorously defended the RSV. Carnell and LaSor even debated their more conservative colleagues Archer and Lindsell on the topic at the Lake Avenue Church. Yet with outside pressure on, the faculty stood basically together. Archer, Harrison, Woodbridge, and LaSor planned a book on the RSV that would present a balanced view,[45] and Lindsell in fact edited *Daily Bible Readings from the Revised Standard Version* (1957), a remarkable affirmation in the face of fundamentalist fire that the RSV was still the Bible and even suitable for devotions.

As usual, such balance was not the road to popularity. "The Old Fashioned Revival Hour" was losing contributions by the bushel. Charles Fuller assured his subscribers that he himself objected to the RSV but that his seminary professors ought to be free to examine the matter without preju-

---

42. *Sword of the Lord*, November 14, 1952. Chester E. Tulga of the Conservative Baptist Fellowship also blasted away at the RSV; see, e.g., his "Information Bulletin of the Conservative Baptist Fellowship" (n.p.), December, 1952.

43. See the *Christian Beacon*, issues from September 25, 1952, to January 8, 1953. See also "Fanfare for a New Bible," *Life*, October 20, 1952, 91.

44. Carnell, "The Grave Peril of Provincializing Jesus," *Presbyterian Outlook*, March 31, 1952, 5, 6, 8, reprinted from the *Pulpit*, May 1951.

45. William LaSor, "Life Under Tension: Fuller Theological Seminary and 'The Battle for the Bible,'" *Theology News and Notes*, Special Issue, 1976, 8.

dice.[46] Such distinctions were lost on most fundamentalists, though. "We do possess copies given to us by Christian friends who did not even want to keep it in their homes," wrote an irate couple, "and we use these . . . [to] warn students and other friends of the deadly unbelief which has been incorporated into this translation."[47]

A member of "The Old Fashioned Revival Hour" board resigned, complaining that Charles Fuller's seminary was one of the few leading conservative institutions not to take a firm stand against the National Council of Churches product. Charles Fuller later told his son that the controversy cost him one hundred thousand subscribers, probably an exaggerated figure but still pointing toward a painful loss.[48] In the midst of all this, Fuller called a moratorium on public faculty discussion of the RSV. E. J. Carnell later wrote that the bitter "war of nerves" of the orthodox against him for defending the RSV was what first made him realize that "othodoxy suffered from a serious illness." Having until then always thought of himself as a great champion of orthodoxy, Carnell began to examine whether he needed to purge himself of the fundamentalist illness. His "much needed catharsis" was a reevaluation of his own attitudes, which forced him to the insight that "Jesus names *love*, not defense of doctrine, as the sign of a true disciple."[49] Thus in Carnell's personal agony came an important turning of a rudder, not at first perceived, that would soon set the seminary on a new tack.

THE PRESIDENCY

Every time there was a crisis at Fuller, which was often, Charles Fuller and members of the faculty would tell Harold Ockenga that they desperately needed him there as a resident president. Almost everyone who later recalled the early years emphasized the assurance they had that Ockenga would move to Pasadena and that the difficulties of operating without a strong executive on the scene would thus pass away. By the 1953–54 academic year, with a full faculty assembled and its own buildings, the seminary had to settle the much-discussed and much-postponed issue of the president. Ockenga was simply unable to make up his mind. His family would find it difficult to leave Boston. Park Street Church was flourishing and continued its remarkable missionary program. And he had already turned down some of the most attractive positions in the country.

In May 1954, after years of indecision, Ockenga came to the annual board meeting still undecided but determined to settle the issue. Two very significant things occurred during his stay, presumably in the following order.

Ockenga, who considered the decision as to who should be president

46. CF, letter to subscribers, 2-27-53.

47. Letter of 3-20-55 in HL's, "letters from malcontents" file.

48. Concerning resignation, letter of about 5-5-54 in CF file. DF interview, fall 1983.

49. Carnell, in *How My Mind Has Changed*, ed. Harold E. Fey (Cleveland: Meridian, 1960), 91-93.

to be entirely his own, met privately with Edward Carnell and asked him whether he would be willing to serve as president, should he himself decline. Carnell later referred to the "unspoken commitments" of "those sacred moments last May," but the two kept the knowledge of this conversation to themselves. Carnell had already written at length to Ockenga concerning the need for him to come out and take up his duties as the full-time president and warning against some faculty sentiment to put a "back-slapping" promoter in the position. Carnell favored a scholar-president and was sure Ockenga would fill the post admirably. Ockenga apparently agreed with the idea of a scholar-president and so turned the option back to Carnell as the person he considered the most promising scholar in sight. That Carnell had no administrative experience and very few such proclivities seemed to be overshadowed by this lofty ideal. Carnell, who a year earlier had cited President Conant of Harvard University as a fit model for Fuller, was in turn attracted to the challenge.[50]

In the meantime, the picture suddenly changed dramatically. One of the reservations that Ockenga had about coming to Fuller was that the seminary presidency by itself might not fulfill his desires to preach and promote the gospel as well as his position at Park Street Church did. One serious suggestion had in fact been that he become pastor of Lake Avenue Church as well as be seminary president.[51] Characteristically, Ockenga was thinking on a grand scale. So he "put out a fleece." Charles Fuller was sixty-seven. Who would be his successor on "The Old Fashioned Revival Hour"? If this door were opened to him to carry on his preaching ministry, Ockenga resolved, he would accept the position at Fuller as well.

Ockenga was staying with the Fullers during the spring board meetings. No doubt they discussed their futures at length. One night, when Charles Fuller could not sleep, the solution came to him. First thing in the morning, he went to Ockenga's room and told him that he would like him to be his successor on the radio broadcast. "That's the fleece," said the startled Ockenga. At last the issue was decided.[52]

The news that Ockenga was coming to Pasadena was announced at the faculty dinner party, given at the Henrys. It was met with great rejoicing by the faculty, for this was what everyone said they wanted. Carl Henry, something of a realist, especially after seven years of Ockenga's assurances, wanted to make sure. He inscribed the living-room chair on which Ockenga had been sitting "Dr. Ockenga's Announcement Chair." The announcement went out over the wire services, and Henry even saw to it that the *Pasadena Star News* carried it in banner headlines in its local section. "He couldn't show his face west of the Mississippi if he backed out now," he assured one colleague.[53]

The world looked different, as it tends to, when viewed from its hub in

50. EJC to HJO, 3-8-53, 1-12-54, 3-6-54, 3-8-53 (O).

51. EJC to HJO, 3-8-53, argues against this and similar suggestions.

52. This account is from Daniel Fuller, *Give the Winds a Mighty Voice: The Story of Charles E. Fuller* (Waco, Tex.: Word, 1972), 224.

53. CH interview, 11-19-82; Henry, *Confessions of a Theologian: An Autobiography* (Waco, Tex.: Word, 1986); DF interview, fall 1983.

Boston. The Ockenga family had ties and affinities to the east. Moreover, the Park Street congregation was not going to let Ockenga go without a struggle. A car caravan of church officers and members visited the Ockengas at their vacation home in New Hampshire, asking them not necessarily to stay but at least to pray about it. Ockenga also had one personal reservation, now that he had what he had asked for. Working at "The Old Fashioned Revival Hour" and as president of Fuller Seminary, he would be working *for* Charles E. Fuller, no matter what the formal arrangements were. Charles Fuller was still a formidable national institution and was used to getting things done his own way. As the history of the seminary had already showed, Ockenga, too, was used to the independence of deciding things on his own.[54] How would a more dependent relationship go? Ockenga fasted and prayed. The fleece had convinced him he should go to Pasadena. Now he was convinced that the Lord was leading him not to go. He thereupon swallowed his pride and in September sent a telegram to Pasadena announcing his change of mind.

54. HJO interview, 11-6-83.

CHAPTER VIII

The Perils of New Departures

And with this we are led to the final element in the glory of a theological seminary. It is this: that the seminary inculcate on its students an attitude of tolerance and forgiveness toward individuals whose doctrinal convictions are at variance with those that inhere in the institution itself.

Edward J. Carnell, "The Glory of a Theological Seminary,"
inaugural address, May 17, 1955.

A prophet is with honor, except . . . —you know.

Edward J. Carnell to Harold J. Ockenga, September 15, 1954.

THE faculty was assembled at the junior retreat when the telegram arrived. While they had heard rumblings of Ockenga's renewed indecision, the news came nonetheless as an unsettling bomb-burst after a summer of optimism about the school's prospects under a strong resident president. Now they were back to square one and faced with the possibly disruptive process of choosing a new president. None of the senior faculty except Carnell (and Wilbur Smith, who had the ear of Charles Fuller and had found out) knew that the issue had already been virtually decided, although, when the telegram was read, Dan Fuller noticed that Carnell gave a great sigh.[1] The faculty held an impromptu session in the evening sketching out what they looked for in a president. The search, they thought, was on.

Carnell immediately wrote to Ockenga, offering "to release you from any unspoken commitments of last May." He had listened carefully to the faculty's statements and had found nothing, except for their agreement that the new president should not be neo-orthodox, that pointed toward him. Moreover, he still thought that the faculty wanted "an evangelical Dale Carnegie," not a "Pusey of Harvard." He also sensed that the elevation of a younger man from within the faculty would create resentment.

Carnell added some criticisms of the rest of the faculty, perhaps thinking that by revealing these he could disqualify himself. They had "fantastic dreams of being America's leading evangelicals" and talked of publishing "world-shaking literature." Yet "in seven years . . . not one man on this faculty

---

1. DF interview, fall 1983.

has published as much as one article in a scholarly journal; let alone publishing a book with a major house. . . . If I were president, I would only irritate them; for I refuse to be party to their fantastic schemes." These are puzzling remarks. On the one hand, it was true that except for Carnell's own *Philosophy of the Christian Religion* (1952) none of the faculty had produced a major scholarly work while at Fuller. On the other hand, Carnell spoke as much as anyone about making Fuller a *"great,* not merely a mediocre, school."[2] Perhaps he recognized that his tendency toward arrogance regarding his own scholarly success would be an irritant. In any case, he was a divided man, agonizing over aspects of the presidency he feared he could not handle yet knowing it was too great an opportunity to resist.

Within the week, the wheels were turning inexorably toward Carnell's elevation to the post he both coveted and dreaded. As was common for him, and as would be normal for almost anyone under the circumstances, he spent sleepless nights as the final announcement approached. Colleagues had commented in the past on his inability to sleep; and in 1952 Wilbur Smith, noting that Carnell had brought a mattress to school to rest during the day, observed that he hoped "he is not approaching any breakdown."[3] Nonetheless, those who knew that Carnell was the chosen one seem to have discounted any intimations they may have had that he lacked the psychological strength for the Herculean task. He was a dynamic speaker and the favorite teacher and idol of many students. In personal relations he was cordial but reserved. He seemed disciplined and in control; indeed, everyone noted that he was slightly the overdisciplined eccentric scholar. He always dressed formally and wore a homburg. In Pasadena he was renowned for his walks to school, totally preoccupied with memorizing words from pages torn from a dictionary. In facing the presidency, he had a perfectionist's zeal to master every task but also some self-doubts. He worried about his scholarly career and his education, which he calculated had cost him between twenty-eight and forty thousand dollars. Could he "throw this away for an office in which I have to decide how many dozen towels the school should order"? He would certainly need a "Dean of Business Administration," and would not divert himself with financial details. Yet could a president really shape educational philosophy? This would take work "just as intense as if I were answering Barth." Perhaps educational philosophy could be shaped better from within his department.[4]

Carnell's relationship to his colleagues was another realistic concern. He knew that Carl Henry "would be crushed." The two were longtime friends but were also so much in the same field and so long sharing the same spotlight as to encourage comparison and a touch of rivalry. Henry, slightly older, also had all the practical and administrative experience for the presidency. He had served, however reluctantly, as the first acting dean of the school and had chaired the Rose Bowl rallies. As a former newspaper editor, he had also

2. EJC to HJO, 9-15-54, 3-8-53 (O). All correspondence between EJC and HJO is from the Ockenga papers.
3. WS to HJO, 5-31-52 (O).
4. EJC to HJO, 9-22-54.

cultivated cordial relations with the press and had aided in seminary publicity. The obvious question was why Carnell, and not Henry, had been chosen.

Apparently with this delicate situation in mind, Ockenga and Charles Fuller called Henry in to talk about their choice of the new president and asked what he would think of Carnell. Henry immediately gave five reasons why Carnell should not be president, emphasizing especially his lack of any administrative and fund-raising experience as well as his value to the seminary as a full-time scholar. The president, Henry thought, should come from the outside. They should try for Frank Gaebelein again. If it had to be from the inside, Woodbridge would be his choice, certainly not Carnell. Having made these remarks in the context of what he thought was a preliminary exploration, Henry was abruptly informed that Fuller and Ockenga had already chosen Carnell. That night, the trustees announced the selection of the new president.

The next day, Carnell asked Henry to help with the school's publicity and promised him a private secretary. Henry observed that when the founding faculty came to Fuller, they had been promised all the secretarial help they might need to support their scholarship. Why should he now take on an extra task in order to get the secretarial help he ought to have anyway? Nonetheless, Henry pledged his support to Carnell. It was clear to everyone, however, that the naming of the junior man had strained the relationship.[5]

Carnell also met with Lindsell and became convinced, as he reported to Ockenga, that "as we both know, [he] was deeply crushed to see one of his juniors elevated over him to the presidency." Carnell proposed that Lindsell be promoted from dean to vice president,[6] but the new position was not created. Despite some initial reserve about handling the administrative details of someone else's presidency, Lindsell, as dean, remained the key practical academic administrator during Carnell's presidency.

Wilbur Smith was also perturbed. He had some reservations about Carnell's outlook and leadership potential; but even though he was the senior man and the confidant of Charles Fuller, his advice had been ignored. With a flair for the dramatic, as always, Smith told Fuller and Carnell himself that he was considering resigning. He often threatened resignation, however, and within a week this storm was past.[7]

SCHOLARSHIP SHALL NOT SUFFER

A honeymoon period set in. The Monday morning faculty prayer meetings were more uplifting than ever, and the morale of the students seemed to be at an all-time high. The latter was appreciably aided by the arrival in the fall of

5. CH interview, 11-19-82; Henry, *Confessions of a Theologian: An Autobiography* (Waco, Tex.: Word, 1986), 140-41. Henry's recollection is substantiated by a letter, CF to HJO, 9-29-54.
6. EJC to HJO, 9-22-54, 4-15-55.
7. EJC to HJO 10-8-54; CF to HJO 9-29-54 (O); Smith's exact objections are not indicated. DF, on draft, notes that Smith often threatened to resign.

The chosen successor. Harold Ockenga invests Edward Carnell as the
new president of Fuller Seminary as Charles Fuller looks on.

1954 of one of Carnell's old Wheaton friends, Lars Granberg, who would teach
pastoral counselling and psychology and would replace Woodbridge as dean
of students. Granberg's expertise in counselling did much to deal with the
pressures on students, many of whom faced the convergence of a demanding
curriculum and the necessity of earning support for themselves and, often, for
new families.[8] Moreover, the addition of a program in pastoral counselling
suddenly put the California seminary up to date with the latest in seminary
education. Despite Fuller's proclivities toward classical theology, another side
of the seminary's impulse was to be thoroughly up-to-date, "a Cal Tech of the
evangelical world," as Charles Fuller often put it. Both Carnell and Henry
were constantly concerned with keeping up with the latest intellectual fashion,

8. EJC to HJO, various letters, 1954; Lars Granberg interview, 6-6-84.

a trait that was expressed in Henry's continuing interests in publicity techniques and in Carnell's publication of *Television: Servant or Master?* intended for
a secular audience.[9]

In fact, the seminary was moving quickly toward the stage at which it
could point toward a "practical department" of some dimensions. The students of the early classes had lamented the almost total neglect of this area.
One remarked that when he got out of seminary he still "found it difficult to
pray in public." Now, during the course of Carnell's first year, the seminary
was lining up a faculty of five in the practical area. In addition to Clarence
Roddy, Rebecca Price, and Lars Granberg, William Carson Lantz was coming as instructor in speech, and the school was setting up a new position in
evangelism. All the same, the dominant view remained that theologians and
biblical scholars were the heavyweights and that the practical people were
likable, but second-class citizens. While for many years to come the image of
Fuller Seminary remained as primarily a center for academic theology,[10] at
least some moves had been made toward establishing some balance.

Carnell recognized the curricular dilemma clearly. The seminary was
"trying to impose a classical education on students raised in a pragmatic
culture." This anomaly was particularly conspicuous in the California setting
where the classical tradition was seldom part of the baggage that the mostly
twentieth-century settlers had brought with them. Fuller Seminary, however,
was holding out for that classical tradition. The standard Bachelor of Divinity
requirements included, for instance, sixteen hours of Hebrew spread over six
courses—two full years in a quarter system. Pressures were great to reduce
this, and Carnell recognized that the students were not going to learn any more
Hebrew than was necessary to use lexicons and commentaries. Nonetheless,
Carnell noted, the faculty already thought of themselves as having "long-
standing traditions," and they "are never weary of referring to that Chicago
meeting."[11] As a compromise, however, the faculty soon dropped two of the
hours of Hebrew, a small concession to an irrestible trend.

In the meantime, with things running relatively smoothly during his
first year, Carnell began to view the presidency with some enthusiasm as an
opportunity to advance his own vision of the seminary as first of all a scholarly
center. With this high goal in mind, he wrote after the first few weeks: "For the
first time in my life I have done something really sacrificial." This was "probably the last chance in our generation to gather a group of scholars in one
company of fellowship for the cause of evangelical work." The sacrifice of the
solitude to do his own scholarship was a great one, but in his typically perfectionist way, he resolved not to slacken his scholarly production. In fact, early
in his presidency he threw down the gauntlet before the rest of the faculty. He
would hold up his end in producing first-rate scholarship and they should do

9. Grand Rapids: Eerdmans, 1950.
10. Granberg interview; Glenn Barker interview at faculty retreat, September
1983.
11. EJC to HJO, 12-15-55.

the same. The trustees, he thought, should demand a report of the results of at least two months' scholarly production at the end of each summer. Moreover, at the beginning of his presidency, Carnell still had to teach full time and he planned to continue to teach as much as was feasible.[12]

One compensation for him in taking the presidency was that it opened up a place in systematic theology for Paul Jewett, another outstanding member of the old Wheaton crowd. Reared in the separatist General Association of Regular Baptists, Jewett, like Carnell, had studied at Westminster Seminary. From there he had gone on to take a Ph.D. at Harvard and was now teaching at Gordon Divinity School, thus completing (as had Carnell) a sort of "grand slam" of schools feeding the early Fuller. Carnell admired Jewett and was fond of saying that he could be "the Charles Hodge of our generation."[13]

HOPES FOR A NEW GENERATION

The beginning of Carnell's presidency was accompanied by such intimations that the new generation of evangelical leaders could reform fundamentalism and bring it back to its nineteenth-century Reformed and evangelical roots. This had always been the vision for the seminary. Although in the past opposition from both the left and the right had forced some contraction of the hopes, now reform was again in the air.

Ockenga was calling this reform movement "the new evangelicalism." He may have used this term in connection with Fuller as early as the fall convocation of 1948, the same year that Carl Henry published his *Christian Life* series of articles on "The Vision of the New Evangelicalism."[14] The phrase seems not to have caught on earlier. Now, however, Ockenga was proclaiming dramatically that "the new evangelicalism has its main fountain in Fuller Theological Seminary." With this term Ockenga had a particular program in mind. He and others at the seminary and in the NAE had long preferred to use "evangelical" as a self-description to escape the stigma of "fundamentalist." The seminary had also always repudiated the "come-out-ism" of McIntire's wing of fundamentalism. Ockenga now repeated the critique of fundamentalism that he and Carl Henry had expressed in *The Uneasy Conscience of Modern Fundamentalism.* "The new evangelicalism," he said, "embraces the full orthodoxy of fundamentalism in doctrine but manifests a social consciousness and responsibility which was strangely absent from fundamentalism." The pro-

12. EJC to HJO, 10-10-54, 11-28-55; Granberg interview.
13. EJC to HJO, 11-19-54; alumni comments.
14. Mildred M. Cook, "Christian Life Visits Fuller Theological Seminary," pamphlet reprinted from *Christian Life and Times,* June 1948, 2, refers to Carl Henry as an advocate of the "new evangelicalism." In his foreword to Harold Lindsell's *Battle for the Bible* (Grand Rapids: Zondervan, 1976), 11, Ockenga said "Neo-evangelicalism was born in 1948 in connection with a convocation address which I gave in the Civic Auditorium in Pasadena." I did not find the manuscript for this address. The earliest printed use of the phrase with reference to Fuller that I have seen is in an article by Ockenga in the *Pasadena Star News* (September 21, 1953, sec. B, p. 1). In a special section on Fuller Seminary, Ockenga elaborates on Fuller as the center for "the new evangelicalism."

gram Ockenga proposed was not new; but there were now intimations of a separate identity from fundamentalism. Nonetheless, the decisive break had not yet occurred. Fuller Seminary had been founded "to express this movement within the fundamentalist wing of the Christian church."[15]

During the first year of his presidency, Carnell seemed full of hopes to make Fuller the source of renewal that Ockenga had been proclaiming. His specific proposals were those of a scholar. While he dreamed of a research center like the Institute for Advanced Studies in Princeton, his specific proposals to the board in the spring of his first year were more modest. Faculty should have more student assistants. The seminary should keep its enrollment at 250 but recruit more outstanding students. Graduate study, the rather meager Th.M. programs that had been ambitiously introduced a few years earlier, should remain meager until the seminary was truly excellent in training B.D. students. The school should have a theological journal. On this latter point, Carnell added rather pointedly that such an important cooperative effort would never materialize until "the faculty have become more willing to lose part of their individuality in favor of the glory of the institution."[16]

THE INAUGURAL DISASTER

Such remarks suggested that beneath the surface tranquility of this apparently "serene year,"[17] the earth was beginning to tremble. The seminary had been built on a fault, a fine ideological fissure that underlay the attempted fusion of the more malleable positive emphases of the new reformist evangelicalism and the hard rock of stricter fundamentalism. The "new evangelicalism" was still part of fundamentalism and so was each faculty member at Fuller Seminary— some more and some less. Personal antagonisms and rivalries would almost inevitably follow the line of the fault, thus magnifying its importance.

This pattern is of immense significance for understanding the dynamics of the institution and of the development of new evangelicalism.

At the end of Carnell's first year as president, the first major quake occurred. The occasion was his address at the formal inaugural on May 17, 1955. For his theme, he returned to the phrase he had used in his recent report to the board: "The Glory of a Theological Seminary." To an outsider, the points that he made would likely have seemed noncontroversial. His vision for the seminary was that it should stand for both the truth of Christ and the spirit of Christ, and that it should be in contact with the whole church.[18] These themes resonated through his inaugural address. Much of what he said was about holding firmly to the truth of Christ. First, commitment to the creed of the seminary, not as an abstraction but in a heartfelt way, was absolutely

15. Ockenga, "Theological Education," *Bulletin of Fuller Theological Seminary* 4 (October-December 1954): 4. This address seems to have been given in New York, but it also sounds as though it may have been used at Fuller earlier.
16. EJC to HJO, 12-7-54; Carnell, The President's Report, April 1954, passim.
17. Carnell, The President's Report, April 1954.
18. R. Donald Weber interview, 10-25-83.

essential to the glory of the school. Second, the glory of the school would be found in honestly arguing for the faith as the best explanation of the facts of human existence. This was vintage Carnell. He had argued such themes forcefully in his two major works, *An Introduction to Christian Apologetics* of 1948 and *A Philosophy of the Christian Religion* of 1952. Fuller students, he said in his speech, must be given all the evidences, "damaging as well as supporting," so that they would be able "freely to decide for or against claims to truth."

Yet the Carnell who displayed this immense confidence in human rationality, the Carnell whose trust in his own logical powers had led him to develop his own apologetic system and to outdistance his colleagues at a school where apologetics was the king of the sciences, lived with a deep sensitivity to the inadequacy of himself and his movement in embodying the spirit of Christ. He had written dissertations refuting Reinhold Niebuhr and Søren Kierkegaard as not being rational enough. Yet he knew that they represented aspects of the great Christian tradition that he did not often see around him at Fuller Seminary. As preachers often do, he preached as much to himself as to his colleagues.

The crowning glory of the seminary, he emphasized in conclusion, must be its spirit of tolerance. Students must be taught "an attitude of tolerance and forgiveness toward individuals whose doctrinal convictions are at variance with those that inhere in the institution itself." Here, characteristically, Carnell turned his talk into an argument. He built a case for "a Christian philosophy of tolerance." The "logic of intolerance," he said, "is deceptively simple." It is founded on spiritual and intellectual arrogance. It forgets that truth is a gift from God and that, while we must make all sorts of *provisional* judgments to maintain the home, the church, or society, final judgments of the heart are reserved for God. The clinching argument was to consider the command to "love your neighbor as yourself" and then to look at the condition of your own heart. Even Jesus' disciples cried "Is it I?" in recognition of their inability to know the inner mysteries of their own hearts. How much less are we able to pass final judgment on the mysteries of the heart of another. We do indeed have "final truth," as fundamentalists were prone to say. But one such unquestionable truth was "Love your neighbor as yourself." This divine command was "both a final truth and a final reason why we should be tolerant of others."[19]

However unexceptionable the principle that only God can judge the hearts of others, to ears attuned to the rhetoric of fundamentalism such talk of love and tolerance smacked of modernism. No one had ever heard Carnell utter an unorthodox word, but they saw the beginnings of a familiar pattern. When Christian leaders start talking about love or the limits of our knowledge, heresy cannot be far behind. Not that anyone would deny the importance of the principles of love and finitude in their proper contexts of personal relationships. But for the fundamentalist, for whom the preeminent cause was preserv-

19. Carnell, "The Glory of a Theological Seminary," Inaugural Address, May 17, 1955 (pamphlet).

ing Christian truth against soul-destroying errors, tolerance could not be the flag to fly highest over an institution.

Wilbur Smith was fuming. He had been unhappy with Carnell's elevation, and this was the last straw. Smith himself had regularly proclaimed who were Christians and who were not. Whatever aversion he had to separatism or to attacking fellow conservatives, he was not ready to give the liberals any quarter of "tolerance." Woodbridge, still an unreconstructed veteran of the Machen campaigns, was beginning to think that Fuller Seminary was all too much like the old Princeton—the old Princeton that went bad in the 1920s. He had already recently advised a prospective faculty member that he should not come to an institution so disloyal to the word of God. As he later remarked to a student leader, he could smell heresy a mile away and the place reeked of it.[20] Smith and Woodbridge apparently took the lead and, finding Henry and Lindsell of like sentiments, they decided to confront Carnell the next morning. So here was the young president, hardly having put away the academic regalia from his inaugural, accosted by a major segment of his faculty. His hopes had been high—if not to be the Pusey of his generation at least to provide intellectual leadership for the institution. Now his key faculty were saying firmly that he did not speak for them. Carnell's presidency never recovered from the blow.[21]

The inaugural was withheld from publication.[22] The seminary's *Bulletin*, a promotional news brochure edited by Woodbridge, Henry, and Smith, did not even mention the speech. On the other hand, William LaSor in his new alumni publication *Theology News and Notes* praised it as "magnificent," an evaluation that echoed a comment LaSor had heard from a visiting academic dignitary. George Ladd also stood firmly with Carnell. Woodbridge, by contrast, was appalled that Ockenga would not demand retraction or resignation for Carnell's stance of "sweet, forgiving *appeasement* toward heretics," and began to resolve to move elsewhere.[23] The faculty was for the first time deeply divided, not so much by doctrine as by attitude. The question of degree of militance, which before had separated them all from stricter fundamentalists, now defined the line of internal division. One person's evangelical could be another's fundamentalist.

Following the catastrophic inaugural, a superficial peace was restored, as though nothing had happened. Carnell wrote to Ockenga in the fall that the presidency was going all right and that he did not want out. He noted, however, especially with reference to a recent faculty discussion of a paper by

20. Conversation with Frederic W. Bush, fall 1983.

21. There is some disagreement as to whether the confrontation came immediately after the speech or in Carnell's office the next day. Woodbridge puts it the next day in "Reaping the Whirlwind," *Christian Beacon*, May 5, 1977, 7. Perhaps the initial remarks and the appointment had been made the night before. EJC to CF, 4-3-59, refers to the inaugural as a turning point in his presidency.

22. David Hubbard had it published after Carnell's death. Carnell had drafted an introduction alluding to the confrontation by his colleagues, but this was not published.

23. William LaSor interview; Woodbridge, "Whirlwind," 7.

Ladd, the presence of a "Fundamentalist" faction, including Woodbridge, Smith, Archer, and Henry.[24]

THE CONFINES OF PREMILLENNIALISM

Carnell did succeed in one initiative to move the seminary a step away from the fundamentalist orbit. Shortly after Paul Jewett joined the faculty in 1955, Carnell made league with Jewett, Ladd, and Dan Fuller to get the premillennial statement removed from the seminary statement of faith. As long as it had the premillennialist restriction, Carnell told Ockenga, the school could not be "prophetic." "As it stands now," he observed, "neither Calvin, Warfield, Hodge, nor Machen could teach at Fuller Seminary." The school thus was "committed to mediocrity."[25]

The Fullers were the key to the campaign. With Dan on their side, the revisionists had a strong entree. Mrs. Fuller, consistently loyal to her son, readily fell in line. Jewett and Dan, she observed, had become "real pals," and she was persuaded that amillennialism was not a heresy. Convincing Charles Fuller was another matter. As fundamentalists of his vintage often did, he had a deep personal attachment to premillennialism. He also delighted in assuring supporters of "The Old Fashioned Revival Hour" that "every professor on our faculty is premil." One evening, after dinner at the Jewetts, Dan Fuller and Paul Jewett attempted to persuade the evangelist with arguments, though when they saw how deeply he felt about it they soon dropped the subject.[26] Eventually, however, the campaigners won a compromise. They persuaded Charles Fuller to sign a statement declaring that after his death the premillennial clause could be removed.[27] The faculty in the meantime agreed on a procedure to amend the creed by a two-thirds vote of faculty and trustees, should the sentiment to do so arise.[28]

While the campaign to drop the premillennial clause was not publicized, it related to longer-range questions concerning the direction of the seminary. Technically, the faculty were all premillennialists, at least to the extent that they could affirm the creedal statement that "the Lord Jesus will return bodily, visibly, and personally to conform believers to His own image and to establish His millennial Kingdom." Yet even this statement allowed some equivocation since it did not specify that Christ's kingdom would be in Jerusalem or even on earth.[29] The literal one thousand-year kingdom in Jerusalem was part of the dispensationalist heritage that had been part of the background of nearly everyone at Fuller. One thus had to be extremely

---

24. EJC to HJO, 11-9-55.
25. EJC to HJO, 10-14-55, 3-7-56. Ladd makes a similar point in *Theology News and Notes* 1 (October 1955): 10.
26. Grace Fuller to HJO, 1-29-56.
27. Document in vault, FTS.
28. Amendment of faculty by-laws, December 2, 1955, as noted by David Hubbard, "The Stange Case of Fuller Seminary," *Theology News and Notes*, Special Issue, 1976, 9.
29. DF, on draft, suggests that the omission was intentional to accommodate Carnell's views.

cautious in attacking this belief. One point on which dispensationalists had traditionally allowed some room for debate was on the doctrine of the "pre-tribulation secret rapture" of the church. According to this view, the Bible taught that immediately prior to the calamitous events ending this age and ushering in the millennium, believers would be caught up "to meet the Lord in the air" (1 Thess. 4:17). At Fuller, even though the full-fledged dispensational-ist view of history was not taught, some on the faculty believed in the coming secret rapture. Lindsell listed himself, Smith, Archer, Henry, Harrison, and Woodbridge as the "Pre-Trib men" and noted that Woodbridge was the most insistent for this view. Except for the irenic Harrison, this was the exact lineup of the militants against Carnell. Ladd, Carnell, Roddy, and Dan Fuller were listed as "Post-Trib."[30] Framing the discussion of millennialism as a debate between "pre-tribs" and "post-tribs" shielded larger differences with the dis-pensationalist tradition.

The degree to which the fundamentalist heritage still set much of the Fuller Seminary agenda is indicated in the fact that the question of the pre-tribulation rapture was then a leading issue. The immediate push that brought the matter up was George Ladd's major attack on pretribulationism, pub-lished in 1956 as *The Blessed Hope*. Ladd argued gently but firmly that there was no biblical basis for belief in a secret rapture preceding the tribulation of the last days. He thus attacked one of the key points in the dispensationalism in C. I. Scofield's notes in the *Scofield Reference Bible;* but he did so with weapons to which in principle every fundamentalist bowed. Only what the Bible says, Ladd insisted, should be decisive. Traditions of interpretation can be mislead-ing, he said; and the modern dispensationalist scheme was a recent invention. On the other hand, Ladd unequivocally affirmed his own belief that Christ would personally return to set up a millennial kingdom. This, he said, was the historic premillennial view. Rather than repudiating fundamentalism, Ladd was, in typical Fuller Seminary fashion, trying to make it more consistent with its own first principles.[31]

Even an attack on pretribulationism, however, was risky business. One admiring reviewer of *The Blessed Hope* observed that "only those who have experienced the ostracism of beloved brethren because of differences in escha-tology can fully appreciate the importance of this."[32] Fuller Seminary was sure to take some heat for attacking even so peripheral a tenet of classic funda-mentalism.

On the other hand, a British reviewer of Ladd's book expressed dis-may that a person of talent would have to waste his time writing such a book. The Britisher said he would be pleased "if this book can save anyone from such

---

30. Typescript copy of letter from HL to alumni, December 1955. DF, on draft, says that he recalls clearly that in 1956 or 1957 Wilbur Smith confessed to him that he did not believe in the secret rapture.

31. George E. Ladd, *The Blessed Hope* (Grand Rapids: Eerdmans, 1956), 140 and passim.

32. Joseph C. Holbrook, Jr., review of *The Blessed Hope* in *Westminster Theological Journal* 19 (November 1956): 83.

pathetic absurdity" but wondered how anyone in the modern age could need such salvation. "The idea that disagreement upon minutiae of prophetic biblical exegesis can involve practical excommunication would be surprising in a totalitarian atheistic tyranny; in an enlightened Christian democracy it seems well-nigh incredible."[33]

In this remark the Britisher revealed his total misunderstanding of the dynamics of American evangelical religion. It was *because* America was "enlightened," had boundless religious freedom, and had no established church that it needed practical equivalents to set boundaries. Theological "minutiae" could play that role. The fundamentalist wing of evangelicalism was a church without a formal creed, but with many informal ones. Standards of the informal creeds could be enforced by appeals to popular opinion. Before that court, even more than before a formal ecclesiastical court, the truly fundamental was difficult to distinguish from the peripheral.

The "new evangelical" reformers at Fuller Seminary felt this pressure from the invisible fundamentalist church authority every step of the way. Any attack on dispensationalism from the seminary would bring a "veritable torrent" of mail to "The Old Fashioned Revival Hour." Early in 1955, after spending an hour calming the soul of the Revival Hour's secretary, Miss Rose Baessler, E. J. Carnell added to a letter to Ockenga a postscript that said much about the Fuller presidency:

> P.S. Oh, Harold, by the way (and I do not want to appear insubordinate in the least) but when you are approached again to write an article in defense of the view that the church will pass through the tribulation, take a rain check on it. . . .[34]

---

33. J. E. Fison, review of *The Blessed Hope* in *Encounter* 18 (Winter 1957): 121.
34. EJC to HJO, 2-11-55.

CHAPTER IX

The New Evangelicalism

As you know, Dr. John Rice, Dr. Bob Jones and Dr. Carl McIntire have kept a running attack on me for the last two years. The things they are telling border on the ridiculous. . . . As the Psalmist said in Psalm 56: "They mark my steps." Again the Psalmist said: "They wrest my words." Every move I make is now under careful scrutiny by these men. They never print but one side of any story. Thus far I have refused to answer them. I have tried to avoid any controversy for fear of being deterred from my God-called mission of soul winning.

Billy Graham to Wilbur Smith, April 9, 1958.

TOWARD THE MAINSTREAM AGAIN

AT Fuller Seminary the struggle to free the fundamentalist heritage from its pecularities was proving more painful than might have been anticipated. Though progress was perceptible, each advance seemed to be met with a reversal. These uncertain efforts at Fuller were representative of a wider movement for refurbishing fundamentalism that had been developing cautiously since the founding of the NAE. Now, dramatically, the national situation began to change.

Several factors opened the door for the change. Most immediate was the rising status of Billy Graham, marked especially by his acceptance by some of America's most powerful business and political leaders. Graham's early evangelistic successes guaranteed him huge press coverage and personal influence comparable to that of a major denomination. His early image, though, was largely that of the hayseed boy evangelist, consistent with the stereotype of fundamentalism as a movement on the fringes of America's culture-shaping forces. Though the image persisted, by the mid-1950s the realities were substantially different.

The Republican victory in the election of Dwight Eisenhower to the presidency in 1952 was a turning point. Before then most fundamentalists had not been much involved in politics since the 1920s. The recent rhetoric of visionaries like Henry and Ockenga had in fact been little more than rhetoric. To the extent that fundamentalists were political, their sentiments were overwhelmingly conservative and (unless they were from the south) Republican. Charles Fuller, for instance, was wholly apolitical publicly. Privately, he was conservative Republican. Billy Graham and Fuller Seminary leaned in a similar conservative direction. Of Fuller alumni from 1950 to 1952 who responded to a 1985 survey, nearly two-thirds described their political position just before coming to Fuller as "conservative," and another tenth recalled being "very conservative." Of the remaining quarter of the student body almost all were "moderate," with only three of some fifty respondents saying they were "liberal" or "very liberal." Unlike their attitudes in almost every other area surveyed, there was virtually no shift from this overwhelming ratio of conservative to liberal during these students' time at Fuller. Alumni from 1957 to 1959 responded in very similar ratios, confirming the overwhelming political conservatism of Fuller's new evangelical constituency.[1]

Such conservative politics gave fundamentalist-evangelicals natural affinities to the Republicans who in 1953 regained presidential power for the first time in twenty years. Billy Graham, perhaps influenced by the fundamentalist reformers' call for reshaping American society, began to cultivate a hearing in Washington. Initially, this strategy may have had more evangelistic than political motivations, just as Youth for Christ or Campus Crusade would work especially hard to convert campus leaders or football heroes. In any case, Eisenhower's election suddenly gave Graham an entree to the White House. Not only did he have ready access to the president, he also developed a mutually beneficial friendship with the controversial vice president, Richard Nixon, who apparently represented himself as something of an evangelical.[2]

Graham's new influence coincided with opportunities for his friends, among whom the Fuller Seminary people were prominent, to make some profitable contacts with the conservative American business community. One of the attractions for the business leaders on the other side was the firm anticommunism of these intelligent fundamentalists. The fundamentalist-evangelicals did not make anticommunism their first concern, and they always made clear that politics was not the ultimate solution to the country's problems. Yet they were totally unified on pointing to the dangers of the communist threat. As we have seen, already shortly after World War II Wilbur Smith had alerted evangelical audiences to the dangers of communist infiltration of the U.S. government. And when Billy Graham spoke at the Mid-Century Rose Bowl Rally, Ockenga preceded him with a discourse titled "The Answer to Communist Aggression." This was a favorite subject with Ockenga, who had studied Marxism in his Ph.D. work at Pittsburgh, and was no doubt a key point in his outstanding ability to line up business support. Carl Henry also routinely cited the Marxist menace, though usually treating it with more

1. Alumni survey. See Appendix.
2. Richard V. Pierard, "Billy Graham and the U.S. Presidency," *Journal of Church and State* 22 (1980): 107-27; see also Pierard, "Cacophony on Capitol Hill: Evangelical Voices in Politics," in *The Political Role of Religon in the United States,* ed. Stephen D. Johnson and Joseph B. Tamney (Boulder: Westview, 1986), 71-92. Graham's later interest in influencing American politics is indicated in several letters to WS. Graham mentions in a letter of 10-26-60 that he almost got involved in the election campaign (see Chapter XIII, below), and in a letter of 9-5-61 he says that "I feel I should spend some time in Washington as quickly as possible to convey my views to those in high office" (S).

nuance under the general topic of the threat of atheistic materialism to Western civilization. A turn to Christ, a sweeping spiritual revival, they all agreed, was the only answer.[3]

Anticommunist themes, while always subordinated to the quest for personal decisions for Christ, were prominent in Billy Graham's early ministry as well. Graham did not hesitate to say that communism was "inspired, directed, and motivated by the Devil himself," and to warn against "the infiltration of the left wing through both pink and red into the intellectual strata of America."[4] Although he had no direct connections with Senator Joseph McCarthy, Graham repeatedly dropped remarks making clear his sympathies with efforts to expose communism in government.[5] In 1952 he wrote from England to Wilbur Smith, by now a trusted counsellor, "In my opinion, England is in such a tragic spiritual state that unless God sends a revival, Britain will go Marxist-Socialist within the next five years. . . ,"[6] Later, during his British campaigns, Graham provoked a small sensation and was forced to back down when he remarked publicly that socialism was doing more damage to Britain than Hitler's bombs had. Graham also had little sympathy for the American labor movement, which he saw as undermining Christianity.[7] He wrote to Smith that Pittsburgh was "completely paralyzed by Roman Catholicism, labor unions, and extreme modernism."[8] One of his first major evangelistic films, *Oiltown, U.S.A.*, was billed as "the story of the free enterprise of America—the story of the development and use of God-given natural resources by men who have built a great new empire."[9]

Such sentiments were not entirely lost on the empire builders themselves. One of the most sympathetic was oil magnate J. Howard Pew, head of the Sun Oil Company. Pew, a conservative Presbyterian, was concerned about the spread of modernism in the northern Presbyterian church and was especially alarmed by the connections of such theology to liberal politics. Even more than the fundamentalist-evangelical leaders themselves, he thought that the answer to socialism was not only to preach the gospel but also to proclaim its political and economic implications, which he saw as decisively supporting free-enterprise capitalism. The Pew Foundation had immense amounts of money that might go to the right religious causes, and before the end of his

---

3. See Wilbur Smith, *The Increasing Peril—Of Permitting the Dissemination of Atheistic Doctrines on the Part of Some Agencies of the United States Government* (n.p., 1947); "Excerpts from Dr. Harold J. Ockenga's Address on 'The Answer to Communist Aggression,' in the Rose Bowl, Thursday night, 9-14 [1950]," mimeograph; Carl Henry, "Christianity and the American Heritage" (July 4, 1953), from *Vital Speeches of the Day* (n.p., n.d.); Henry, "Christianity and the Economic Crisis," *United Evangelical Action*, May 1, 1955, 7-8.

4. Quoted in Pierard, "Billy Graham and the U.S. Presidency," 109; quotations of Graham are apparently from the 1949 to 1951 era.

5. William McLoughlin, *Billy Graham: Revivalist in a Secular Age* (New York: Ronald Press, 1960), 111-12.

6. BG to WS, 9-27-52 (S).

7. McLoughlin, *Billy Graham*, 99-105.

8. BG to WS, 9-27-52 (S)

9. Quoted in McLoughlin, *Billy Graham*, 98-99.

presidency, Harold Ockenga was assiduously courting Pew on behalf of Fuller Seminary.

EVANGELISM AND CONSERVATIVE POLITICS

Close to the heart of Charles Fuller was the idea that the seminary should have a chair of evangelism. Fuller himself, however, was running too low on Fuller Evangelistic Foundation funds to keep up his usual support of the seminary. So the school was, for the first time, actively seeking other major contributors. Pew was one of the major prospects. For him, the anticommunist credentials of the school had to be stressed. In June 1954 Ockenga wrote to Charles Fuller telling him of his upcoming address to a businessmen's luncheon in New York at which Pew would be present. Ockenga said his address would present "the spiritual nature of the present oil threat and the Scriptural antidote to the infiltration of such corrupting ideas in American life." He would stress the importance of sound seminary education for rebuilding spiritual leadership, especially pointing out "the connection of sound theology, sound economics, politics, and diplomacy, with the idea of getting them to underwrite either a professional chair at Fuller or setting up a particular department for the training of evangelists."[10] In a later account published in the seminary *Bulletin,* Ockenga underscored that he had dealt with "the Christian answer to the international challenge of communism and the insidious internal threat to our heritage of liberty." Of his business-leader audience he observed, "To say that these men were disturbed over the outlook for democracy, peace and freedom is to put it mildly. They were agitated." When Ockenga talked about "the new evangelicalism" and Fuller Seminary around this same time, his list of the issues that the new social consciousness would address was safely conservative and included a prominent reference to "creeping socialism."[11] J. Howard Pew apparently agreed with Ockenga that evangelism and sound theology were important for protecting the free enterprise system against communism, and by the fall of 1954 the seminary had the promise of a gift to set up a position in evangelism.

The oil magnate was convinced that some pumping would help sustain the flow of ideas from old-time evangelism to free enterprise. In connection with his main gift he contributed to the seminary one thousand dollars per year (double the stipend for the Payton Lectures) for a series of presentations to be entitled "The American Heritage," though to avoid confusion with another organization the faculty changed the lecture series title to "The Christian Heritage."[12] In either case the "heritage" seemed to have a good bit to do with free enterprise. The first speaker was Howard Kerstner, editor of *Christian*

---

10. HJO to CF, 6-11-54.
11. *Bulletin of Fuller Theological Seminary* 4 (July-September 1954): 2; *Bulletin* 4 (October-December 1954): 4.
12. Faculty minutes, 4-12-55.

Economics, a Pew-supported periodical that unrelentingly championed the free market as God ordained.

Along with this medicine of a stronger political stance for the seminary came the sweet strains of evangelism. The Pew grant, which could be renewed on a yearly basis, stipulated that the evangelism position had to be filled by the next fall. The faculty first approached Charles Woodbridge, who was largely engaged in outside practical activities anyway. Woodbridge seemed interested at first but soon turned them down. Next they turned again to Paul Rees, whom Ockenga had contacted earlier about other positions. This time Rees was interested. The faculty then had to face squarely the problem that Rees regarded himself as an Arminian, not a Calvinist, especially on the question of the perseverance of the saints. The faculty nonetheless dearly wished to enlist him as a colleague. President Carnell, who ultimately opposed the appointment, saw himself and the faculty as caught in a truly tragic situation. In order to protect the seminary for future generations, they wished to keep their Calvinist identity, even though their official statement of faith did not mention perseverance directly. "I have never seen a vote of the faculty taken with such sorrow and hesitation," wrote Carnell.[13] In the end, they turned Rees down.

Just when it looked as though the position might go begging, the faculty met with a happy solution. They heard that J. Carlton Booth was looking for a new position. Booth had taught for many years at Providence Bible Institute (later Barrington College) in Rhode Island and was very widely known on the evangelistic circuit as a soulwinner and as a music director and songleader. Booth had worked especially with Jack Wyrtzen, but also with most of the other major evangelists of the era, including Billy Sunday, Gypsy Smith, Charles Fuller, Percy Crawford, and Billy Graham. He was also a personal friend of about half the Fuller faculty and brought the enthusiasm and practical touch needed for organizing the evangelism department. Once he started, Booth frequently brought Charles Fuller to lecture to his classes. Fuller was always the model of simplicity: "Preach the word, boys, preach the word," was his refrain. Booth soon expanded the curriculum in evangelism and also organized summer internships for Fuller students to assist in Graham crusades.[14]

AN EVANGELICAL *CHRISTIAN CENTURY*

With Pew lining up behind Ockenga and Graham, new possibilities were opening for reshaping the fundamentalist heritage. Pew, a layman in the Presbyterian Church in the U.S.A., was eager to shore up the intellectual foundations of broadly conservative theology and politics; but he had rela-

13. EJC to HJO, 2-11-55 (O).
14. Booth, manuscript of autobiography. Charles Fuller's Gospel Broadcasting Association published Booth's *Helps and Hints to Soul Winning* in 1956.

tively little interest in the specific controversialist or separatist emphases of mainstream fundamentalism. The Sun Oil Company executive was frankly interested in name-brand religion.[15] His interests could thus be mobilized to coincide with those of the reforming evangelicals.

One crucial project, long a dream of Wilbur Smith, came to fruition with the advent of the Pew money. Smith wished for a monthly periodical that would raise the scholarly level of fundamentalist-evangelicalism. In February 1951 he outlined his dream to Billy Graham: we need "a periodical so important that it would be absolutely indispensable for every serious-minded Christian minister in America." It would be devoted to Biblical exposition and prophecy (always Smith's major interests) but would also have religious news and reviews of important books, with "no attention to trash."[16]

By 1954 Graham had become convinced that such a substantial theological voice would be an important follow-up to his revivals, and so he began to lay plans with his father-in-law, L. Nelson Bell, a retired missionary doctor and an active conservative leader in the southern Presbyterian church. Their model for the new journal was, explicitly, the *Christian Century*. To ensure maximum impact, they would publish it in Washington, D.C.[17] Appropriately, they offered the editorship to Wilbur Smith. Smith accepted, but after a few weeks of planning meetings he changed his mind. By now he was in his sixties and comfortably settled in California.[18]

In January 1955, Harold Lindsell wrote to Bell and Graham suggesting that Carl Henry would be an excellent editor. Graham's reply was most revealing of the current dynamics of fundamentalist-evangelicalism and of his own vision for its future. Henry, he said, in effect, might be too fundamentalistic. The new periodical, as Graham envisioned it, would "plant the evangelical flag in the middle of the road, taking a conservative theological position but a definite liberal approach to social problems. It would combine the best in liberalism and the best in fundamentalism without compromising theologically." It would see good as well as bad in the World and National Councils of Churches. More specifically, "Its view of Inspiration would be somewhat along the line of the recent book by Bernard Ramm, which in my opinion does not take away from Inspiration but rather gives strong support to our faith in the Inspiration of the Scriptures."[19]

Graham's reference to Ramm was remarkable. A Baptist teaching at Baylor (and a good friend of Carnell), Ramm had just published *The Christian View of Science and Scripture* in which he challenged the fundamentalist assumption that a high view of biblical inspiration implied that the Bible was a reliable source of scientific data. He thus called for a return to the "noble tradition" of

15. J. Howard Pew to BG, 1-13-65: "I am a Presbyterian, and one of my greatest ambitions is to help establish a Presbyterian seminary" (S).

16. WS to BG, 2-22-51 (S).

17. BG to HL, 1-25-55 (L).

18. Graham, "Tribute to Dr. Wilbur Moorehead Smith," in *Evangelical Roots: A Tribute to Wilbur Smith*, ed. Kenneth Kantzer (Nashville: Nelson, 1978), 13.

19. BG to HL, 1-25-55 (L).

the relation of the Bible to science, the tradition characteristic of late nine-teenth-century evangelicalism. Among other things, such a view meant that Christians might properly believe in a divinely guided development of spe-cies.[20]

Though Wilbur Smith had given Ramm's volume a laudatory ad-vance notice in *Moody Monthly,* the young theologian's views were bound to cause a furor in many fundamentalist circles. "Inerrancy" was often taken to imply Biblical accuracy in scientific detail, and total opposition to biological evolution had become a major test of the faith since the era of the Scopes trial of 1925. By the next summer Ramm's book had indeed caused the largest stir in fundamentalism since the RSV controversy.[21]

Graham's initial fears that Carl Henry might be too conservative signaled the direction he was about to move and thus also the impending larger break between the new evangelicalism and separatist fundamentalism. Despite the antagonism between McIntire's American Council of Christian Churches and Ockenga's National Association of Evangelicals, they were still generally regarded as rival parts of the same movement. McIntire, in addition, did not speak for all separatist fundamentalists, and relatively few followed him strictly. Bob Jones, Sr., of Bob Jones University, for instance, a militant fundamentalist if there ever was one, nonetheless maintained ties with the NAE into the 1950s. So did John R. Rice, who, through his paper the *Sword of the Lord,* with a circulation in the hundreds of thousands, was the most influen-tial fundamentalist publicist of the era. Though Rice was an archetypically strict fundamentalist, in the 1930s he had experienced the pain of a split with his more volatile mentor, J. Frank Norris. In the 1950s, while McIntire, Ches-ter Tulga (a Conservative Baptist militant), and others were attacking Graham for his associations with Ockenga and his lack of militance toward some modernists, Rice still backed Graham and helped keep most of funda-mentalism solidly in Graham's camp.[22]

During campaigns in England in 1954 Graham received broader church support than his fundamentalist supporters would have allowed him in the United States. Such successes in culturally influential religious circles were leading Graham toward the conviction that he could make marvellous inroads into America's major denominations if he could only jettison the disastrous fundamentalist images of separatism, anti-intellectualism, and contentious-ness. As his letter to Lindsell indicated, this would also involve at least distanc-ing himself from some of the more restrictive shibboleths. He would not tie his ministry to a narrow view of the implications of the inerrancy of Scripture for modern science. He would not identify evangelical Christianity with only the

20. Ramm, *The Christian View of Science and Scripture* (Grand Rapids: Eerdmans, 1954), 9-10, 347-48.
21. Butler Farley Porter, Jr., "Billy Graham and the End of Evangelical Unity" (Ph.D diss., University of Florida, 1976), 107-16. Smith's review in *Moody Monthly,* October 1954, was quoted on the jacket of the 1955 printing of Ramm's book.
22. Porter, "Billy Graham," 44, 61-90. I am indebted to Porter for his fine account of these relationships between Graham and fundamentalism.

most conservative politics. His recent stand for racially integrating his crusades exemplified this point. Nor would he totally condemn the ecumenical movement. Graham himself was ready to weather the storms that such moderate stances would surely bring. So in speculating to Lindsell about Carl Henry he asked: would he "be ready to take a certain amount of criticism from typical fundamentalist leaders?" More basically, "Would he be willing to recognize that fundamentalism is in need of an entirely new approach and that this magazine would be useless if it had the old fundamentalist stamp on it?"[23]

When the search turned explicitly to Carl Henry the next summer, Graham was still worried that Henry might be "too well known as a fundamentalist" and even wondered if the magazine might not be edited under an assumed name for a year or two.[24]

Henry had his own reservations about the direction the new journal was pointing. Two things had happened that spring to affect his thinking. One was the break with Carnell over his inaugural address and its failure to make clear that intolerance was sometimes a virtue.[25] The other was that J. Howard Pew, who was making his very conservative economic views felt at Fuller, was now apparently a force in shaping the magazine as well. Henry wrote to Graham that he might be disqualified from the editorship on two counts. On the one hand, he might be disqualified for his convictions: "that the authoritative Scripture is the watershed of theological controversy" and that "Liberalism and Evangelicalism do not have equal rights and dignity in the true church." On the other hand, Henry had reservations regarding the place of his own politics in the magazine: not that he was too conservative but (presumably with an eye to possible conflicts with Pew in mind) that he believed "that capitalism is not beyond Christian criticism." On this latter point, Henry referred Graham to his recent address to the NAE entitled "Christianity and Economic Crisis."[26] There he had criticized American conservative Protestants who "too often implied that American capitalism was the ideal economic form of the Kingdom of God." Moreover, he had said that Christians must be indignant about "injustices and inequities in the world of labor and economics." Christians should not put their trust in any economic system. Yet Henry still came down soundly for capitalism as opposed to socialism and took a firm stand for aggressive anticommunism.[27]

Militancy against communism was still an important test among the fundamentalist-evangelicals who were founding the new journal, now designated *Christianity Today*. One of the first of the influential fundamentalists to shed his fundamentalism openly was Donald Grey Barnhouse, editor of *Eternity* magazine. In March 1954, in reference to the then much-maligned inves-

23. BG to HL, 1-25-55 (L).
24. BG to L. Nelson Bell, 6-6-55, as quoted in Henry, *Confessions of a Theologian: An Autobiography* Waco, Tex.: Word, 1986), 141.
25. CH, comment on draft, February 1986, summarizes his objection this way.
26. CH to BG, 6-20-55 (L).
27. Henry, "Christianity and Economic Crisis," *United Evangelical Action*, May 1, 1955, 7-11.

tigations of Senator Joseph McCarthy, Barnhouse had written an article agreeing with liberal church leaders that anticommunists were becoming a greater threat than the communists themselves. Barnhouse's remark caused a considerable stir in fundamentalist-evangelical circles. Wilbur Smith, for instance, responded to an inquiry from a businessman friend and supporter by reassuring him that he and Ockenga had recently argued with Barnhouse on this very point—"one of the most miserable and irritating half-hours we had spent with anyone for a long time."[28]

Carl Henry and the founders of *Christianity Today* found no insurmountable conflicts regarding their respective economic views; but they did differ on how they thought the magazine should discuss theology. After meeting with Graham and Bell in August 1955, Henry wrote to them insisting on a firmer stance were he to be editor. Apparently their proposed strategy was that for the first two years they would emphasize points of commonality with ecumenical Christians, thus establishing the widest possible hearing for the magazine. Henry found this totally unacceptable.

> It allows men whose theological perspective is, at best, gray, to appear to receive special distinction because, here and there, they maintain partial points of contact with evangelical theology. It offers no clear and decisive criticism of that false doctrine of ecumenical unity which not only treasures a minimal of doctrinal agreement, and even rejoices in (rather than merely tolerates) an inclusivistic theology, but which militates against a sound evangelical witness except where that witness lends itself without protest to the platform and service of ecumenical outlets.

Henry suggested that perhaps after the two-year concessive period he might be interested in the editorship, but that he could not accept their present strategy. He then added a paragraph that echoed his reaction to the Carnell inaugural just a few months earlier. "The truth is still the indispensable human factor in Christian apologetics; truth without love will be usually ignored, but love without the truth is not even real love."[29]

The founders of *Christianity Today* conceded to Henry's terms and named him editor. So, though greatly reluctant to interrupt his academic career, Henry asked for a one-year leave of absence to edit the magazine, beginning in the fall of 1956. As editor, Henry immediately established some independence from his board. Ockenga, the board chairman, told Henry that Pew wanted to see advance copy of the first issue. Henry made clear that this would mean the end of his editorship, and he went ahead on his own terms.[30] For the first several years, he remained simply on leave from Fuller, which gave him some leverage in such matters.

28. WS to Douglas Ober, 3-16-54 (S).
29. CH to BG and L. Nelson Bell, 8-18-55 (L).
30. CH interview, 11-19-82; See Henry, *Confessions of a Theologian*, for his account.

THE IRREPARABLE BREACH

In the meantime, the tensions between the new evangelicals and the strict fundamentalists were mounting toward a major explosion. What long had been treated as differences in emphasis now were leading toward an irreparable breach. The open controversies surfaced at two levels, theological and practical, with the practical forcing the decisive break.

In 1955 Graham finally repudiated efforts to bring his crusade to New York City under strictly fundamentalist auspices and accepted instead an invitation from the Protestant Council of the City of New York to hold a crusade there in 1957. Working with the Protestant Council meant cooperating with a group that was predominantly nonevangelical and even included out-and-out modernists. It also meant sending converts back to their local churches, no matter how liberal those churches might be. Fundamentalist evangelists, such as Jack Wyrtzen, who had led the great New York campaigns of the 1940s, were irate.

While this crisis was brewing, the popular fundamentalist monthly *Christian Life* increased the consternation with its publication in March 1956 of the article "Is Evangelical Theology Changing?" The article allowed that fundamentalism had started out well when leaders such as J. Gresham Machen were defending the essentials of the faith. But soon after 1925, "fundamentalism began to be the catch-all for the lunatic fringe," which was "why to the man on the street *fundamentalism* got to be a joke." After World War II, however, "out popped a young generation." These younger theologians agreed with their elders in opposing the mishmash of liberal Protestantism; but they wanted a more positive emphasis. "In short," the magazine explained in a key sentence announcing the revolution, "fundamentalism has become *evangelicalism.*" The major difference between the two was that the fundamentalist watchword was "Ye should earnestly contend for the faith," while evangelicals emphasized "Ye must be born again." Accompanying this major shift were a number of lesser departures from fundamentalism, advocated variously by younger theologians such as Bernard Ramm, Vernon Grounds, E. J. Carnell, and Carl Henry. These innovations included moving away from dispensationalism, taking more positive views of science, scholarship, and social concern, reconsidering the role of the Holy Spirit (in regard to holiness and pentecostal groups), and reopening discussions about the inspiration of Scripture.[31]

The fundamentalist old guard were understandably outraged. This seemed a pop caricature of their movement. Didn't they too preach being "born again"? John R. Rice in a letter of response jumped on the article as "sophomoric." He said it was based on the opinions of men who, with a few exceptions, were not only young but "rather unknown and cocky." Bob Jones, Sr., also wrote a letter the next month to protest a companion article in the April issue of *Christian Life* entitled "Is Liberal Theology Changing?" The

31. "Is Evangelical Theology Changing," *Christian Life*, March 1956, 16-19.

current optimism about liberal change, he said, was just a case of "mind-worshippers" becoming soft on neo-orthodoxy in order to win approval as scholars.[32]

With the way prepared by the accusations against fundamentalism in the March issue, Billy Graham took the opportunity of an interview in the June issue of *Christian Life* to take the offensive against his critics. His travels abroad had convinced him that "the fighting, feuding and controversies among God's people . . . is a very poor example to our governments." He was "sick and fed up" with these controversies. Most importantly, he thought that one of the primary reasons why revival had not come to the evangelicals of America was their "name-calling and mud-slinging." The key to revival, he was sure, was for evangelicals to repent and to spend the time in prayer that they had before spent in controversy. As to the sponsorship of the New York meetings, "What difference does it make who sponsors a meeting?" Paul preached under the sponsorship of the philosophers at Mars Hill, and White-field said he would preach to the Pope if he got an invitation.[33]

Graham's repudiation of the controversialism so central in his fundamentalist heritage predictably launched the most heated controversy of his career. To the controversialists, the point was not at heart a love of controversy but the salvation of souls. Joseph T. Bayly, the very conservative editor of Inter-Varsity's *His* magazine, made just this point in a letter to *Christian Life*. Paul may have been "sponsored" by the philosophers at Mars Hill; but the crux of the problem was whether he turned over the names of converts to non-Christian synagogues.[34] To the full-fledged fundamentalists, this central issue had already been translated into painful breaks with America's traditional denominations. The hottest current battle was in the overwhelmingly conservative Southern Baptist Convention. Militant fundamentalist Southern Baptists were unhappy with some convention programs and opposed contributing to the Cooperative Program, which financed convention-wide activities. Lee Roberson, who had built a fundamentalist empire at his twelve thousand-member Highland Park Baptist Church in Chattanooga and his Tennessee Temple Schools, was in April 1956 forming the independent Southern Baptist Fellowship and moving toward a complete break with the Southern Baptist Convention. Behind Billy Graham's general attack on fundamentalist controversialism lay this issue within his own denomination. In the April issue of a denominational magazine, he enthusiastically endorsed the Cooperative Program as "the greatest means ever devised by the church for giving one's tithe."[35]

---

32. Rice, letter to *Christian Life*, May 1956, 3, in response to "Is Evangelical Theology Changing"; Jones, letter to *Christian Life*, June 1956, 4, in response to "Is Liberal Theology Changing," *Christian Life*, April 1956, 20-22. Porter, "Billy Graham," provides useful accounts of these and the subsequent controversies.

33. "What's the Next Step," interview with Billy Graham, *Christian Life*, June 1956, 20-23.

34. Bayly, letter to *Christian Life*, August 1956, 4.

35. *Baptist Standard*, April 7, 1956, quoted in Porter, "Billy Graham," 158.

This was the last straw for Rice. Through the spring of 1956 he had been faithfully defending Graham from the mounting fundamentalist criticisms. Pointing to a growing liberal Protestant outcry against Graham over his upcoming cooperative New York crusade, Rice had been arguing that such attacks were reassuring evidences that "Dr. Billy Graham is a fundamentalist." Now, however, the Southern Baptist issue led Rice to request privately from Graham a reaffirmation of the fundamentalist statement of faith of the *Sword of the Lord*. Graham responded bluntly by asking that his name be dropped from the cooperating board of this leading fundamentalist publication.[36]

In the swirl of such exchanges, the first issue of *Christianity Today* finally appeared in October 1956. The new magazine clearly intended to rise above the accusations and counteraccusations now spicing up most fundamentalist and recently fundamentalist journalism. John R. Rice took the advent of the new journal as the opportunity to publicize his break with Graham. Graham's new magazine, he said, was "highbrow and formal in tone," more scholarly than spiritual, and for schools, not for churches and soulwinners. Almost as though Rice had seen Graham's earlier correspondence, he observed that the new journal seemed as though it was "intended to be a middle-of-the-road publication not offensive to modernism and only slightly offensive to fundamentalists." It would disagree with modernists, but not denounce them. This was "Billy Graham's viewpoint." He wrote directly to Graham that Graham clearly did not share the *Sword*'s "opposition to the young 'intellectuals,' the left-wing fringe including Bernard Ramm, Dr. Carl Henry, Dr. Vernon Grounds, etc."[37]

Christianity Today, eager to establish itself as of *Christian Century* quality, immediately distanced itself from the fundamentalism with which everyone but the hard-line fundamentalists would identify it. Carl Henry in one of his earliest editorials warned of "the perils of independency." During the next year he reiterated the point, using primarily the relatively safe example of Carl McIntire. By this time McIntire had alienated himself even from many of his closest associates, although he still had a large popular constituency. McIntire's *Christian Beacon*, said Henry, was "a religious smear sheet in the worst traditions of yellow journalism."[38] The more responsible fundamentalist critics of Graham's new tactics were a greater problem, however. *Christianity Today* published a defense of Graham's cooperative evangelism in January 1957 and in April reported at length Graham's own answer to his critics in a recent speech to the National Association of Evangelicals. "The one badge of Christian discipleship," Graham proclaimed in what was becoming a refrain, "is

36. See Porter, "Billy Graham," 147-60; quotation from Rice, *Sword of the Lord*, April 6, 1956, 5, cited by Porter, 151. Porter provides a detailed account of this episode.

37. See Porter, "Billy Graham," 166-68; quotation from *Sword of the Lord*, November 23, 1956, 2, cited by Porter, 167.

38. Henry, "Theology, Evangelism, Ecumenism," *Christianity Today*, January 20, 1958, 23.

not orthodoxy, but love."[39] Carl Henry himself picked up the same theme in a major critique of fundamentalism, published in June. Fundamentalism as a theology should be distinguished from fundamentalism as a temperament. The problem was with the latter. "The real bankruptcy of fundamentalism," said Henry, "has resulted . . . from a harsh temperament, a spirit of loveless-ness and strife. . . ."[40]

NEW LINEUPS

By the time Graham's New York crusade opened in the spring of 1957, it was all over for the classic fundamentalist coalition, though the shouting continued for two more decades. Polemics on both sides proliferated as the old fundamentalist community sorted itself out into two camps. The pivotal question was what one thought of Billy Graham. The evangelical coalition that emerged could be rather simply delineated as those who were enthusiastic about Graham. At the center of this group were former fundamentalists such as those who produced *Christianity Today*. But evangelicalism, like enthusiasm for Graham, was much wider, drawn from many denominations and traditions. So the new evangelicals could plausibly claim to speak for a large portion of American Protestantism, even though their own fundamentalist heritage gave their emphases less universality than they sometimes presumed.[41] The strict "fundamentalists" were now a considerably smaller group, probably only a few million, who shared a fundamentalist heritage with the new evangelicals but unlike them disapproved of Graham. Separatism, accordingly, now became a chief test of "fundamentalism."

Of course the lines were not immediately clear, nor was it immediately evident which direction everyone would go. Wilbur Smith, since he seemed to know everyone, was particularly important for reassuring conservative evangelicals who might be wavering about their group loyalties. Graham was close to Smith and cultivated his counsel and support. In May 1958 Smith wrote to Graham a characteristic letter that revealed the tenor of their relationship.

> My beloved Friend:
> I had intended to write to you long before this, but these have been rather stormy days in my own soul, and I have not had the liberty for much work. First of all, I want to thank you for the great privilege of spending those few hours with you recently. It was one of

39. News, "The Lost Chord of Evangelism," *Christianity Today*, April 1, 1957, 26; *Christianity Today*, January 21, 1957, 28, 33.

40. Henry, "Dare We Renew the Controversy?" *Christianity Today*, June 24, 1957, 26.

41. Joel Carpenter explores the development of this relationship in "The Fundamentalist Leaven and the Rise of an Evangelical United Front," in *The Evangelical Tradition in America*, ed. Leonard I. Sweet (Macon, Ga.: Mercer University Press, 1984), 257-88.

the most spiritually refreshing times I have had in years. I shall always cherish, but never be able to repeat to anyone else, the very gracious words you spoke regarding our friendship, sentiments that I do not deserve. To summarize everything, I would like to say that after talking with you that day, I came away with a greater feeling of confidence in you and your ministry than ever—and you know that confidence has always been strong and deep. Upon returning, I called Dr. Fuller to give him my reactions to our conversation.

Last week I opened up to my English Bible class this whole problem of modernism on a committee as distinct from modernism on the platform, and also spoke to the faculty about this with real earnestness.[42]

Smith had long been a trusted counsellor to Graham, and now his support was especially crucial. In April Graham had written Smith soliciting help from him in an upcoming speech that the elder statesman was to give at the NAE convention. Graham lamented the constant barrage he was receiving from John R. Rice, Bob Jones, and Carl McIntire and noted that the secretary of the NAE had told him "that about twenty percent of the evangelicals are becoming disturbed and many others are confused." "I feel that a strong statement by you, . . ." Graham told Smith, "would have a tremendous and telling effect."[43]

As fundamentalists were sorting themselves out from evangelicals, the key institution caught in the middle was Moody Bible Institute. Graham was especially disturbed by his breach with what had been the central fundamentalist institution. He repeatedly asked Smith to do what he could to regain its support. During a remarkably successful crusade in San Francisco in 1958, Graham noted that *Moody Monthly* was silent, even though some on the staff deeply wanted to support him. Explaining the situation to Smith in a letter, he wrote:

You have been so wonderful and helpful to me that I hesitate to call upon you to help in yet another matter. However I feel that this is extremely important. I would hate to see the Institute make a serious mistake in joining hands with these extremists who are not interested in facts and who, I believe, are taking an unscriptural position.[44]

Smith did what he could; but not until 1962 did Moody's president William Culbertson finally gave in and pledge full support for a Graham crusade.[45] In the meantime the lines of the borders between fundamentalism and the new evangelicalism were far from settled.

42. WS to BG, 5-5-58 (S).
43. BG to WS, 4-9-58 (S).
44. BG to WS, 6-21-58. Graham makes a similar request in his letter of 4-9-58 (S).
45. BG to WS, 5-17-62; WS to BG, 5-3-62 (S).

THE NEW EVANGELICALISM ARRIVES

During 1957 and 1958, when this crisis was particularly intense and the initial alignments were taking shape, Graham and Fuller Seminary were thrown into each others arms. They were fully agreed that they had to jettison the counterproductive negativism of extreme fundamentalism and that they had to be open to sympathizers in ecumenical old-line denominations. They were in fact moving into the mainstream of American life. Graham recognized that he had to repudiate the anti-intellectual image associated with fundamentalism. Endorsing the overt intellectualism of *Christianity Today* and Fuller Seminary was an important step in that direction, one that he could take without sacrificing the simplicity of his own preaching. At the crusade in San Francisco in the spring of 1958 Charles Fuller visited Graham. On the platform he leaned over to Graham and suggested that he join the Fuller board of trustees. He would not have to do anything but lend his name and make an occasional cameo appearance. Graham accepted. The leading evangelists of the two generations were thus symbolically united and Graham lent his endorsement to Fuller Seminary as a leading institution in the emerging new evangelical coalition.[46]

As Graham wrote to Charles Fuller, confirming the arrangement, "There is no doubt that the extreme liberals and the extreme fundamentalists are unhappy about the particular road down which the Seminary is going. I, for one, believe you have taken a New Testament position and will stand with you all the way."[47]

Ockenga in the meantime took the opportunity to attempt to give the movement a distinct identity as "the new evangelicalism." He himself had played a leading role in the NAE, Fuller Seminary, Graham's early ministry, and as chairman of the board of *Christianity Today*. In a lengthy press release of December 1957, labeled in an Associated Press dispatch as from "the originator of 'the New Evangelicalism,'" Ockenga defined the term. The new evangelicalism, he said, was distinguished from three movements: neo-orthodoxy, modernism, and fundamentalism. The difference with fundamentalism, he said, was primarily in the application of biblical teaching to society and not just to individuals. Billy Graham, said Ockenga, was "the spokesman of the convictions and ideals of the new evangelicalism."[48]

The rhetoric was much the same as in 1947; but now in the late Eisenhower years and behind the momentum of Graham the reformers of fundamentalism seemed on the verge of gaining the place in American life that they claimed as their rightful heritage. They still had a long way to go with the secular media—and even further with the militantly antifundamentalist Protestant establishment—but they could demonstrate some sophistication, as the

46. Daniel Fuller, *Give the Winds a Mighty Voice: The Story of Charles E. Fuller* (Waco, Tex.: Word, 1972), 226; *Bulletin of Fuller Theological Seminary* 8 (Summer 1958): 1-3.
47. BG to CF, 9-4-58.
48. Ockenga, quoted in *Christian Beacon*, January 9, 1958, 1, 8; Robert P. Lightner, *Neoevangelicalism Today* (1965; Schaumberg, Ill.: Regular Baptist Press, 1978), 28.

*Charles Fuller, Billy Graham, and Edward Carnell shortly before
Graham addresses the chapel at Fuller Seminary (Graham carries a
cane because of a minor accident a few days previously)*

well-edited pages of *Christianity Today*, ranging over a broad spectrum of theological, political, and ethical topics, evidenced.

Their political conservativism limited their acceptability to the liberal press and media. Writings of J. Edgar Hoover, head of the FBI, sometimes graced the pages of *Christianity Today*, reflecting sentiments close to those of J. Howard Pew. On the other hand, despite such pressures from the polemical right, Carl Henry attempted to maintain some balance in dealing with the American heritage. American materialism received some criticism alongside polemics against Marxist materialism. Politics was not the major priority, however. Preaching personal commitment to Christ always came first. After that, the weapons for battling modern culture should be primarily theological and intellectual.

This tempered outlook helped dispel fundamentalist stereotypes and, although not always pleasing the press and the religious establishment, opened up other doors. Billy Graham was, after all, a regular guest at the White House and a friend of the vice president and heir apparent. Though Graham had emerged out of fundamentalism, his branch of the movement was shedding much of its Bible institute and store-front image. Instead, it was reflecting the values and aspirations of an important segment of middle-class America. At the end of the decade, *Christianity Today* could proudly contrast the reception of Graham's 1960 Washington crusade with that he had received there in 1952. On the earlier date he had preached on the Capitol steps, and a local sponsor had to warn Graham and his staff that "Washington would look askance at the brilliant ties and gabardine suits they were accustomed to wearing." Now he was speaking in Griffith Stadium, and the president himself was expected to attend. When he spoke at a banquet for government employees at the Statler Hilton, the invitation specified "Black Tie."[49]

In some respects evangelical Protestantism was returning both in theology and in status to positions it had held as recently as forty years earlier. This was a point that defenders of the "new evangelicalism" sometimes emphasized, at least in regard to their theology. When fundamentalist detractors jumped on the word "new" and said that "neo-evangelicalism" was a lot like "neo-orthodoxy" and that both departed from the old-time gospel, the new evangelicals could reply that what they advocated was not new at all. In fact, they could claim with some legitimacy that they represented the original fundamentalism more faithfully than the latter day fundamentalists did.[50] Recent fundamentalists had added separatism, unloving militancy, and an insistence on the details of dispensationalism to the original orthodox evangelical defenses of the fundamentals. A return to a more balanced fundamentalism shaped Carl Henry's earliest conceptions of *Christianity Today* and provided his strongest critique of current fundamentalists. He envisioned a return

49. *Christianity Today*, June 20, 1960, 23-34; cited in Porter, "Billy Graham," 286.
50. See, for example, Ronald H. Nash, *The New Evangelicalism* (Grand Rapids: Zondervan, 1963), 161. E. J. Carnell makes a similar point in *The Case for Orthodox Theology* (Philadelphia: Westminster, 1959), 113-26.

to standards much like those of *The Fundamentals,* the twelve-volume series published from 1910 to 1915 that had presaged the fundamentalist movement. Following the example of that earlier publication, he lined up for *Christianity Today* an impressive international array of scholars as contributors. The predominant tone was gentle and, even more than in *The Fundamentals,* most of the strongest stands were carefully qualified.[51]

BREAKING AWAY FROM FUNDAMENTALISM?

The ideal of turning back the clock to before the fundmentalist era—to a time when evangelicals combined substantial scholarship with fervor for action—nowhere had greater appeal than at Fuller Seminary. The shapers of Fuller had long hoped that the attitudes and emphases that had grown up in the fundamentalist decades of the 1920s, 1930s, and 1940s could be repudiated and that evangelical orthodoxy could return to the balances of its earlier days. With the exception of Woodbridge, who went over to the fundamentalist side, each of the Fuller faculty identified to some extent with the new evangelicals and hence with a version of this ideal. What they did not entirely reckon with, however, was their own history. Though Fuller was new and in a seemingly historyless part of the country, its faculty was made up of people who were all powerfully shaped by the fundamentalist heritage. Fundamentalism was not just something external that could be abandoned at will.

Moreover, the new evangelicals at Fuller were far from willing to adandon the essence of fundamentalism. Even the most progressive of them was conservative on this score. While they objected to certain aspects of dispensationalism and to certain traits of the fundamentalist heritage, they still firmly identified themselves with what they saw as central to the fundamentalist cause. William LaSor, for instance, always regarded as a progressive, expressed alarm at responses to a survey of the class of 1950 in which some graduates indicated that they felt that the critical tools they had acquired at Fuller would force them to "leave Fundamentalism." LaSor retorted that this was a non sequitur since he himself and many other conservative scholars knew biblical criticism yet had not abandoned fundamentalism. Despite this concern, the Old Testament professor was gratified by a number of comments indicating that alumni were getting "both more rigid and more tolerant." They were "holding the line" on their theological framework but since leaving Fuller had acquired a greater sense of love and humility in applying this theology.[52]

For all the Fuller faculty members, fundamentalism was still, in varying degrees, an inescapable, internalized reality, intimately related to their deepest spiritual commitments. As far as their movement was concerned, they

51. Henry, "Dare We Renew the Controversy?" *Christianity Today,* June 24, 1957, 24-25. See the appeal to the model of *The Fundamentals* in CH to BG and L. Nelson Bell, 8-18-55 (L).
52. LaSor, *Theology News and Notes,* January 1956, 1-2.

all sided firmly with Graham against the separatists and the militant dispensa-tionalists. But for some, as for Graham himself, this inclusivism did not mean abandonment of militant fundamentalist defenses of the faith and its key symbols, especially the inerrancy of Scripture.

The neo-evangelicals were thus still torn internally over variations of the same issues that were dividing them from separatist fundamentalists. Their one impulse was to insist that the exact positions won in the fundamen-talist stand against modernism were too important ever to abandon. At the same time, they clearly wished to purge themselves of all the unessential traits acquired during the fundamentalist era, especially the spirit of belligerence. To put their dilemma in a question, To what extent was their movement a reform of fundamentalism and to what extent was it a break with it? The "new evangelicals" had no easy rules by which to settle these issues.

CHAPTER X
The Tensions of the New Evangelical

I have dedicated the whole of next summer to writing. *You cannot dissuade me from this purpose. I have no intention of giving a week of my time to a conference where water-soaked saints gather to check on the heresy of the speaker.*
E. J. Carnell to R. Donald Weber, interoffice memo, April 16, 1957.

A PRESIDENCY IN RUIN

NO one was more in accord with Harold Ockenga's "new evangelicalism" than Edward J. Carnell. Fuller's president was deeply indebted to the Boston preacher and was his protégé and admirer. When, in the midst of the break between Graham and the fundamantalists, Ockenga reemphasized his designation for the new party, Carnell followed suit. "What Is the New Evangelicalism?" is the title he gave to a Fuller promotional speech in Chicago in October 1958. He was, he admitted, uneasy with calling the movement "new." Echoing a famous remark by Charles Hodge a century earlier that there had never been a "new" idea at Princeton Seminary, Carnell stated, "We have nothing new at Fuller Seminary and God help us when we do." Nonetheless, Carnell defined his own calling and the mission of Fuller Seminary exactly in the terms that Ockenga had long been proclaiming.

As the son of a fundamentalist minister, Carnell said, he had found it a shock to discover that the cause to which he was committed was intellectually mediocre. In graduate school he realized that in America's theological centers no one read the works of living evangelicals. Machen was the last to whom they paid the slightest attention. Fundamentalist evangelicals had "forgotten the dictum that great ideas are going to rule the world." While university professors had left the faith because they thought it was intellectually indefensible, Carnell, by contrast, declared with characteristic new evangelical confidence that any fairminded person who looked honestly at the facts will become convinced of the biblical worldview. But "evangelicalism has surrendered its leadership," he warned. While theologians at Union Seminary in New York were producing great ideas, evangelicals were still arguing about when the rapture would occur. They had substituted orthodoxy for love as the chief mark of the faith. They emphasized minor virtues while cultivating major vices.[1]

Less than two months after this impassioned defense of the new evangelicalism, the young Fuller president sent to his faculty and board an order that the term "new evangelicalism" was no longer to be used in connection with Fuller Seminary. He explained that the term had been chosen to stimulate interest in new approaches to the eternal gospel; but it had caused "no small misunderstanding in the field." Henceforth the seminary would refer to itself as the "Home of Historic Christianity" (a phrase that never caught on). The pronouncement concluded by reaffirming the seminary's loyalty to the vision of Charles E. Fuller, thus revealing what part of the constituency the problem was coming from.[2]

Dropping the term *new evangelical* was by this time one of the least of Carnell's problems, though it was symptomatic of the intense irritations of working with a constituency that could not tolerate the most innocent innovations. By the winter of 1958–59 he was exhausted from constant tension and inability to sleep.[3] In early March 1959 he wrote to Ockenga:

> I am feeling somewhat better, thanks to sleeping pills every night. I hope to find relief from the tension in this office some time next summer. I am a misfit as president, that is the trouble. My temperament is monastic and academic; I have no natural desire to command, to assume authority. If I could get out of this job gracefully, I would do it with no small joy.[4]

And in early April he recounted to Charles Fuller some of the irritations that accentuated his long-standing sense of isolation from his colleagues:

> Since the night I tried to express a few fresh ideas about the law of love in my inaugural address as president, I have had to stand alone in the defense of the classical tradition, and in the persuasion that we ought to express the more gracious and gentle attributes of Christ as well as thunder in the defense of doctrine.[5]

By this time, Carnell, who was his own most acute critic, was losing his ability to remain either gracious or gentle. In his letter to Fuller (who, one must recall, was a close friend of Wilbur Smith and no intellectual himself) he wrote: "Dr. Smith will probably raise a big fuss about parts of my new book. I really hope you will ignore him, for he simply does not have the mental equipment to understand the issues that are transpiring in the modern ideological struggle."[6]

1. Carnell, "What Is the New Evangelicalism?" address at the Union League Club, Chicago, October 10, 1958 (tape recording).
2. EJC to the trustees of FTS, 12-4-58 (O).
3. EJC to HJO, 1-12-59, 2-6-59; see also 3-26-59 (O).
4. EJC to HJO, 3-2-59 (O).
5. EJC to CF, 4-3-59.
6. Ibid.

In late April he wired Ockenga, pleading desperately for relief from the presidency.[7] In May, he resigned. But it was too late. Even out from under the presidency he could not fight off an impending psychological collapse.

The forces that occasioned the demise of Carnell's presidency and his psychological break tell us much about the dynamics shaping Fuller Seminary and the movement of which it was a part. Carnell was a perfectionist,[8] unable to compromise happily on any front. Intellectually he stood for all the highest ideals of the Fuller tradition, but as president he had to relate these to practical realities far from the ideal. Carnell hoped to lead Fuller to full acceptance by the largely nonevangelical American theological establishment. At the same time he was singlehandedly trying to develop a whole new apologetic that would triumph over liberal and neo-orthodox alike. Yet as president he faced the irritating everyday problems of keeping the peace with a fundamentalist community that was notoriously suspicious of change and in the midst of the trauma of breaking up into warring camps. To add to these Herculean tasks, Carnell was the chief financial officer of a sizable institution. He recognized all too well that financial health was essential for independence in other domains. Finances were, however, an area where perfectionism was likely to be most severely tried. Constant storms on this front, punctuated by the quakes of the fundamentalist–new evangelical splits were enough to permanently shatter any hopes of tranquility.

AN EARLIER CRISIS

Carnell's resignation in 1959 was not his first attempt. Though it remained a well-kept secret, in January 1957 he had informed Ockenga, and later the board, of his "irreversible" decision to resign. Only after half a year of negotiations did he withdraw this resignation in July 1957.[9]

Things had been going badly as Carnell entered his third year as president in 1956–57. While others who had protested his inaugural address had made peace of one sort or another, the dispute with Woodbridge was still festering over a year later. As early as the spring of 1955 Woodbridge had advised Carlton Booth not to come to the seminary because of its apostasy. Yet Woodbridge himself remained on the faculty, a constant thorn in the flesh of the president. The subtle warfare between the two was becoming intolerable, and Carnell resolved that by the end of the fall Woodbridge would have to resign or be fired.

The real issue, as Carnell himself remarked, had to do with the fundamentalist–neo-evangelical crisis. As the trauma of the break between Billy Graham and the fundamentalists was reaching its peak, Woodbridge was doing all he could to aid Graham's opponents.

7. Telegram, EJC to HJO, 4-25-59 (O).
8. Interviews with HL, 10-28-83; with J. Laurence Kulp, 3-19-85; and with others.
9. EJC to HJO, 1-23-57 (O). Ockenga informed the trustees in early March. Carnell withdrew his resignation in a letter to the board of trustees, 7-31-57 (O).

In particular, he had, in Carnell's words, "sold a bill of goods" to Jack Wyrtzen, a central figure in shaping fundamentalist opposition to Graham's upcoming New York crusade. Wyrtzen, in turn, was putting pressure on his good friend Charles Fuller to cut off support for Fuller Seminary. Carnell thought that Fuller, who would be seventy in the spring, was demoralized by this attack from a fellow evangelist. Fuller seemed worn and in the early weeks of the term had not put in one of his usual appearances in chapel. Carnell feared that the pressure would bring the evangelist to an early grave, a possibility that for various reasons brought dread to Carnell throughout his presidency. On the broader front, Carnell saw such incessant controversies as illustrating evangelicalism's tendency to "self-disembowelment." As a result, he even feared, in classic evangelical terms, that "our land is swiftly turning Roman Catholic . . . by default."[10]

Woodbridge, however, unlike the Catholics, was right down the hall. To Carnell he was the very embodiment of the fundamentalist self-destructive problem. He acknowledged that the man had some endearing personal qualities but thought he had "suffered a traumatic experience as a result of the Machen incident" (the ouster of Machen and Woodbridge from the Presbyterian Church in the U.S.A.), from which he had never recovered.[11]

To the relief of nearly everyone, Woodbridge offered his resignation in November 1956. Carnell eagerly accepted. Woodbridge, however, only increased his polemics against the school. He still taught Sunday school at Lake Avenue, and there he proclaimed that he was leaving the nearby seminary because of its tolerance of apostasy.

Such accusations, made while Woodbridge was still on the Fuller payroll, destroyed much of the remaining goodwill between him and his colleagues. Harold Lindsell, with his usual thoroughness, reported to Ockenga in the spring: "I have checked as carefully as I know how and feel that his opinions are not validated by the facts."[12] Wilbur Smith, on the other hand, who had lost none of his abilities to sense the slightest doctrinal tremor, harbored suspicions that Paul Jewett was "not sound on inspiration." Charles Fuller was assured of Jewett's soundness; but Woodbridge had succeeded in raising lasting doubts about the seminary in the minds of two trustees, Herbert J. Taylor and Edward L. Johnson, an important supporter from Lake Avenue Church.[13] To add to the frustrations, the usual wearying story of taking losses on both the right and the left continued.

As all this was going on, everyone at the seminary was exceedingly eager for accreditation from the American Association of Theological Schools. Recognition by the national agency was a crucial step in putting the new-style evangelicalism solidly on the map of respectable American Protestantism. The school was academically qualified and, by all accounts, Dean Lindsell had

10. EJC to HJO, 10-1-56 (O).
11. EJC to HJO, 10-5-56 (O).
12. HL to HJO, 3-8-57.
13. CF to HJO, 3-4-57. EJC to HJO, 3-17-58 (O).

The Carnell trademark

done a marvellous job of putting the application in order. Yet full approval seemed inordinately delayed. Everyone at Fuller was sure that ideological opposition from the Presbyterian seminaries was behind these roadblocks. In December 1956, when hopes were especially high for approval, they once again got the disappointing news. Though they were not rejected, final accreditation was once more postponed.[14]

Such irritations were compounded by minor anxieties. There was a slight drop in student applications. Carnell also felt some uneasiness over his own relationship to students. The ideal president who did everything would keep close touch with students, but Carnell was irrepressibly formal. He deplored the "open-shirted informality" and "brilliant sport shirts" that students wore. He himself was always immaculately attired and had even been seen so, complete with the homburg, black suit, and cane, at the beach.[15] He was appalled by some students' use of "you," rather than "thee," in prayers, which he condemned as a "shocking informality when addressing God." One student retorted that it was easier to teach his small children "you," to which Carnell countered that it would be easier to teach them to spit on the floor too. Though he remained revered by students as a great teacher, he hardly knew what to say to them when he was not behind a podium. As president, he dutifully organized regular times when they could come and chat with him; but the occasions were so stiff and formal that few came.[16]

14. EJC to HJO, 12-21-56 (O).
15. Lars Granberg interview, 6-6-84.
16. Carnell, The President's Report, April 1955, 8; conversation with Frederick Bush, fall 1983; and other alumni comments.

CHIEF FINANCIAL OFFICER

Such frustrations were trivial compared with Carnell's sense of incompetence in dealing with finances. While he was enough of an intellectual to feel that he could ride out the ideological struggles and eventually defeat his opponents by argument, here was a field in which he had no expertise, in which rationality did not always prevail, and which he had found to his sorrow that he could not avoid.

When Carnell accepted the presidency, he did so with the assurance that the budget was balanced and the seminary rested on a firm financial base. Sound finances were important to his highly ordered view of things, and, consistent with his personal conservatism, he deplored venturous financial arrangements. He even opposed buying on low down payments and any credit.[17] Up until then Fuller Seminary had been in an extraordinarily favorable financial situation. At the outset, the school, despite having its own board, was legally just a part of the Fuller Evangelistic Foundation. Charles Fuller had guaranteed to Ockenga that the foundation would designate for the seminary at least $150,000 per year, plus the buildings. In 1947 $150,000 was a lot of money, and the amount well exceeded the seminary's operating budget for each of about the first five years. Moreover, the foundation financed most the building program, contributing some $900,000 there. In 1951 the foundation board and the seminary board were legally separated and, when Carnell became president, he made sure that the buildings were transferred to the seminary debt free. With the expansion of the seminary beyond the original projection of 150 students and ten faculty, the foundation had also increased its contribution to the operating expenses.[18]

Early in Carnell's presidency it was becoming apparent that something was going awry and that the days of financial ease were over. By 1955–56 the $160,000 that Charles Fuller could provide from the foundation was more than $50,000 under the net expenses for the year.[19] The seminary had always received other gifts as well as a moderate tuition income, but for the first time the administration had to consider aggressive fund raising, a prospect that Carnell found exceedingly distasteful. For this purpose, he persuaded Fuller to allow him to hire a fund-raiser, Donald Weber, a good friend and also his brother-in-law.

By the end of the 1955–56 school year a financial crisis was looming. While faculty salaries and work loads were still relatively good, the salaries had been frozen since 1947. Moreover, Charles Fuller now could promise no more than $150,000 per year to the school. At the 1956 board meeting a proposal for a $500 raise for Carnell brought so much haggling by the trustees that he felt deeply humiliated and withdrew the request.[20]

17. Carnell, "Personal Happiness and Prosperity," *Christian Economics*, September 3, 1957, 4.
18. HJO to HJT, 6-27-59 (T); CF to HJO, 9-22-55 (O).
19. CF to HJO, 9-22-55.
20. EJC to HJO, 3-17-58 (O). The details of this matter are vague, but Carnell saw it as a turning point in his presidency.

Even more frustrating difficulties were afoot. As the seminary leadership began looking for major alternative funding, they found that some foundations to which they appealed for funds required them to supply a complete financial disclosure, including a disclosure for the Fuller Evangelistic Foundation as well. Charles Fuller, who managed some of the FEF funds personally, repeatedly refused to do this. More importantly, the American Association of Theological Schools was putting pressure on the seminary to establish its total financial independence from the foundation. They feared that otherwise they would be accreditating a ghost institution, subject to the whims of an outside agency.[21]

This latter point was becoming a major preoccupation of Carnell. He frequently observed in his correspondence that Charles Fuller's health seemed to be failing. What would happen should the evangelist suddenly be taken from them? By early 1956 Carnell was seeing this as a major issue in his presidency. Miss Rose Baessler, second in command at the FEF, had "repeatedly warned that if the Seminary ever departs from the purposes set down by Dr. Fuller, the Foundation money will go elsewhere." With the split between the fundamentalists and the new evangelicals heating up, this could leave the seminary in an impossible situation. Once Charles Fuller was gone, said Carnell, the foundation might decide to cut off the seminary simply for refusing to discipline a faculty member for using the RSV in his preaching, or for some other celebrated cause, just as trivial. With Carnell convinced that the evangelist was fading fast, the problem of achieving financial independence was becoming "a race against time."[22]

Charles Fuller, however, had other problems. He apparently agreed in principle that the seminary should become independent, either by the merger of the foundation board into the seminary or by a simple transfer of funds. But, much to Carnell's chagrin, whenever the evangelist actually agreed to move in that direction, he would soon back out. The main issue was the disclosure of the financial situation of the foundation, which had become something of a disaster area. Fuller had been a successful businessman before he was an evangelist, and business ventures were still his avocation. In the early 1950s, during the building campaigns, he had discovered a marvellous way to advance the foundation's cause—investing in oil wells. In 1951 he wrote to Ockenga that "God has answered believing prayer in a wonderful way for he has allowed me to raise the sum of $200,000 for the new administration building."[23] By 1955 it was another story. A major investment in a company somewhat inaptly named Providential, through which Fuller owned sixteen wells, had gone bad because of mismanagement. As losses for the foundation accumulated, Fuller began investing from his personal fortune to recoup them, even borrowing against his life insurance. Good money went after bad. The

21. HL to Walter M. Roberts, executive secretary, American Association of Theological Schools, 2-22-56 (A).
22. EJC to HJO, 1-9-56, 3-19-56 (O).
23. CF to HJO, 9-25-51. Presumably this windfall was from oil-well investments.

more he tried to recover, the more embarrassing the situation became. He could not understand "why the dear Lord has permitted adverse results." Only the Lord knew "why almost overnight salt water was permitted to enter certain wells and make them worthless."[24]

Fuller told only Ockenga and Carnell about his financial plight, and all they could tell others was that he had good reasons for his endless delays in turning over the major share of the foundation funds to the seminary. Even Ockenga and Carnell could not find out the actual amount of the foundation's assets. In fact Charles Fuller was trying to save face with them as well, but he was doing so by cutting into the principal in order to keep up at least the promised $150,000 per year.[25]

For Carnell, the impasse over the foundation funds, combined with all the other frustrations he faced, became more than he could tolerate. So, in early 1957, he offered his resignation. It was a terribly difficult decision, for he had considerable affection and respect for Fuller—as did everyone that knew him well. In fact, a year earlier Carnell had remarked to Ockenga that he thought it would be "catastrophic" to resign the presidency during Fuller's lifetime, since the evangelist now depended so greatly on him.[26]

Carnell clearly intended his resignation to be "final and irreversible." What turned him around is not altogether clear. In a conversation with Charles Fuller in the spring, he emphasized that, while some lack of acceptance by the faculty had hurt him, by far his largest problem was in finances. As always, he emphasized that he was not a fund raiser. More fundamentally, he felt he did not get any respect in the financial area. He felt he was treated "like a little boy." At a trustees dinner, three or four people had been asked to get up and speak, but not him, the president. As Fuller observed, "he is a sensitive man."

On the other hand, Carnell seemed surprisingly open to reconsideration. When asked who else might be president, he observed that he could think of *no* one and then threw up his hands and said "*No* one but I am the indispensable man! I have the education—the vision—am qualified except in money raising. I am treated as a little boy."[27]

With some assurance that his concerns would be taken seriously, Carnell reconsidered. One important reason to stay was the pending accreditation (which in fact was received in December 1957). Charles Fuller had also strengthened the foundation's commitment to the seminary and was taking some definite (though preliminary) steps toward transferring some of the funds. Student enrollments were up again. The immediate crisis was past.

The long-range financial situation was as intractable as ever, however. Ockenga and Don Weber were going after some big donors, but seldom with major success. They were constantly running into obstacles such as the

24. CF to HJO, 9-4-55; Rose Baessler to HJT, 6-15-59 (T).
25. HJO to HJT, 6-27-59 (T).
26. EJC to HJO, 11-9-55 (O).
27. CF to HJO, marked 1957, apparently in the spring.

Edward Carnell and Harold Lindsell with the letter granting Fuller Seminary full accreditation in 1957

wife of one donor who was distressed when she heard that Fuller professors used the RSV. Apparently, in the euphoria of his renewed commitment to the presidency, Carnell even agreed to go on a fund-raising tour with Weber in the fall. This was totally uncharacteristic. More typical was his irritated retort, quoted at the outset of this chapter, that he was not going to waste his precious time with heresy-hunting saints at the Winona Bible Conference.

The fifteen hundred-mile trip in the fall met with Carnell's usual expectations. They called on some very wealthy cattlemen, dealers in rice and cotton, ranchers, oilmen, and custodians of foundations. He "kissed babies, inspected turkey hatcheries, rode around vast ranches, listened to small talk, and sat hours in an unventilated room with children who were in the last stages of Asian flu." Despite all this, "we brought no direct gifts into the Seminary."

The fact was, "Fuller Seminary has no real constituency." They were not connected with a denomination or anything else, and "the wealthy have no conception of the new evangelicalism." As they faced being on their own, constructing a new base of support became ever more pressing.[28] Don Weber had hoped to build a more solid structure of trustee support, but as yet little had happened on that front.

AN INTELLECTUAL THOREAU

For E. J. Carnell, deep personal tensions over these issues, plus his struggles to master the world of finances, coincided with his emergence as the recognized

28. EJC to board of trustees, 11-5-57 (O).

leading scholarly spokesman for the new evangelicalism. With opportunities for the hearing that he had worked so hard for now opening up, he could not allow the mere duties of an administrator to distract him from his primary work of writing. Both his own expectations for himself and those of others were extremely high. Harold Lindsell wrote in 1957, with typical Fuller Seminary confidence, that Carnell could do for evangelicalism what Tillich and Niebuhr had done for other schools of thought.[29] In this, Lindsell was simply echoing Carnell's own assessment.

The big breaks began to come around 1956 as the religious establishment started to recognize the new-style sophisticated fundamentalism as a serious phenomenon. The *Christian Century* began asking Carnell to write for them. Moreover, his latest apologetics book, *Christian Commitment: An Apologetic,* which Carnell considered his best, had been accepted for publication in 1957 by Macmillan in New York. To be published by a major secular publisher was a great triumph for the new evangelicals. Soon they were congratulating themselves on this as another sign of reaching maturity.

Christian Commitment was a highly original volume, directed toward winning for traditional Christian belief respect from its cultured despisers. As in all his apologetic works, Carnell emphasized the points of commonality between the experiences of the believer and those of the unbeliever. In seeking a hearing in the mainstream of American life, he played down the gospel's offenses to secular culture—at least the *needless* offenses—and stressed the harmonies of Christian belief with what secularists already believed. Thus his apologetic books were conspicuous among evangelical literature in their relatively sparse references to Scripture. The hypothesis that Carnell defended was the truth of biblical Christianity. For the defense to be successful, he was convinced, he had to appeal, not to the authority of Scripture itself, but to truths derived from some common human experience.[30]

A related trait, found widely in neo-evangelicalism, was a relatively limited sense of history or tradition. The immediate fundamentalist traditions were something of an embarrassment, and in the mid-twentieth century appeals to Calvin did not enhance one's prestige. So in their efforts to refurbish their movement, evangelicals tended to go it alone. Carnell epitomized this tendency. He believed his calling was to construct a whole new apologetic from scratch. This was one of the American evangelical traits that had most startled Béla Vassady, whose confessional European heritage encouraged a strong appreciation of historical traditions. The new evangelicals, on the other hand, typically saw the central issues confronting Christianity as matters to be settled by arguments abstracted from historical contexts.

This trait was most conspicuous in the tendency to see the crucial

29. HL to HJO, 3-8-57.
30. This interpretation, together with some of what follows, has been aided by the insights of John G. Stackhouse, Jr., "Pioneer: The Reputation of Edward John Carnell in American Theology" (M.A. thesis, Wheaton College, 1982). I have also been helped by Gordon R. Lewis, *Testing Christianity's Truth Claims: Approaches to Christian Apologetics* (Chicago: Moody Press, 1976).

questions regarding the faith as questions of epistemology. Carl Henry and Carnell both stressed this point. What was inadequate about the contemporary modes of knowing, they asked, and what was the evidence for the superiority of the Christian mode? Consistent with this approach to the central issue was the new evangelical emphasis on the inerrancy of Scripture. Lacking in theory a place for the authority of tradition and seeing the chief problems of modern thought as various epistemological abysses that dropped into relativism, they could find in an inerrant scriptural revelation a firm epistemological foundation for fixed religious truth.[31]

All these traits were apparent in Carnell's early work. In *An Introduction to Christian Apologetics,* he had sought to appeal to the common affirmations of humanity via their virtually universal acceptance of the law of noncontradiction. While he had given up the naive common sense empiricism of nineteenth-century American evangelical apologists and their hope to build solid proofs for Christianity simply on the basis of objective examination of the evidence, Carnell in this early work was heir to their general confidence that the superiority of Christianity could be demonstrated rationally. Following roughly the path set by Gordon Clark, Carnell argued that the Christian hypothesis best stood the test of "systematic consistency." For Carnell, however, systematic consistency involved both logical consistency with the law of noncontradiction and also accounting for all the facts of experience.[32] The Christian hypothesis, Carnell thought he could show, could meet this test better than any alternative worldview. Hence it had a strong rational presumption in its favor.

The real originality in Carnell's work came as he moved beyond the appeal to human rationality to other dimensions of common human experience for which Christianity provided the best explanation. He thus was beginning to wrestle with the tendency toward abstractness that characterized most of the intellectual efforts of fundamentalism, its newer evangelical offspring, and even some of his own work. In *A Philosophy of the Christian Religion* he had dwelt on how Christianity best satisfied the human heart's quest for meaningful values. Now, in *Christian Commitment,* he was providing a more personal exposition of how Christianity best accounts for universal human moral sentiments, especially the sense of moral outrage at injustice.

Carnell was increasingly striving to take into account the existential dimensions of Christianity. His concerns fit the spirit of the times that many Fuller people were so eager to keep up with. In the mid-1950s existentialism was at the height of its influence in American thought. In theology, neo-orthodoxy stressed this dimension. Symptomatic of the spirit that Carnell wished to cultivated was Paul Jewett's 1957 address "What Is Right with Existentialism?" Jewett was second to none in emphasizing the importance of

---

31. William J. Abraham suggests these points in *The Coming Great Revival: Recovering the Full Evangelical Tradition* (San Francisco: Harper and Row, 1984).

32. Carnell, *An Introduction to Christian Apologetics* (Grand Rapids: Eerdmans, 1948), 56-64.

Paul Jewett delivering his address "What Is Right with Existentialism?" on the occasion of his installation as Associate Professor of Systematic and Historical Theology

classic systematic theology. Nonetheless, as evangelicals long had said and existentialists now were saying, propositional truth was not enough. True knowledge, the two traditions agreed, demanded "personal commitment."[33] What was significant was that at Fuller, unlike in most of fundamentalism, scholars were now asking what they could learn from contemporary thought, even though they were still resolved not to compromise. Carnell himself had studied Kierkegaard and Reinhold Niebuhr in graduate school, and, although he translated them into his own categories and offered the usual orthodox critique of their lack of solid foundations, he was struggling to find in evangelicalism a way to deal with the dimensions of Christian faith that Christian existentialism and neo-orthodoxy had recovered.

So, while on the one hand *Christian Commitment* took the classic form of evidences and arguments for orthodox Christianity, on the other it was a personal, often autobiographical, attempt to penetrate to the essences of universal human experience. While some of his illustrations of a universal sense of justice were trivial—such as one's irritation at someone cutting into a line, or

33. Paul K. Jewett, "What Is Right with Existentialism," convocation address, FTS, October 3, 1957.

at being repeatedly distracted by a noisy pencil sharpener in a library—others revealed a soul in agony. Already in graduate school, Carnell confessed, he had suffered from insomnia and a resulting physical state that colored his most fundamental perceptions of reality: "Everything I conceived became a burden; every anticipated obligation threatened to impale me. Even so ordinary responsibility as conversing with others overwhelmed me with consternation. Nor dare I conceal the fact that even suicide took on a certain attractiveness."

So, Carnell argued poignantly, our affections are basic to our most elemental knowing, so that there are levels of knowing that transcend the merely rational. Among these levels, he maintained in his central thesis, was "knowledge by moral self acceptance, and moral responsibility."[34]

While *Christian Commitment* received some approval, it was not lauded as the breakthrough in conservative apologetics that Carnell supposed it was. He thought that he had found a whole new level of knowing and had related it successfully to orthodox Christianity. Yet most orthodox reviewers received it with some caution. Even *Christianity Today* did not give the book prominent coverage and chose as reviewer Gordon Clark, a polemicist who was predictably disturbed by Carnell's turn from his earlier apologetic appeal to the law of noncontradiction. Carnell's former mentor suggested that Carnell might be weak on the doctrine of salvation by Christ alone. Clark also observed that Carnell's derivation of theology from ethics was the standard modern procedure since Kant, used by all sorts of heretics whom Carnell would oppose.

Mainline reviewers were not swept off their feet either. Probably the most damaging criticism came from William Hordern in the *Christian Century*. Hordern, neo-orthodox, but in many ways a conservative theologian, might have been expected to sympathize. Yet he found Carnell weak on some philosophical matters, even in his understanding of Kierkegaard and Kant. He too regarded Carnell as too concessive in his central argument. Carnell's reliance on humanity's intuitive moral sentiments took insufficient account of humanity's depravity and capacity for self-deception. So, while Hordern welcomed the move from fundamentalism by men like Carnell and Henry, he ended with what he saw as a haunting "paradoxical suspicion." "Could it be that the errors of earlier modernism, such as overconfidence in man's goodness and rationality and an uncritical view of the immanence of God, are going to be brought back by the new fundamentalists?"[35]

Despite some such critical remarks, *Christian Commitment* did not even manage to create controversy. As with most books, it was simply noticed and then ignored. Macmillan soon gave up on it and sold off the stock as remainders. To Carnell this failure in big-time publishing was a great blow. Some who knew him thought it was hardest blow for him to sustain. Until now everything he had done academically had brought success. But here was

---

34. Carnell, *Christian Commitment: An Apologetic* (New York: Macmillan, 1957), 29.
35. Gordon H. Clark, review of Carnell's *Christian Commitment* in *Christianity Today*, September 2, 1957, 36-38; William Hordern, review of Carnell's *Christian Commitment* in *Christian Century*, September 4, 1957, 1042. Stackhouse, "Pioneer," 29-51, summarizes reviews of Carnell's work.

failure—and with the work for which he had hoped the most. Exactly when the blow fell is not entirely clear, though it certainly compounded his anxieties about failure in the presidency.

The tepid reception for *Christian Commitment* exemplified one of the basic difficulties in the work of Carnell, of Fuller Seminary, and of all neo-evangelicalism to the extent to which it aspired to be a positive intellectual movement. As John G. Stackhouse, Jr., has suggested, Carnell was a sort of intellectual Thoreau, working out his individual insights and then generalizing them for all of humanity. He was, as was the rest of the Fuller community and, for that matter, most of neo-evangelicalism, largely individualistic in his approach to theology. Although Fuller itself was part of a wider attempt to build an intellectual community, its attempt was not based on the awareness that ideas do not get accepted by force of abstract argument alone but rather must take their place as part of a previously existing community tradition.[36]

In this respect Fuller scholars were thoroughly American and thoroughly modern. They assumed, as Americans characteristically had, that in the realm of ideas one could start again from the beginning rather than standing on the shoulders of their predecessors. They assumed, as modern people tended to, that scientifically—that is, rationally—defended truths, if well enough defended, would make it on their own. The fact was that they needed a living tradition to which to speak. This was for Fuller a parallel in the intellectual realm of the problems it faced in the financial realm. When breaking away from fundamentalism, would the school have any financial community of support? Cut off from both fundamentalism and mainline Protestantism, the seminary was in danger of having no intellectual constituency as well, as Carnell was discovering with painful chagrin.

Fortunately these liabilities were partially offset by some assets. Although largely cut off from the major institutions of American Protestantism, the new evangelicals were part of a genuinely conservative movement. Despite their rhetoric of newness and their apologetics that purported to start from scratch, much of what the neo-evangelicals promoted was broadly rooted in the American evangelical Protestant and Reformed traditions. These traditions had well preserved some intellectual interests, as the enthusiastic reception of *Christianity Today*, soon surpassing the *Christian Century* in paid circulation, testified. Moreover, an institution such as Fuller that promised liberation from the strictures of fundamentalism without abandoning evangelical orthodoxy had appeal for many young people. So the school was assured of student support, even as it suffered from some financial, institutional, and intellectual isolation.

THE TOKEN EVANGELICAL

Despite his continued frustration over not being taken seriously by the mainline Protestant intellectual community, Carnell's work cracked open the door

36. Stackhouse, "Pioneer," 65 and passim.

of the establishment's club. Like the token negroes who might grace a mainline church of the day, so long as they did not shout or clap, Carnell was becoming the "token fundamentalist" whose manners were good enough to grace the pages of mainline publications. To their credit, the ecumenists saw that the dialogue must turn to the right as well as to the left, as long as the right was willing to participate civilly for a change. For the neo-evangelicals, to have one of their own treated as though he were an equal in such august company was a novelty that had not been seen since Machen's early days. Generally they considered it a great triumph; though some warned that it was a danger, simply inviting concessions.

Carnell was using his opportunity not simply to impress the establishment with his urbanity and scholarship but also to present a real challenge. As Billy Graham's New York crusade approached, he wrote an article in the *Christian Century* in answer to a critique of Graham by Reinhold Niebuhr. Carnell conceded some of Niebuhr's points, agreeing that Graham promised too much to converts, as though personal and even social problems would disappear with the acceptance of the gospel. This amounted to a dangerous perfectionism, he acknowledged. On the other hand, while he heard a loud "No" from the dialectic theologian, he could hardly hear any "Yes." Preaching for decisions, as Graham did, was biblical, said Carnell. Moreover, when Niebuhr called upon Graham to do more for racial justice, he was not sufficiently taking into account the complexity of such problems. Negroes surely deserved equal housing opportunities, Carnell agreed; but if there were resultant declines in property values—itself a question of justice—the problem became immediately more complex.

Predictably, this latter remark obscured for his liberal audience everything else Carnell said and brought some indignant letters to the editor. It also illustrated once again that when the new evangelicals called boldly for more responsible evangelical social involvement, the applications of their principles were usually both cautious and conservative.[37]

Carnell repeated his central challenge to Niebuhr the next spring in *Christianity Today*. "If *Reinhold Niebuhr* has not succeeded in stirring New York City for Christ," he taunted, "what chance has Billy Graham?" The difference between Graham and Niebuhr for Carnell was that Neibuhr's profound Christian realism was little help to the man on the street.

> This, I assert, is the grand irony of Christian realism. Reinhold Niebuhr can prove that man is a sinner, but man already knows this. Reinhold Niebuhr can develop the dialectical relation between time and eternity, but this is beyond the tether of a dime store clerk or a hod

---

37. Carnell, "A Proposal to Reinhold Niebuhr," *Christian Century*, October 17, 1956, 1197-99; letters to the editor, *Christian Century*, November 21, 1956, 136. See also Lindsell, "The Bible and Race Relations," *Eternity*, August 1956, 12-13, 43-44, which, while condemning race prejudice, ends up saying that it would be more practical to have whites join black churches than the reverse.

carrier. When it comes to the acid test, therefore, realism is not very realistic after all. A concrete view of sin converts to an abstract view of salvation. And all of this is a direct fruit of realism's decision to mediate problems of Scripture from the perspective of man and history. For example, Reinhold Niebuhr does not speak about Christ's literal cross and resurrection at all. He speaks, at most, of the "symbols" of the cross and resurrection. But of what value are these symbols to an anxious New York cabby?[38]

Niebuhr did not reply; but the Protestant establishment was at least taking the new-style fundamentalists somewhat seriously. During 1958 *Christian Century* published two analyses of the strange phenomenon. Arnold Hearn reported in the first article that, contrary to the popular notion in mainline seminaries, fundamentalism was not dead and buried. Indeed, there was a "Fundamentalist Renascence," as evidenced by the impressive collection of authors that Carl Henry had assembled in two recent volumes he edited, *Contemporary Evangelical Thought* and *Revelation and the Bible*. Liberals, said Hearn, might have their own thinking honed by encountering this new generation of serious defenders of orthodoxy. "Given the right twist," Hearn ventured, " 'respectable' fundamentalism" might catch on.

The second *Christian Century* article was, from the Fuller Seminary point of view, a more painful critique. The author, Sherman Roddy, was the son of Fuller professor Clarence Roddy. The younger Roddy had little but disdain toward his former community, which he implied was psychologically destructive. The fundamentalist, he said in a standard formula for dismissing the entire movement, was "unable to come to terms with modern life. He is victim of fear at heart." Such fears distort their theology so that "God becomes the supreme sadist of the universe." While the neo-evangelicals had shed some of the fear and hence could be a bridge to ecumenical Christians, Roddy argued, they nonetheless lived in two worlds and did not seem to realize "that they have already destroyed fundamentalism's *raison d'etre*."[39]

Despite cultivating such critiques, ecumenical leaders were making some efforts to extend their dialogue to include these more civilized fundamentalists. The outstanding symbol for the new evangelicals of having "arrived" with the mainline establishment was the Westminster Press's choice of Carnell to write a volume on the topic "the case for orthodoxy." This would appear along with a volume on the case for neo-orthodoxy by William Hordern and one on the case for liberal theology by L. Harold DeWolf. Just to have orthodoxy presented as an option on a par with the other two was a triumph.

38. Carnell, "Can Billy Graham Slay the Giant?" *Christianity Today*, May 13, 1957, 3-5.
39. Arnold W. Hearn, "Fundamentalist Renascence," *Christian Century*, April 30, 1958, 527-30; Sherman Roddy, "Fundamentalists and Ecumenicity," *Christian Century*, October 1, 1958, 1109-10.

MILITANCY AGAINST FUNDAMENTALISM

Carnell was determined to make his book (given the final title *The Case for Orthodox Theology* and published in the spring of 1959) not only an engaging presentation of the faith but also a landmark in the new evangelical break from fundamentalism. This in itself was no small move psychologically for a fundamentalist preacher's son. Yet, since the RSV controversy and then the Woodbridge furor, Fuller's president was absolutely fed up with the fundamentalist mentality. He had already said as much in a scathing polemic in his article on fundamentalism in Meridian Books' *Handbook of Christian Theology*, which appeared early in 1958. But by the end of the year, Carnell observed to his surprise, no one had noticed. He was also a bit surprised that the fundamentalists semingly had not noticed that Fuller had hired as Woodbridge's replacement Geoffrey Bromiley of Scotland, an orthodox Calvinist who was also the translator of Karl Barth into English and thus might have been accused by the ultra-orthodox of aiding the enemy. Bromiley, however, proved to benefit from the diplomatic immunity that Britishers had always enjoyed in the fundamentalist world and from his own unimpeachable orthodoxy.[40]

That fundamentalists would notice *The Case for Orthodox Theology*, however, Carnell was making sure. Even Frank Gaebelein, known for his balanced opinions, was critical of an advance draft with its polemic against fundamentalism. Carnell dismissed such criticisms by remarking bluntly to Ockenga that this book would "separate the men from the boys theologically." He was convinced "that the hour to speak has come." He could easily have left out the polemic, but he thought it crucial to his appeal to a broader audience. The uncommitted university student, he argued, must be assured that biblical Christianity is not necessarily associated with "the intellectual dishonesty and the ethical hypocrisy of fundamentalism." Without courage to speak out, he told Ockenga, "sick and desperate" orthodoxy "will lose to either Rome or Neo-orthodoxy by default." Ockenga wrote that he was "in agreement with you on almost everything," save for a certain ex cathedra tone that was too biting. Carnell replied that from his experience with *Christian Commitment* he knew how disappointing it was to say provocative things and get no reaction. This time he would be heard.[41]

Carnell said a number of startling things in his volume. First, despite the nature of the series, he did not concentrate as much of his fire-power on neo-orthodoxy and theological liberalism as on fundamentalism. Clearly his major motive was to try to dislodge the notion, now fixed in the American religous mind for a generation, that all Protestant orthodoxy was a subspecies of fundamentalism. He would show that on the contrary fundamentalism was an aberrant subtype of orthodoxy. He thus defined fundamentalism as "orthodoxy gone cultic." It was characterized by "ideological thinking," which "is

40. EJC to HJO, 12-11-58, 8-1-58 (O)
41. EJC to HJO, 11-24-58; HJO to EJC, 12-9-58; EJC to HJO, 12-11-58 (O).

The British connection: Geoffrey Bromiley

rigid, intolerant, and doctrinaire." It is given to black and white views, "exempts itself from the limits that original sin places on history," ignores the role of self-interest and pride in its holy crusades, and hence "creates new evils while trying to correct old ones."

Fundamentalist ethics were just as intolerable, in his view. Their condemnations of smoking were necessary for status in the cult, but the same people said nothing of the similar dangers of coffee or tranquilizers. They would not be caught dead in a movie theater, but they watched movies on television in their homes. "Fundamentalists defend the gospel, to be sure, but they sometimes act as if the gospel read, 'Believe on the Lord Jesus Christ, don't smoke, don't go to movies, and above all don't use the Revised Standard Version—and you will be saved.'"

Carnell also repudiated the other fundamentalist distinctives: dispensationalism, separatism, and their handling of Scripture. He dismissed dispensationalism with some peremptory remarks, leaving the substantive attack on that issue to George Ladd and others. Nor was his attack on fundamentalist separatism a new departure. Ockenga had said as much in his "come-out-ism" speech of 1947, and now the Graham forces were raising a chorus against separatism as a test of faith. The *way* in which Carnell attacked separatism was, however, startling. He zeroed in on J. Gresham Machen, the apostle of intellectual fundamentalists, as the culprit. Machen, he said, manifested the very "cultic mentality" that was the worst feature of fundamentalism. He "took an absolute stand on a relative issue, and the wrong issue at that."

Machen's misguided campaign against the Presbyterian church, said Carnell, simply reflected a defective view of the nature of the church.[42]

Such rough treatment of the hero of his own movement risked alienating even some who agreed in principle. Those who did not agree were, of course, thoroughly outraged. A reviewer in the theological journal of Westminster Seminary, where Machen was considered only to have restated the views of the apostle Paul, said that he shuddered every time he looked at the chapter entitled "Perils" and saw the listing: "1. Fundamentalism, 2. J. Gresham Machen, 3. Dispensationalism, 4. Intellectual Stagnation. . . ."[43]

Not only did Carnell guarantee alienating several constituencies by his dismissive treatment of various pillars of fundamentalism, he also raised some questions about the nature of his belief in the inerrancy of Scripture, thus allowing everyone offended room for counterattack. While not giving up his commitment to "inerrancy," Carnell seemed determined to allow as much latitude as possible in interpreting what that meant. In his earlier work, he had simply endorsed the classic Princeton view of B. B. Warfield and A. A. Hodge. Now, however, he presented Warfield and Hodge as only one orthodox option. Another school within orthodoxy, he emphasized, was that represented by James Orr, the turn-of-the-century Scottish apologist. Orr had argued that defending the " 'inerrancy' of the Biblical record, down even to its minutest details," was "a most suicidal position." Carnell simply said that "the dialogue betwen Orr and Princeton Theology was never successfully terminated."

The relationship of the very highest views of inspiration to obvious difficulties in reconciling conflicting biblical accounts had been a matter of intense discussion among Fuller faculty. Carnell now thought he had a solution. Authors of Scripture who used written sources (such as the author of the Chronicles) might have given infallible accounts of what the fallible sources had said, just as the author of Acts may have unerringly reported the sermon of Stephen, which appeared to contain a misquotation. This solution, said Carnell, would have allowed Hodge and Warfield to face the inductive difficulties of Scripture more frankly, and it might have allowed Orr to affirm inerrancy.[44]

This compromise, which Carnell himself admitted might seem "like a very desperate expedient," was too clever to appeal to very many readers. A generally sympathetic reviewer in a Southern Baptist journal remarked that Carnell's way around the issue "leaves us still blushing."[45]

From real fundamentalists the chorus of protest was sustained and scathing. Probably most damaging to Fuller Seminary was that of John R. Rice of the *Sword of the Lord.* Still smarting from the Billy Graham split, Rice headlined his attack, "FULLER SEMINARY'S CARNELL SNEERS AT

42. All quotes in the above three paragraphs are from Carnell, *The Case for Orthodox Theology* (Philadelphia: Westminster, 1959), 113-26.
43. Robert E. Nicholas, review of Carnell's *Case for Orthodox Theology* in *Westminster Theological Journal* 22 (November 1959): 91.
44. Carnell, *The Case for Orthodox Theology,* 101, 111.
45. Dale Moody, review of Carnell's *Case for Orthodox Theology* in *Review and Expositor,* April 1960, 204.

FUNDAMENTALISM." Rice provided lengthy quotations to show that Carnell attacked Warfield and Hodge, claimed that all of Scripture was not equally inspired, endorsed organic evolution, repudiated premillennialism, and derided fundamentalist mores and separatism. Rice aimed his attack where it was sure to hurt most, at Charles Fuller. The seminary, he pointed out, was "made possible only by the support of fundamentalists." "What will Fuller Seminary do about Dr. Carnell?" he asked. If it did not repudiate him, then it must be officially endorsing him. In that case, said Rice, "I do not believe that out-and-out Bible believers can safely send students to Fuller Seminary or send any money to support the seminary. . . ."[46]

The usual flood of mail to Charles Fuller followed. Harold Lindsell, as dean of the faculty and chief executive on the scene at the seminary, drafted replies. In a general statement, he explained that there were two kinds of fundamentalists. "Right wing" fundamentalists "not only fight unbelief or modernism but Bible-believing Christians who do not follow them in all their opinions." By contrast the "orthodoxy" that Carnell defended, while not differing on fundamental doctrines, was marked by an attitude of love. Lindsell himself, however, was not any more gentle toward fundamentalists such as John R. Rice than Carnell had been. In a letter to Rice he wrote that he considered him highly inconsistent in lauding Warfield, Hodge, and Machen who were not premillennialists and who did not share the characteristic fundamentalist mores. "Moreover," said Lindsell, "you have either ignorantly, or deliberately, but falsely accused Dr. Carnell of saying that all parts of the Bible are not equally inspired." A born debater, Lindsell turned Carnell's most vulnerable point into an asset. "Dr. Carnell is so strong for the inspiration of the Scriptures," he argued, "that he insists that in some instances we have an infallible record of error."[47] As he and Charles Fuller always did in their standard responses to inquirers, Lindsell enclosed a copy of the Fuller doctrinal statement, noting that the faculty signed it each year. Rice refused to publish Lindsell's entire letter, however, and added his own commentary.

Fuller Seminary continued to get it from all sides of fundamentalism. At Wheaton, Illinois, home of both the *Sword of the Lord* and of Wheaton College, Fuller's key supporting college, the seminary sponsored a roundtable discussion including some particularly vocal critics from Grace Theological Seminary in Winona Lake, Indiana. George Ladd stood in for Carnell, who by then was attempting to get some respite. Grace Seminary later held its own follow-up roundtable to once again rake the book over the coals.[48]

The evangelist Bob Jones, Sr., culminated a long-impending break with Charles Fuller over the Carnell book. Writing to Fuller early in 1960, Jones recalled their earlier days when they both had high hopes for the NAE.

46. John R. Rice, review of Carnell's *Case for Orthodox Theology* in *Sword of the Lord*, October 30, 1959, 1, 7, 11.
47. HL, draft of statement, n.d.; HL to John R. Rice, 11-10-59, 12-30-59.
48. The Wheaton discussion was held December 4, 1959, and was financed by the new Fuller trustee, Gerrit Groen of Wheaton. The Grace Seminary discussion was held December 15. See Charles Fuller papers, "Carnell and Controversy" file.

Now, however, he asked him as an old friend whether he would provide a statement denouncing compromise to be read in the Bob Jones University chapel. Otherwise, he said, he would take "The Old Fashioned Revival Hour" off the school's radio station. Too many students, said Jones, kept asking whether Fuller's program endorsed Fuller Seminary and, if so, how the university could continue to broadcast it. Fuller would not comply. The two old evangelists parted cordially and a bit sadly. To another inquirer, Fuller drafted a letter excusing Carnell on the grounds that he had completed the assignment when he was suffering from a nervous breakdown, and hence "he did not always express himself too clearly."[49]

COLLAPSE

The real psychological crisis for Carnell, however, did not come until after he had completed the book and left the presidency. At that time he immediately took a sabbatical leave in order to rest, devote himself to writing, and especially to try to gain some tranquility. While he was not in a state of total collapse and did continue to write, he was staggering from periods of deep depression. To Charles Fuller he wrote in January 1960 that he was recovering from the strains of the past years except for insomnia but that he had inherited from his mother a "nervous temperament" and that "the various crises of the presidency . . . stripped me of courage to face responsibility without nervous fear."[50]

With the assumption apparently prevailing that Carnell would be fine after a little rest, his neo-evangelical colleagues became concerned about his theological stability. After leaving the presidency, Carnell published in the *Christian Century* two articles repeating many of his accusations against "cultic fundamentalism." Even Ockenga, formerly Carnell's chief promoter, now spoke as though Carnell's views might be threatening both the seminary and the evangelical cause. Ockenga had recently been taking sharp criticism about Carnell, not from fundamentalists, however, but from some of the key friends of the new evangelical cause. "One of our very good friends of Fuller," he told Carnell, thought he was conceding too much to the enemy. Another "erudite friend of yours and mine" suggested that Carnell must be angling for an appointment at a liberal school. Another said simply, "This is treason." Ockenga had clearly cooled in his support. While he agreed with many of Carnell's points, he disagreed with using a modernist journal to wage a running battle against fundamentalists. He told Carnell that he should not forget that "our real enemy is the modernist." Implying that Carnell might need some help, Ockenga offered to read the manuscript of his present book and suggested that at least he submit it to his colleagues.[51]

49. Bob Jones, Sr., to CF, 1-16-60, 1-25-60; CF to Bob Jones, Sr., 1-22-60; draft of letter, CF to "Brother Mills," n.d.
    50. EJC to CF, 1-2-60.
    51. HJO to EJC, 5-6-60 (O).

Carnell replied coolly that the "verdict of history" was not yet in on the wisdom of attacking the cultic elements in fundamentalism. He had received many letters of encouragement concerning the substance, if not always the tone, of what he had written. As to Fuller Seminary, he thought there were now signs pointing toward the long-standing goal of acceptance by mainline denominations. Had Ockenga changed his mind about that goal?[52]

Despite such displays of confidence, the world was on the verge of caving in on Carnell mentally. In his academic life, he still felt the wound over the failure of *Christian Commitment*. His subsequent apologetic work, *The Kingdom of Love and the Pride of Life* (1960) was more modest, gentle, and artful than his other books. He had been reading Freud and was impressed by the coincidence of the insights of modern psychology and what he himself was seeing more and more as the heart of the gospel. Christian apologetics, he argued, picking up the theme of his ill-fated inaugural address, must add to its repertoire an appeal to the universal need for love. Jesus' observation that we must become like little children to overcome our self-destructive pride and lust for power was only repeated in modern psychology's recommendation that we must recapture childlike openness and spontaneity.

Carnell himself, rather than mastering such spontaneity, and perhaps because at the same time he saw the ideal so clearly, was being destroyed by an inwardness that bred guilt and anxiety. At age forty, with spectacular successes behind him, he felt not only a sense of nowhere else to go, but even a failure at what he had already done. His books, while gaining polite respect, had not made him the Tillich of evangelicalism. He was too liberal for the fundamentalists and too fundamentalist for the liberals. His attempts to temper fundamentalism with charity had only focused fundamentalist wrath on himself. His old nemesis Charles Woodbridge, for instance, was now proclaiming that neo-evangelicalism with its "love, not doctrine," was "the worst menace that has confronted the church since the time of Luther."[53] And the presidency? Carnell had fled in disarray. "At times I suffer great guilt feelings," he confided to Ockenga. "But I could not help myself. My emotions simply got out of hand." He had "never realized that it was possible to suffer such intense inwardness, while all the time giving the outward impression that all is well." Anxiety sometimes overwhelmed him "with the force of a terrible tidal wave."[54]

By this time, early in 1961, he was undergoing therapy with the same psychiatrist who had brought Clarence Roddy out of a long depression. Carnell and Roddy were only the two best-known cases from what over the years was a distressingly high number of serious psychological crises or breakdowns among Fuller's faculty. Carnell's case was the most severe. By the summer of

52. EJC to HJO, 5-14-60, 5-9-60 (O).
53. G. Archer Weniger, "New Evangelicalism: Trusted Leaders Say," *Sword of the Lord*, clipping, ca. fall 1962, quoting Charles Woodbridge, March 1961 statement "before three thousand people" at Bob Jones University.
54. EJC to HJO, 1-23-61 (O).

1961 he had to be hospitalized and was brought out of deep depression only by a major series of shock treatments. He was also put under the care of a psychoanalyst, reputed to be a Freudian. After his release from the hospital, Carnell still suffered guilt feelings "for having failed as president," and for his inability to take speaking engagements. "I am afraid I am going to vomit if I try to preach," he wrote to Ockenga.[55] In February 1962 he was hospitalized again for five weeks and after his release continued to receive weekly shock treatments.

"ONCE MORE TO THE LISTS"

In between recurring bouts of depression he continued to function more or less normally. By late April he had remarkably pulled himself together enough to make his last major appearance in his controversial role as guest evangelical in the ecumenical lion's den. The occasion was Karl Barth's much-heralded tour of the United States. Carnell had received the great honor of being asked to be one of the "young theologians" to question Barth during the Swiss theologian's appearance at the University of Chicago. For Carnell, the exhilaration of the honor was soon tempered by the usual sharp fundamentalist, and now also evangelical, criticisms.

Appearing before overflow audiences that jammed the University of Chicago's Rockefeller Chapel, the panel of young theologians included Jerald Brauer, Hans Frei, Jakob Petuchowski, Bernard Cooke, Schubert Ogden, William Stringfellow, and Carnell. Each could ask Barth several written questions submitted in advance. Central to Carnell's questions was the intellectual point around which the new evangelicalism had come to center, the inerrancy of Scripture. "How does Dr. Barth," asked Carnell, "harmonize his appeal to Scripture, as the objective Word of God, with his admission that Scripture is, indeed sullied by errors, theological as well as historical or factual?" No doubt fearing that he would look like an unthinking fundamentalist, Carnell added to his written question the candid parenthetical observation "(This is a problem for me, too, I cheerfully confess.)" Barth answered that the Bible was a true and fitting instrument to point man to God, who alone is infallible. So the Bible contained "'errors' in its time-bound human statements." To this latter remark Barth added: "Is that enough to encourage you to continue to cheerfully confess that here is a problem for you?"

Jaroslav Pelikan, moderating the sessions, underscored this concluding comment more than Carnell might have wanted. "That is just another way of saying 'Welcome to the Club,'" he quipped. Carnell declined to press the subject further.[56]

55. EJC to HJO, 6-25-61 (O).
56. "Introduction to Theology: Questions to and Discussion with Dr. Karl Barth, Wednesday April 25, 1962 and Thursday April 26, 1962" (transcript), *Criterion*, Winter 1963, 11, 18.

Gordon Clark was in the audience and let those around him know his displeasure with Carnell's soft stance on Scripture.[57] Apparently he also confronted Carnell between the sessions and told his former student how distressed he was by his recent stances. Any line of intellectual succession that might have been thought to run from Machen to Clark to Carnell was absolutely severed as far as Clark was concerned. Clark also wrote a news story on the event for *Christianity Today* in which he made clear that Carnell seemed to make some concessions to Barth and had declined to argue for an inerrant Bible.[58]

The fundamentalist network of innuendo went into operation as word went around that Carnell had confessed that there were errors in the Bible and had been welcomed into the Chicago liberals' club.[59] Carnell returned to Fuller both as a hero and amid fears that he had once again created a scandal. At a special semimary chapel gathering he reported on his encounter with Barth. Concerning his views on Scripture, he said that anyone who read his *Case for Orthodox Theology* could see what he meant by having problems; but then he added, "I want to make it as clear as the English language can put it, that I now believe and always have believed in the plenary inspiration of Scripture and the inerrancy of Scripture." He signed the seminary statement of faith each year with full sincerity, he noted, and suggested that "if anybody in any part of the country is interested in what I believe, I hope he will be man enough to write and ask me." The seminary made Carnell's remarks available on tape for alumni and, in response to Clark, Harold Lindsell wrote to *Christianity Today* quoting the text of Carnell's statement on Scripture.[60]

Carnell also expressed his criticism of Barth in the *Christian Century*. He said that Barth's approach to Scripture could not keep evangelicals from falling into the morass of subjectivism in determining what of Scripture they should accept. On the other hand, Carnell strongly affirmed that he was not going to join the fundamentalists' "holy war" against Barth. Barth was "an inconsistent evangelical," Carnell insisted, not an inconsistent liberal. Here he took the occasion to vent some of his suffering at being cut off from his former mentors and from much of fundamentalism. "I felt actual physical pain," he wrote, "when I read in *Time* magazine that Cornelius Van Til, one of my former professors, had said that Barthianism is more hostile to the Reformers than is Roman Catholicism." Van Til, Carnell proposed, should "ask God to forgive him for such an irresponsible judgment."

As to "extreme fundamentalists," Carnell summarized his agonized conclusion at what was virtually the end of his productive career:

57. Conversation with Richard Mouw, 1983. Mouw claims to have sat beside Clark at the forum.
58. Gordon Clark, "Special Report: Encountering Barth in Chicago," *Christianity Today*, May 11, 1962, 35-36.
59. Vernon Charles Lyons, "Fuller Professor Denies Bible," typed reprint from *Sword of the Lord*, ca. May 1963.
60. Tape of Carnell's report on Barth discussion, FTS chapel, May 1962; Lindsell, letter to the editor, *Christianity Today*, June 8, 1962, 19-20.

Awaken from slumber! If you try to upgrade your own estate by downgrading the estate of others, God will see to it that you become a victim of your own cruel standard. Scripture is clear: "judge not, that you be not judged. For with the judgment you pronounce you will be judged, and the measure you give will be the measure you get" (Matt. 7:1-2, RSV).[61]

61. Carnell, "Barth as Inconsistent Evangelical," *Christian Century*, June 6, 1961, 713-14.

CHAPTER XI

The Crisis and the Turning

So you see, as everyone realizes, our Seminary is split straight down the middle on the most important single question, apart from the Deity of Christ, that can be considered by Christian people.

Wilbur Smith to Billy Graham, December 3, 1962.

INTERREGNUM

CHARLES Fuller was worried about his seminary. During the 1959–60 school year the aging evangelist had on his hands an institution that lacked leadership and any clear direction. Not only had its youthful president suddenly resigned, he had left a whirl of controversy that was costing "The Old Fashioned Revival Hour" painful losses with each day's mail. Ockenga was acting president, but was busy with other things and was still living in Boston. Fuller's son Dan, on whom his parents' hopes for the seminary's future rested, was in Switzerland studying with Karl Barth. Dan had argued persuasively that he must have the highest European credentials if he and the seminary were to make an impact in the scholarly world, and the elder Fullers were confident that he would stand strong in the den of neo-orthodoxy. They were proud to learn that he had won a coveted fellowship, but saddened also that this honor guaranteed that their only son and his family would be away a second year or longer.

The elder Fullers had by this time come to rely on Dan for most of their opinions about the seminary. Among these was the assurance that, despite the current storm from irate radio listeners, Carnell had carried the seminary in the proper direction. Whoever the next president should be, Charles Fuller had remarked on a number of occasions, he should continue Carnell's policies.

Harold Lindsell, as dean, was filling much of the power vacuum by taking over many of the executive functions. In February 1960 he wrote to Fuller, with some apparent unease, about the oft-repeated statement that the seminary should continue the thrust of Carnell's policies. "I think a most useful purpose would be served if you would put down on paper what you think this thrust is. It will serve as a useful guide now and in the future, for we would like to have such an expression from the Founder. And who is better equipped than our Founder to do this?" Drawing on his debating skills, Lindsell—who considered himself in the Ockenga camp and opposed claiming

Carnell as a champion of real change—put Fuller in the corner with his next paragraph. "It seems to me that it would be well to ask, at the same time, whether the thrust you have in mind is the same as that enunciated by Dr. Ockenga when the school was founded. If it differs from Dr. Ockenga's thrust in what do these differences consist?"[1]

The next month yielded a flurry of discussion, enough of which has survived to provide revealing insights into the seminary's dynamics at this crucial juncture.

Precipitating the intense reflection on the seminary's future was not only the discussion about Lindsell's request, but, far more importantly, Charles Fuller's announcement that he thought he had found his candidate for the next president. His choice was David Hubbard, a Fuller graduate only thirty-two years old. Hubbard had unusual promise. He was well-known around the seminary, having stayed on after graduation in 1952 to serve two years as student assistant to William LaSor and to complete a Th.M. He then studied at St. Andrews University in Scotland where he received a Ph.D. in Old Testament and Semitics in 1957. Since then he had been teaching at Westmont College in Santa Barbara, where the Fullers had one of their homes. When they were there, the Fullers attended a local Evangelical Covenant church where Hubbard sometimes preached. Fuller was so impressed that he tried out the idea of a Hubbard presidency on a number of the faculty and then in February 1960 met with Hubbard himself, for whom the suggestion came as a bolt from the blue.

At a second meeting Charles and Grace Fuller met with Hubbard and a fourth person, who was doing his best to manage the direction of the seminary and yet remain in the shadows. Paul Jewett, who had become the confidant and advisor of the Fullers, was frankly filling in for the absent Dan, with whom he had formed a close alliance. Jewett's presence at this crucial moment was a sign that a minor revolution had already taken place and that the scene was set for a major struggle for control. Ten years earlier, it would have been Wilbur Smith advising the Fullers. Indeed, just before his presidency Carnell had explained how to advance a policy: "Convince the trustees; sell it to the Fullers and the Smiths; persuade the faculty." Now Smith was no longer in the inner circle and could only guess at the inside stories. Jewett meanwhile had become the key liaison with the Fullers; he had even ghost-written a number of their recent publications.[2]

The same evening as this second Hubbard interview, Jewett and the Fullers discussed Lindsell's letter. Jewett viewed it as ominous. It might, he thought, be an attempt to get Charles to reaffirm as founder the school's commitment to premillennialism, thus reversing the hard-won victory of Car-

---

1. HL to CF, 2-15-60. Perhaps related is a letter from CH to HJO, 2-7-60 (O), suggesting that under Carnell's presidency the seminary had departed from its original vision regarding faculty memberships in major denominations, corporate production of seminary-level literature, and a strong positive voice on social issues.
2. PKJ to HJO, undated (ca. 4-60?) (O). EJC to HJO, 2-12-54 (O).

All on the same stage—the seminary faculty in 1959 with the founder and the chairman of the board of trustees. Seated: Rebecca Price, Harold Lindsell, Edward Carnell, Harold Ockenga, Charles Fuller, Wilbur Smith, Clarence Roddy, William LaSor; standing: Geoffrey Bromiley, Carlton Booth, Everett Harrison, Gleason Archer, Lars Granberg, Paul Jewett, William Lantz, George Ladd, and Daniel Fuller. Absent is Robert Bower.

199

nell and Jewett, who had persuaded Fuller to say that premillennialism could be abandoned after his death. Jewett in fact thought there should be an entirely new creed, primarily to eliminate premillennialism though secondarily because he thought the article on Scripture inhibited honest discussion. Jewett's overall agenda was to commit the school to classic Calvinism without any of the additional doctrinal tests devised in the fundamentalist era.

With this program in mind, Jewett was tepid about the proposal of Hubbard for president. While he liked much of what Hubbard said, the young man's background was dispensationalist, and he still bore some of the marks of his fundamentalist heritage. Hubbard admired Carnell but was sharply critical of his recent attacks on ecclesiastical separatism in *The Case for Orthodox Theology*. Moreover, Hubbard, who was a biblical scholar, was unwilling to say that systematic theology was the queen of the sciences. Most importantly, though, he was only vaguely Reformed theologically.[3]

THE HEIR APPARENT

The Fullers and Jewett both reported the conversations to Dan, who was still pivotal to any decision making despite his absence. Dan himself had not sought leadership. He was a scholar's scholar, retiring and modest, eager to stay out of the limelight that his worldwide fame as part of a radio family had thrust upon him. One of his great fears was that, upon his father's passing, he might be expected to take over "The Old Fashioned Revival Hour." Popularity, with the maneuvering and role-playing it took to sustain it, held no appeal for him. He distrusted popular scholars who wrote "flashy books that will create a quick big splash." Brought up in a fundamentalist environment where the "truth" was always proclaimed as paramount, the younger Fuller had an unrelenting dedication to principle. In his biblical scholarship his goal was no less than to find the objective truth, what actually happened. Salesmanship, political intrigue, and the wheeling and dealing of those in power were alien to his spirit.[4]

Dan's response to his parents' account of the Hubbard conference was that it might take a while for Hubbard to learn the realities of what could be changed in a seminary curriculum but that, despite his lack of Calvinism, he would be satisfactory if he was truly dedicated to taking the seminary in the direction Carnell had pointed it. Dan's main concern, though, was to see that, in answer to Lindsell's inquiry, his parents fully understood what Carnell's direction implied. To Dan this meant not the details of Carnell's apologetic but the larger issue that had put him and the seminary in so much hot water: his challenge to the fundamentalists to stop relying on stock formulas and name calling and to defend the truth intellectually.

3. PKJ to DF, 2-22-60; PKJ to HJO, undated (ca. 4-60?).
4. DF interviews, fall 1983; quotation from DF to CF and Grace Fuller, 2-25-60. Daniel Fuller's candor and his view of history was evident throughout my interviews with him and was well summarized in his remark, "I don't care how I look, as long as it is the way it was."

With characteristic candor, Dan bared his heart in a letter to his parents concerning his whole intellectual outlook and how it bore on his views of Scripture. His outlook was indeed alien to the European intellectual environment. It was closer to the philosophical base that had long nourished much of American evangelicalism and fundamentalism: Scottish Common Sense philosophy. As nineteenth-century American evangelical apologists typically had done, Dan insisted on starting with the "canons for verifying truth which all men agree to except those who are insane." If the Bible were indeed God's book, superior to all merely human writings, then the Bible should be capable of defense in the open market of ideas according to intellectual standards on which all candid inquirers could agree. If Christians were faithful to this principle, then only the lack of grace and hence fallen humanity's perverse love of untruth, not the lack of good arguments for Christianity, could explain unbelief.

To maintain this high ideal, however, evangelicals would have to face up to one colossal error in the way they typically defended the faith. By insisting that the "Bible is without error 'in whole and in part,'" and at the same time paying lip service to their openness to the latest archaeological findings, fundamentalists had made a joke of their claims that Scripture met the highest intellectual standards. "Unbelief laughs and I see no reason why I should not laugh with them."

Some of the chronologies in Scripture, Fuller explained to his parents, were simply wrong, and, although the errors were innocent bookkeeping errors, it was an apologetic disaster to act as though such errors in detail did not exist. It made a sham of evangelical claims to take history seriously on such vitally important matters as the fact of the Resurrection. So the Fuller Seminary creed should be revised to say that the infallibilty of the Bible had to do with its statements on faith and practice, not its precision of historical detail. "How tragic," he observed, "that we went overboard so on this in order to make it too hot for Vassady." He also knew, as a matter of fact, that the current creed made it too hot for Jewett as well, who had resorted to letting Carnell teach the parts of his systematics course that dealt with the doctrine of Scripture. As for Dan, he was anticipating trying out his views on his seminary colleagues to "see whether the Faculty can blow holes in it."

Dan's remaining suggestions were consistent with his high view of truth seeking. Fuller should hire only the best scholars, he said. They must be pious evangelicals but should not be limited in their intellectual explorations by an arbitrary test of premillennial beliefs. The school furthermore should pay them enough to enable them to write only technical theological works, not pot-boilers. Sabbatical policy should also encourage study outside the Anglo-Saxon world, in contrast to what had become standard for the faculty. The scholars should always be ready to defend the logic of their position to all comers, especially students.[5]

5. The quotations in the above paragraph are all from DF to CF and Grace Fuller, 2-25-60.

Filled with these lofty ideals for the seminary and his own scholarly future, Dan received the next day Jewett's largely negative account of the Hubbard interview. From Jewett's account, Hubbard did not sound like the person who would take the uncompromising stands for the truth and technical scholarship that Dan envisioned. Besides, he was not a dedicated Calvinist and he also sided with ecclesiastical separatists against Carnell.

Discouraged, then, by the dashing of some of his high hopes for Hubbard, Dan had a brainstorm. He himself could become president once he had finished his studies. Being the heir apparent, he would have the leverage and the respect to bring to pass the reforms he envisioned. He had always assumed, as had everyone else who knew him, that he would be miserable in administration. But why not carry out the vision?[6] Although Dan's presidential aspiration proved short-lived, it apparently did launch something of a "draft Dan Fuller" movement during the spring of 1960, of which Paul Jewett was among the supporters.

At about the same time, Jewett mentioned to Ockenga that he was hearing, especially at Lake Avenue Church, of a "draft Lindsell" movement.[7] Ockenga himself looked favorably on Lindsell as a possibility, and many people thought Lindsell was a candidate. In April 1960, however, Ockenga conducted a poll of the presidential choices of board and faculty members. Eleven names were mentioned: Dan Fuller led the list with five nominations, David Hubbard still had four, and Carl Henry had two, but Lindsell was not mentioned.[8]

Hubbard's candidacy, in the meantime, had been put on the shelf. Charles Fuller—who had, in an apparently ghostwritten answer to Lindsell,[9] left the door open for a change of mind—went personally to the faculty in early April to say that Hubbard's candidacy had met "a definite check from the trustee's level." Wilbur Smith, clearly no longer on the inside, could remark only that "suddenly something happened, exactly what I do not know and the whole matter was dropped."[10] Speculations about Dan Fuller's presidency continued to be widespread at least into the summer, though Dan himself soon thought better of the idea.

A POWER BASE

By now the faculty was roughly aligned into progressive and conservative camps over the choice of president, and a full-scale power struggle, replete with maneuvering and intrigue, was building. Crucial to the outcome was that the progressive side was beginning to build up some organizational structure. Donald Weber was the key figure. Intensely devoted to his brother-in-law Carnell, and in full agreement with Carnell's break with fundamentalism,

6. DF to CF, 2-26-60.
7. PKJ to HJO, undated (ca. 4-60?).
8. HJO interview, 11-6-83; HJO report on presidential preferences, 5-12-60 (O).
9. CF to HL, 3-16-60.
10. WS to CH, 6-30-60 (WS).

Weber filled as much of the power gap as he could when Carnell abdicated. This brought him into intense conflict with Lindsell, as both were trying to run the school during the interregnum.

In this cool war atmosphere, Weber was building structures to support the progressive cause. Late in Carnell's presidency he had initiated a successful program of dramatically increasing the strength of the board of trustees. Prior to Carnell's presidency, having a board had been largely a formality, since the real decisions were made at Charles Fuller's dining room table—as was still the case to an extent in the spring of 1960. In the early days the support from the Fuller Evangelistic Foundation meant that the trustees did not need to be a major source of funds. Now, with that support fading, Weber was in the process of putting the seminary on a new financial base of wealthy and loyal trustees.

Finances were a major concern, but Weber and Carnell were also looking for the right sort of loyalty. Just as Carnell retired in the spring of 1959, they secured his legacy with the addition of two especially capable and distinctly nonfundamentalist trustees. Gerrit P. Groen was a highly accomplished patent lawyer with a national reputation. He was a member of the Christian Reformed Church, a denomination that had long guarded classic Calvinist orthodoxy but that also included a talented and scholarly progressive party. Formal contacts with the Christian Reformed Church had been limited at Fuller because the denomination contained few premillennialists. In Groen's case, the premillennial requirement was, in effect, quietly ignored.[11] Groen was also enthusiastic about Carnell's critique of fundamentalism; in fact, he hosted and financed George Ladd's December 1959 appearance at Wheaton College to defend Carnell's views.[12] His early death from cancer in 1964 removed Groen from Fuller, but he played a significant role for the progressives during some crucial years.

Unquestionably the most important addition to the board of trustees was C. Davis Weyerhaeuser, director of the immensely successful Weyerhaeuser Timber Company of Tacoma, Washington. Weyerhaeuser had a full-fledged fundamentalist background, though contrary to stereotypes about fundamentalism he had also been educated with America's elite at Phillips Academy, Andover, and Yale. When the Fuller people first contacted him, he was on the board of Moody Bible Institute, a fact that made Ockenga wary of Weyerhaeuser's leanings. "I am anxious to know if he entertains the mentality of fundamentalism," he wrote to Carnell in December 1958. "One such man on our Board is enough for me—Ed Johnson. . . . If we don't get men who are clearly behind classic orthodoxy, we will invite a scrap between administration and the Board."[13]

Ockenga soon found that "the mentality of fundamentalism" was

11. PKJ to DF, 2-22-60.
12. George Ladd to CF? 12-59 (Charles Fuller papers, "Carnell and Controversy" file).
13. HJO to EJC, 12-8-58 (O).

hardly his worry about Weyerhaeuser. The lumber executive was in the midst of his own break with fundamentalism. Shortly after accepting the Fuller position, he resigned from Moody, offering its president, William Culbertson, a lengthy explanation. Though he could still call himself a "fundamentalist," he thought that fundamentalism had warped the Christian message by majoring on the minor in its demand for "separation" as the mark of the Christian life. As fundamentalists stressed the "big five" sins—smoking, drinking, dancing, card-playing, and theater attendance—they neglected the weightier fruits of the spirit.

> I became increasingly aware that the average man on the street possesses an extremely distorted notion of what Christianity is because of fundamentalism's emphasis on certain specific don'ts, its divisiveness, and the tragic lack of manifest Christian love. In the experience of many unbelievers, a fundamentalist is one who will not smoke but who will not hesitate to split a church; who will not go near a theatre, but who sees nothing wrong in murdering another person's character; who will not play cards, but who will make no effort to establish helpful social contacts (outside of his narrow circle) according to the admonition of our Lord that we should be the salt of the earth.

Weyerhaeuser thought it more important, for instance, to learn to play bridge with his son or to go out to a movie with his daughter than to continue to hold the line on the fundamentalist "separated life."[14]

Weyerhaeuser's candid sentiments illustrate that the new evangelical break with fundamentalism was quietly attracting a new constituency as well as driving away part of the older one. A generation that had been raised on the fundamentalism of the 1930s and 1940s was coming to maturity. Some kept to the letter of the faith; others left it entirely. An important segment, however, had broadening experiences like Weyerhaeuser's. They were deeply committed to the evangelical faith but desperately wanted to be free from needless stumbling blocks. The Carnell–Fuller Seminary agenda fit their outlook exactly.

The break with fundamentalism, however, was also fostering among the new evangelicals a coalition of persons with somewhat differing positive programs. The early Fuller had been dominated by those, such as Ockenga, who broke with classic fundamentalism in order to get back to something more truly conservative: classic Calvinist orthodoxy. Some of the new generation of reformers, especially Jewett and Dan Fuller, also had this motive in mind. On the other hand, the early Fuller had always tempered zeal for orthodoxy with the openness necessary for effective evangelism in the style of Charles Fuller and Billy Graham, a concern that the new reformers also shared. Outside the circle of professional theologians, the latter motive for openness was more

14. CDW to Moody president William Culbertson, ca. 1-60; see also a similar letter to President V. Raymond Edman of Wheaton College, 1-4-60, from which a phrase or two in this summary is taken (SS).

compelling than any zeal for Calvinism. Protestant orthodoxy held the attraction of not being fundamentalism; and the evangelical flexibility on detail fit the practical emphases of the tradition. The movement was thus able to embrace a wide coalition. The original generation of Fuller's founders were divided on how far to stray from fundamentalism, especially regarding the doctrine of Scripture; and even the more progressive among them were divided over whether the revolution should lead to classic Calvinism or a more pragmatic openness.

MANEUVERING

The power vacuum remained the outstanding immediate issue. As always, the chief hope for many was that Ockenga could be persuaded to become resident president and thus restore the peace. With this in mind, the thc board issued him another formal invitation early in 1961. Ockenga declined, but in doing so forged a temporary compromise. He would again serve as president in Boston (he was already acting president); but Lindscll would be promoted from dean to a strong on-the-scene vice president. At the same time Dan Fuller would be appointed dean of the faculty.

   The latter part of the compromise required some persuasion of Dan Fuller, who remained engrossed in his beloved scholarly pursuits in Switzerland. Since his flirtation with the presidency, Dan had concluded with some certainty that scholarship rather than administration was his calling. Ockenga visited Dan in Europe and asked him to become dean, but Dan turned him down. Nonetheless, during the board meetings in the spring of 1961 Don Weber sent an urgent special delivery letter to Dan insisting that he accept the deanship to prevent a takeover by Lindsell as the on-campus executive backed by a distant Ockenga's presidential power. The result, Weber warned, would be the elimination of freedom of speech and an insistence on the strict old Princeton party line on Scripture.

   Receiving this unwelcome appeal in the midst of studying critiques of Bultmann, Dan turned to prayer to confirm his resolution to stick to scholarship and teaching. His earlier decision had been based on the verse in Romans 12 in which the apostle Paul said that those who had the gift of teaching should teach. At prayer, however, Fuller asked that the Lord send him a Scripture verse to tell him if he were wrong. All of a sudden a verse that he had not thought of for years popped into his mind—1 Timothy 5:17, which said that those who both taught and ruled should be worthy of a double portion. With this apparent answer to his prayer, Dan felt that he could no longer say no, despite his sense that he had no administrative talents and despite his deepest desire that someone else head off the Lindsell-Ockenga takeover. So, while the board was still meeting, he reluctantly wired back that he would accept the nomination, effective upon his return the next year.[15]

   Placing Dan in the deanship was a crucial part of the efforts to

15. Interview with DF, 10-21-83.

strengthen the progressive party. Already at the same 1961 board meeting another major gain had been secured with the election of Weyerhaeuser as chairman of the board. Weyerhaeuser had great interest in the seminary, amplified by great resources that enabled him to effect his vision. Thanks to his leadership, the seminary was set for groundbreaking for a new library in the fall.

In addition, the board also added J. Laurence Kulp, who would be another immensely influential member in the coming years. Kulp, professor of biophysics and director of Lamont Geological Observatory at Columbia University, had, like so many of the Fuller people, been at Wheaton in the pre–World War II era. In the fundamentalist-evangelical scientific community he was one of the outstanding progressives, controversial for his defenses of theistic evolution and the leading opponent of Henry Morris's fledgling "creation-science" movement. In the early 1950s he had associated with Jim Rayburn of Young Life in founding the Young Life Institute in Colorado. Young Life was a rather sophisticated evangelistic agency for reaching young people, and its institute was a summer school for training its leadership at roughly seminary level. Kulp knew Weyerhaeuser as another Young Life board member and was also well acquainted with Jewett, who taught regularly at the Young Life Institute. Jewett had kept Kulp up to date with the party conflicts at Fuller and, with aid from Weyerhaeuser, convinced him to join the board. When he did, Kulp immediately threw himself into what he saw as a mammoth struggle for control. His superb academic credentials and educational experience soon placed him in a leadership role on the board second only to that of Weyerhaeuser.[16]

Despite the apparently interim character of Ockenga's second presidency, the seminary was advancing aggressively on a number of fronts. In 1961 it announced the acquisition of the Winona Lake School of Theology as the seminary's own summer campus. The Indiana school had been founded in 1920 by G. Campbell Morgan, a British Bible teacher. Its most recent president, John A. Huffman, a friend of Ockenga, had been negotiating with Fuller people for years about a possible merger or acquisition (the difference was not always made clear). In the arrangement finally reached, Huffman remained at Winona as director of the Fuller Summer School Division. Students could receive full seminary credit for courses at Winona, though a year of course work in Pasadena would be required for graduation. Huffman and another Winona trustee would also be represented on the Fuller board. Huffman definitely stood with the conservatives on the faculty, such as Smith, Archer, and Lindsell, who in turn tended to do their summer teaching at Winona while the progressives were more likely to be found at the Young Life Institute.

16. Interview with J. Laurence Kulp, 3-19-85 (DF, in interviews, notes Kulp's leading role). The same year (1961) Donald Weber brought W. Robert Stover to the board. A San Francisco businessman, Stover was a friend of the Rev. Robert Munger, an influential Presbyterian pastor who had supported the seminary since its founding. Though theologically conservative himself, Stover was opposed to rigidity and supported the progressives. Stover interview, 11-4-83.

The question of political conservatism loomed again when the first Winona trustee designated for the Fuller board was Howard E. Kershner, editor of the politically conservative journal *Christian Economics*. The Kershner connection aroused some alumni protests about a possible identification of Fuller with a conservative economic party line, an impression the seminary made some genuine effort to play down.[17]

More momentous was the announcement in 1962 of tentative plans to found a school of psychology. This initiative arose almost solely from Davis Weyerhaeuser and his wife Annette, who promised to finance the founding of the enterprise. Plans for one new school also revived Charles Fuller's original dream of founding another, a school of missions and evangelism. Early in 1962, a committee headed by Everett Harrison was appointed to consider such satellite schools. The possibility of a school of Christian education received little support; but that of a mission school was seen as worth continued consideration.[18]

Even as Fuller was moving ahead, all such planning was over-shadowed by the outstanding issue: which party would control the seminary? This debate, in turn, seemed more and more to hinge on the doctrine of Scripture. The conservative neo-evangelicals were emphasizing the doctrine of inerrancy as firmly as ever, thus severely limiting how far the break with fundamentalism might go and insuring against any general drift toward doctrinal laxity. The progressive neo-evangelicals, on the other hand, were ready for a clean break with fundamentalism and were willing to let the chips fall where they might.

Ever since the publication of Carnell's *Case for Orthodox Theology* the biblical inspiration question had been a substantial public relations problem for the seminary. Between 1960 and 1962 the school seemed constantly to be publishing its statement of faith and assuring its constituents that all its faculty and trustees indeed signed it every year. During 1961 and 1962 the public relations department distributed twenty thousand copies of brochures containing the statement of faith and fifteen thousand scrolls containing the statement with faculty and board signatures.[19] In addition, the faculty members together were preparing a book with the reassuring title *Things Most Surely Believed*, edited by Clarence Roddy, in which each offered an exposition of one article of the Fuller creed.

Just as things might have been settling down, Carnell blew the lid off again with his Barth encounter in April 1962. He said nothing really sensational; but by this time things were at such a pass that even his silence against Barth was taken as evidence of insufficent zeal to defend inerrancy. Even

17. CDW to HJO, 6-27-62 (S); HJO, "The Fuller Image," speech to board of trustees, October 1962, explicitly disclaims any political implications of the connection with *Christian Economics*.

18. Report of Committee III on the Planning of Associated Schools, December 1, 1962.

19. Report of Committee on Church Polity, Relations to Denominations, Public and Alumni, December 1, 1962.

though he reaffirmed his unqualified commitment to the Fuller statement of faith—which, after all, he had written—the inerrancy issue remained a source of constant strain.

BLACK SATURDAY

At this juncture came the most dramatic moment in the seminary's history. The tensions over the struggles for control and the parallel tensions over differing views on Scripture suddenly erupted in a scene that left everyone shaken. After "Black Saturday," as the incident came to be called, little hope remained for reconciliation.

The outburst took place at a special "ten-year planning conference" for faculty and trustees, held at the luxurious Huntington Sheraton Hotel, December 1 to 3, 1962. That the seminary's future was being plotted contributed to the import of the occasion; but far more important was the pressure of the renewed presidential search, now reaching a most critical stage.

Despite the compromise of the past year, C. Davis Weyerhaeuser had kept pushing for a resident president. When, in the spring of 1962, Ockenga reaffirmed his unwillingness to move, Weyerhaeuser as chairman of the board appointed a formidable search committee to find a replacement. The majority were dedicated progressives, including Larry Kulp, Dan Fuller (who was still in Europe), and himself. The committee also included Dr. R. C. Logefeil (one of the original trustees) and Billy Graham. Weyerhaeuser, backed closely by Kulp, was in a position to do most of the committee work himself and was determined to make something positive happen soon.

Within a few months most of the well-known possibilities had been eliminated, so the committee turned back to considering David Hubbard. Weyerhaeuser decided that Hubbard was the man and by early November was pressing the committee for quick action.

Almost simultaneously a major crisis surfaced at Westmont that threatened to eliminate Hubbard from the Fuller presidential picture entirely. A few years earlier Eerdmans Publishing Company had contracted with Hubbard to write an Old Testament survey. Hubbard asked his friend Robert Laurin, the son of a well-known Westmont trustee and a teacher at the American Baptist Seminary of the West in Covina to assist in this considerable task. As they completed drafts of the various chapters they made copies to use as a syllabus that they could try on their students. In the Westmont context a number of the statements in the syllabus were startling. It asserted outright that the Bible was totally reliable only in its theological or spiritual content— that part designed "to make better men and women out of us"—but not inerrantly reliable in its historical and scientific content. Specifically, it stated that the first eleven chapters of Genesis were myth, or epic, meaning that they dealt with things that really happened in the spiritual realm but which did not need to be regarded as history in the ordinary modern sense. The syllabus also called into question the Mosaic authorship of the Pentateuch and assigned a late date to the prophecies of Daniel.

All this was especially surprising at Westmont since the school had been founded in 1940 precisely to counter theological drift at other Christian colleges and had a strong inerrancy clause not only in its creed but in its articles of incorporation. Already in the summer of 1962 one of the founders got wind of what was being said in Bible courses and complained. The administration met with Hubbard but were satisfied that the issues at this point only had to do with subjects on which fundamentalists still allowed some discussion, such as the length of the "days" of Genesis 1 and the extent of the flood. The continued use of the syllabus was also discussed. Hubbard pointed out that the offending parts were all written by Laurin, that he disagreed with some, especially on the date of Daniel, and that his sections of the work would be clearly distinguished from Laurin's. He himself affirmed the doctrine of inerrancy. Nonetheless, he also acknowledged some responsibilites for coauthorship and defended a general policy of openness in discussing such questions. The Westmont administration backed him, and in his teaching he distinguished between his own views and those of Laurin. Nonetheless, the use of the syllabus sparked a small furor, eventually leading two families to remove their daughters from the school.[20]

The Westmont situation was connected directly to that at Fuller. Just when the presidential search committee began to push for Hubbard, the Westmont situation was reaching a crisis point. Upon hearing of Hubbard's renewed candidacy, Charles Fuller wrote to Dan in early November expressing the gravest reservations. While he had been the first to propose Hubbard some years earlier, he had been rebuffed. Now, moreover, he heard from Rolf Jacobsen, a leading defender of inerrancy on the Westmont board and also the head of the ten-year planning conference for the seminary, that Hubbard and Laurin denied the historicity of Adam and Eve and other similar points. He had also heard a rumor that Jewett had said something shocking about the doctrine of Scripture at the Young Life summer conference. Jewett was also in Europe for the year, so Charles Fuller had reverted to the opinions of his older friends.

Harold Ockenga had looked at the syllabus himself and concluded that its teachings were incompatible with the Fuller statement of faith. Even though the authors of the chapters were designated, he felt it impossible to distinguish Hubbard's and Laurin's views in a joint work of this sort.[21]

With both the founders now upset about Hubbard's candidacy, the progressives saw their cause in deep trouble. They had no other candidate and were convinced that, if there were an impasse, Lindsell, on whom Ockenga looked kindly, would emerge as a dark horse. Or perhaps Ockenga would remain president in absentia, allowing a virtual Lindsell takeover. Lindsell subsequently denied that he was ever an active candidate. Since he actively supported Ockenga as his own first choice, his own candidacy, if any, was

20. DF to CDW, 11-30-62 (draft); DH to President Voskuyl of Westmont College, 12-13-62; Rolf Jacobsen to DH, 2-10-63. See also several other documents that discuss the syllabus, Charles Fuller papers, "Presidency" file.
21. CF to DF, 11-9-62; HJO to CDW, 11-16-62.

likely passive. Also, by this time any presidential aspirations he may have harbored (Carnell thought he was "crushed" at being passed over in 1954) may have been tempered by realistic assessments of the depth of the opposition. Nonetheless, Lindsell had steadily moved up the administrative ladder to the vice presidency, he was the leading figure in the interregnum power struggle with the progressives, and he was at least *perceived* by all his opponents as an active candidate. Someone in fact gave his name in nomination to the search committee by the summer of 1962. In any case, whether in actuality a dark horse or a red herring, Lindsell's candidacy had taken on for the progressives immense symbolic importance as the central feature of the disaster they feared.[22] In Europe, just before Dan Fuller returned in late November, Jewett speculated on whether he would have a seminary to which to return.[23]

This latter fear was not altogether extravagant. In fact, Lindsell as vice president and Archer as acting dean until Dan Fuller's return had within the past year met with Ockenga to tell him frankly of their alarm about the erosion of belief in the doctrine of inerrancy among the faculty. They suggested that they directly confront those who they thought were signing the creed with reservations. If they could not be brought to sign it in good conscience, they should be encouraged to leave. Ockenga said in effect that he did not have the stomach for such a purge.[24] At the same time, however, he privately put pressure on the progressives, intimating that there might be a crackdown. To Jewett he said bluntly, "If you don't break off from the Fullers and stop trying to influence them, I'll fire you—tenure or no tenure. Is that clear?"[25] It was clear. By this time, everyone knew that one side or the other might have to leave, depending on who the new president was.

On Saturday December 1, as the emotions over the struggle were reaching a peak, the faculty and board met for their ten-year planning conference.[26]

By all accounts, especially his own, Dan Fuller's personal role was crucial to what ensued. Still suffering from the culture shock after three and a half years immersed in European scholarship, he suddenly found himself the seminary's chief academic officer in the midst of a titanic struggle. His inaug-

22. Lindsell denies that he was seeking the presidency, interview, 10-27-83. Many other people in interviews volunteered the opinion that Lindsell was actively seeking the position. Lindsell's own first choice for the presidency was almost certainly Ockenga, thus perhaps explaining how his position could simultaneously be regarded as a candidacy and not a candidacy.

23. DF interviews.

24. GA interview, 6-15-83.

25. PKJ, remarks to ad hoc committee of trustees, faculty, and administration meeting with him, 1-20-76 (transcript of tape) (P).

26. Most of the following account of the planning conference and the quotations in it are based on an interview with DF, 10-21-83. Fuller's memory of this event seemed particularly sharp and fits the vaguer recollections of other participants. Lindsell, *The Battle for the Bible* (Grand Rapids: Zondervan, 1976), 110-11, contains a useful brief account. GA added a number of details. WS immediately wrote a detailed second-hand account to BG, 12-3-62 (this and other WS correspondence with BG on the crisis are in the Charles Fuller papers).

uration as dean was to be the following Monday night. He was convinced he knew nothing about the job and in Europe had already gone through some dark moments of depression when he thought of the overwhelming administrative tasks.

During the day-long planning discussions, several occurences heightened the tension for the fledgling dean. Gleason Archer, secretary of the faculty and a champion of inerrancy, remarked cheerily, "We're going to have a special signing of the creed for you to see if you are still with us." Dan assured him "I am not signing anything, Gleason," though realizing that he would have to sign sometime.

During the day, the faculty and board discussed business matters: proposed curricular changes, questions of possible expansion, the proposed new schools of psychology and missions, whether to cultivate major denominations or separatists, and issues of priorities. Dan felt that everyone would be looking at him and asking, "What kind of dean is he going to be." He had hoped to offer perceptive remarks on each subject; but through the day he could think of little to say. Finally, late in the afternoon, only one committee report remained, that on the creed. At the break just before the final session, Don Weber, the chief political coordinator of the progressive takeover, found Dan and read him the riot act. "What on earth is the matter with you," he asked. "You're the number one man in the room, yet you sit there like a bump on a log and say nothing. . . . You have got to get off it and get rolling here. You're failing before you begin." The remark hit Dan where it already hurt. He had to assert his leadership. The final session was on the creed, and he knew about theology.

Nothing much was expected of the late afternoon session on the creed. Some of the faculty, especially Jewett, had been pressing for a new statement of faith, an adaptation of a classical creed. The creed committee, headed by Harrison, suggested certain ground rules should a new creed be adopted, including an understanding that anyone who disagreed with any essential provision would be expected to resign. Since Jewett, a key committee member, was out of the country, however, the committee recommended delaying any revisions until he returned. The session, accordingly, looked so unpromising that Wilbur Smith decided to go home, presumably to read a book.

While Ockenga, as chairman, could have left it at that, he opened the door for major debate by asking immediately, "But why do we need a new creed?" He could see no such need. Dan Fuller, the model of candor, and now on his own terrain of theology, saw his chance to assume his new leadership role. He pointed to what he saw as a vital need to revise the statement on inerrancy. "Dr. Ockenga," he asserted before the whole faculty and board, "there are errors which cannot be explained by the original autographs. It is simply not historically feasible to say that these errors would disappear if we had the autographs." He went on to explain his whole theory of the nature of biblical inerrancy—essentially, that the Bible claimed inerrancy only for its "revelational" teachings, that is, matters that make one wise unto salvation. On incidental matters, such as cosmological theories or historical details,

Fuller stated, God accommodated himself to the imperfect standards of the day. The Bible thus contained incidental errors; but these did not hinder God's revelational purpose.

Ockenga responded with thinly veiled indignation. "Well, what are we going to do then? Dan Fuller thinks the Bible is just full of errors."

"That is a gross distortion," Fuller retorted. He was pleading only that they take the historical method seriously. After all, he said, what else distinguished an evangelical view of Scripture from liberal and neo-orthodox views? B. B. Warfield said that the faith was grounded on empirical evidence, so that the Bible could be and should be subjected to the most rigorous historical investigation. Fuller was determined to follow Warfield's empirical historical approach to Scripture "right down to the bitter end," thus necessitating "facing squarely" that the Bible did contain errors in nonrevelational matters. His three years in Basel had confirmed his dedication to this forthright interpretation of biblical historicity. This view was not simply a revision of the neo-orthodox position. In fact, it was directly opposed to the method of Karl Barth, who started with the Holy Spirit's witness to the authority of Scripture but who would not let the historical method say anything about basic revelational truth.

At this point, Carnell jumped in with considerable irritation. In what Wilbur Smith later heard was a "magnificent speech," Carnell opened up his rhetorical guns on Dan Fuller. He was convinced that a purely inductive defense of the truth of Scripture was philosophically disastrous. Rather, one should come to the Bible with the hypothesis that it was the indeed the word of God. Only then do we frankly admit that we have some unsolved problems. "My list of discrepancies is longer than yours, Dan Fuller," Carnell insisted. But that did not matter, because if we come to the Bible as the verbally inspired word of God we find that we have fewer major problems with our system than with any competing system.

By this time, almost everyone was ready to join in the fray. LaSor stood up for Fuller, arguing as an example that there was no honest way to get around the fact that Luke in the book of Acts reports Stephen's sermon as authoritative, even though it relied on the Septuagint and thus got some of the Genesis chronology wrong.[27] Such classic conundrums had been discussed frankly within the faculty for years, especially by a mostly progressive group that gathered over lunches. Everett Harrison, in fact, had written about the problem of mistakes in the sources in a volume entitled *Revelation and the Bible,* edited by Carl Henry. Harrison's moderate approach was to look at the actual phenomena of how the Bible was revealed to determine what inerrancy meant. "We may have our own ideas as to how God should have inspired the Word, but it is more profitable to learn, if we can, how he actually inspired it."[28]

27. HJO to DF, 12-19-62.
28. Harrison, "The Phenomena of Scripture," *Revelation and the Bible,* ed. Carl Henry (Philadelphia: Presbyterian and Reformed, 1958), 249. See also "Presentations by Faculty Members," June 7, 1960, which includes Harrison, "What Is the Word of God? What Are Some of the Problems Christian Scholarship Must Face in the Study of the Bible."

Whether such issues could be discussed on their own merits, however, depended on who raised them and in what context. The discussion of Carnell's *Case for Orthodox Theology* had illustrated this. At a faculty meeting in late 1960, when the Carnell crisis was at its peak, George Ladd frankly stated his own opinions about inerrancy, prefacing them with the remark that he realized that his views could cost him his job. Nonetheless, he insisted that there was no way, for instance, to reconcile some of the discrepant accounts of the same event in the Gospels. This point was within bounds. What was not was his conclusion: that, strictly speaking, one of the accounts must be in error. Jewett added similar remarks. The seminary was in the midst of its campaign to quell the fallout from the Carnell crisis by publishing its statement of faith. Jewett and others had refused at first to re-sign the statement for the Christmas publicity mailing. Only after "extensive discussion" did they agree to re-sign for publicity purposes. Even then, the faculty disagreed on the implications of signing. Rumors circulated of a crisis at Fuller, and Wilbur Smith described the event to Carl Henry as a "very disturbing hour." This incident also apparently sparked the unsuccessful effort by Lindsell and Archer to bring an administrative crackdown.[29]

On Black Saturday, then, Dan Fuller was putting fire under an issue already approaching the boiling point. Inerrancy itself was a deeply important subject to everyone, but at Fuller it could never be discussed as an isolated intellectual question. In this setting it was always tied to political, personal, and other doctrinal concerns.

C. Davis Weyerhaeuser, who had been dealing with these same issues in the matter of the Hubbard-Laurin syllabus, also rose to Dan Fuller's defense. Weyerhaeuser's view was that the resort to the inerrancy of the original autographs was artificial, since it would have been odd of God to create inerrant texts but then not preserve them for succeeding generations. Moreover, he saw the heart of the matter in the definition of *error. Discrepancies,* he thought would be a better word for matters reported under the looser standards of accuracy of biblical times. If these were "errors," he agreed with Fuller, they were incidental to the point of the Bible. In any case, the assertion of the statement of faith that the autographs were "free from all error in the whole and in the part," was at best misleading.[30]

The conservative side heard these open attacks on the creed and on the traditional reading of "inerrancy" with consternation. In their view, inerrancy was the logical implication of the statement in 2 Timothy that "*all* Scripture is inspired by God" (3:16). God would not inspire an error, small or large. Furthermore, Jesus' use of the Old Testament implied that he regarded it as historically accurate in detail. In the end, if one said that parts of the Bible

29. WS to CH, 1-31-61 (WS). GA, interview, refers to Ladd's remarks about this time, which seem to be part of the same event. Lindsell, *Battle for the Bible*, 110, also refers to Ladd's remarks, as does an earlier undated memo by HL that he furnished to me.

30. This summary is an approximation based on the letter from CDW to Edward L. Johnson, 12-10-62. DF, interview, recalled that CDW refined the discussion by talking of "discrepancies," rather than errors.

were inerrant and other parts had error, who was to decide which was which? What standard higher than the Bible itself was to be used? Christians would be left in a morass of subjectivism and fallible human opinion.

Just as important as the specific arguments, and surely a reason why they seemed so compelling, was the conservatives' knowledge of the history of American Protestantism. Beginning with the gradual slippage of Harvard into Unitarianism, the past two hundred years had seen an endless repetition of the same story. Most of America's greatest academic institutions had been founded by conservative Bible-believing evangelicals. But nearly every one of these schools had eventually fallen to the onslaughts of theological liberalism, and then to outright secularism. A vast empire lay in ruins. Except in a few cases, such as Wheaton College or Moody Bible Institute, where conservatives had kept the tightest control on innovation, their efforts at institution building had proved futile.

A favorite example was Andover Seminary, which was founded early in the nineteenth century to counter the liberalism of Harvard. Its founders made every effort to bind the school to New England orthodoxy, and faculty had to sign a strict creed each year. Nonetheless, by the end of the century, liberalism had triumphed at Andover. In the early days of Fuller, E. J. Carnell had enunciated this familiar story. Fuller Seminary, its founders had been aware, was the latest Andover and so needed to be guarded with extreme care.[31]

Many of the Fuller leaders, moreover, remembered first-hand the mammoth twentieth-century struggles that brought on the necessity of building their own institution. Yet in their telling of the history they tended to project the recent emphasis on inerrancy onto the past. Prior to 1870, inerrancy, while often assumed, was not often used as a test of orthodoxy. But with the rise of higher criticism in America it had indeed become central. A pivotal episode was the debate in the 1880s and 1890s between Benjamin Warfield and Charles Briggs of Union Theological Seminary in New York. Warfield used the inerrancy issue to attack Briggs's moderate revisionism. Once the battle line was so drawn, there was no backing down. Conservatives widely believed that any weakness regarding inerrancy would leave an opening through which liberalism would inevitably rush in. The demise of Princeton Seminary as a strict conservative school was one more case in point. As Harold Lindsell later wrote, the lesson was plain. "Down the road, whether it takes five or fifty years, any institution that departs from belief in an inerrant Scripture will likewise depart from other fundamentals of the faith and at last cease to be evangelical in the historical meaning of that term."[32]

As the heated discussions of Black Saturday went on into the evening, preempting the planned program, Lindsell and Archer were the chief faculty proponents of a strict inerrantist position, with some help from Carnell and

31. Carnell, "Entrust the Same," speech at FTS, December 1952. WS cited the Andover Seminary case in his letter of resignation to CF, 6-4-63.
32. Lindsell, *Battle for the Bible*, 120-21 and passim.

Bromiley. Most incensed about the episode, however, was Edward L. Johnson, vice chairman of the trustees. Johnson was president of Financial Federation, Inc., a member of Lake Avenue Church, a friend of Harold Lindsell, and one of the major financial supporters of the seminary. He was also the Moody Bible Institute board member whom (as mentioned earlier) even Ockenga had found too rigid. What Johnson now plainly heard from the Fuller faculty and its incoming dean was more than he could tolerate. In his view, the inerrancy issue was like a surveyor's benchmark. Once the benchmark was changed, the institution was sure to go off course. Those who were not in accord with the creed should, in honesty, leave. Since they obviously were not going to, Johnson himself would resign.[33]

The next morning, Sunday, as the conferees gathered for breakfast, they were still in a state of shock. Several said they had hardly slept. The only relief was that Wilbur Smith finally bustled in late and was asked to give the opening prayer. Having missed the entire disruptive proceeding, Smith thanked the Lord for the harmony that had prevailed at the conference thus far.

He was quickly filled in and joined in the alarm. Earlier in the week Lindsell had already told Charles Fuller that he would resign if Hubbard were chosen as president. Now Johnson was ready to resign. Smith was privately considering it himself. In fact, he later said, he would quit "within twenty-four hours" if Hubbard were chosen. "What tragic days we have come upon!" he wrote to Ockenga on Monday morning. "How different from the early years of the seminary."[34]

Charles Fuller was distressed by this episode that was driving a wedge among his friends. If news of it came out that his son was at the center of the controversy it would cost "The Old Fashioned Revival Hour" dearly. As a matter of course, stenographers had made a shorthand record of the entire planning conference. Within a few days the elder Fuller had gathered all the notes and the transcripts typed from them and placed them in his safe. Eventually they disappeared.

THE PRESIDENCY

Meanwhile, there was the even more pressing matter of the presidency. The board met all day the Monday after Black Saturday, and Weyerhaeuser and Kulp pushed hard to resolve the issue. The board now told Ockenga definitively that, as Saturday's breakdown illustrated, the seminary could not go on without a resident chief executive.

On Monday evening Daniel Fuller was inaugurated as dean. A few days later Ockenga called him in and asked him if he could sign the statement

33. Ibid., 110; Edward L. Johnson, letter to *Theology News and Notes*, March 1963, 23-24; GA, interview, also describes Johnson's views. WS to BG, 12-3-62, provides a detailed second-hand account of the episode.
34. WS to BG, 12-3-62; WS to HJO, 12-3-62 (O).

of faith. Fuller said "sure" he could. He observed that Article II of the creed, that concerning Scripture, combined the statement that the Bible was inerrant with the classic formula that it was "the only infallible rule of faith and practice." That phrase, Fuller argued, implied that it was as a rule of faith and practice that the Bible was "free from error in the whole and in the part." About the same time Lindsell privately checked the new dean for heresy by asking whether he believed that Peter had written 2 Peter. Fuller said he did.[35]

With another of their key people finally in place, the progressives knew they had a chance for total victory if only they could secure the presidency. Ockenga, however, was standing in the way. Just after the board meetings, he and the search committee had a stormy meeting about the Hubbard candidacy. Though Ockenga was not always a strict hard-liner, sometimes attempting to mediate between the two parties, when the chips were down he was squarely on the side of the conservatives. At the committee meeting he took a firm stand against Hubbard, which he documented by reading from passages from the disputed syllabus. The progressives were ready. Kulp had carefully analyzed and underlined the syllabus, distinguishing Hubbard's from Laurin's views. After Ockenga had read several passages that he found unacceptable, Kulp pointed out triumphantly that every quotation he had offered was from Laurin, not from Hubbard.[36]

Moreover, to each person who interviewed him, Hubbard was giving impressive assurances of his personal conservatism on the biblical issue.[37] His view was most carefully expounded in a memorandum to President Roger Voskuyl of Westmont. He affirmed the "*plenary, verbal inspiration* of the Scriptures." By that he meant that "the Bible is exactly what God wanted it to be to the very word, that is infallible in its teaching, completely accurate in its historical statements, and fully and finally authoritative in matters of faith and practice."

Hubbard's position was formulated in a way importantly different from that of Dan Fuller. While in substance it was much the same as Fuller's, in the logic of its statement it was much more compatible with classic Princeton orthodoxy. All the flexibility in Hubbard's view was in the domain of interpretation. The Holy Spirit made the central redemptive message of the Bible plain to the simple believer, he believed; but other parts took great skill to interpret, and some still remained difficult. Biblical scholarship might yet turn up fresh insights into the meaning of Scripture that differed from traditional interpretations. In regard to these differences, however, "it is not *inspiration* which is at stake but *interpretation*. The two must not be confused."[38] This was the crucial distinction. This position was similar to Harrison's and was a more sophisticated version of Weyerhaeuser's observation that it was difficult to define what an "error" was. Both Hubbard and Weyerhaeuser wished to

35. DF interview, 11-11-83.
36. Ibid.
37. HJO to DF, 1-3-63.
38. DH to Roger Voskuyl, 12-13-62.

preserve a conservative view of the authority of Scripture in which a clear claim of Scripture could not be written off as "error." On the other hand, a high view of the authority of Scripture did not resolve the many interpretive differences that conservative evangelicals might have over what exactly Scripture claimed.

The revolutionary aspect in Hubbard's way of describing the unerring authority of Scripture was that it had built into it a principle of tolerance. Interpretive differences, such as those concerning the early chapters of Genesis, did not imply any departure from the authority of Scripture, only a new understanding of what Scripture meant. Even then, Hubbard had his own interpretive limits. For example, he disagreed with Laurin's view that the book of Daniel was written at a late date after many of the events it prophesied had already taken place. Nonetheless, consistent with his character, Hubbard was willing to tolerate this interpretation as long as he thought Laurin was trying to remain essentially orthodox.

The pressures at Westmont together with the prospect of the Fuller presidency, however, caused Hubbard to back away from his characteristic tolerance. Recent criticisms, he said to President Voskuyl, "have brought the matter into sharper focus." Accordingly, he had agreed with Laurin and the publisher to take out Laurin's part of the contract and to complete the volume by himself or with others. He still intended to use the mimeographed syllabus in his classes, though, a stance that the Westmont board, led by Rolf Jacobsen, eventually rejected. Yet by separating himself from Laurin and through assurances regarding his own view of Scripture, Hubbard had considerably boosted his eligibility for the Fuller position.

Meanwhile the conservatives mobilized for a last stand to stop the progressive offensive. With Ockenga unable to stem the tide, they still had one last hope—Billy Graham. Immediately after the planning conference, Wilbur Smith sent Graham a long tale of woe about the tragedy that had befallen the school. Graham was apparently alarmed about the gravity of the situation. Within a week he had a six-hour conference with Ockenga, followed by a half-hour phone conversation with Smith. Earlier in the year he had told Smith that he would fight for the authority of Scripture if he were the last man alive. Now he was ready to enter the fray to save Fuller Seminary.[39]

Graham was on the search committee and in November had written to Smith lamenting the difficulty in finding qualified men for evangelical leadership.[40] In December, however, the newly mobilized conservatives came up with a bona fide candidate, a sophisticated southern Presbyterian clergyman who identified himself thoroughly with the old Princeton theology. The problem was, this candidate lacked an earned doctorate and experience as an educator.

Everything came down to a final test on January 10, 1963, at a special board meeting called to select a president. Both sides were at full strength as

39. WS to William Culbertson, 12-13-62.
40. BG to WS, 11-20-62.

Billy Graham made a rare personal appearance. Graham was working closely with Smith and Ockenga to hold things together, and Smith was confident that Graham could save the day. "Your place in our Seminary's history," he wrote with his typical hyperbole, "is as that of one of the judges called of God in Israel's often repeated times of weakness and compromise, a Saviour sent to deliver."

After the board meeting, Smith actually thought the victory had been won. A week later he was still effusive in his praise of Graham. "I am absolutely certain that, at least, as far as human factors are concerned, our school was saved from disaster solely by your vigorous, wise and powerful intervention. . . ." He said this because Graham had persuaded the board to reaffirm its allegiance to the present statement of faith. More importantly, Smith thought that the presidential choice, once announced, would bring resignations from two or three "that should really go." Thanks to Graham, said Smith, "for the time being, at least, our school is safe."[41]

His sense of victory was short-lived.

The struggle could have gone either way until the last moment. The two sides were evenly matched. Each had three or four strong advocates on the faculty. The conservatives had President Ockenga, who could still be a dominating influence; but the progressives had Dan Fuller. Though a fledgling as dean, Dan had the loyalty of his parents, which both prevented them from lining up with the conservatives and gave him job security. Any conservative regime would have to work with and around him. The progressives also had the most influential trustees, Weyerhaeuser and Kulp, though these could be, as Smith had hoped, outweighed by Graham.

While Smith was originally optimistic about the board meetings, the outcome was more of a compromise than he realized. In addition to reaffirming the statement of faith, the board also interviewed both candidates. The southern Presbyterian was found lacking in his response to too many questions about his academic credentials to have a chance to win. Hubbard, on the other hand, did well. Billy Graham explained his impressions to Smith some days later:

> To be very frank with you . . . I was somewhat impressed with Dave Hubbard's presentation to the Board. He stated outright that he believed in the inerrancy of the Scriptures and that he could support the doctrinal statement. If words mean anything, then he must be a strong conservative. My doubts arise concerning his ability as an administrator and from the fact that he allowed his name to be associated with a manuscript which was extremely doubtful. This indicates to me that when the chips are down he might give in on certain strategic points.[42]

41. WS to BG, 1-8-63, 1-15-63.
42. BG to WS, 1-21-63.

In an exhausting session that stretched over twelve hours, the board found itself unable to agree on Hubbard directly, given that this choice was sure to bring a split. After lengthy debate, Billy Graham, though not absolutely opposed to Hubbard, began leaning heavily on Ockenga to persuade him that only he could save the day. Ockenga was finally persuaded that at last the situation might be grave enough that he should come out as resident president. He called his wife, who reportedly had long been cool to the idea, and got clearance to give the offer serious consideration.

The Hubbard people, led by Kulp and Weyerhaeuser, were troubled by this last-minute counterstroke that threatened to destroy their carefully planned campaign. Charles Fuller, fearing that his board would be split down the middle, helped them forge the compromise.[43] Ockenga would have to let his decision be known within ten days; should he not accept, the nomination would go to Hubbard. The board accepted this proposal, leaving both sides with some hope.

Ockenga's move to Pasadena would have been far more difficult now than at any earlier juncture. He had always wondered whether he could work so closely with Charles Fuller;[44] now, moreover, the crisis had put him on the side opposite Fuller's son. Charles Fuller still hoped that the president of the seminary, whoever it might be, would eventually take over "The Old Fashioned Revival Hour"; but Ockenga could see that radio evangelism was not what it used to be. So the reasons he had to come to Pasadena were now largely to prevent negative developments. Most importantly, moving would mean leaving his ministry at Park Street Church, which was still at its zenith.

After "a long period of prayer and fasting," with these considerations weighing heavily on him, Ockenga had what he described as a "mystical experience" perhaps occasioned by unexpectedly seeing one of his elders on a street corner while he was driving to church. Jesus was telling him, he was sure, that Boston still needed him.[45] He decided to turn the board down.

Once again, an apparent leading of the Lord played a major role in the history of the seminary. Though Ockenga saw the leading as sufficient to justify turning the seminary over to Hubbard, not all his cohorts were convinced that that was what the Lord had willed.

---

43. DF, on draft. Kulp, interview, suggests that he and Weyerhaeuser were architects of this compromise.
44. HJO interview, 11-6-83.
45. HJO to DF, 12-3-71; interview with HJO and Audrey Ockenga, 11-6-83.

CHAPTER XII

The Changing of the Guard

We established the seminary in 1947 in order to maintain an institution committed to the absolute authority of Scripture. This view had been maintained at Princeton until its reorganization and then had been eroded until 1947. I felt that it was necessary to have a new institution fully committed to the authority of Scripture and fully positive in its testimony. This we expressed in our Statement of Faith and it is our keen desire to maintain it.

Harold J. Ockenga to David A. Hubbard, letter of congratulation,

January 19, 1963.

EXIT OF THE OLD ORDER

THE morning after his mystical experience, Ockenga called Charles Fuller and Weyerhaeuser informing them of his decision. Then he wrote a gentlemanly letter to Hubbard, saying that he had been impressed by his sincerity, candidness, and ability. He encouraged him to accept and urged him to keep the seminary on its original moorings.[1] There was no doubt that the younger man would take the challenging position.

Despite the cordiality, Hubbard was walking into a storm, the full force of which had not yet been measured. All the signs indicated, however, that the worst was yet to come. The one hope was that as it ran its course it might bring a brighter and clearer atmosphere.

Hubbard's acceptance brought the resignation of another trustee, Charles Pitts. Would faculty resignations soon follow? None came during the spring term, at least. Meanwhile the seminary was moving rapidly toward reorganization for the new regime. In the process, each of the key conservatives got the subtle but unmistakable message that, while they were free to stay, their services were not nearly as indispensable as they had been in earlier days.

In the summer came the first faculty resignation as Wilbur Smith led the way. Since Black Saturday in December he had been contemplating resignation, and in fact made the gesture at that time of handing in a note of resignation, which Charles Fuller and Ockenga convinced him to take back.

1. HJO to DH, 1-19-63 (P).

*Turning over control: Harold Ockenga invests David Hubbard as
president of Fuller Seminary*

Meanwhile, Smith was playing his cards (Rook) close to the vest. He was
sixty-nine—only one year from required retirement—and was already slated
for a reduced teaching load.

In addition to his deep concern over the doctrinal trend at Fuller,
Smith may well have been chafing over his loss of status. In the early days he
had been the celebrated senior professor, who held his own in student respect

and influence despite his lack of degrees. He had also been Charles Fuller's most influential confidant. Now he may have sensed that he was tolerated by seminary sophisticates as an amusing eccentric, a dinosaur from the fundamentalist days before the seminary arrived at its mature scholarly standing.[2]

The convergence of several events led him to take the decisive step. To start, he was presented with what he described as a wholly unexpected opportunity. Kenneth Kantzer of Wheaton, who had just accepted the deanship of Trinity Evangelical Divinity School in Illinois, asked Smith if he would be willing to join that faculty. The Evangelical Free Church, which operated Trinity, had decided that the seminary should be expanded from a small denominational school into a major evangelical seminary. Kantzer's willingness to take on this task was directly related to the Fuller situation. Kantzer had taught at the Fuller summer school at Winona Lake, where the summer faculty was of a distinctive conservative bent. Gleason Archer, Gordon Clark, and J. Oliver Buswell had been at Winona with Kantzer and together they openly discussed the demise of Fuller Seminary over the inerrancy issue.[3] The new Trinity under Kantzer was transparently an attempt to build a new Fuller: bringing in Wilbur Smith clearly signaled this intention. Smith hesitated. Nonetheless the call was a great affirmation. Once again he was being asked to anchor a well-trained theological faculty.[4]

The next Tuesday after Smith heard from Kantzer, two things happened to push him in the direction of Trinity. First, he received from Charles Fuller a curt rebuff to a note he had sent requesting to see the transcript of the December 1 faculty meeting (from which he was absent). Fuller, who had locked all the transcripts in his safe, simply replied formally that the case was closed. While Smith was still steaming about this, Dan Fuller came to his office on a difficult mission. As part of its planning, and to help reduce the recurring budged deficits, the seminary had hired an independent agency, Studies in Higher Education, to evaluate the school and recommend changes. Among the recommendations was that there be an extensive revision that would streamline the curriculum by consolidating core courses and allowing fewer electives. Though the revisions were still in their early stages, Dan Fuller had to inform Wilbur Smith that the curriculum committee was recommending that the English Bible requirement (twelve hours during the junior year) be dropped. "We'll see about that," Smith harrumphed.[5]

The very same day Smith dictated a long letter of resignation to Charles Fuller. In his view, the troubles at the seminary began with Carnell's attacks on fundamentalism and the school's subsequent support. "You, Dr. Fuller, and I," wrote Smith, "and some others connected with our school are Fundamentalists. . . ." The balance of the faculty, the implication was, were now something else. Smith noted that Fuller himself had estimated that the

2. These observations were suggested in conversations with Smith's former secretary, Delores Loeding, fall 1983.
3. GA interview, 6-15-83.
4. WS to CF, 6-4-63; see also WS to Kenneth S. Kantzer, 6-14-63 (T).
5. DF interviews, fall 1983.

seminary's policies had cost him 40 percent of his support for "The Old Fashioned Revival Hour." Now they had driven off two trustees. People everywhere were asking him, "What is wrong with Fuller Seminary?" Yet no one stopped this antifundamentalist course.

Inerrancy, of course, was the paramount question for Smith, and he reviewed the intraseminary controversies on the subject. Then he took the new president to task. Hubbard, he argued at great length, was suspect because he had defended the use of the controversial syllabus at Westmont and only when forced by the administration did he abandon it.[6]

When Charles Fuller received this letter, he tried once again to convince Smith to withdraw his resignation; but it was too late. The July 1963 *Bulletin* of the seminary included a special insert with the headline "Tribute Paid Retiring English Bible Professor Wilbur M. Smith." Hoping to cut its public relations losses, the school mentioned Smith's resignation only as though it were part of his "retirement." Though this infuriated some of his friends, Smith himself vowed not to go around, à la Woodbridge, running down Fuller. A brief news story in *Christianity Today* made clear, however, that Smith had resigned in protest of the school's view of Scripture; and it added a note on Edward Johnson's resignation from the board as well. An adjacent story announced that Smith was going to Trinity.[7]

Harold Lindsell was next. With Hubbard as president-elect, Lindsell remained as vice president. While Hubbard assured him in March 1963 that no changes would be made for a year, everyone, including Hubbard, wondered whether the two could work together at all, given their strong differences. The control was taken from Hubbard's hands, however. At the spring board meeting, held while both Hubbard and Lindsell were traveling, the board voted to terminate the office of vice president immediately, though continuing Lindsell's administrator's salary. When Lindsell got word of this, he was irate. Hubbard then got the board to back down and reverse its decision, thus allowing Lindsell to continue for the next year as vice president. His former administrative powers were greatly limited, though, and the position was little more than assistant to the president. Since Lindsell's best gifts were in administration, it was clear that there was little future for him at Fuller.

By the next winter Lindsell had an offer of a position at *Christianity Today*, which he promptly accepted. In his letter of resignation in February 1964, he cited both the positive opportunities he had elsewhere and the seminary's "failure to maintain Article II of the Statement of Faith either in letter or in spirit."[8]

Gleason Archer was on sabbatical in Beirut while these rumblings were going on; but he too soon got the message that he was dispensable. First, he heard from Dan Fuller that the radical revision of the curriculum consoli-

6. WS to CF, 6-4-63.
7. *Christianity Today*, July 19, 1963, 36.
8. See the letter of resignation, HL to DH, 2-5-64; see also HL to HJO, 10-19-64 (letters furnished by HL). Also, HL to DH, 8-9-63, DH to HL (draft), 8-13-63, and DH to Ralph C. Hutchison, 4-18-63 (all P); and DH interviews, fall 1983.

dated the Old Testament offerings into large blocks organized around groups of Old Testament books and also dropped all topical courses. This meant the demise of Archer's most prized course, his four-hour required senior course in Old Testament Introduction. Archer viewed his principal goal in teaching Old Testament as apologetic. In the tradition of old Princeton, he answered one by one the objections of higher criticism. Under the new curriculum there would be no course devoted to this purpose.

The sequel to his strong protest against this change seemed to him to make the message even clearer. Dan Fuller wrote again asking whether, since the changes were definitely going through, Archer would consider the direc-torship of the library. However well intentioned this offer may have been, it immediately led Archer to conclude that it was time to leave. He wrote to Kenneth Kantzer who was already interested in bringing him to Trinity, and by February he had settled on going there. Trinity's expansion, however, was just getting underway, so Archer and Kantzer agreed to postpone the appoint-ment until the fall of 1965. In the spring of 1964 he accordingly resigned from Fuller, effective at the end of the next year.[9] Unlike Smith and Lindsell, Archer had apparently been prepared to remain at Fuller as a voice for the conserva-tive old Princeton view of inerrancy. Fuller, however, clearly no longer wanted such a polemical approach to the subject. In a statement explaining his rea-sons for leaving in *Theology News and Notes*, Archer too cited his discontent over the seminary's stand on inerrancy.[10]

THE FUNCTIONS OF INERRANCY

As these three of the old guard were leaving, the new regime was consolidating its gains. One quiet move that especially irritated the conservatives was that the administration unilaterally removed from the 1964–65 catalog the sen-tence explaining that when the faculty signed the statement of faith each year, "this concurrence is without mental reservation, and any member who cannot assent agrees to withdraw from the institution." The removal of this elabora-tion, which had been added when the creed was first published during the Vassady crisis, appeared particularly ominous to the conservatives in the light of another episode of 1963–64.[11]

Calvin Schoonhoven, a Fuller graduate of 1958, had been filling in teaching some courses in biblical intepretation since 1962. He was a friend of Dan Fuller and a devotee of his inductive method of biblical hermeneutics. When Hubbard arrived as president, there was no room to add Schoonhoven as another full-time faculty member, but a way to keep him on was eventually devised. He could fill the vacant library directorship and continue to teach

9. GA interview.
10. *Theology News and Notes*, May 1964, 2.
11. Note, however, that Carnell was also unhappy about this administrative ac-tion, EJC to HJO, 10-7-64.

Two of the victors—Trustee J. Laurence Kulp and Dean Daniel Fuller

part time. In his interview with the library committee (composed of Dan Fuller, LaSor, Jewett, Carnell, and Lindsell) he caused real sparks to fly. This interview preceded Lindsell's resignation and perhaps hastened it. Lindsell pressed Schoonhoven on the question of biblical errors and was entirely unsatisfied by the replies, which revealed his reservations about the inerrancy article. When LaSor and Jewett added remarks that upset Lindsell even more, Jewett observed that, given his views, Lindsell ought to bring charges against some of his colleagues. Lindsell replied that either he would do so or he would withdraw from the faculty.[12] Schoonhoven was in the end appointed to the

12. Memo by IIL (early 1964?) (furnished by HL).

library position and as assistant professor of biblical interpretation, though, as a compromise, he was put on a tenure track for the library post only.

Schoonhoven also helped precipitate the next—and the fiercest—storm of Hubbard's young presidency. At Winona Lake during the summer of 1964, Schoonhoven mentioned to the director, John Huffman, that he would like someday to get back to full-time teaching. The conservatives at Fuller thought they had won a guarantee that Schoonhoven had no such option, as long as he had mental reservations about the creed. This was the last straw for Huffman, who was already persuaded that laxity on inerrancy meant that Fuller was lost to the evangelical cause.

Immensely complicating the picture was that since the Fuller-Winona merger, John Huffman had run up a debt of nearly $100,000 for the seminary. At the end of the summer of 1964 the Fuller trustees came to Winona for its commencement exercises and for a meeting at which they were prepared to play hardball with Huffman on the matter of the debt. Huffman, however, managed to bat first.

Davis Weyerhaeuser described the scene in detail to Harold Ockenga:

> At the Friday noon luncheon, following commencement when many friends were present, John left the head table to take a position in the middle of the dining room so everyone could hear better. Then he proceeded to tell of a drowning of a young medical missionary prospect—the first accident in 44 years—we were all deeply moved by this—following which he told of the extensive activities and plans he is carrying on with Jerome Hines to go to several cities to hold concerts, all of which was very exciting, but made us wonder whether in view of our financial crisis his time might not better have been spent otherwise. I knew practically nothing of this and I think Dave knew very little either.
>
> Then came the blow. John closed his remarks by referring to our Fuller board expressing appreciation for its stand on our doctrinal statement, but went on to say that there was need to put a stop to what was being taught in the classroom on inerrancy and that he, John, was dedicating himself to do something about this and asked the prayers of all who were there. Harold, I could hardly believe my ears and the other board members present felt the same. I almost rose to protest, but did not feel sufficiently led to do so.

After lunch, the stunned Fuller board met with Huffman and let him know clearly what they thought of his publicly attacking an institution of which he too was a board member. Huffman for his part had a list of grievances concerning inerrancy, the Schoonhoven remark being only the latest. He would not back down.[13]

Within a few days Huffman met with his Winona board who voted to

13. CDW to HJO, 9-8-64 (P).

terminate unilaterally the merger with Fuller Seminary. They cited a reversion clause stating that the Winona board could dissolve the union if Fuller Seminary altered the basic operations of the original Winona Lake summer school. The Winona board cited Fuller faculty departures from a strict doctrine of inerrancy as primary evidence that their operations were being altered by the merger.

To complete the coup, *Christianity Today*, which now had two of the Fuller founding faculty as its top editors, immediately published a brief news story reporting Huffman's reasons for the dramatic break—but with no comment from the other side. Huffman's reasons for the "drastic and necessary" actions included the " 'gradual deterioration' of Fuller's doctrine of Scripture, the signing of the statement of faith with 'mental reservations' and the elimination of the English Bible requirements."[14]

The three-year financial controversy that followed nearly went to court. Only the intervention of Herbert J. Taylor prevented that embarrassment.[15] The episode was thoroughly unedifying except in one respect. It illustrated the way in which the doctrine of inerrancy was coming to be used in the new evangelical coalition. Having broken with fundamentalism, the conservative wing of the new evangelicals needed a meaningful test to limit how far reforms of fundamentalism might go. Inerrancy could play that role. It was a distinctive of the fundamentalist movement, yet shared by some other conservative traditions. Unlike premillennialism, it was close to the center of the movement's teachings. It was also logically connected with the crucial question of authority, which was central to the debates with liberals and secularists. Since fundamentalist evangelicals usually lacked authoritative church bodies, inerrancy was an effective tool for drawing a boundary for the movement. Nor was this boundary arbitrary: those who would not affirm the conservative version of inerrancy were usually progressive on other issues as well.

The doctrine of inerrancy was thus functioning at several levels at once. At the most academic level, many conservatives saw it as simply a logically necessary doctrine of the faith. Many progressives, on the other hand, viewed it as confusing, misleading, or simply wrong. But the academic discussions were seldom simply academic. The doctrine also functioned at ecclesiastical and para-ecclesiastical institutional levels. That in turn meant that it was becoming the chief symbol for party divisions within institutions.

The Winona controversy exemplified some further dynamics of the multiple-level functioning of inerrancy. Conflicts over practical institutional policy and financing could very easily be translated into high principle. Such translation did not necessarily imply that the commitment to inerrancy, or opposition to it, was any the less sincere. It did mean, however, that an

14. *Christianity Today*, September 11, 1964, 47. Dropping the Winona master's degree program (which FTS could not get accredited) was also mentioned as a reason for the break. FTS's side of the story is published in an interview with DH, *Theology News and Notes*, February 1965, 2-5.

15. Correspondence on this case can be found in the Charles Fuller papers, "Winona Lake" file.

inerrancy controversy was one form that a policy conflict could take, should tensions between conservatives and progressives arise over other matters. High principles, then, were mixed both with tangible interests and deep feelings.

RECONCILIATION ATTEMPTED

Harold Ockenga, who had done as much as anyone to put together the new evangelical coalition, was especially distressed by its threatened breakup over the inerrancy conflict. He himself cultivated cordial contacts with both sides. In fact, he was in the awkward position during the Winona furor of being chairman of the board both at Fuller and at *Christianity Today*. Although Ockenga sided with the conservatives, he seldom stressed inerrancy as such, and in the early 1960s he may have been genuinely perplexed by some of the difficulties in stating the doctrine to everyone's satisfaction. In any case, his proposed solution was that the contending parties should get together to talk about the issues in a controlled setting where only the theoretical issues themselves would be at stake. The Winona case gave impetus to this plan.

The result was a scholar's conference, initiated substantially by Fuller people and privately funded by Weyerhaeuser, J. Howard Pew, Billy Graham, and Charles Fuller. Even this arrangement caused controversy in Pasadena. The decision by the Fuller Evangelistic Foundation to help fund this conference was the last straw for Charles Fuller's good friend James Henry Hutchins, who resigned from his long-held position on the board of the FEF in 1965. The inerrancy issue at the seminary was his main concern.

In such an atmosphere of ongoing tensions that could divide long-standing friends, fifty-one evangelical scholars from ten countries gathered for discussions at Wenham, Massachusetts, in June 1966. There for ten days they had it out on the doctrine of Scripture. Though Ockenga had been hoping to bring peace, the issues had become too hot to keep at the dispassionate level. Some of the key people in the Fuller controversies, including Lindsell, Henry, and Jewett, did not attend. Daniel Fuller did attend, and again his views and others like them were in for scathing criticism from some conservatives. The party that had coalesced around Trinity Evangelical Divinity School, including Kenneth Kantzer, Gleason Archer, and John Warwick Montgomery, an argumentative historian, made clear that they were going to give no quarter to those who would not affirm inerrancy. Though the discussions were largely cordial, occasional blowups dashed hopes to issue a meaningful collective statement. The issues continued to smolder.[16]

One of the difficulties that plagued even constructive efforts to resolve the issue was that the differences between the inerrantists and those who were uncomfortable with the term were rarely clear cut. C. Davis Weyerhaeuser, who took great personal interest in trying to resolve the differences, pressed this point to little avail. Part of the problem was the adversarial nature of the wider discussion.

16. Information on this conference is in the "Wenham Conference" file (P).

After Black Saturday, Weyerhaeuser had written to Edward Johnson, trying to explain how he could both honestly sign the statement of faith and yet be uncomfortable with its inerrancy clause. The famous discrepancies in Scripture were not errors by the standards of the time; but to speak of the Bible as "inerrant misled people into thinking that it had a precision that would preclude even such discrepancies."[17] At the time, Weyerhaeuser's letter was widely circulated and was used as evidence that Fuller trustees were indeed signing the statement of faith with reservations

Three years later, however, Kenneth Kantzer, dean of Trinity Evangelical Divinity School, published in *His* magazine a very similar view of the relationship of biblical discrepancies to error. The difference, however, was the context. Kantzer was a leader in the inerrantist camp and was writing— within this camp—for college students in defense of the authority of Scripture. Weyerhaeuser sent the article to Ockenga with the comment that he agreed with "practically every statement" in it and that it was one of "the best short statements on inspiration" he had seen. Weyerhaeuser was particularly interested in the way Kantzer qualified the meaning of inerrancy. For example, Kantzer said that "if the Bible is verbally inspired and inerrantly true, yet expresses its truths from different viewpoints and from various cultural backgrounds, this type of problem ["apparent discrepancies"] should be common."[18] Wasn't this a sensible qualification, asked Weyerhaeuser, a type of mental reservation? Wasn't it misleading, then, to affirm inerrancy in a wholly unqualified way? One person's qualification could be another's "mental reservation."[19]

One of the factors that confused the discussions, then, was that the views of the inerrantists who made careful qualifications were not substantially different from the views of many conservatives who did not like the word *inerrancy*. The real issues could not be easily resolved among this large group of centrists among the new evangelicals, partly because of confusions over terminology, but mostly because the substantive question among these centrists was not so much theoretical as practical: which wing of the movement did one want to be identified with? Of course, on each extreme were those for whom the affirmation of "inerrancy" or the lack thereof had significant hermeneutical implications and could lead to wide differences in attitudes toward other subjects, such as higher criticism or prophecy. These really were substantive, theoretical questions. For the great majority in the middle, however, the real question was what kind of movement the new evangelicalism would be. Would it continue as essentially a refurbished version of fundamentalism, with a conspicuously defensive stance? If so, a stress on inerrancy would serve to guard the movement from innovation. Or would openness and tolerance be the more immediately conspicuous traits of the new evangelicals? These questions were especially important since the neo-evangelicals were concerned not

17. CDW to Edward L. Johnson, 12-10-62.
18. Kenneth Kantzer, "Christ and Scripture," *His*, January 1966, 16-20.
19. CDW to HJO, 2-24-66 (P).

just to refurbish their Reformed branch of classic fundamentalism but also to take the lead in building a wider evangelical coalition.

A BROADER EVANGELICALISM

Though it was not much recognized at the time, American evangelicalism in the 1960s was a vast, largely disconnected conglomeration of widely diverse groups. Only some of these had been touched substantially by classic fundamentalism. Most were shaped more by other denominational or ethnic traditions, though these may have been formed or modified by prefundamentalist American revivalism. So, in addition to the "new evangelical" coalition that was central to Fuller's origins there were American evangelicals with much different identities and networks of contacts. Among these groups were Methodists, holiness churches, pentecostals, various nonfundamentalist conservative Baptists, Restorationist Christians, Disciples of Christ, conservative Episcopalians, new charismatics and other theological conservatives in mainline churches, Lutherans, and peace churches. Some of these had ethnic subgroups. Baptists, Methodists, and pentecostals also included major separate black denominations that, while often antimodernist, were seldom directly connected to organized white fundamentalism. Few of these had much to do with the "new evangelicalism." Yet they were all evangelicals.

The dominant leadership of the original new evangelicalism hoped through the influence of Billy Graham and *Christianity Today* to mobilize these diverse evangelicals into an effective coalition. Despite some openness, however, their emphasis on inerrancy kept them close to classic fundamentalism and limited their influence largely to those traditions that had shared these concerns. Fuller Seminary under Hubbard's leadership, on the other hand, took the principle of openness one more step and simply dropped the distinctly fundamentalist agenda. In doing so, they cut themselves off from the strict inerrantists. But at the same time they were opening themselves to forming other alliances within many-faceted American evangelicalism.

This outlook, which shaped Fuller Seminary through the next decades, was a reflection of David Hubbard's own background, experience, personality, and religious commitments. His heritage was thoroughly evangelical, but it was also a long way from the Machen movement that had shaped so many of the earlier leaders of the seminary. His father was a Methodist pastor, and his mother was equally a leader in their church as a brilliant, well-read, and indefatigable Bible teacher. After a stint on the mission field in Puerto Rico, they took a Methodist church in California. There in the early 1920s they came under the spell of Aimee Semple McPherson's revivals and adopted her pentecostal emphases. They remained in Methodist churches, but transormed them into essentially pentecostal-Methodist congregations, emphasizing prayer meetings, healing services, casting out demons, speaking in tongues, and other signs of the power of the Holy Spirit. They also taught dispensational theology. Eventually in the 1930s, the Hubbards were forced to turn their church in Oakland, California, into an independent pentecostal congregation, since a nearby Methodist pastor saw it as infringing on his domain.

David Hubbard attended Westmont College in the late 1940s. When he heard of Fuller Seminary, he was immediately attracted by its combination of piety and intellect. He was also impressed by Carl Henry's *Uneasy Conscience of Modern Fundamentalism*. At Fuller itself, he was especially inspired by Carnell, though he also came under the tutelage of William LaSor in Old Testament studies. He then joined the Conservative Baptist Association, which put him into the network of Reformed groups that had shaped Fuller Seminary. Nonetheless, despite his identification with the new evangelical reformers, he retained sympathies not often found in their heritages.[20]

Hubbard was also among the first in the second generation of new evangelicals, that is, he was among the first students of the founders of the movement. So was his dean, Daniel Fuller. The original new evangelicals themselves had been second generation fundamentalists. As the first generation organizers of their own movement, their agenda was, as we have seen, dictated by fundamentalism—they still saw themselves fighting for the fundamentalist cause in the fundamentalist-modernist controversies. For most of them it was thus extremely important not to move too far from fundamentalism—to put a left boundary on the course they set. Inerrancy served this purpose. Their protégés, however, were one more step removed from the fundamentalist-modernist wars: those contests were for them second hand. Their experiences had been more exclusively shaped by the wars against the strict fundamentalists. So when they set boundaries on the left they tended to be less concerned with where their fundamentalist forebears had drawn the line.

Probably also relevant to Hubbard's broader view was that, unlike every other major figure in the seminary's history excepting the Fullers, he was a native Californian. California seemed on the edge of Western civilization in that its institutional traditions were not firmly fixed. Hubbard clearly reflected this trait of the region. Like Charles Fuller before him, he saw that with the proper resources institutions could become almost anything one wanted. Unlike the easterners (and vastly more than the Britishers), both Fuller and Hubbard tended not to see traditional structures as inevitable.

Hubbard evidenced this innovative vision from the outset. In June 1962, as part of the early campaign for his presidency, Don Weber had arranged for him to address the alumni association. In addition to setting a broad agenda of theological education balancing scholarship with love, practicality, and ministry to the whole person, Hubbard suggested a radical vision of what a theological seminary could be. The universities of the twentieth century, he observed, had unfortunately become multiversities, where the disciplines had been separated and specialized. The academic world needed

20. Hubbard, "The Life of Helena White Hubbard," draft of chapel address, FTS, May 22, 1984; DH interviews, fall 1983.

David Hubbard in the classroom

reintegration of the disciplines. It could be, therefore, that the theological seminary would "bring into life the true meaning of the word university where the whole process of learning sings one song, where truth is seen as a whole not as a series of fragments."[21]

Though Hubbard did not describe the implications of this ideal in quite the grandiose terms that might have been heard in the Ockenga-Henry-Carnell era, the vision still persisted that Fuller Seminary should be a lighthouse on the hill, a model of Christian charity, piety, intellect, and practicality.

What made plausible this expansion of the founders' view of the role of theological education was the prospect of the other schools to be added to the theological school. Already in 1962 there were plans for the School of Psychology and serious talk of a school of missions. Coming into this situation, Hubbard soon envisioned a sort of theological university. As he put it on an early chart, the School of Theology would be at the core surrounded by satellite graduate schools in other fields, not only psychology and missions, but conceivably in social work or even Christianity and literature. At one time in the later 1960s there was even some consideration of calling the school Fuller University. Hubbard, however, thought that theological seminaries repre-

21. Hubbard, "The Question of Wholeness in Theological Education," address delivered at the annual alumni association luncheon in June 1962 (mimeograph).

sented a valuable heritage that should not be treated as though it were second best. The eventual compromise, when the other schools were in fact added, was to refer to each of the three "graduate schools" of the seminary and the idea of a larger theological graduate center or university faded away.

Hubbard's earliest efforts in setting up the new schools coincided with new faculty recruitment policies that reflected the suddenly broadened operative concept of who the evangelicals really were. Up to the Hubbard era Fuller had found new faculty almost entirely through a narrow network of acquaintances connected with Wheaton, Westminster, Gordon, or related evangelical organizations. Usually those hired were already known to several of the faculty. In theory the neo-evangelicals claimed to speak for a wide constituency; in practice, however, they had kept the leadership on a narrow foundation.

CHRISTIANITY AND THE SCIENCE OF PSYCHOLOGY

A preliminary step toward broadening the bounds of evangelicalism was taken in large part through the influence of the Weyerhaeusers. The emergence of the School of Psychology, which admitted its first class of students in 1965, evidenced the large impact a few individuals could have on the course of events. Annette Weyerhaeuser's role was central. She herself had suffered from some debilitating anxieties since early in their marriage, among which was a fear of heights. This phobia became a major problem when a ferry to their summer home in Tacoma was being replaced by a high bridge. She found dramatic help, however, from a Christian psychiatrist, John Finch, who eventually suggested that Fuller found a Christian school of psychology.

Finch was an evangelical, but of an ilk much different from that which had shaped Fuller Seminary thus far. He was born and reared in India and had a strict old-style Methodist upbringing, which he considered repressive. He studied theology in India and then pastored several Methodist churches there. He came to the United States in 1946, and in the following years he pastored a Methodist and then a Presbyterian church in New Jersey. Throughout his ministerial career he had always been deeply interested in relating Christianity to contemporary psychology. While still in India, he had studied philosophy and psychology at Calcutta University, and in this country he eventually received a Ph.D. from Drew University. In 1954 he came to Tacoma and began counselling.

Finch was especially concerned with the philosophical issues that underlay the divergence of the Christian and contemporary psychological worldviews. His dissertation was a critical assessment of Freud's assumptions about human nature and included suggestions for an alternative Christian view. Finch viewed humans as made up of body, mind, and spirit together, and he deplored any worldview that did not integrate and balance the three. Modern psychology, in his view, had neglected the spiritual dimension that was necessary to self-transcendence. He was especially critical of modern psychology's positivistic pretensions to be a natural science. He was convinced that this approach, reflecting strong trends in modern thought since at least Descartes, overestimated the importance of the cognitive.

Impressed by Finch's insights, the Weyerhaeuser's sponsored him in a series of lectures at Fuller in 1961. Consistent with his Methodist background, his psychological training, and his expansive personality, Finch deplored highly cognitive theology. Viewing Fuller in 1961 as still essentially a "fundamentalist" institution, he feared—not altogether without reason—that he might be "tarred and feathered" when he spoke there. His lectures, which raised some essential issues about the relationship of Christianity to modern psychology, were received with considerable interest, though not with entire approbation from the more cognitively oriented members of the theological faculty. Oddly, Carnell, who was then himself deeply involved with modern psychology, was one of Finch's more severe critics. Finch's call for a sort of Christian existentialist rethinking of human nature might have seemed to fit some of Carnell's own proposals in his later works. Yet Carnell was both less critical of the presuppositions of Freudian psychology than was Finch and also, despite his best efforts, irrepressibly cognitive.

Some students asked where to go to study this sort of integration of psychology and Christianity. Finch replied that no such place existed. "If we want to have those in the field who will practice Christian psychology, we must grow our own." The Weyerhaeusers took the idea to heart and proposed a school to teach Christian views of psychological counselling.[22]

Finch was too much the outspoken outsider to control the direction of the school; but he was an important force in broadening the early outlook. From the outset the founders envisioned the School of Psychology not as a center for pastoral psychology, but as a bona fide Ph.D. program in clinical psychology, to which they would add substantial theological perspectives. The planners eventually designed a formidable six-year program, including a large portion of the B.D. curriculum at the School of Theology. Symptomatic of the rigor was that Ph.D. students in psychology would be required to know four languages: Greek and Hebrew in addition to two modern ones. The latter years of their program would involve an extended series of "integration seminars" in which professors from the two schools would attempt to relate their disciplines to each other.

"Integration" of psychology and theology was at the heart of the enterprise as Finch had conceived it; but those who planned the school quickly found that this was a vexing topic. They realized that little had been done by way of integrating even the first principles of the two fields, and so they designed a curriculum that involved extensive exploration of this largely uncharted territory. They also recognized, however, that there was little consensus as to what integration would involve, or what it would lead to. Some

22. Interview with John G. Finch, 9-23-83; William T. Weyerhaeuser, "The Significance of John Finch for a Christian Psychology," 3-14, and Annette B. Weyerhaeuser, "Vitality and Power," 89-96, both in *A Christian Existential Psychology: The Contributions of John G. Finch*, ed. Newton Malony (Lanham, Md.: University Press of America, 1980). See also Finch, four lectures, FTS 1961, mimeograph (School of Psychology archives).

regarded psychology as a more-or-less autonomous science into which it would be an intrusion to introduce theological presuppositions. Others wanted to know exactly what edge, if any, a Christian perspective provided the therapist. The curriculum forced continuing attention to questions of integration; but even so these did not bring easy or early results to revolutionize the field.[23]

Paul Fairweather, professor of pastoral counselling and psychology at the School of Theology, played a major role on the planning committees along with Finch, Hubbard, Weyerhaeuser, and numerous distinguished consultants. Together they decided to begin in 1964 with the formation of the Pasadena Community Counselling Center. Especially influential in pushing in this direction was another one of the distinguished new trustees, Stanley W. Olson, dean of the Baylor University College of Medicine. Olson insisted that the school should have the counselling center to provide a research base prior to admitting students the next year. Donald F. Tweedie, Jr., was subsequently hired to head the center. Tweedie had attended Fuller in the early 1950s and came from Gordon College and thus was part of the original neo-evangelical network. His principal coworker at the counselling center, Paul F. Barkman, a specialist in children's counselling, was the first staff member to evidence the opening up process in Fuller's concept of evangelicalism. Barkman was an ordained minister in the Evangelical Mennonite Church. Although he was a full-fledged evangelical doctrinally, at Fuller he always felt, according to his own later account, an outsider theologically. He considered himself an Arminian and not a Calvinist, and an Anabaptist rather than a pietist.[24]

Much more important for building a broader evangelical base for Fuller was the selection of the dean for the new school. They had to find someone with a national reputation who could help gain early accreditation, for without it the program would be almost worthless. After a lengthy quest, the search committee found an ideal candidate close at home. In the fall of 1964 Lee Edward Travis was appointed dean, to assume his duties at the beginning of 1965.

Travis was known among his peers as one of the leading figures in the history of American psychology. In 1957, 1,350 American psychologists were asked in a survey who had most influenced their involvement in psychology. Travis was ranked thirteenth in influence. He was the first American to engage in brain wave (EEG) research and had long been the dominant figure in the field of speech pathology. For many years he taught at the University of Iowa and later at the University of Southern California. Since 1960 he had also established a private clinical practice.

In the spring of 1961, just as he was approaching sixty-five, Travis and his wife, Lysa, attended church for the first time in forty years. As a boy in the

23. The FTS archives contain detailed reports of early psychology school planning discussions, at which these topics were well rehearsed.
24. Conversation with Paul Barkman and School of Psychology faculty members, 12-1-83.

rugged land of western Nebraska, Travis was baptized by a Mormon elder. He went through an extended time of religious belief and eventually attended Graceland Academy in Iowa, a school of the Reorganized Church of the Latter Day Saints (which was more like an evangelical Christian sect than was the Utah Church). But since then he had fallen away from church attendance. The church that he attended in 1961 was the Bel Air Presbyterian Church, where Louis H. Evans, Jr., was pastor. Travis found himself overwhelmed by a profound sense of transcendence in which he felt found by God. He had a sense, rare among psychologists, of the emptiness of modern human attempts to gain mastery over the ultimately fatal human condition. He eventually let himself travel "the road of wonder over the road of logic" and accepted the evangelical gospel of grace.[25]

During the search for a dean for the School of Psychology, a Fuller graduate who was one of Travis's patients told the seminary people about him. The committee leaped at the chance and eventually persuaded him to begin at age sixty-eight what became an extensive new career. Travis's leadership undoubtedly was largely responsible for the rapid accreditation of the School of Psychology, in marked contrast to the earlier problems for the theological school. The School of Psychology in fact paved the way for the accreditation of doctoral programs at all three school by the Western Association of Schools and Colleges in 1969. In 1974 the American Psychological Association also approved the clinical program of the School of Psychology, the first such approval of a school not connected with a university. Travis's leadership thus proved an invaluable asset.

At the Bel Air Presbyterian Church Travis was already in more or less the same religious orbit as Fuller Seminary. Although his interests were wide and his theological instincts sound by Fuller standards, he was a new Christian and first had to learn theology in order to talk about integration. While he took up this task with eagerness, his policy for the school itself was that it first had to excel by conventional standards in clinical psychology before it could expend its energies in the unexplored areas of theoretical integration. The theoretical explorations were thus an added-on part of the program, but always a serious concern for attacking unresolved problems.

The addition of Paul Clement to the faculty in 1967 was symptomatic of the move away from Finch's original speculative integrationist vision toward professionalization. Recently out of graduate school, Clement was, according to Travis, a key person in setting the standards necessary for accreditation. On the other hand, Clement had put considerable thought into relating Christianity to psychology and had concluded that the task was impossible. Some of the School of Theology people said that he was a behaviorist.

25. See two essays by Lee Travis: "An Answer to a Stuggle for Immortality," 39-48, and "Belief in God: My Field of Reality," 199-203, both in *Psychologist Pro Tem: In Honor of the 80th Birthday of Lee Edward Travis*, ed. Donald F. Tweedie, Jr., and Paul W. Clement (Los Angeles: University of Southern California Press, 1976). See 122 and passim for other information.

Lee Travis: science and piety

This he denied. He did hold, though, that psychology and theology were separate diciplines with different rules that could not be synthesized.[26]

WORLD MISSION AND CHURCH GROWTH

If Travis was a distinguished outsider who was happy to learn from the Fuller version of evangelicalism, Donald McGavran, his contemporary and counterpart at the School of World Mission, was a long-time missionary who represented a tradition of evangelicalism remarkably independent of the Fuller ex-fundamentalist variety.

Shortly after assuming the presidency, David Hubbard appointed a

26. Travis interview, 11-28-83; see also the manuscript chapter from his autobiography that details his early days at FTS; Paul Clement, interview at faculty retreat, 9-16-83.

committee to lay plans for an "Institute for World Evangelism." J. Kenneth Strachen, general director of the Latin American Mission who had recently been teaching missions at the seminary, was an early inspiration for the project before his untimely death in 1965 and was the first chairman of the planning committee. In the fall of 1964 William LaSor, one of the leaders in the early faculty's widespread enthusiasm for missions, became chairman.

In its early days, the seminary had prided itself on the number of its graduates who went on to the mission field. According to a 1960 board report 100 of 570 graduates had gone into missions. But the numbers had been dropping off noticeably since about 1956.[27] Hoping to regain this earlier emphasis, LaSor's committee, together with Hubbard and Daniel Fuller, sought extensive advice from expert missiologists.

From a number of directions they began hearing about McGavran and his "church growth" movement. McGavran already headed a small organization called the Institute for Church Growth, which he had founded in 1961 at Northwest Christian College in Eugene, Oregon. In the spring of 1965 the Fuller people met with him and soon persuaded him to move his institute to Pasadena. He insisted, however, on maintaining the integrity and identity of his school.[28] To emphasize his point that the move to Fuller was a merger, not an absorption, the name for his institute would become the School of World Mission and Institute for Church Growth.

So, unlike the School of Psychology, where the integration of psychology with the evangelical tradition was a distant goal to be pursued, McGavran's school came to Fuller with a distinct evangelical viewpoint in which most of the conclusions had already been drawn. In the long run, the merger of this outlook with the rest of the Fuller heritage proved as difficult as the more obviously Herculean task of integrating the largely opposed assumptions of modern psychology and evangelical theology.

Of missionary parentage himself, McGavran belonged to the Disciples of Christ. He was educated at some of the best American liberal theological schools and, during about the first ten of his thirty years as a missionary in India, he held liberal Christian beliefs himself. During the 1930s, however, he concluded that the liberal view of the Bible, which seemed to allow one to dispense with any passage one did not like, was not viable. Unless there was an infallible and authoritative Bible, there was no reason for Christian missions at all. He thus worked his way to a traditional evangelical position, though he had never been a fundamentalist.[29]

---

27. Annual Report to the Board of Trustees, May 1960, 2. An alumni survey in 1962 located 486 graduates in full-time religious work, 113 of whom were with missions agencies.

28. McGavran to DH and Ross J. Griffith, 5-10-65 (McGavran papers, Billy Graham Center, Wheaton, Ill.). See also Daniel Fuller, *Give the Winds a Mighty Voice: The Story of Charles E. Fuller* (Waco, Tex.: Word, 1972), 230-34.

29. McGavran, "That the Gospel Be Made Known," *Theology News and Notes,* June 1985, 10-13; McGavran interview, 11-18-83.

McGavran, accordingly, was in the rare position of combining a thoroughgoing evangelical zeal for spreading the old-time gospel with a background that provided perspectives more common to the liberal theological position. One such perspective was a sensitivity to anthropology and the cultural context in which Christianity develops and missions take place. Such sensitivities had been almost exclusively the property of the liberal side of the American Protestant tradition. At Fuller Seminary, for instance, the new evangelicalism, relative to most of twentieth-century thought, had involved remarkably little sense of the culturally conditioned aspect of human belief. One of the intellectual traits that had most distinguished fundamentalism from modernism was the fundamentalists' emphasis on timeless truth as opposed to the cultural relativism of the liberals. Because of their emphasis on the original biblical languages, the Fuller new evangelicals, like their sophisticated fundamentalist forebears, knew that one had to study ancient culture to understand biblical meanings. But they had not developed a critical awareness of the cultural roots of their own heritage, and they dealt with cross-cultural issues at only an elementary level. McGavran, on the other hand, saw such understandings as central to properly carrying out the Christian mission. Accordingly, the first colleague he brought with him was an anthropologist, Alan Tippett, an Australian who had been among McGavran's first students at the Institute for Church Growth. The early addition of Charles H. Kraft in the field of Missionary Anthropology added to the school an aggressive proponent of recognizing the culturally conditioned aspects of *all* theological and ethical statements.

In this respect, the parallel to the School of Psychology was instructive. A chief theoretical question at each school was how to integrate evangelical theology with contemporary social sciences, based as they were on vastly different and often opposed premises about human nature and standards of evaluation. In the School of Psychology this divergence of assumptions was considered a central problem to be addressed. Even if there were internal disagreements as to whether integration was possible, the search for it continued and was in fact built into the curriculum. Lee Travis, for instance, was quite ready to say that psychology had "hardly any answers" and that one then needed to look to theology on the underlying issues.[30] A lack of a clear tradition in the School of Theology as to how Christian assumptions might alter another "science" hampered this enterprise; but constructive efforts continued.

At the School of World Mission, on the other hand, integration took place at the practical level. Church growth came first, and anthropology was to be used in its service. The anthropology itself tended to be taken as a given— as an autonomous scientific discipline—to which, according to Kraft at least, evangelical theology ought to adjust. Kraft freely expressed the opinion, apparently shared by most of the early faculty at both of the new schools, that the

30. Travis interview.

Mission work got a new emphasis at Fuller with the arrival of Donald McGavran and the Institute for Church Growth. Here David Hubbard (left) and Donald McGavran (right) see off the Latin America Research Team

theologians "across the street" regarded them as second-class citizens.[31] In response to the problematic relationship of the new schools to the older one, the new schools carefully guarded their autonomy during their early years, not even allowing theology students to take their courses.

McGavran's own original vision departed from the fundamentalist-evangelical heritage in another important respect. When he was asked what was wrong with current missions, one of his major answers pointed directly at a central aspect of the American evangelical fundamentalist heritage: its view

31. Kraft interview, at faculty retreat, 9-16-83. Kraft's views are summarized in "Can Anthropological Insight Assist Evangelical Theology?" *Christian Scholar's Review* 7, nos. 2, 3 (1977): 165-202.

of the church. The most aggressive modern missions, McGavran observed, were dominated by the "gathered church" ideal. This concept—that the church should be made up only of well-qualified and well-tested believers—was a reaction to inclusivist state church practices. The gathered church ideal had been an important factor in American Protestant thought since the days of the Puritans and was reinforced by the Great Awakening. It also dominated much of early American evangelicalism. Indeed, Protestant church membership in America through the mid-nineteenth century remained relatively low in part because it was so hard to join most evangelical churches. Often each individual member was required to recount a definite conversion experience.

The liberalization of American Protestantism in the late nineteenth and early twentieth centuries involved abandonment of this gathered church tradition in favor of easy, inclusivist membership. By contrast, one of the important features of fundamentalism was its reemphasis of the gathered church tradition. Dispensationalism put special emphasis on this theme, seeing the church as a "remnant" of true believers, not to be confused with the decadent inclusivist organizations that called themselves "churches."

Without specifying this background, McGavran identified the gathered church concept as one of the chief defects of modern missions. Missionaries set up "gathered colonies" and tried to win individual converts here and there. This sectarian and individualistic approach reflected ideals that might be appropriate to "discipled nations" with nominal Christianity, but it was inappropriate for non-Christian lands. What McGavran wanted was a revolutionary concept of evangelical missions as directed toward "peoples" rather than individuals. Each nation was made up of groups and sub-groups of peoples. The characteristics of each of these and their openness to the gospel could be identified. Then, building on the "bridges" that connected people, such as kinship lines, missionaries could concentrate their efforts on whole peoples who appeared especially responsive, rather than continuinng to rely on their hit-or-miss methods among generally unresponsive populations.

In McGavran's view, then, missionaries should concentrate on "discipling" whole peoples. In contrast to traditional evangelical concepts, such discipling did not involve leading each church member to a documentable conversion experience. Rather, more in tune with the open-church tendencies of twentieth-century liberal Christians or the methods of Christian advance in the early middle ages, all the missionary should require for "discipling" a people was that they collectively agree to abandon their old religion, to identify with Christ, and to claim the Bible as their authority and the church as their institution. The evangelical aversion to "mass produced" conversions and the demands for "solid foundations" of Christian maturity as a precondition for admitting individuals to church membership were, in McGavran's view, the standards of "ice-age missions."[32]

32. This summary of McGavran's views is based primarily on his two major early works, *The Bridges of God* (New York: Friendship Press, 1955) and *How Churches Grow: The New Frontiers of Mission* (London: World Dominion Press, 1955).

McGavran's outlook differed with the dominant view of the church at Fuller Seminary. The statement of faith, for instance, described the church as consisting "of all those regenerated by the Spirit of God, in mystical union and communion both with Christ, the Head and the Body, and with their fellow-believers," but it made no mention of the church as a visible organization. On the other hand, the faculty had never been committed to the sectarian view of the church, even though they tended to be sectarian in practice. The school had long been working, after all, for acceptance by America's more inclusivist denominations.

The whole emphasis and rationale for the School of Theology, none-theless, had been to build a solid base of quality for American evangelicalism. Revivalist fundamentalism's growth in numbers had not been enough for the neo-evangelicals. They insisted on rigorous theology and scholarship for just this reason. It would require a good bit of flexibility on both sides to accept that such strategy might be appropriate for a discipled land but inappropriate to export to the mission field. On the face of it, however, the two schools would coexist while teaching very different views of the importance of theology as such, and with the School of World Mission far more open to innovations that promoted church growth. McGavran made clear in his earliest contacts with Fuller that the "best" methods would not be taught if they did not work, that is, if they did not foster the "supreme aim" that "multitudes be added to the Lord."[33] How much the interests of growth would determine the boundaries of acceptable Christian practice and how much they would be set by the "best" theoretical theological concerns was left unsettled.

Even for the evangelistic side of the Fuller-fundamentalist tradition, McGavran represented at least a change in tone. The aging Charles Fuller had always dreamed of a school of missions and evangelism, and he was delighted with the prospect for the new school and with the veteran missionaries who enrolled. But on the other hand it was no secret that McGavran was something of a disappointment to Fuller. McGavran was frankly a technician of church growth. He lamented that while Christians would support careful research to develop a synthetic fabric or to deliver mail faster, they would not invest the same effort in finding out what made missions successful. In 1965, such scientific approaches to the work of missions was unfamiliar and could easily be regarded as insufficiently pious. Even though Charles Fuller had been something of a master of technique in his generation, he had always regarded the warmth of the Holy Spirit, projected toward each individual who heard his broadcast, as overwhelmingly the most important key to his success. Symptomatic of Fuller's concern for individuals was his long-standing interest in evangelism in isolated areas too poor to sustain a church—among just the sorts of people whom market analysis would suggest neglecting.[34]

33. McGavran, "Purpose, Objectives, Curriculum, and Staff for the Graduate School of World Mission and Evangelism being proposed at Fuller Theological Seminary," statement sent to DH, 3-5-65.
34. Daniel Fuller, *Give the Winds a Mighty Voice*, 191.

In the summer of 1965 McGavran came to the Fuller Conference at Mount Hermon to tell supporters about the new school. He illustrated his talk on church growth with numerous charts and graphs. When McGavran was finished, Charles Fuller got up and, without the usual thanking of the missionary for his wonderful presentation, suggested that everyone just sing a chorus of "Heavenly Sunshine" and then turn around and shake hands with their neighbors.[35]

Despite these differences in the two styles of evangelicalism that were now converging at Fuller, they had enough in common to be able to blend. McGavran was personally warm and optimistic. Moreover, his pragmatism was a version of a trait long near the heart of American evangelicalism. Evangelical and fundamentalist revivalists had always worked on a free enterprise system. Marketing considerations had often influenced gospel concerns. And revivalists were typically better at numbering converts than in nourishing them in deep spiritual communities. Charles Finney in the early nineteenth century was in fact the first technician of winning converts, saying it was as much a science as growing grain was. Finney's "science" suggested the importance of personalistic methods in gospel preaching, and his concern for the market was important in replacing Calvinism with milder, more preachable, doctrines in most of American revivalism. Finney's successors, such as Dwight L. Moody and Billy Sunday, adopted many of his innovations, even if the popular romanticism of their personalistic message did not fit with emphasizing that soul winning was a science. Behind the scenes, however, even the most pious segments of big-time evangelism, such as the Billy Graham enterprises, had developed scientific methods of gauging response or potential response. McGavran could thus resonate with a pragmatic, sometime-scientific theme in the tradition, even if his application of it to missions called for some rethinking.

Most importantly, MacGavran was, in his innovative way, a great proponent of soul winning. Winning converts, he insisted, was what missions was all about. In this respect he passed with flying colors one of the central evangelical and fundamentalist tests, especially for anyone dealing with the mission field. He was, in this, distinctly antiliberal. Although he indeed criticized the fundamentalist gathered church idea as well-meaning but misapplied, his other major critique of modern missions was directed at the liberal missionary establishment. Their typical fault was that they mixed the true purpose of missions—to win converts—with other laudable causes like doing good or spreading peace and justice. These important concerns might legitimately be advanced after populations were converted; but by making them primary the liberal churches were turning missions into simply a massive interchurch aid program.[36] Perhaps as good an indication as any that McGavran seemed "safe" to traditionalist fundamentalist evangelicals was a review of

---

35. DF interview. See also interview with McGavran, 11-18-83, which confirms the general feeling of cordial coolness from Charles Fuller.

36. McGavran often makes such points, e.g., in *How Churches Grow*, 182-85.

one of his works by Harold Lindsell, published in *Christianity Today* in May 1965. Lindsell had nothing but praise for McGavran and his coauthors. McGavran, the volume's editor, had provided a "spendid overview" of the church growth views of the book. The volume, said Fuller's former professor of missions, "should be required reading for every missionary, missionary administrator, and every pastor."[37]

Though Fuller Seminary under Hubbard would in many ways differ from the institution in the era of Lindsell, Smith, Archer, and Henry, important continuities remained.

37. Lindsell, review of *Church Growth and Christian Missions,* ed. Donald McGavran, in *Christianity Today,* May 21, 1965, 30.

CHAPTER XIII

End of an Era

It is almost self-evident that we shall do nothing but articulate empty sounds if we speak about moral and spiritual values without defining exactly what we mean when we speak. Our modern young people are already confused about who they are and what purpose life has, if any, without adding the confusion of a moral sermon which makes no effort to explain the ground of morals and why it is necessary that we strive more seriously to be moral.

Edward J. Carnell, manuscript entitled "Moral and Spiritual Values," April 1967.

OPEN EVANGELICALISM

ALUMNI returning to Fuller in the mid 1960s would have found the seminary little changed since the mid 1950s. Though the presence of the two new schools altered the overall picture, the size of the theology school remained much the same. In 1951–52 the seminary enrolled 245 students. In 1966–67, the School of Theology enrolled 243 (down about sixty from a peak just after the Carnell era). The School of Psychology in 1966–67 enrolled 52 students, including a number of former pastors, not always the strictest evangelicals, who wished to change fields. The School of World Mission added 41, almost entirely veteran missionaries.[1]

The most evident difference would, of course, have been the disappearance of the whole right-wing of theological stalwarts: Henry, Woodbridge, Smith, Archer, and Lindsell. Moreover, an acute observer in the mid-1960s would soon note that no one talked anymore about Fuller being the continuation of the old Princeton. Nor did the faculty any longer give artifical respiration to the accompaning myth that Fuller was a gentleman's school.

A returning alumnus would also have noticed a general loosening of the evangelical ethos. The numerous statements of Fuller's platform during the 1960s typically included planks promoting such traits as "loving kindness," "balanced judgment" (in distinguishing between primary and second-

1. "Quarter Century of Growth, "*Bulletin of Fuller Theological Seminary* 21 (December 1971). As late as 1971 the School of Theology enrolled only 315, indicating a slow growth comparable to the population expansion of the past twenty years. The comment on psychology students is from interview with Lee Travis, 11-28-83.

ary teachings), and "an open mind."[2] These emphases, which continued President Carnell's concerns, presumably also reflected some reactions of the two early graduates, David Hubbard and Daniel Fuller, against the tighter, rule-oriented atmosphere of the earlier years. The most conspicuous change, however, was the demise of compulsory chapel, a transition culminated at the outset of the Fuller-Hubbard years. During his student days, Dan Fuller had been a champion of student spiritual life. Though he did not change his view of the importance of chapel, he nonetheless sympathized with the student leaders of the early sixties who argued that compulsion was no way to ensure spirituality. Students promised to keep up attendance and such voluntary support seemed far more meaningful. Within a few years, though, the attendance had dwindled embarrassingly. Even well-known missionary speakers, who would have excited campus-wide enthusiasm in earlier eras, might draw only handfuls.[3] Complaints about the spiritual atmosphere cropped up as usual. On the other hand, some alumni recalled striking personal contacts. David Hubbard knew every student and spouse by name, and the aged Fullers made special efforts to meet seminary students and to make them feel at home.

The more open atmosphere of the early Hubbard years could also have a welcome impact on students. "I found F.T.S. to be a breath of fresh air," one student who had transferred from a more conservative seminary later wrote. "I felt as free to be myself at Fuller as I've ever felt before or afterward," commented another alumnus. This latter remark suggests the degree to which the mood at Fuller was responsive to the changing student atmosphere nationally. More and more people were setting values on the basis of personal commitment rather than strict rules. Fuller students who used such language of personal fulfillment, however, still tended to find freedom within largely traditional structures of rules.

Though a survey of alumni recollections of their views as students has obvious limitations, we can draw from it rough estimates of the extent to which the atmosphere at Fuller has changed over the years.[4] The biggest doctrinal changes, as one might expect, were regarding the inerrancy of the Bible. Three-fourths of the students coming to Fuller in its earliest days, in the graduating classes of 1950 to 1952, came with a solid belief in inerrancy. At the time they left Fuller about 60 percent of them still remained firm in this view, while almost all the rest held something like a limited inerrancy view. By the 1960s, on the other hand, limited inerrancy was the overwhelmingly dominant, though not undisputed, view. Less than half the students entering Fuller held to strict inerrancy and only about one-fourth left with the view intact.

Consistent with the stance of the school's leadership, the large changes on inerrancy appear not to have been accompanied by comparable changes concerning the evangelical gospel message. Eighty-five percent of the

---

2. "The Philosophy of Fuller Seminary," in FTS Catalog, 1964–66, 13-15.
3. DF interview, fall 1983.
4. See the Appendix for survey details.

1960s students, for instance, believed in hell as "a place of eternal torment for those who do not believe in Jesus Christ." This was down from 94 percent in the 1950 to 1952 group, but still showed solid support for a crucial element in the tradition. Almost all Fuller students still affirmed that "the only hope of Heaven is through person faith in Jesus Christ." One-fourth of the alumni from 1950 to 1952 said that when they graduated they would have preferred to add to this affirmation the qualifier "*except* those who have not had the opportunity to hear of Jesus Christ." By the later 1960s about one third of the students would have preferred adding this qualifier.

On behavioral matters, the patterns of continuity and change were similar. On most questions of mores the students of the 1950s were overwhelmingly conservative. The student body of the 1960s, including some reputedly more progressive School of Psychology students, was much the same except for the presence of about 10 percent who took more progressive views. In the early 1950s, according to the survey, 96 percent said homosexual and extramarital sexual relationships were "always" wrong. Of students surveyed from the 1960s, slightly less than 90 percent said "always wrong." Views on premarital sex loosened somewhat more. Seventy-seven percent of the 1960s students said "always wrong," compared with 92 percent from the first classes.

Predictably, the biggest change came regarding a leading behavioral badge separating fundamentalism from much of the Christian heritage. At the early Fuller only 10 percent of the students would have said that drinking alcohol was "rarely" or "never" wrong (and those who did have a drink must have been closet drinkers, since nearly half the student body said it was "always wrong"). By the late sixties over a third thought that drinking was permissible, and only one Fuller student in seven would insist that drinking was always wrong. Significantly, this change, like that regarding inerrancy, reflected not only differences in what was being taught at Fuller, but also differences in the students being attracted to Fuller.

This greater openness was bound to bring some conflict with those used to the fundamentalist ethos. Now some of the progressive faculty were no longer teetotalers; and the old guard got wind of other changes as well. In 1966 Harold Ockenga and Herbert J. Taylor became agitated over some things they heard about James Daane, who was being hired to head a new four-year pastoral doctorate program. Daane, who had been pastor of a Christian Reformed church in the Los Angeles area, had long had contacts with Fuller people and had worked with Lindsell and Henry at *Christianity Today*. Now he was becoming slightly controversial, though. Through the evangelical network, Ockenga and Taylor heard that Daane was amillennial, that he did not affirm inerrancy, and that he smoked. Apparently they did not hear that he took a traditional Calvinist view toward drinking as well. Daane's aversion to the term *inerrancy* was nothing new at Fuller. That a faculty member was known to smoke was. Hubbard was sure Daane would exercise discretion and argued, as Carnell apparently agreed, that the smoking issue was among the "adiaphora," not a question central to the faith. Ockenga maintained however that the "habitual use of tobacco," although not a sign of a lack of Christianity, was a matter of a lack of consecration.[5]

Some students were also quite puzzled by the transition from the fundamentalist to the more open atmosphere. One former School of Psychology student recalled that "a rather large percentage (but still a minority) of the students at the then-new School of Psychology retired from a day of theological/psychological studies to a bar down the street on Walnut." Such signs of the times contrasted particularly with the warm traditionalist piety that was still openly expressed at Fuller. The same student was deeply impressed by the tearful testimony of Donald Cole, a School of Psychology professor, that his deep assurance of the truth of the gospel had come from hearing children singing "Jesus Loves Me."

GEORGE ELDON LADD

One professor whose paradoxical contrasts became legendary was George Ladd. Ladd's academic rigor was at once both intimidating and a great inspiration to many students. A grade of B from him was considered the equivalent of an A in other courses. He could demolish students by saying one of their papers "sounds more like a sermon than scholarship" or for using a Bible handbook for research. Every preacher, he insisted, must be a theologian. Paul and Moses, he argued, were learned men with the best training of their days.

At the same time, Ladd never ceased to be the Baptist preacher, a man of deep sentiments. He was known to weep in class when telling how God had given him the opportunity to leave his small New England pastorates and become a scholar. He had also retained through Fuller's transitions a deep love for the evangelical cause. "We're in the business to save souls," he told the students, "and let's not forget it." One alumnus recalls that at the opening of a class "he counseled us that we must make our peace with God about missions before we consider an academic teaching ministry."[6]

George Ladd also went through some personal struggles, and the several sides of his personality were not always well integrated. His outlook was in a number of respects parallel to Carnell's, though Ladd was more the pastor, more sensitive, rather than always appearing rigidly in control. Ladd had almost exactly the same high aspirations for evangelical scholarship as did Carnell and the other new evangelicals. In 1960 he noted that a *Life* magazine list of one hundred outstanding young men included no evangelicals, even though it included some theologians, such as Martin Marty and Jaroslav Pelikan. Ladd saw his calling as above all to correct evangelical scholarship's general lack of prestige. His ambition, as he sometimes told his students, was to write a book in biblical studies that every scholar in the field would have to

5. HJO to DH, 1-7-66, 1-19-66 (P); HJO to DH 1-28-66 (T); DH to HJO, 4-12-66 (P).
6. Alumni comments. Ladd quotation from sermon at new student retreat, fall 1960 (tape) (S).

respect. This was a Herculean task, since he also had to work within the parameters of conservative evangelical views of Scripture. Automatically, these conservative commitments would raise opposition from more progressive critics.

As Carnell had pinned his hopes on *Christian Commitment*, Ladd pinned his on *Jesus and the Kingdom: The Eschatology of Biblical Realism*, published in 1964, also by a secular press. Whereas most of Ladd's other work was directed toward evangelical problems and audiences, this volume reflected over ten years of scholarship and was directed at the wider community of New Testament interpreters. Its theme was that which Albert Schweitzer had put at the center of twentieth-century discussions of the origins of Christianity: What was Jesus' own view of the coming kingdom? Ladd wished to show how Jesus' view differed from that of Old Testament prophets and Jewish apocalyptists. Even more centrally, he hoped that his tour de force would be a demonstration that the higher critics who were preoccupied with finding the "Jesus of history," were in the process failing to discover the Jesus of the New Testament. Their problem was that they had employed secular scientific presuppositions that eliminated the possibility of God acting in history. While resolving to be equally scientific, Ladd proceeded on the assumption that the New Testament was an authoritative interpretation of God's entry into history through the Incarnation. Contrary to the secular presuppositions of the critics, then, Ladd asserted that the New Testament interpretation of the kingdom corresponded with Jesus' own view.[7] Ladd was thus taking up at least one aspect of the task set by Machen: providing for his generation a defense of the divine origins of the New Testament that effectively answered the best scholarly critics of the day.

An unfortunate set of circumstances contributed to the failure of Ladd's magnum opus to have anything like the impact for which he had hoped. First, shortly before his book was completed, two new major studies of Jesus' view of the kingdom appeared. Ladd could only mention these latest works in his notes, and thus his intention to definitively answer the latest scholarship was undercut.

Most importantly, the highly regarded author of one of the new volumes, Norman Perrin, a British scholar recently teaching at the University of Chicago, attacked Ladd's work unmercifully in the important American journal *Interpretation*. Perrin castigated Ladd on the same grounds that Ladd had attacked secular historicist criticism—that he had let his conclusions be controlled by his presuppositions. Perrin moreover found Ladd's exegesis "unusual." Ladd, he claimed, took passages and "simply extracts from them what he needs at that point, ignoring everything else." Probably more damaging, however, was that Perrin argued that Ladd actually had a most ambivalent attitude toward the twentieth-century critics. While "dismissing contemptuously aspects of their work which do not support him," Perrin said, Ladd demonstrated "what seems to be a ruling passion with him: the search for

7. Ladd, *Jesus and the Kingdom* (New York: Harper and Row, 1964), xi-xv.

critical support for his views." Perrin documented this tendency by citing several examples and implied there were many more. This passion for approval, he alleged, led Ladd to misconstrue some of the more liberal scholars in order to make them support his own views.[8]

To George Ladd, the impact of this review was devastating. Even though his reputation as the leading evangelical New Testament scholar was already solidly established, he saw Perrin's review as crucial in denying him prestige in the larger academic arena. Though other reviews were mixed, Ladd overreacted to this early review and never quite got over it. The problem was the old one of the neo-evangelical efforts to reestablish world-class evangelical scholarship. Fundamentalists and conservatives did not trust them (though Ladd and the more trusted Harrison had a major impact in bringing evangelical biblical studies into touch with modern scholarship), and the mainline academic community refused to take them seriously.

Perhaps Perrin had correctly perceived a trait of the new evangelical movement when he described Ladd as torn between his presuppositional critique of modern scholarship and his eagerness to find modern critical scholars on his side. At Fuller, scholars tended, through a variety of intellectual stances, to try to have a foot firmly planted in each community, the community of secular scientific academia and the community of fundamentalist-evangelical faith. No one quite succeeded philosophically in mapping the way this was to be done, though. The result was confusion, as became apparent with subsequent efforts to relate evangelical theology to the social sciences at the new schools. For Carnell and Ladd, who had the highest hopes for managing to be in both camps with the full respect of each, the difficulties of maintaining the balance contributed to deep personal anxiety.

In Ladd's case, the painful lack of enthusiasm from the larger academic community contrasted sharply with his immense prestige within his own evangelical domain. By the end of his career, he had clearly become the biblical scholar most respected by other evangelicals in the field. He was not content, however, to be a prophet with honor only in his own country.[9]

THE LOGICAL SEMINARY

At the School of Theology the new curriculum of the 1960s reflected the neo-evangelical intellectual agenda of being distinctly evangelical while at the same time producing scholarship so scientific that everyone would have to

8. Perrin, review of Ladd's *Jesus and the Kingdom* in *Interpretation* 19 (April 1965): 228-31.

9. In a later survey of evangelical biblical scholars, Ladd was ranked as "most influential" by scholars in the progressive evangelical organization Institute for Biblical Research and was placed just behind John Calvin as "most influential" among the scholars in the more conservative Evangelical Theological Society. See Mark A.Noll, "Survey of Evangelical Bible Scholars," appendix in *Between Faith and Criticism: Evangelicals, Scholarship, and the Bible in America* (San Francisco: Harper and Row, 1986), 209-14. Noll's book makes a major contribution toward understanding twentieth-century evangelical scholarship and is an important source on this major dimension of thought at FTS.

listen to it. The school catalogs of the era begin with a several-page disquisition, drafted by Geoffrey Bromiley, on the crucial importance of theology. The curriculum itself was highly standardized, with many core requirements and few electives. Academic idealism had prevailed over the general trends of the day toward openness. One of the outstanding features of the requirements was that each theology student started with a heavy dose of Daniel Fuller's hermeneutics. Fuller's approach represented yet another way of trying to give total allegiance both to warm evangelicalism and to scientific academia.

Daniel Fuller was the seminary's leading champion of an objectivist historical approach to Scripture—attempting to determine exactly what the writers intended to say without imposing our presuppositions or preconceptions on them. He maintained also that Christianity must be defended according to straightforward, ordinary standards for testing historical claims. So he argued, for instance, that if one did not arbitrarily exclude from the start the possibility of supernatural events, then the resurrection of Jesus was the only cause sufficient to explain the disciples' faith.[10]

In the academic reception of his scholarship, Daniel Fuller encountered obstacles similar to those that plagued his colleagues. Theological liberals and the neo-orthodox admired his careful work but did not find his empirically based proofs convincing. Moreover, because of who he was and his role in the seminary's controversial history, fundamentalist-evangelicals were especially ready to pounce on him. Thus when he publicly aired his views of inerrancy in December 1967 at a meeting of the Evangelical Theological Society in Toronto, rumors quickly flew again through the fundamentalist-evangelical network. David Hubbard, who was on a trip to the Orient, soon found to his chagrin that the word about Daniel Fuller was quite literally abroad. In Tokyo or in Saigon at the height of the Vietnam War, evangelical talk soon turned to Dan's views of inerrancy. About this time, Bill Bright, who had been hearing rumblings about Dan ever since Black Saturday, dropped his erstwhile classmate from the board of advisors to Campus Crusade.[11]

The irony of all this was that Daniel Fuller was, more than many of his critics, attempting to be wholly consistent with the essentials of the apologetics of B. B. Warfield, the great Princeton champion of inerrancy. With Warfield and against evangelical presuppositionalists and popularizers, as well as against neo-orthodoxy, Fuller argued for a rigorous "empirical" defense of Scripture. With Warfield and Machen, Fuller was willing to say boldly that "one should let one's faith stand or fall with the verdict of historical reasoning." Of course he differed from his predecessors in many specifics. Nonetheless, he was a latter-day champion of the classic American evangelical apologetic enterprise.

10. See Daniel Fuller, "The Resurrection of Jesus and the Historical Method," *Journal of Bible and Religion* 34 (January 1966): 18-24; and his *Easter Faith and History* (Grand Rapids: Eerdmans, 1965).
11. DF interview, fall 1983; Daniel Fuller, "Benjamin B. Warfield's View of Faith and History: A Critique in the Light of the New Testament," *Journal of the Evangelical Theological Society* 11 (1968): 75-83.

A small incident from the mid-sixties was later reported by a number of alumni as encapsulating the academic ethos of that time. A student noticed that the seminary's sign could be much improved with a small scribal emendation. For several days it read, appropriately, FULLER THE LOGICAL SEMINARY.

THE 1960s

In fact the 1960s turned out to be the last era when closely reasoned apologetics was a dominant motif in the Fuller curriculum. Not many of the signs of the school's future course—toward more practical and relational concerns—were yet present, though, except in the founding of the two new schools. Nonetheless, the seminary was beginning to be touched, at least in small ways, by the activism of the cultural revolution of the era.

To appreciate these changes, one must recall how politically conservative and withdrawn Fuller Seminary had been in the 1950s. According to the alumni recollections, about two-thirds of the students during the 1950s would have rated their political views as "conservative" or (for a few) "very conservative," outnumbering those who were "liberal" or "very liberal" by about ten to one.

In 1960 a classic fundamentalist pattern of political behavior recurred for the last time. Fundamentalists, and now their neo-evangelical offspring, were typically politically conservative but seldom politically active unless an "evangelical" issue was at stake. The prospect of the election of John Kennedy, a Catholic, aroused them from their political slumbers. At Fuller Seminary, opposition to Rome had always been part of the outlook, as it had been in Protestant education from the beginning. Fuller students who wished to learn something about Catholicism could do so in Harold Lindsell's elective entitled "Modern Cults." Point one of Lindsell's lecture notes on the Church of Rome was simply "It had Christian beginnings."[12] Though such views were tempered in various ways, they were the point of departure on which virtually everyone agreed.

Harold Ockenga, who had long been an ardent Catholic fighter in Boston, entered the lists with vigor during the Kennedy-Nixon campaign. Recalling for Protestants the atrocities of the Duke of Alva in the Netherlands and of the St. Bartholomew's Day massacre of 1572, Ockenga argued, in characteristic evangelical fashion, that if the Catholic hierarchy had its way in America, "the Protestant churches will be reduced to sects." No American president should be subject to a foreign ecclesiastical power, he said; and the best protection against that event was a "wall of separation" between church and state.[13]

Billy Graham was especially torn over what to do. He liked Nixon,

12. HL, lecture notes (L).
13. Ockenga, "Religion, Politics and the Presidency," sermon preached at Park Street Church, Boston, June 5, 1960, 11, 15.

favored Republicanism, and opposed Kennedy's Catholicism. He deeply wished to influence American politics for the good. On the other hand, he was a Baptist and interpreted separation of church and state to mean that he should not formally endorse a political candidate. Yet during 1960 he did everything but endorse Nixon. Finally, he gave in and prepared an article for *Life* endorsing the vice president. The contest was so close that his endorsement might have turned the tide, but at the last moment the Kennedy people objected and the article was withdrawn. Graham was deeply disappointed by the election result and remained ambivalent about what separation of church and state meant for the relationship between evangelicalism and politics.[14]

At Fuller Seminary there was similar disappointment and concern over the Kennedy victory. In *Theology News and Notes* of January 1961 Bill LaSor noted jokingly that the new decade had arrived despite the outcome of the last election. Perhaps not entirely facetiously, he added that "according to the Communist timetable, it will be America's last decade as an unfreed nation—so get busy."

As some alumni have noted, progressive social concerns were almost wholly absent from Fuller in the 1950s. The problem of racism and the current civil rights movement was one issue not squarely addressed by the school. Billy Graham had integrated his campaigns and the new evangelicals did list opposition to racism as one of their causes. Moreover, a few black students had attended Fuller and one was even elected student body president. Yet, according to the recollections of a black graduate of the late 1950s, the seminary, while not overtly racist, gave next to no recognition of the depths of the race problem. Despite neo-evangelical rhetoric, and an occasional article emphasizing that the race problem *was* a problem,[15] the seminary had, in the view of the alumnus, virtually nothing to offer on this front. As he recalled, "I could see little difference between the 'neo-evangelicalism' of Fuller and high-class fundamentalism."

In the early 1960s the new student newspaper, the *Opinion,* itself a sign of the times, carried a few articles on social concern. In May 1963 a black senior, Ralph S. Bell, felt impelled to write a piece with the central thesis, "the Negro is a human being." The point still had to be argued, he felt. "What are we to feel," asked Bell, "when we hear about the love of God in class and know that most of the faculty would be shocked if a Negro moved next door to them?"[16]

With the arrival of Hubbard, the seminary's public stance began to

---

14. Richard V. Pierard, "Billy Graham and the U.S. Presidency," *Journal of Church and State* 22 (Winter 1980): 107-27; Pierard, "Cacophony on Capitol Hill: Evangelical Voices in Politics," in *The Political Role of Religion in the United States,* ed. Stephen D. Johnson and Joseph B. Tamney (Boulder: Westview, 1986), 71-92. In a letter to Nixon, 6-19-61, Graham detailed the events preceding the election. This account is based on a summary provided by Richard Pierard in a letter to me, 10-21-86.

15. For examples see Harold Lindsell, "The Bible and Race Relations," *Eternity,* August 1956, 12-13, 43-44; and E. J. Carnell, "A Christian Social Ethics," *Opinion,* November 1962, 1-2.

16. Bell, "Christianity's Untouchables," *Opinion,* May 1963, 1-6.

change markedly. The 1964 catalog included "social action" (defined essentially as antiracism) as a major point in the seminary's philosophy. Though in 1965 the seminary was embarrassed by not having any black American students, it did adopt a formal statement, drafted by Paul Jewett, condemning racism at the seminary. It also gave its formal blessing, through a letter of introduction from President Hubbard, to a trip by student Bruce Crapuchettes to participate in Martin Luther King's march to Selma, Alabama. During the next years the seminary sponsored conferences on the race question as part of a concerted effort to change its image and outlook. Most importantly, in 1966 the seminary called to the faculty one of its recent graduates, Jaymes P. Morgan, Jr., a social ethicist with strong progressive concerns for justice. During his brief tenure, ended by his untimely death from cancer in 1970, Morgan argued passionately for evangelical social action and led the seminary in developing evangelical versions of the concerns that were preoccupying so many young American in that turbulent era.

Such pioneering efforts took place in the context of a movement that remained predominately conservative. Fuller students from the classes of 1965 to 1967 who were politically "conservative" (49 percent) and "very conservative" (5 percent) still outnumbered the "liberal" (11 percent) and "very liberal" (1 percent) by over four to one. Nonetheless, this was a considerable change from the ten to one ratio that had held up throughout the 1950s. Political activism was more acceptable also. In the earliest days almost half the students would have said that political protests were usually or always wrong. Now only one in six said that.

Perhaps most revealing of both the degree and the limits of the change concerned the question of the importance of social justice in relation to evangelism. Throughout the 1950s fewer than 10 percent of Fuller students would have said that social, economic, and political justice was "just as important" as evangelism, and just an additional 15 percent would have said it was "almost as important." Three quarters of the students would have said that social justice was simply "less important" than evangelism. Similar percentages of entering students in the 1960s held these views. By the time the sixties students had left, however, only a little more than half still said social justice was clearly less important. About 20 percent of these mid-sixties students had changed their views while at Fuller. On the other hand, an alternative way of reading the statistics is that, despite the changing political mood of the time, over half of Fuller students still saw evangelism as clearly the top priority.

One instance of the modest, but in the long run momentous, shifts that were taking place was the opening of the B.D., the pastoral degree, to women. The faculty in fact backed into this innovation. The 1962 catalog still said "Fuller Seminary recognizes the need for adequately trained women for positions of Christian service other than the pastoral ministry." In addition to the Master of Religious Education degree open to women, the seminary now instituted the Bachelor of Sacred Theology degree, which it described as "for women" who would complete the standard theological curriculum, but with substitutes for pastoral courses. A male student from Taiwan, however, asked if he could take this "more academic course." Granting this permission opened the door for a line of men during the next years wishing to take the S.T.B. and thus avoid the pastoral courses. According to Paul Jewett's recollection, "this so upset the practical division that they came before the faculty recommending that the S.T.B. degree be dropped."[17] So, primarily in order to solve a problem for the men, beginning in 1966 the S.T.B. disappeared and the catalog read, "Fuller Seminary welcomes women students, who may enroll for any of the degrees offered."

TOWARD THE MAINSTREAM

As much as anything signaling the end of the fundamentalist-evangelical era at Fuller and marking an entry into the mainstream of American religious life was the school's acceptance by the Los Angeles presbytery of the Presbyterian church. At the outset of the Hubbard administration, in the fall of 1963, the seminary commissioned a small survey entitled "The Element of Divisiveness in the Image of Fuller Seminary." The survey revealed that, although mainline Christian leaders who knew about Fuller usually referred to it as "fundamentalist," they typically qualified it with expressions like "sincerely and pacifically fundamentalist." Correspondingly, there had already been some signs of a thaw with the Presbytery of Los Angeles. Hubbard's openness and irenic spirit accelerated this trend. The seminary also put together dossiers on a hundred of its graduates who had loyally served the United Presbyterian Church. By 1964 Eugene Carson Blake, now famous for the Blake-Pike proposal for church mergers, and Ganse Little of the nearby Pasadena Presbyterian Church took the lead in reversing the stance of the Los Angeles presbytery. By 1965 the presbytery was ready to accept Fuller students as candidates for the ministry under their care, and in 1967 William LaSor, followed soon by Everett Harrison, was at last admitted into the presbytery's membership.

This small revolution coincided with the Hubbard administration's efforts to broaden the seminary's constituency. Known sometimes as "the Presbyterian strategy," this was an effort to realize the original Fuller vision of an independent seminary loyally serving mainline as well as more strictly evangelical denominations. In the past, the realities of Fuller's character and the relationship of fundamentalist-evangelicalism to mainline churches had forced the seminary on a more independent course. Now, as it was becoming alienated from the fundamentalist side of evangelicalism, it was beginning to take up the slack with a new, more moderate evangelical constituency. Whereas Baptists outnumbered Presbyterians by about three to two in the alumni of the pre-Hubbard years, the ratio was now on its way to being reversed.[18]

17. Paul Jewett, interview in *Women: A Newsletter on Women's Concerns* (Fuller Seminary, Fall 1985), 1.

18. "Initial Survey of FTS Alumni," October 1962, lists 149 Baptists and 95 Presbyterians of the 486 alumni surveyed. Seventy-nine of the Presbyterians were members of the the United Presbyterian Church (U.S.A.), the largest single denomination represented. In 1974 the report "Fuller, the Decade Ahead: Report of Joint Research and Planning Committee," 1, reported about 30 percent Presbyterian students and 20 percent Baptist in the current student body.

The formal acceptance by the Los Angeles Presbyterians was just one sign that the old Fuller of the "new evangelical" era was giving way to yet another, newer, sort of evangelicalism—an outgrowth of the 1950s version but not identical with it. Already during the Carnell era the seminary had felt constrained to drop the term *new evangelicalism* from its public references. David Hubbard followed this up with an effort to eliminate it internally as well, quipping that there would be a five-dollar fine for those who called themselves "new evangelicals" or "new" anything else.

A major difference between the prematurely passé neo-evangelicalism and the newer open or progressive evangelicalism was that while the former was preoccupied with its relation to fundamentalism, the latter had moved a step away from that connection. Positively, the open evangelicals were open to broader alliances. On the negative side, their preoccupation now was with their relationship to conservative neo-evangelicalism. Some of the old guard of conservative neo-evangelicalism were now beginning to play the role that fundamentalists had played in the seminary's early days.

CLOSING SCENES

Among the most momentous milestones in the journey away from old-style fundamentalism was the passing of the elder Fullers themselves. Grace Fuller took ill in the spring of 1965 and died a year later. Her influence on the seminary had been formidable, especially her personal concern. One former Fuller student's wife wrote of Grace Fuller's unforgettable manner in inquiring after the well-being of each student's family: "Grace Payton Fuller had a greater impact on me after just several brief encounters than any other individual in my experience."

Charles Fuller was conspicuously lonely in his bereavement. He was still an active evangelist, though. He kept up his radio broadcasts, and in 1966 he accompanied David Hubbard to the Berlin Congress on Evangelism, where the elderly evangelist was lauded by many whom he had influenced and was pleased to see the extent of Fuller-related influences in world evangelical work. In April 1967, twenty years after the seminary plans had been initiated, the school held a "Founders Day" banquet honoring Ockenga and Charles Fuller. Less than two months later Charles Fuller suffered a heart attack that effectively ended his career. He died March 18, 1968.

The twentieth anniversary banquet on April 7, 1967, was part of the closing scene for a number of the key people in Fuller's history. Clarence Roddy, who long had been the leading figure in the practical department, was retiring. Harold Ockenga would soon effectively bow out of the Fuller picture, accepting in 1969 the presidency of the reorganized Gordon-Conwell Theological Seminary near Boston, yet another school (together with Trinity Evangelical) devoted to the original Fuller Seminary vision. Ockenga remained an active Fuller trustee, though, largely as a signal that he was not repudiating the school. Billy Graham, who likewise had stayed on the Fuller board as a gesture of nondivisiveness, also paid his respects to Charles Fuller by speaking

Charles Fuller, Billy Graham, David Hubbard, and Gary Demarest at the Founders' Day Banquet on the twentieth anniversary of the founding of Fuller Seminary

at the Founders Day banquet. E. J. Carnell, the other leading figure in the seminary's brief history was also given a role at the banquet, presenting to the founders volumes of pictures relating to the seminary's history.

Carnell had been a shadow of himself since his mental breakdown. He nonetheless struggled on, teaching and writing. Remarkably, he remained the seminary's most influential professor among the students (just ahead of Ladd, Hubbard, Jewett, and the ever-respected Harrison), though student opinions were now strongly divided about him.[19] His teaching was becoming a matter of deep distress to all concerned, including certainly Carnell himself. Once the master who could hold everyone enraptured, he now sometimes had difficulty in getting through a sentence. Students sat in pained silence, hoping he would say something as he paused searching for a word, often ten or fifteen seconds, sometimes for two or three awful minutes. At times he would literally stagger through a lecture, showing the effects of his unshakable addiction to sleeping pills.

Yet in the spring of 1967 Carnell seemed in good spirits and was thought to be somewhat improved. He had even accepted with some enthusiasm an invitation to be one of the three keynote speakers for a Roman Catholic National Ecumenical Workshop to be held in Oakland, California, later in April.

19. Survey (see Appendix) and alumni comments.

At the Founders Day banquet he had shown good humor, joking about his illness as he presented the volumes of pictures of past seminary highlights. "My psyche is very severely traumatized," he quipped, "that my picture doesn't appear more frequently." Carnell completed his very brief remarks with the hope that the Lord would give all those present the grace and wisdom to build on the founders' example "as we face a future filled with exciting challenges and yet threatened by demonic uncertainties."[20]

Two weeks later he flew to Oakland for the ecumenical workshop, held at the luxurious Claremont Resort Hotel in the Berkeley hills overlooking the San Francisco Bay. He arrived on Sunday, checked into the hotel, and called home to say that he had safely arrived. He did not appear, however, at the speakers' table for the Sunday evening banquet. The Rev. Duke Robinson, a Fuller graduate of the 1950s who had been influential in getting Carnell to the conference, saw him sitting alone near the back of the room. Robinson had not seen Carnell for several years and had the impression "that he had lost some weight, his face looked very drawn and frowning or scowling." As Carnell was leaving, Robinson and his wife met him and identified themselves. "Dr. Carnell did not look at Robinson for more than 2 or 3 seconds, took his hand, shook it, then turned away and walked by." Robinson's wife, a nurse, felt something was wrong. Carnell seemed to walk with a limp, like someone who had had a stroke.[21]

No one at the conference saw him the next day and he had not been answering his phone. At Tuesday noon he was scheduled to speak. With the time approaching, the Monsignor in charge decided to check the room. There he found Carnell dead. Although the cause was not immediately apparent, the coroner determined that he had died the evening before from a moderate overdose of sleeping pills. "I find death undetermined whether ACCIDENTAL or SUICIDAL," his report concluded cryptically.

No one ever got beyond this verdict. The issue of suicide is moot. Carnell died as the result of acute depression that one way or another overwhelmed his rational control. He was in a state in which desperation could have obliterated normal categories of intention. If his death was in any sense willed, it was not premeditated. It had none of the Carnell organization. The overdose was "moderate," and the room showed signs that the seizure was unexpected.[22]

All the symptoms point in any case to Carnell's having lapsed once again into the abyss of depression, after a spring of good spirits. Though he had initially accepted the invitation with eagerness, a few days before the conference he attempted to withdraw from it. He had attended another conference the week before, and, according to a priest who was also there, he left early

---

20. Transcript of Founders Day banquet.
21. DH, summary of telephone conversation with Andrew (Duke) Robinson, 4-26-67 (P).
22. I am indebted to Rudolph Nelson for furnishing me with a copy of the coroner's report and for his insights regard the circumstances of Carnell's death.

without attending his discussion group, remarking with irritation about the changes initiated by VaticanII, "You Catholics are not Catholics any longer." Carnell had been every bit as anti-Catholic as the other evangelicals. To speak to sophisticated Catholics in an ecumenical setting when he deplored the old Catholicism and distrusted the new was a formidable assignment.

Carnell's misgivings about Vatican II mirrored his deep ambivalence about the changes he had done so much to initiate at Fuller. Occasionally he would blow up in irritation over some seemingly minor innovation. He complained that the new type of students were not interested in his apologetics.[23] Nor was he happy with the changes taking place in American society. It was 1967 and he was upset, as most in his generation were, at the conspicuous flaunting of traditional moral values by the younger generation. Law and order were not cliches for Carnell and his new evangelical peers; they were keystones of their thought, the guidelines within which any reform must take place. Deep depressions, however, go vastly beyond identifiable public causes, even though these may give them part of their immediate shape.

All too typically, some were ready to make the most of Carnell's death. The seminary, of course, minimized any intimations of suicide. Yet rumors quickly spread. The extent of the interest was discovered ten years later by Rudolph Nelson in the course of research on a biography of Carnell. Nelson went to the Alameda County courthouse to see the coroner's report on Carnell. When handing it to him, the medical examiner remarked that there was something strange about this report. Whereas for most reports there might be requests for six or seven copies, this unsensational report had been requested dozens of times by people from all over the country. Nelson immediately recognized some of the names: "the nationally famous pastor of a large Southern Baptist church, a fire-breathing Fundamentalist college president, a writer of militant religious tracts, an executive of a hyper-conservative separatist denomination." One pastor from an independent fundamentalist church requested several copies.[24]

NEO-EVANGELICALISM IN DISARRAY

Though hard-core fundamentalists kept up their polemics against "neo-evangelicals" for years, the death of Carnell was a signal that the new evangelicalism was near its end as a unified and progressive enterprise. The movement had never sailed far enough from the fundamentalist shores to avoid breaking up on surrounding rocks, set there ostensibly to protect the Rock of Ages. Shipwrecks were frequent.

A major one was Carl Henry's editorship at *Christianity Today*. When Henry came to the magazine there had been fears that he was too "fundamen-

23. DF, on draft; DF also comments on EJC's views of Catholics.
24. Rudolph Nelson, early draft of biography of Carnell. See Nelson's completed work, *The Making and Unmaking of an Evangelical Mind: The Case of Edward Carnell* (New York: Cambridge University Press, 1987).

talist." Through the 1960s he remained solidly conservative and sided with the party that was ousted from Fuller. Nevertheless, as American politics polarized in the 1960s, J. Howard Pew, backed by L. Nelson Bell, saw Henry as insufficiently zealous to take a hard line against ecumenical churches that endorsed liberal and radical political causes. Henry, who had always carefully guarded his editorial independence, reacted with some pique. Ockenga, the chairman of the board, fearing loss of the Pew support, did not clearly back Henry. After a series of misunderstandings between these two principal organizers of the new evangelicalism, Henry finally left the magazine in 1968, offically resigning but regarding the action as "involuntary termination after twelve years of sacrifical labor."[25]

The *Christianity Today* board initially planned to offer the editorship to G. Aiken Taylor, a southern Presbyterian champion of rigid antiecumenical theological and political conservatism. After the threat of rebellion among the staff at such a precipitous move to the far right, however, the board finally settled on Henry's longtime friend and colleague, Harold Lindsell. By this time there was an important difference between Henry and Lindsell that made Lindsell more attractive to the supporters of *Christianity Today*. Lindsell was willing to be more explicit and aggressive both in ecclesiastical and political conservatism.[26]

Though neo-evangelicalism was no longer a unified movement, it had left a considerable heritage. Remnants of the movement survived more or less in its original form at Trinity Evangelical Divinity School, at Gordon-Conwell Seminary, at many colleges, such as Wheaton, Westmont, and Gordon, and in many organizations and individuals. This intellectual legacy was, however, much broader and more amorphous than mention of these schools suggests. The number of self-conscious "evangelicals" who had earned college and graduate degrees had increased manyfold since mid-century. While this marked a triumph for neo-evangelicals (who had first proclaimed that fundamentalist-evangelicals should think), higher education broadened the range of options within the bounds of evangelicalism. No longer was there a semblance of one unified school of evangelical thought, even within the network once administered by Harold Ockenga.

The national cultural revolution of the 1960s sped up this change. Evangelicals, like other Americans, were politicized and divided (partly along generational lines) by new issues, especially Vietnam, the merits of violent demonstrations, and "the American way of life." For evangelicals these new divisions compounded the already existing theological divisions focused on the debate over inerrancy. Often, political and theological dispositions coalesced. Progressives, including those at Fuller Seminary, were often, though not always, more open regarding both Scripture and politics. Conservatives, such as Lindsell, now fused militancy on both cultural and biblical questions.

25. Carl Henry, *Confessions of a Theologian: An Autobiography* (Waco, Tex.: Word, 1986), 264-87, esp. 281.
26. CH interview, 11-19-82.

The new evangelical legacy was by 1970 too diverse to categorize neatly. Surely it was very different from the simple combination of Machen's scholarship, Macartney's ecclesiology, and Charles Fuller's evangelism that had provided the models for the early ideals. That the later products did not look exactly like what the founders of neo-evangelicalism had anticipated was best exemplified by Fuller Seminary. Nonetheless, what was happening at Fuller was typical of the legacy. The new evangelicals had sparked a revolution, or perhaps a renaissance. What in the 1930s had appeared to many cultured people as the wasteland of fundamentalist-evangelicalism now bloomed. But as always in the history of the church, the tares grew with the wheat. Not everyone agreed about which was which.

EPILOGUE

The Mega-Seminary

What models do we follow? I've often been puzzled by this. I know of no institution in the world of which I can say, "I would like Fuller to be like that." Our commitment to an evangelical tradition distinguishes us from a great many mainline and university-related seminaries. Our willingness to take risks in churchly relationships, in graduate programs, in the quest for justice makes us somewhat different from a great many of the evangelical seminaries. Our graduate character sets us apart from the Christian colleges of liberal arts, while our theological confession separates us from the structures of the universities.

David Allan Hubbard, "Destined to Boldness: A Biography of an Evangelical Institution," the Ezra Squier Tipple Lectures, Drew University, October 23, 1979.

CATCHING A WAVE

WHILE a student returning to Fuller in 1967 after a decade's absence would have needed to make only rather simple adjustments, a counterpart leaving in 1967 and returning ten or fifteen years later would have been confronted by a revolution. The sheer size of the seminary would be most startling. At the School of Theology alone, the total fall enrollment for 1977 was 1,051 (762 full time equivalent). The School of Psychology added 125 students and the School of World Mission 157. By now Fuller had started extension ministries in seven cities enrolling a total of 188. An in-service program added 51, and 225 clergy were enrolled in continuing education in the Doctor of Ministry program. Adding 99 from a new cooperative program with the Young Life Institute for Youth Ministries, the total enrolled in the various Fuller programs was almost two thousand. The vast growth was quite recent. As late as the fall of 1972, the total enrollment in the three schools was only 474. But by the fall of 1975 President Hubbard was reporting succinctly: "Our place has burgeoned beyond belief."[1] Fuller Seminary had caught a huge wave, the impact of which was enough to change its character.

The growth itself, however, was also the *result* of changes in character

---

1. Enrollment figures of 1977 from President's Annual Report, October 31–November 1, 1977, 7; quote from President's Annual Report, November 9–10, 1975, 4.

263

that had already taken place. One important aspect of these changes would be immediately apparent to anyone setting foot on campus during Fuller's fourth decade. The seminary was no longer a school designed for white gentlemen, with women only tolerated and students and staff from minority races a rarity. By the school's thirty-fifth anniversary the new style was fully evident. In the fall of 1982 over five hundred women enrolled, constituting 19 percent of the M.Div. students, 30 percent of M.A. students, and 24 percent of those in the School of Psychology. By now Fuller had so many extension and special programs that much of its over three thousand enrollment was part-time, its full-time equivalent being 1,332.

Growth through diversification was evidenced as well in the presence of significant numbers of students and staff from American minority races. Embarrassed in the late 1960s by its almost exclusively white character, Fuller set out to diversify. In 1970 William Pannell was the first black elected as a trustee, and in 1974 he became the first black member of the regular faculty. Also in 1974 the seminary added a program for black pastors, supported with funding from the Rockefeller Foundation. During the next half dozen years the administration instituted similar programs for Hispanic pastors and then Asian pastors. By 1982 over two hundred members of these American minority races were enrolled in these and other Fuller programs. A campus visitor in the 1980s could drop in on classes in which the instructor gave the lectures in Korean or taught New Testament Greek in Spanish.

The phenomenal growth of Fuller did not come primarily from the addition of these new groups, however. Rather, the bulk of the growth in the great surge of the 1970s came from the traditional constituency of white males. The reasons for this remarkable surge in Fuller's popularity involve a combination of factors that can provide important clues to the character both of Fuller and of a major segment of American evangelicalism during this era of rapid change

A simple factor, although not altogether informative as a reason, was that Protestant seminary enrollments throughout the nation were rising in the mid-1970s.[2] Fuller, however, far surpassed almost everyone else, becoming the largest independent, regularly accredited theological seminary in the world, surpassed in enrollment in the United States only by Southwestern Baptist Theological Seminary of the Southern Baptist Convention. The growth at Fuller, as elsewhere, was part of a religious revival among young college-educated people. This revival, growing out of the late 1960s, was one manifestation of the widespread disillusion (on both the left and the right) with the mid-century liberal-secular consensus. Evangelical religion was one way of finding alternate values without necessarily adopting counterculture styles or attitudes. Emphasis on more meaningful and "authentic" interpersonal relationships, as reflected in the immense popularity of pop psychology, might be just as important in characterizing the new mood as political concerns were. In either case, personal conversion and commitment were crucial for many

2. News, *Christianity Today,* May 21, 1976, 34.

college and university students. While mainline seminaries benefited peripherally, most of the revival was by its very nature evangelical.

This spiritual revival coincided with and contributed to a remarkable new role of evangelicalism in American life as a more or less respectable national phenomenon. In 1976 Americans elected a president who proclaimed himself "born again." *Newsweek* declared 1976 "the year of the evangelical." The news media began to notice the forty million or more evangelicals and, for the first time since before World War I, talked about them as a force to be taken seriously. Though evangelical memberships were growing at about the same rate as the general population, their visibility was growing much faster. Moreover, evangelical churches maintained growth even as mainline Protestant denominations were steadily losing members.

Evangelical seminaries generally benefited from these national developments. There was growth at all the schools that were part of the traditional fundamentalist-evangelical network, such as Asbury, Dallas, Westminster, Trinity Evangelical, Gordon-Conwell, Covenant in St. Louis, and (the newer) Reformed Seminary in Jackson, Mississippi. But none of these flourished quite the way that Fuller did. In part this may have been due to the fact that these more conservative evangelical seminaries were all competing with each other and other conservative evangelical seminaries while Fuller, as a moderate independent evangelical seminary, had almost no competition. Geography helped as well: 40 percent of the population of the eight most western states lived in southern California, Fuller's backyard.[3]

More than the other seminaries in the evangelical network, Fuller was expanding its concept of evangelicalism to fit more closely the actual diversity of the national phenomenon. All the denominations in the National Association of Evangelicals (roughly two million members) plus all the strictly fundamentalist churches (perhaps four million more) did not nearly account for all the evangelicals in the nation. Many of the remaining were denominationally oriented evangelicals, such as Southern Baptists or Missouri Synod Lutherans, who tended to stay within their denominational institutions. And there were even more besides. Fuller Seminary looked beyond its traditional constituency to include these. Partly out of principle and partly out of necessity when the inerrancy controversy made Fuller's relationship to its traditional constituency tenuous, the seminary was developing a broader evangelical base not always so directly influenced by fundamentalism.

By far the largest portion of this potential evangelical constituency was in the mainline denominations. From these Fuller drew most of the students who accounted for its remarkable growth. From 1972 to 1982 the American Baptist enrollment at Fuller increased from 16 to 109; Disciples of Christ from 4 to 37; United Methodist from 16 to 160; Protestant Episcopal from 10 to 71; and the United Church of Christ from 6 to 50. By far the largest block of students, however, came from the United Presbyterian Church. Fuller's

3. Figures compiled by Ross Kinsler, Southern California Extension Center of San Francisco Theological Seminary, Sept. 5, 1985, furnished by Jack Rogers.

"Presbyterian strategy" had been reaping dividends since the 1960s. The already sizable United Presbyterian block of 140 students in 1972 grew in ten years to over five hundred, thus making Fuller one of the largest centers for Presbyterian seminary education in the country. Appreciable numbers of students from traditionally evangelical denominations were now attending Fuller as well. Missouri Synod Lutheran enrollment went from 3 to 37, and Southern Baptist from 20 to 85. Among the most rapidly increasing groups were the pentecostals and charismatics, often difficult to identify by denomination. Also by 1982, the representation of American racial minorities, though still not large, was appreciable, including 79 Blacks, 78 Hispanics, and 53 Asians.[4]

OPEN EVANGELICALISM

Reviewing the seminary's history in 1979, David Hubbard emphasized this success first as "an ecumenical experiment" rare in American religious experience (except as theory and at conferences). "We are bold enough to believe," he could state confidently, "that at Fuller we take more realistically the pluralism of our American churches and denominations than do many church agencies." Hubbard himself, more than anyone else, had cultivated this vision for Fuller. Not only had he been a participant at the major world evangelical gatherings, including the World Congress of Evangelism in Berlin in 1966 and the Lausanne World Congress for Evangelization in 1974, he was also a regular advisor and observer at gatherings of the World Council of Churches. The days when the seminary had to chasten Béla Vassady for his ecumenical interests were long past. Hubbard was in fact implementing an aspect of Ockenga's earliest vision that the school had been unable to sustain in its fundamentalist-evangelical days. The parachurch agency, Hubbard was demonstrating, while sometimes acting like a church, could also display some loyalty to established denominations. Though still subject to residual criticism from both stricter evangelicals and broader ecumenists, Fuller was helping to build a new transdenominational coalition of open evangelicals.

Equally as important for Fuller's growth as this ecclesiastical inclusiveness was the more generally open attitude that underlay it. Consciously reacting against fundamentalist negativism, the seminary attempted to cultivate a positive evangelicalism, open to almost any trend or movement that did not involve overt heresy. The one major exception was the more conservative evangelicalism from which Fuller had split. Though they continued to draw many students from this tradition, they no longer admitted faculty who were not at least open to progressive stances on controverted issues such as the inerrancy of Scripture or the ordination of women.

The openness necessary to shaping a new evangelical coalition was

4. On mainline denominations, see Board Report, July 1, 1981 to June 30, 1982, table H; see also "Facts and Implications of Growth," position paper, FTS, January 19, 1976, 3. On pentecostals and charismatics, see below. On minorities, see the 1982 Board Report, table C. These groups had not grown much since 1978.

frankly risky. It involved building an institution for which there were no precedents.[5] It also meant that a new emphasis might get out of hand. Whereas the fundamentalist stance had been to see a lurking heresy in practically every neighboring movement, even in those that might appear healthy, Fuller's stance seemed almost the opposite. There one could learn from diversity and hope that the peculiar emphases of various movements, if all brought together in one place, would balance against each other.

Fuller was fostering a comparable revision in understanding evangelicalism's essential relationship to American culture. Fundamentalists had often spoken of modern culture as simply of the devil, although in practice they were selective in applying that principle. Neo-evangelicals tempered that tradition by building bridges to modern thought and culture, still condemning it as under God's judgment but hoping also to renew it. Their undogmatic premillennialism symbolized this ambivalence. At Fuller Seminary by the 1970s and 1980s, however, premillennialism had disappeared as a creedal test and the residual belief in that doctrine had little to do with cultural attitudes. Fuller Seminary—indeed, all of evangelicalism—was a full-fledged part of American culture. The seminary leadership saw this as a mixed blessing but tended to take it as an opportunity rather than a danger. There was much wrong with current trends; but there were also things right too—points where one could make common cause. Open evangelicals felt the responsibility to raise the spiritual and moral level of an imperfect culture of which they were a part.

Symptomatic of this outlook was a document carefully crafted by Fuller administration and faculty and published in the fall of 1983 as "Mission Beyond the Mission." Recognizing that the primary mission of Fuller was to educate its students, the authors attempted to define the context of larger commitments within which that education takes place. Evangelization of the whole world was, as always, the preeminent goal; but with that evangelization came other major responsibilities. The Fuller Seminary community, the document stated, must work for the renewal of all the church, "ecumenical" and Catholic as well as evangelical. It must also promote the moral health of society, pursue peace, and champion justice throughout the world. Few causes that evangelicals, left or right, might support were omitted. Family issues were just as prominent as "peace and justice" concerns. And while the document definitely had a politically progressive tone, it avoided any party line, also calling, for instance, for respect for government. As the document put it, Fuller wished to include the concerns of evangelical political moderates and conservatives, especially since "there are many persons, agencies, institutions, and churches which have found themselves under-represented in any narrower evangelical call to action."[6]

5. David Hubbard suggests this theme in "Destined to Boldness: A Biography of an Evangelical Institution," the Ezra Squier Tipple Lectures, Drew University, October 23, 1979.

6. "Mission Beyond the Mission," *Theology News and Notes*, October 1983, 4-17.

REFORMING FUNDAMENTALISM

Open evangelicalism did have definite limits. Doctrinally the boundaries were roughly those of Nicene orthodoxy. The seminary accordingly revised its statement of faith to make it fit better with these actual boundaries in practice. Around the time of the death of the elder Fullers, the faculty revived this controversial project which had sparked such a conflagration on Black Saturday. Unquestionably the chief point of dissatisfaction with the statement was still the affirmation of biblical inerrancy. There was also the long-standing campaign to remove the premillennial requirement after Charles Fuller's death. Another concern was that the original statement suggested a non-institutional definition of the church, describing it simply as all regenerated persons. All these issues were addressed in the revision; and, also consistent with a slightly milder evangelicalism, the original statement's reference to the "eternal punishment" of the lost was changed to "the wicked shall be separated from God's presence."

Although there was a time lag in bringing the statement of faith into conformity with the actual standards of the faculty (the revision was finally adopted in 1972), Fuller Seminary clearly intended to take seriously its actual standards. Prospective faculty members might be accepted despite relative innocence of theology; but any who could not affirm the Nicene and broadly evangelical formulae would be rejected.[7] Decline in interest in theology as such was a more serious change at Fuller. And in the new schools and in other practical areas this decline inevitably introduced some looseness. Nonetheless, the administration and board occasionally brought formal or informal pressures on those who seemed overtly to depart from the creed.

Fuller's openness regarding mores was also limited by some more traditional boundaries. In 1982 the administration declined to reappoint a School of Psychology faculty member who had publicly advocated a positive, accepting attitude toward homosexuality.[8] The School of Psychology, dealing with a discipline in which moral values were usually defined relationally rather than by any other law, was under particular pressure to abandon strict evangelical standards on such issues. In 1979 a group of five of the school's students actually brought formal charges to the American Psychological Association against the School of Psychology, accusing it of violating academic freedom by requiring its faculty to sign a statement of faith. Under the leadership of Dean Neil Warren, but only with the greatest difficulty in a year-and-half struggle, Fuller's position was narrowly sustained, thus allowing the school to preserve both its creedal boundaries and its academic standing.

At the School of Theology the student constituency continued to be distinctly and overwhelmingly evangelical in their views but (like the administration and faculty) tolerant on matters of intraevangelical debate. Predictably, commitment to the inerrancy of Scripture continued to drop, so that by 1982 only about 15 percent of the students held that view. According to James

7. DH cites such instances, interview, fall 1983.
8. *The Stimuli* 13 (Fall 1982): 15-29, contains interviews with the faculty member, Phyllis Hart, and with the retiring dean, Neil Warren.

Davison Hunter's "Evangelical Academy Project," on which these 1982 figures are based, 51 percent of seminarians at other evangelical seminaries surveyed still held to inerrancy (about the percentage at Fuller in the 1950s). Nonetheless, at Fuller in 1982 the overwhelming choice was for a limited inerrancy view—"The Bible is the inspired Word of God, not mistaken in its teachings, but is not always to be taken literally in its statements concerning matters of science, historical reporting, etc."—and hardly any students held clearly neo-orthodox or more liberal views.[9]

Whatever the changes regarding the doctrine of Scripture, Fuller theology students were still within the broad evangelical movement. Ninety-four percent of them claimed a "born again" experience (close to the 97 percent at other evangelical seminaries). Just about the same percentages (96 percent at Fuller, 98 percent elsewhere) affirmed the orthodox statement "Jesus Christ is fully God and fully man." Ninety-six percent of Fuller students said they believed that "Jesus Christ will physically return to earth," while a substantial 75 percent still believed in the strict premillennial doctrine of a one thousand-year reign. On the question whether "Hell is a place of eternal torment," 86 percent of Fuller students still said yes, thus taking a stricter view than the new statement of faith did. Student views on this subject had changed little since the late 1950s and early 1960s. In fact, the alumni from those eras were more progressive on this issue in the 1980s than the current Fuller students of 1982 were.

One of the most striking differences between the Fuller student bodies of the 1980s and of the 1960s revealed a movement counter to many progressive trends. In 1982, an astounding 44 percent of Fuller theology students said they considered themselves "a pentecostal or charismatic Christian," and 43 percent said they had spoken in tongues. These numbers were considerably higher than those at other evangelical seminaries (27 percent charismatic, 32 percent tongue speakers) and far higher than they would have been at the early Fuller.[10] The seminary's open stance had attracted not only a small minority of progressives but also many students whose departures from the old evangelicalism were in a more overtly spiritual direction.

A similar mixture of continuity and change in student attitudes shows up in the responses to behavioral questions. More Fuller students than ever, though not much over half, were tolerant of drinking alcohol. At other evan-

9. See Appendix for this and other survey details.
10. James Davison Hunter survey, see Appendix. Unfortunately we do not have a complete comparison with the earlier eras on this point, but in 1982, 14 percent of Fuller students said that "charismatic" comes *closest* to their doctrinal preference, as opposed to "evangelical," "fundamentalist," "traditional/confessional," and other options. Less than 3 percent of alumni from 1950 to 1967 characterized their present position as "charismatic," although in its early decades the seminary included a few charismatics or pentecostals. See alumni comments.
One curious statistic, possibly related to the higher number of charismatics or pentecostals at Fuller is that 1982 Fuller students included 40 percent who said they had their "born again" experience between the ages of 14 and 17, while at other seminaries this number was only 27 percent. See Hunter survey.

gelical seminaries only about a third were so tolerant, but this was still a big change from the evangelical students who came to Fuller in the 1940s. Sexual mores had changed little at Fuller since the 1960s. Other evangelical seminary student bodies were more solidly conservative on these questions; but still in the 1980s higher percentages of current Fuller students than of alumni took the strictest views.

Although four out of five of Fuller students favored ordination of women (as opposed to less than half at other evangelical seminaries), many students at Fuller were hardly feminists. On the question of whether "a woman should put her husband and children ahead of her career," 56 percent of Fuller students agreed and only 20 percent disagreed. On the other hand, these figures appear progressive relative to other evangelical seminaries, where 81 percent of the students agreed and only 6 percent disagreed. A bigger difference was on the issue of whether the husband should have the "final say" in family decision making. At the other evangelical seminaries four times as many agreed as disagreed; at Fuller more disgreed than agreed.

On political issues, the number of "moderates" at Fuller climbed considerably since the 1960s, from about a third to over half. The number of moderates at evangelical seminaries as a whole also rose. The emphasis on social justice versus evangelism grew stronger as well. The number of Fuller students who would say that social justice was "just as important" as evangelism rose from one in seven to one in three. Still, almost none said it was more important.

Significant in providing a conservative to moderate counterbalance to some of the progressive trends at Fuller was the board of trustees. Following the way pointed by Donald Weber, Hubbard continued to build a strong board. He was also a master at cultivating the loyalty of its members, thus providing a base for his personal leadership in an institution tied down to few traditions. The board reflected Hubbard's own emphases. While it contained representatives of all sorts of minority groups, at its core was a group of leaders, typically businessmen who were key supporters of the seminary and who were also more conservative than most of the faculty. While their conservatism, combined with their resources, provided some insurance that Fuller would not go off the deep end, Hubbard's extensive efforts at keeping them open to any nonheretical innovation allowed the seminary to expand rapidly in many directions at once.

TOWARD THE PRACTICAL

At the School of Theology the new openness also took the form of a curricular revolution in the mid-1970s, coinciding with the growth during that era and likely contributing to it. During the first Hubbard decade, while Daniel Fuller was dean, the School of Theology maintained notably rigorous and standardized academic requirements. For instance, entering students usually had to study Greek the summer before their first year in order to keep pace with the other requirements. The School of Theology accordingly retained its earlier reputation as a good place for capable students to do graduate study in theology but not a strong center for preparation for practical ministries.[11]

A new generation of key personnel was especially important for revolutionizing both the atmosphere and the curriculum. Preparing the way was Robert Boyd Munger, who came in 1969 as professor of evangelism and church strategy. Munger was a renowned west coast Presbyterian pastor, long close to the Fuller orbit. He was the first person in the practical field who was formidable enough to stand up to and effectively counterbalance the theologians who had long dominated seminary policy. Mainstays of the faculty such as Geoffrey Bromiley, a staunch champion of no-nonsense classicist theology, had "met their match," as David Hubbard later observed.[12] The times were right for such a revolution. Munger's theological emphases were "relational," fitting the therapeutic style of thinking so popular in the early 1970s. He especially cultivated spiritual development and growth as a Christian community, ideals that the school had always talked about but seldom had achieved. Some of the gains in building community, however, were offset in the mid-1970s by the vast expansion, which perpetuated a sometimes impersonal, even if accepting, atmosphere.[13]

No one did more toward revolutionizing the Fuller curriculum than Glenn W. Barker, who came in 1972 as dean of the faculty at the School of Theology, succeeding Daniel Fuller. In a subsequent reorganization in 1974 Barker was named provost, the academic officer and primary coordinator of the three schools.[14] Barker was the last of the old Wheaton tribe to shape Fuller's history, though he arrived after most of his contemporaries had left. He had, nonetheless, pure neo-evangelical credentials. As so many of his peers, he had studied at Harvard in the 1940s. Then from 1950 to 1972 he taught New Testament at Gordon Divinity School (later Gordon-Conwell Theological Seminary). Essentially conservative in his theology, yet much like Hubbard in his openness to any nonheretical innovation, Barker was filled with imaginative ideals as well as sound administrative sense for moving the seminary in new directions. Upon his arrival he immediately oversaw the broadening of the M.Div. curriculum, the encouragement of more flexible

11. Glenn Barker interview at faculty retreat, 9-16-83.
12. DH interview at faculty retreat, 9-16-83.
13. See the report of Lars I. Granberg to DH on faculty interviews conducted November 8-11, 1976, which found these traits prominent. In earlier correspondence Granberg remarked: "Your observations on the paucity of friendship and mutual support suggest that matters have not changed a great deal over the years"; see Granberg to Robert Munger, 9-22-76 (documents from Granberg). See also James Hunter's 1982 Evangelical Academy Project survey. While over 40 percent of Fuller students found "social life" there either fair (37 percent) or poor (6 percent), 14 percent more liked it, 14 percent finding it excellent and 43 percent good. Other evangelical seminaries were similar: 34 percent fair, 6 percent poor, 16 percent excellent, and 45 percent good. On "Christian fellowship" there was more satisfaction, but also a slight difference with other seminaries. The figures (with Fuller first and others second) are 22 percent/30 percent excellent, 46 percent/46 percent good, 27 percent/21 percent fair, 5 percent/4 percent poor.
14. *Theology News and Notes,* October 1984, is dedicated to Barker, who died suddenly in May 1984.

M.A. programs, and the addition of the host of specialized programs and institutes. Leadership in these years of expansion was shared with deans Arthur Glasser and Paul E. Pierson in the School of World Mission, Neil Warren and Archibald Hart in the School of Psychology, and Robert Meye in the School of Theology.

The preponderance of the changes in the School of Theology during the Barker era were in the direction of adding practical programs. Whereas in 1972 the school still appeared heavily intellectual and cognitive, the Fuller of the early 1980s was most notable for its emphasis on practical training. Yet most of the tradition of a substantial academic theological program survived, and faculty in the theological disciplines were still expected to meet university standards for tenure. Accordingly, they continued to produce a formidable array of scholarly and popular works, mostly directed toward evangelical audiences. Nonetheless, sabbatical policies were tightened and class sizes increased, so that the commitment to pure scholarship was sometimes submerged in other important concerns. Faculty often wondered aloud how they were to keep up university standards without university perquisites.

The positive side of this transition was well summarized by Lewis B. Smedes, successor to Carnell as professor of theology and ethics and another of the leading figures in the changing emphasis. Alluding to the history of Fuller in connection with "Mission Beyond the Mission," Smedes saw three "minds" that might characterize an evangelical school's sense of itself. First was the "mind of safety," which clearly referred to an aspect of the outlook of the Lindsell, Henry, Smith, Woodbridge era. Second was "the mind of excellence," also a leading trait in the neo-evangelical days through the era of Daniel Fuller's deanship. During this period the primary goal in determining academic policy was to produce outstanding evangelical scholarship and students who could command that scholarship. Smedes, however, saw the dominance of this ideal as a thing of the past. "We are not here," he said with clear reference to the early Fuller, "to manage a stage for evangelical stars to strut their splendid evangelical stuff." Rather, in his view, the outlook of the new Fuller was defined by its "Mission Beyond the Mission"—its commitment to the "mind of servanthood." The school now saw itself "as a community of learning located on one corner of the global village." Not only did it attempt to inform itself "by the best that has been taught and said in the history of culture, but by the cries of spiritually lost, physically undernourished, politically oppressed people." This commitment to servanthood is "the awesome mission beyond religious safety and academic excellence." Servanthood, in Smedes's view, did not replace academics so much as underlie it and thus reshape its goals.[15]

As Smedes's observations suggest, the seminary was struggling to make two important breaks with the past. The lesser of these was the effort to free itself from the dominance of "the mind of excellence." In fact, the semi-

15. Lewis B. Smedes, "An Introduction to Mission Beyond the Mission," *Theology News and Notes*, October 1983, 2-3.

Glenn Barker

nary was searching for a new concept of what a theological seminary should be. At the School of Theology this search involved a reappraisal of the role of the clergy. Inheriting the Princeton model, the ideal for the clergy had been the gentleman theologian. In the American Puritan and Calvinist tradition the preacher was expected to be an intellectual leader of the community as well as a spiritual leader. The assumption was that intellect was one key to cultural and hence spiritual influence. Seminaries, according to this model, were havens away from the pressing demands of a dying world. Much as Paul spent time in the wilderness after his conversion, one should take time to be thoroughly prepared. Seminaries should also be theological graduate schools, fostering the general enterprise of intellectual leadership for the Christian community and judicious theological leadership for the church.

Lewis Smedes

This ideal, so pervasive in the first decades of Fuller's history, survived into the 1980s among an important segment of the faculty of the School of Theology. Elsewhere it was difficult to find. Probably the majority opinion was that traditional emphases on simple excellence in theological training were overly abstract, intellectual, and impractical. As we have seen, the School of Psychology and the School of World Mission were, by their very natures, oriented toward the practical, and many of their faculty had little patience with the old seminary ideal. Now, however, at the School of Theology itself, such views were common. Especially in the practical field, spokespersons such as the influential Roberta Hestenes, a Robert Munger protégé, emphasized that a seminary was not just the intellectual center of the Body of Christ but also a theological resource center for *ministry* or service in the broad sense. For this purpose, spiritual formation was probably more important than theological precision.

That the once-conspicuous theological emphases were now overshadowed by programs for practicality and service reflected a number of trends in the American evangelical tradition and in American cultural generally. American evangelicals had always been oriented toward the practical. The orientation at the early Fuller toward the theoretical was an exception, not the rule. Moreover, important segments of American academia as a whole, including much of the social sciences, had long made practical applications the test of all theory. At Fuller, the School of World Mission was built around this principle, always testing ideas by measurable results. Similar outlooks appealed to practical business people who might support Fuller and to many of its students who, like most Americans, wanted evidence of what theory would do.

Such tendencies were amplified by the spirit of the times. Since the 1960s the spirit of the counterculture, which was eventually synthesized in diluted form into the mainstream of American life, had been warning against the dangers of the "head-trip" or "Western linear thought." The even more popular psychological theories of the day reinforced the theme. So, for better or for worse, traditionalist conceptions of theology were in for hard times in any community that prided itself in the least in staying au courant.

Moreover, the reevaluation of what a seminary should be was necessitated by the ever-present factor in Fuller's history of its peculiar relationship as an independent seminary to the organized church. Fuller Seminary was not, like old Princeton, one department of a church that supported other ministries. Rather, it was in many respects a church itself: it was the headquarters for a spiritual movement. Though Fuller vigorously encouraged loyalty to traditional denominations, created an Office of Church Relations, had an Office of Presbyterian Ministries, and in 1985 entered into a formal adjunct relationship with the Reformed Church of America, it was at the same time inevitably nourishing a new type of Fuller-evangelical quasi denomination that would be superimposed on the traditional structures. So, for instance, local churches of different denominations pastored by Fuller graduates of similar vintage might well have more in common with each other than with many churches of their own denominations. More than would be true for a seminary under denominational control, Fuller's self-definition would shape the practical emphases of parish ministries.

In the 1980s Fuller Seminary seemed headed in the direction of more practical programs and increased emphasis on service. Since the two newer schools fit this model so well, there was less thought of Fuller as a quasi university, in the sense of a theological center for the theoretical study of the disciplines. At the School of Theology, however, the issue of the future course was far from settled. The 1980s in America has seen many institutions consider recovering fading identities. The older classicist view of education had the early Fuller tradition on its side and persisted as a considerable force. Indeed, the appointment in 1985 of Lawrence DenBesten, professor and chief of gastrointestinal surgery at UCLA, as Fuller's provost pointed toward renewing the school's early mission as an intellectual center. In the meantime, nonetheless, most of what had been added through the previous decade was in the practical domain, so that tensions remained unresolved between the older tradition of the theoretical and the newer trends toward the practical.

This, however, was not the first conflict between past and present in the seminary's recent history.

The Last Battle with Fundamentalism

Down the road, whether it takes five or fifty years, any institution that departs from belief in an inerrant Scripture will likewise depart from other fundamentals of the faith and at last cease to be an evangelical institution in the historical meaning of that term. This is the verdict of history.
        Harold Lindsell, *The Battle for the Bible* (1976).

Lindsell has a gas-balloon theory of theology. One leak and the whole Bible comes down. As a result he spends all his time patching.
        David A. Hubbard, as quoted in *Time*, May 10, 1976.

"THE STRANGE CASE OF FULLER SEMINARY"

AFTER leaving Fuller, Harold Lindsell was rather suddenly elevated to eminence in the evangelical community when in 1968 he succeeded Carl Henry as editor of *Christianity Today*. The heyday of Lindsell's editorship was in the Nixon-Agnew, Vietnam era of deep polarization in American life, and Lindsell made the magazine unmistakably a voice for the conservative side of this polarization, politically as well as ecclesiastically.

By the early seventies the political backlash against the counterculture and sympathetic liberals had its ecclesiastical counterparts in resurgent fundamentalistic movements in some major American denominations. In both the the Missouri Synod Lutheran Church and the Southern Baptist Convention a fierce struggle focused on the question of the inerrancy of Scripture. In 1970 Lindsell addressed these issues in a *Christianity Today* article entitled, "Whither Southern Baptists?" As an aside, the editor launched a direct attack on his former institution. Fuller Seminary he pointed out, was close to adopting a new statement of faith, thus sealing the departure from one of the main purposes for founding the school, "to defend the old Warfield view of the Scriptures."[1]

In the early 1970s, one might well have supposed that Lindsell and allies were fighting a rear-guard action in a last stand to make inerrancy a test of evangelicalism. This conclusion would have seemed particularly appropriate if one held, as almost all fundamentalists did, that modern religious organi-

---

1. Lindsell, "Whither Southern Baptists?" *Christianity Today*, April 24, 1970, 3.

zations tend to drift to the left unless rigidly held in place. In conservative denominations, such as the Missouri Synod Lutheran Church and possibly the Southern Baptist Convention, there might have been the machinery for such checks, though in 1970 the potential effectiveness of such machinery was not yet clear. But what about evangelicalism as a whole? How could such a piecemeal conglomeration of institutions and individuals be anchored to anything? Lindsell insisted that the only solid ground was the unshakable authority of Scripture. Almost all evangelicals agreed on this point. But when the debate turned from the affirmation of the Bible's authority to the question of what exactly the Bible *claims* for its own authority, then the matter became less clear. On what further authority could such a debate be adjudicated? Could anyone dictate one interpretation for the whole of evangelicalism?

In fact, the trend in evangelicalism in the early 1970s appeared to be toward increasing latitude. Since Carnell's day, evangelicals had been tolerating, or had been forced to live with, more and more flexibility on the inerrancy question. The open break at Fuller with its old creed was just one instance. The spirit of the times seemed to be well characterized by the titles of two new books on recent evangelicalism. In 1973 Donald G. Bloesch spoke of *The Evangelical Renaissance*, and in *The Young Evangelicals*, appearing the next year, Richard Quebedeaux told "the story of the emergence of a new generation of evangelicals." Bloesch, somewhat confusingly, referred to the new post-1960s outlook as "the new evangelicalism," as though the new outlook were simply an extension of the movement of the 1950s but with a broader view of Scripture. Quebedeaux cited and retained Bloesch's usage of "new evangelicalism" but made a helpful distinction between the progressives, or "young evangelicals," and "establishment evangelicalism," which was associated with Billy Graham, *Christianity Today*, and the NAE. Quebedeaux implied that the future lay with the progressives, nowhere better represented than at Fuller Seminary, which he praised extravagantly. His panegyric for Fuller reads like copy from an immodest public relations department:

> By their stature, teaching, publications, and their loyalty to the institutional church and the Church universal, the faculty of Fuller Theological Seminary has provided a model to its students and graduates, and through them to the Young Evangelicals in general, of what modern biblical Orthodoxy can be—of its explicit revolutionary potential. Unlike the Fundamentalist schools, Fuller is not polemically anti-intellectual. And in contrast with the mainstream Ecumenical seminaries and their Liberal denominational counterparts, it still regards theology as *serious* business, involving questions of ultimate significance. Social concern is most certainly important at Fuller, but not to the exclusion of its fostering personal Bible reading and a meaningful devotional life. The faculty of Fuller Seminary tend to inspire their students in the Christian faith rather than encourage their doubts. Unlike Fundamentalist institutions, differences of opinion among faculty at this school are tolerated and discussed

openly. . . . And all this is done within a community of faith which is mutually supportive of the needs of both faculty and students.[2]

Such positive images certainly contributed to the seminary's growth and made it appear that indeed it represented the wave of the future and the true heirs to neo-evangelicalism.

Harold Lindsell and his confederates were determined that the party represented by Fuller would not take over evangelicalism as a whole. The internal struggle at Fuller was thus extended to a wider struggle for dominance in the transdenominational movement. The party that hoped to control that movement, centered at *Christianity Today* and Trinity Evangelical Divinity School, was deeply committed to inerrancy as the touchstone of the faith. They also correctly saw that this doctrine could be used effectively both as a test by which to distinguish between two major parties of former fundamentalists and as a banner under which to rally wider conservative support.

This struggle turned into warfare with the appearance of Harold Lindsell's all-out assault, appropriately titled *The Battle for the Bible.* Appearing in the midst of the evangelical decade, it drew immense attention. No one who was the object of Lindsell's bombardments could easily ignore them.

Although addressing his work to the entire evangelical community, Lindsell left little doubt that it was Fuller Seminary's departure from the doctrine of inerrancy that disturbed him the most. The former vice president devoted a full chapter to "The Strange Case of Fuller Theological Seminary." Lest any insider miss the point, Lindsell also dedicated the book "to four of my teaching colleagues, all of whom stood or stand steadfastly for biblical inerrancy—Gleason L. Archer, Edward John Carnell, Carl F. H. Henry, and Wilbur Moorehead Smith." To claim Carnell, who surely stood up for inerrancy but just as surely meant something different by it than Lindsell did, rubbed salt in the wounds of those at Fuller who claimed to be carrying on in the spirit of their departed president. To complete the salvo, Lindsell persuaded his old friend Harold Ockenga to write the foreword. Ockenga was president of Gordon-Conwell divinity school, but he was also still active on the Fuller board. To the chagrin of the Fuller leadership, Ockenga had nothing but praise for Lindsell's work and mentioned the Fuller case directly. This was full-scale civil war.

Lindsell argued that commitment to inerrancy was essential to any claim to be "evangelical." Moreover, he revealed that he held an even stricter view of inerrancy than had prevailed in the heyday of early Fuller. Whereas Carnell, in his notorious chapter on "difficulties" in his *Case for Orthodox Theology,* had resorted to the expedient that the Old Testament chronicler might have given us "an infallible account of what was said in the public registers and genealogical lists," which themselves might have been inaccurate, Lindsell would allow no such equivocation.[3] He implicitly rejected, for instance, Ever-

2. Richard Quebedeaux, *The Young Evangelicals: The Story of the Emergence of a New Generation of Evangelicals* (New York: Harper and Row, 1974), 71-72.
3. Quote from Carnell, *The Case for Orthodox Theology* (Philadelphia: Westminster, 1959), 111.

ett Harrison's principle of interpretation published in Carl Henry's *Revelation and the Bible,* published in 1958. Harrison, a solid inerrantist, had said that the way to deal with such problems as the apparent disharmony of the Gospels was to avoid imposing our own ideas on Scripture: to look at the phenomena of Scripture itself to determine how God actually inspired it.[4] Lindsell, by contrast, looked for logically consistent harmonies. So, for example, he suggested that one good way to solve the problem of the seemingly contradictory accounts of the timing of Peter's three denials of Christ was to posit that there had actually been six denials, with no more than three mentioned in any one Gospel.[5]

Lindsell had an easy time showing that the seminary had changed its stance on Scripture since the early days. In "The Strange Case of Fuller Seminary," he reviewed most of Fuller's main debates on inerrancy, beginning with that over Béla Vassady, whom he praised for at least not signing a creed in which he did not fully believe. Lindsell then leveled his strongest attacks against the positions of Weyerhaeuser, Schoonhoven, Daniel Fuller, Paul Jewett, and George Ladd. He also accused David Hubbard of duplicity, both in his handling of the Hubbard-Laurin syllabus and especially in what Lindsell regarded as a hollow claim that the faculty was still loyal to the doctrine of the inspiration of Scripture. A number of the Fuller faculty, said Lindsell, as well as the administration that protected them, had been dishonest during the 1960s when they signed a creed with which they partly disapproved. That they later repudiated that creed, Lindsell added with the force of an experienced debater, demonstrated their earlier dishonesty.

PAUL JEWETT AND THE APOSTLE PAUL

The timing of this assault on Fuller turned out to be perfect for Lindsell. The seminary, in its rapid advance as the leader of progressive evangelicalism, had just left one of its flanks wide open. In 1975, in time for Lindsell to take advantage of it in his polemic, Paul Jewett published his landmark defense of the equality of women and men, *Man as Male and Female.* The volume proved beyond all doubt that, despite his rigorous Calvinist conservatism on most doctrinal points, Jewett had long since repudiated the role of "the Charles Hodge of our generation." Lindsell pointed out that when Jewett was brought to Fuller he was thoroughly identified with the champions of the old Princeton tradition. His book on Emil Brunner's concept of revelation, published in 1954, reflected his Westminster Seminary training and was dedicated to the inerrantist Calvinist mentor of early Fuller, Gordon H. Clark. As had been characteristic at the early Fuller, Jewett had rejected the neo-orthodox suggestion that the Bible was humanity's word about God's Word and hence subject to imperfections. Jesus, said Jewett, "appeals to Scripture, to each part of

---

4. Everett F. Harrison, "The Phenomena of Scripture," in *Revelation and the Bible,* ed. Carl Henry (Philadelphia: Presbyterian and Reformed, 1958), 249.
5. Lindsell, *The Battle for the Bible* (Grand Rapids: Zondervan, 1976), 174-76.

Scripture and to each element of Scripture as to an unimpeachable authority."[6]

Now Jewett had quite frankly changed his position. Since he had arrived at Fuller, other faculty had been noticing this transition. Its full extent, however, now became dramatically (and for some disconcertingly) apparent in his efforts to reconcile what he saw as the dominant biblical teaching of equality of the sexes with the apostle Paul's statements apparently to the contrary. Jewett's way of resolving this conundrum was, in the evangelical context, startling. Rather than claiming that the apostle was saying something other than what he seemed to be saying or that Paul's statements about the subordination of women had only local or temporary application, Jewett argued that the apostle was simply mistaken in these passages. Paul supported his views, for instance, with an appeal to Genesis 2, which indicated that Adam was created before Eve. Jewett claimed, however, that Paul's reading of this passage as implying the necessary subordination of women was incorrect. Paul was relying on faulty rabbinic interpretations of Genesis and thus asserted teachings that contradicted the preponderance of biblical teaching about women as well as his own statement in Galatians that in Christ there is no male and female.[7]

By May 1975, well before Fuller people knew of Lindsell's impending cannonade, internal unrest began to shake the seminary. Even without Lindsell's prodding, Jewett's book was bound to be a public relations problem. Moreover, some key administrators and faculty were themselves upset by Jewett's view, despite their deep respect for him and their commitment to tolerance. The real trouble came from C. Davis Weyerhaeuser, the school's primary benefactor who had long been active in the inerrancy debate. Weyerhaeuser felt that his perennial efforts on behalf of progressive openness at Fuller were now being undermined by Jewett's dismissal of Paul's arguments about the role of women. Weyerhaeuser had gone out on a limb to insist that the seminary's commitment to the authority of Scripture had not essentially changed over the years—even with the change of the creed—and that the Bible was still an infallible authority on the matters of faith and practice on which it spoke. Jewett's approach, however, seemed to go beyond the latitude for which Weyerhaeuser had fought. Though affirming the authority of the *overall* testimony of Scripture on the question of women, Jewett was saying that Paul was simply in error in certain pronouncements and that consequently they need not be made a matter of faith and practice.[8]

In the midst of this discussion came word of the impending publication of *The Battle for the Bible*. The internal distress made the external threat

---

6. Jewett, *Emil Brunner's Concept of Revelation* (London: Clarke, 1954), quoted in Lindsell, *Battle for the Bible*, 117.

7. Jewett, *Man as Male and Female: A Study in Sexual Relationships from a Theological Point of View* (Grand Rapids: Eerdmans, 1975).

8. Weyerhaeuser's views were spelled out at a meeting of an ad hoc committee of trustees, faculty, and administration with Paul Jewett, January 20, 1976, transcript (P). Weyerhaeuser had raised his objections the previous spring.

seem more ominous. A special committee of trustees, administration, and faculty was apppointed in January 1976 to deal with the Jewett case. Disciplinary action was a real possibility, though dismissal was unlikely. After lengthy discussion, the majority of the committee concluded that Jewett was wrong in claiming that the apostle Paul was mistaken. Nonetheless, they were also convinced that he sincerely subscribed to the statement of faith's article affirming that "Scripture is the only infallible rule of faith and practice." Jewett, they pointed out, defended his view by an appeal to the long-standing principle that "Scripture should be interpreted by Scripture." Even though the committee "sharply disagreed" with Jewett's specific application of this rule, they construed his purpose, however mistakenly carried out, to be to defend the overall authority of Scripture, not to undermine it. No disciplinary action was taken.[9]

THE COUNTEROFFENSIVE

The seminary nevertheless had a major public relations problem. Student enrollment, as it turned out, was not appreciably hurt by the notoriety—more likely it was enhanced. The one exception, however, was, of all places, at the School of World Mission. Despite its own generally broad theological stance, its conservative missionary and new church constituency was especially vulnerable to polemical propaganda. Some prominent faith missionary societies and some churches discouraged their students from attending Fuller. Even so, the steady growth of the School of World Mission was only slowed.[10]

The real fear, however, was that Lindsell might succeed in discrediting Fuller among the majority of its traditional evangelical constituency and supporters from the Weyerhaeuser generation. With its denominational ties always tenuous, such a maneuver could leave the school in a no-person's land.

There also seemed to be no way to stay on high ground by ignoring such polemics, as had been the seminary's policy in earlier days. The conjunction of Jewett's book and Lindsell's attack with the seminary's growth and a split over inerrancy in the Missouri Synod Lutheran Church made the case national news. *Time* magazine immediately picked it up. On the one hand it called Fuller "probably the best U.S. evangelical divinity school" and quoted Hubbard's observation regarding Lindsell's "gas-balloon theory of theology." Yet on the other hand it called attention to the startling fact that an evangelical professor openly disagreed with the apostle Paul.[11]

The seminary accordingly launched a massive counteroffensive. In a special convocation in April 1976, the same month *The Battle for the Bible* appeared, Hubbard mapped out the major points of response. He lamented evangelical divisiveness, deplored Lindsell's "unbiblical view of Scripture,"

9. "The Authority of Scripture at Fuller," *Theology News and Notes*, Special Issue, 1976, 20-22, provides report of the ad hoc committee.
10. Arthur Glasser interview, 12-12-83; and report from Arthur Glasser furnished by DF, 7-14-86.
11. *Time*, May 10, 1976, 57.

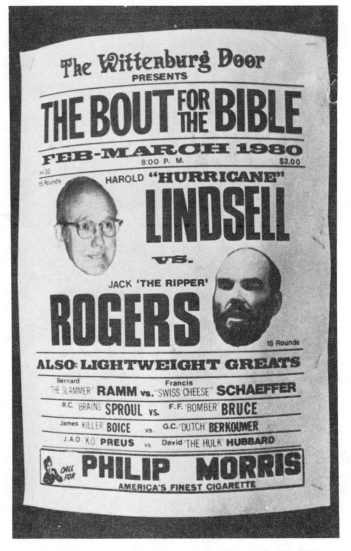

The Wittenburg Door*'s view of the battle for the Bible*

defended the seminary's right to be called "evangelical," and affirmed the continuity with the school's pre-1963 past. Notably, contrary to Lindsell's claim of Hubbard's personal hero Carnell for his side, Hubbard enlisted the Carnell of the 1950s, specifically the Carnell of the much controverted inaugural, as the prophet who had pointed the way for the Fuller of the 1970s.[12]

12. Hubbard, "Reflections on Fuller's Theological Position and Role in the Church," seminary convocation, April 8, 1976 (P).

"The Strange Case of Fuller Seminary"

Following the same line of defense, the seminary prepared a concerted reply to Lindsell in a special issue of *Theology News and Notes* dedicated to "The Authority of Scripture at Fuller." Hubbard again defended the seminary against Lindsell's accusations. William LaSor added a lengthy historical recollection, countering some of Lindsell's accounts with colorful anecdotes and observations. Clark Pinnock, a former champion of inerrancy, was enlisted to counter Lindsell's understanding of the biblical view of the nature of Scripture. Paul Rees, representing old-guard evangelicalism, added his views as did the more progressive Donald Dayton, representing the "young evangelicals." All this surrounded the publication of the ad hoc committee's report on the Jewett case.

In the meantime the seminary's philosopher of religion, Jack Rogers, was mobilizing a larger scholarly response to Lindsell. He edited a book of essays entitled *Biblical Authority*, ready by 1977 to be included with a packet of materials to be sent to inquirers. Rees wrote the foreword; Hubbard, Pinnock, and Rogers contributed; and to the lineup of Fuller defenders were added Bernard Ramm, Berkeley Mickelsen of Bethel Theological Seminary in St. Paul, and Earl Palmer, the popular pastor of First Presbyterian Church in Berkeley. Rogers and his former student Donald K. McKim were at the same time preparing an even more formidable scholarly attack on inerrancy, published in 1979 as *The Authority and Interpretation of the Bible: A Historical Approach*.[13] In an extensive historical survey, Rogers and McKim argued that the dogma of inerrancy was the product of seventeenth-century Protestant scholasticism which was later falsely equated with classical orthodoxy by nineteenth-century Princeton Seminary theologians. Inerrancy, they argued in answer to Lindsell, had not been the teaching, or even the view, of those such as Augustine and Calvin whom evangelicals typically cited as great champions of the historic faith. Rather, it was a modern invention reflecting later philosophical commitments, notably Princeton's commitment to Scottish Common Sense Realism and its related attempt to ground the faith on indubitable principles of human reason.

Rogers and McKim's volume immediately gained wide attention. Eventually it received *Eternity* magazine's "Book of the Year" award and was chosen as the subject of a special symposium in the mainline journal *Theology Today*. Rather than quelling the controversy, however, the book raised a chorus of protest from conservative reviewers and set off a minor industry of essays and volumes defending the view that inerrancy was always regarded as, or at least assumed to be, essential to orthodox Christianity. In the meantime, champions of the inerrancy test had organized themselves in 1978 into the International Council on Biblical Inerrancy. At their first summit meeting that year they produced a definitive concord: the "Chicago Statement on Biblical Inerrancy."[14] Prominent in this movement were a number of people with close connections to Trinity Evangelical Divinity School, including Kenneth Kantzer, who in 1978 succeeded Lindsell as editor of *Christianity Today*, philosopher Norman Geisler, who signaled the new direction of alliances by moving to Dallas Theological Seminary, and the stalwart Gleason Archer.

13. Jack Rogers, ed., *Biblical Authority* (Waco, Tex.: Word, 1977); Jack Rogers and Donald K. McKim, *The Authority and Interpretation of the Bible: An Historical Approach* (San Francisco: Harper and Row, 1979).

14. The "FACT Sheet," of the International Council on Biblical Inerrancy (P.O. Box 346, Walnut Creek, CA 94596) lists the Council's publications and leadership.

Jack Rogers

Moreover, the most industrious of the respondents to Rogers and McKim was Trinity's historian, John D. Woodbridge, son of former Fuller professor Charles Woodbridge.[15]

ATOM BOMBING AND PRECISION BOMBING

The aging Charles Woodbridge had become the most fundamentalist of fundamentalists. Since leaving Fuller, he had moved almost as far to the right as it was possible to go. His sometime allies Bob Jones and Carl McIntire could not outdo him in separatist zeal. For Woodbridge, separatism was so crucial that he could not tolerate even the most orthodox evangelicals who did not sever all connections with moderates. This was "second-degree separationism": separation from those who would not separate, even though they might agree on all else. His own son John, though an indefatigable champion of inerrancy, fell

15. John Woodbridge's major contribution is *Biblical Authority: A Critique of the Rogers/McKim Proposal* (Grand Rapids: Zondervan, 1982).

into this category. In what might seem the reductio of our story, Charles repudiated John as insufficiently orthodox, even while John remained one of the most vocal critics of Fuller Seminary's views on Scripture.[16]

Harold Lindsell had not moved as far as Charles Woodbridge; but he had taken at least a half step back toward fundamentalism. Accordingly, his estimate of his former colleague had changed considerably since the late 1950s when he was defending Fuller Seminary against Woodbridge's gibes. Now Lindsell himself had surpassed Carl Mcintire and John R. Rice in his zeal to criticize Fuller and was saying that Woodbridge had left Fuller in 1957 "presciently."[17]

Furthermore, Lindsell stated in a sequel volume, *The Bible in the Balance* (1979), which included a withering sixty-page attack on Fuller, that he now preferred to call himself a "fundamentalist" rather than an "evangelical." After again arguing at length that "evangelicalism" properly understood entails inerrancy, he acknowledged that no one could legislate the meaning of the term and that its meaning had become "so debased that it has lost its usefulness." In his view, the "new evangelicalism" of the early Fuller had been intended to repudiate only "fundamentalist sociology," that is, its rigid separatism and the party spirit of its subgroups. Now that various new evangelicalisms were, in his view, repudiating one of the very fundamentals, it was time to abandon the term *evangelical*. "Fundamentalism," he affirmed in this postmortem for neo-evangelicalism, "at the very least, lets everyone know they believe in a Bible that is free from error in the whole and in the part."[18]

The one member of the ex-Fuller old guard not to enlist on either side of this latest evangelical civil war was the former commander of the army, Carl Henry. Henry's ouster from *Christianity Today* was related to basic neo-evangelical strategy. As Henry explained in a published interview after Lindsell's book appeared, his vision for *Christianity Today* had been to support an orthodox center for a wide evangelical coalition. Henry said he had championed inerrancy "as a test of Evangelical *consistency*," but he refused to use it to set the boundary of the broad evangelical coalition he envisioned. So at *Christianity Today* some of the key contributing editors did not believe in inerrancy. This policy was strikingly different from what Henry advocated at Fuller Seminary at the same time; but he regarded a seminary and a magazine as playing quite different roles. Under Lindsell the conception of the nature of the evangelical coalition had changed; the standard that Henry would have applied to the seminary alone was now applied to the whole coalition.

Reflecting on this question of evangelical identity, Henry observed in an interview at Trinity Evangelical Divinity School early in 1976 that Lind-

16. I discovered this when, in an August 1984 phone conversation asking for an interview, I mentioned to Charles Woodbridge that I knew his son John. That set off a lengthy polemic against all such evangelicals. Charles Woodbridge refused to be interviewed or to do anything that would appear to be cooperating in the Fuller history project.

17. Lindsell, *Battle for the Bible*, 111.

18. Lindsell, *The Bible in the Balance* (Grand Rapids: Zondervan, 1979), 319, 322, and passim.

sell's editorship had brought changes at three points. First, *Christianity Today* contributors were now drawn more from independent sources than from ecumenically oriented denominations. Second, there was less willingness "to reexamine the evangelical socio-political stance" (the falling out between Henry and J. Howard Pew was related to Henry's insistence that even capitalism is subject to biblically based critiques). And third, there was the change in the role of inerrancy from a test of evangelical *consistency* to the determinant of evangelical *authenticity*.[19]

Carl Henry accordingly lamented, as he said to *Time*, that his former colleague was "relying on theological atom bombing" in which "as many Evangelical friends as foes end up as casualties." In Henry's view, Lindsell was destroying evangelicalism as a coalition by demanding uniformity to the standards of one of its parties. Moreover, in a review of *Battle for the Bible*, Henry suggested that Lindsell's way of defending inerrancy was shoddy and unpersuasive.[20]

On the other hand, Henry let it be known that he too belonged to the inerrancy party and that he shared much of Lindsell's alarm over some of the current trends. Specifically, he remarked to the interviewer at Trinity that he thought the assessment of Fuller Seminary was "one of the finest sections in Dr. Lindsell's book." Despite many other reservations, Henry said, he shared Lindsell's "domino-theory" with respect to institutions and saw Jewett's recent position on apostolic error as a case in point.[21]

So while Henry deplored the indiscriminate inerrantist "atom bombing," he still considered Fuller Seminary a proper target for more selective conventional theological attack. Especially disturbing, he found, were the views of Charles Kraft of the School of World Mission, published most fully in *Christianity and Culture* (1979). Two Christians who affirmed similar evangelical confessions could hardly have been further apart philosophically. Kraft rejected virtually everything epistemological that Henry stood for. Whereas Henry in his five-volume magnum opus *God, Revelation, and Authority* emphasized the propositional character of Christian truth, Kraft dismissed all systematic theologies as culturally bound, overly cognitive products of Greek cultural categories that encouraged intolerance of deviations. He saw Scripture as inspired of God and "accurate," but only as a "record of the Spirit guided perceptions of human beings." Enamored of anthropological emphases on the relativism of human perceptions, Kraft went all the way in rejecting the epistemological realism that had long been a chief feature distinguishing evangelical from dominant trends of modern thought.

Evangelicals had long affirmed that humans, despite their cultural

19. "Whose Battle for the Bible?" interview with Carl Henry, "syndicated article" typescript, 3. This interview was first published in *Scribe*, a publication of Trinity Evangelical Divinity School. Henry, "Decade of Gains and Losses," *Christianity Today*, March 12, 1976. CH, comments on draft, January 1986.
20. Henry, review of Lindsell's *Battle for the Bible* in *New Review of Books and Religion* 1 (September 1976): 7.
21. Henry, "Whose Battle?" 4-5.

Charles Kraft

limitations, had some access to knowing reality as it actually is, including historical reality or spiritual truths revealed in Scripture. Scottish Common Sense philosophy had only reinforced this long-standing belief, which seemed central to Protestant affirmations that individuals could rely on the Bible alone for knowledge of Gods redemptive acts. Kraft, on the other hand, started with the thoroughly modern assumption that *"we see reality not as it is but always from inside our heads."* Nevertheless, Kraft affirmed his faith in an important core of truth referred to in traditional evangelical statements about God, human sinfulness, and the necessity of faith in God for salvation. In Henry's view, published in a scathing review in the *Trinity Journal* of Trinity Evangelical Divinity School, such affirmations, when taken together with Kraft's frequent suggestions that modern anthropological categories should be normative for reevaluating Christian theology, reflected simply a "schizophrenic mentality."[22] Though Henry did not allude to the point, Kraft's epistemology incorporated on behalf of evangelicalism the very trends that Henry had polemicized against in 1946 in *Remaking the Modern Mind.*

Lindsell also cited Kraft in his expanded catalog of noninerrantists at Fuller in *The Bible in the Balance.* According to Lindsell, Kraft had told a missionary gathering that a Muslim might not have to be convinced of the death of Christ, or even of the deity of Christ, to have an initial saving faith.

The difference between Henry's and Lindsell's criticisms of Fuller was that Henry's were more selective. Lindsell saw Kraft's views as sufficient to demonstrate "the continuing Fuller drift away from the authority of Scripture."[23] Henry, on the other hand, recognized that few people at Fuller, especially in the School of Theology, shared Kraft's views. Accordingly, he held fast to his principle that, while deviations away from the old "neo-evangelicalism" produced an evangelicalism at Fuller that was not *normative,* the school must still be considered part of the authentic evangelical coalition. So Henry maintained cordial but cautious relations with his former institution. He continued to affirm that the school was an important contributor to the evangelical cause, even if it contained elements Henry himself considered beyond the evangelical pale. The other key leaders of the now-defunct "neo-evangelicalism" apparently took much the same view. Billy Graham, despite endorsing *The Battle for the Bible,* remained on the Fuller board of trustees, essentially as an honorary member but thus providing a ratification of the school's credentials as more evangelical than not. Harold Ockenga, too, remained convinced that the seminary was doing more good than harm, and continued as an active member of the board until his death in 1985.[24]

FREE AT LAST?

The fact of the matter was that the battle for the Bible proved to be Fuller's war of independence. When the smoke had cleared by about 1980 the gap between tolerance allowed by Fuller evangelicalism and the strictness demanded by the fundamentalist evangelical right was so great that the right seemed no longer able to rock the seminary with its blasts. So, for example, a well-documented one hundred-page polemic, *Is Charles Kraft an Evangelical?* from the Carl McIntire camp in 1985 went virtually unnoticed at Fuller.[25]

Everything had been said already, often with inflated rhetoric. So any conservative support that the seminary had depended upon had been either

22. Henry, "The Cultural Relativizing of Revelation," *Trinity Journal* 1 (1980): 153-64.

23. Lindsell, *Bible in the Balance,* 226-27.

24. CH interview, 11-19-62; HJO interview, 11-6-83.

25. Edward N. Gross, *Is Charles Kraft an Evangelical? A Critique of Christianity and Culture* (Elkins Park, Pa.: Christian Beacon Press, 1985). Gross had connections with Faith Theological Seminary and the Independent Board for Presbyterian Foreign Missions.

long since alienated or proven impervious to fundamentalist critiques. More-over, the students who now flocked to Fuller were evangelicals who, although largely conservative themselves, no longer cared whether the school met the fundamentalist standards of the 1940s. A generation had arisen who knew not Wilbur Smith.

An additional reason why Fuller was relatively invulnerable to attack from the right was the peculiar nature of its financial base. In the late 1970s, Fuller was dependent on fewer than two thousand contributors. Moreover, during these years approximately one-third of the school's gift income was coming from the trustees.[26] Careful cultivation of trustee loyalty, which David Hubbard carried out with great skill, could protect the seminary against the whims of popular opinion.

Fuller had thus established itself in a position highly unusual for evangelical institutions. As Nathan Hatch and Mark Noll have pointed out, one of the peculiarities of American evangelicalism is that its theological dis-putes are often settled in the court of popular opinion.[27] Whereas evangelicals appeal to the "Bible alone" for authority, they lack adequate mechanisms for settling differences on how the Bible is to be understood. Typically having weak views of the church or of central ecclesiatical authority, they cannot depend on synods or councils to adjudicate their disagreements. Nor is there any clear principle for establishing the authority of the expert theologians. The authority of anyone in most of evangelicalism thus depends on winning popu-lar support. Losers in disputes among theologians, or among competitors for theological influence, can always go to the court of popular opinion, as so often happened in the history of Fuller Seminary. Popular opinion has thus func-tioned as the evangelical pope, the ultimate court of appeal. *Vox populi vox papae.* Or perhaps popular opinion has more often provided, as in the late middle ages, multiple popes, each denouncing the others.

Like almost all evangelical institutions, Fuller Seminary was in its early days subject, at least partially, to such evangelical authority. While the funds from the Fuller Evangelistic Foundation provided it with some valuable immunity from those who would fan the fires of negative public opinion, Charles Fuller's radio ministry was especially vulnerable to the condemna-tions of the latest bull *vox populi* (à la Carl McIntire). Through its first two decades Fuller Seminary constantly operated in the shadow of such threatened censures. A decade later, when the pattern was repeated in the Lindsell at-tacks, the seminary reacted as though nothing much had changed and the threat was as great as ever. In fact, however, except for the real danger of losing

26. Figures for 1976–77, 1977–78, 1978–79, President's Board Report, October 26-28, 1980, addendum D, addendum E. Most of the trustee contributions, however, went to "restricted operations," and less than 10 percent of the "current operations" income came from trustees.

27. Nathan O. Hatch, "Evangelicalism as a Democratic Movement," in *Evangelicalism and Modern America*, ed. George Marsden (Grand Rapids: Eerdmans, 1984), 71-82; Mark A. Noll, *Between Faith and Criticism: Evangelicals, Scholarship, and the Bible in America* (San Francisco: Harper and Row, 1986).

trustee confidence, the seminary was now standing on a base of student and contributor support upon which old-line fundamentalist appeals could have little impact.

By the 1980s, the fundamentalist-evangelical versus progressive evangelical categories, though not forgotten, were no longer as central for understanding what was going on at Fuller. These categories had taken their classic shape in the storm surrounding Princeton Seminary in the 1920s, and they had dominated perceptions of Fuller through the 1970s. By then, however, the new broader evangelical coalition that Fuller had put together included many new concerns—especially in practical fields, charismatic ministries, and church growth—that raised issues that cut across the old lines of debate.

SIGNS OF A NEW ERA

Perhaps most telling in pointing out the departure from the old categories was that the primary controversy at Fuller in the mid-1980s was an anomaly in terms of the traditional fundamentalist-progressive disputes. These recent debates centered around a course, first introduced experimentally at the School of World Mission in the winter quarter of 1982. The course was "Signs, Wonders, and Church Growth," taught by C. Peter Wagner, a School of World Mission professor widely known for his writings on church growth, and John Wimber, a local charismatic pastor who in recent years had also been working with the Fuller Evangelistic Association (formerly Foundation). The unique feature of the course was that, not only did it analyze "signs and wonders" in Christian churches today, it also included "practical sessions" in which signs and wonders, including actual healings, were performed in class. The course was immensely popular, especially with the many charismatic students at the seminary. The seminary administration, characteristically, was at first willing to "hazard the risks" of such innovation, observing that indeed much of the church growth around the world was associated with charismatic signs.[28]

The questions that had separated fundamentalists from modernists through the first half of the twentieth century could typically be reduced to their different emphases on the natural and the supernatural in Christianity. Liberal Christianity emphasized the natural human elements in the development of biblical religion. Fundamentalists, partly by way of reaction, heightened traditional emphases on the supernatural. The "fundamentals," such as the virgin birth, the miracles of Christ, his bodily resurrection, and his second coming, all focused on miraculous divine interventions. Dispensationalism likewise stressed divine interventions in human history. The debate over inerrancy reflected the same issues. Inerrantists emphasized divine intervention and guidance in the inspiration of Scripture while extreme liberals saw it as a wholly human product. Progressive evangelicals stood somewhere in between.

---

28. See *Signs and Wonders Today*, compiled by Christian Life Magazine (Wheaton: Christian Life Magazine, 1983), 31-34, 63, and passim.

C. Peter Wagner

They wanted to affirm the divine origins of Scripture but give more practical weight than did the inerrantists to understanding it as also the product of human cultural circumstances. Prior to the 1980s, then, virtually all the debates at Fuller had centered around the efforts of the progressives to steer a course between the hypernaturalism of liberalism and the hypersupernaturalism of fundamentalism.

The signs and wonders controversy, however, involved new versions of the old issues and so changed some of the lineups. Charles Kraft, for instance, who would appear extremely progressive in terms of the theological categories of fundamentalist evangelicalism, was a vocal champion of the signs and wonders course (which he found nicely non-Western).[29] He was thus as much a champion of heightened supernaturalism as any fundamentalist.

29. Ibid., 62.

Some of the evangelical progressives of the School of Theology, on the other hand, were adamantly traditionalist in most of their theology. They were consequently chagrined at Peter Wagner's suggestion that Christians would be wise to exorcise their homes from demons, especially if they had traveled to pagan temples in foreign lands where the demons might have attached themselves to persons or luggage.[30] While classic fundamentalism placed great emphasis on miraculous signs and wonders during the New Testament era, it denied that they continued after that time. Progressive evangelicals on the other hand, because of their general principles of openness, had generally been more cordial toward pentecostalism and charismatics. But when it got down to debate over what was genuinely miraculous today, the old fundamentalist-progressive lines could no longer serve.

Yet there was some continuity in the signs and wonders debate insofar as the chief opponents of the course were the progressive veterans of the wars with fundamentalism. They had won the hard-fought battles for a moderate evangelicalism, in tune with classic Protestant-Augustianian theology and free from modern innovations from the right. Though they were eager for alliances with other evangelicals, such as with moderate pentecostals or charismatics, they feared new imbalances with the heightened supernaturalism of the signs and wonders party. These traditionalists were in control of the School of Theology and ultimately the School of Theology set the theological standards for the seminary as a whole.

In early 1987 the seminary accordingly issued a major statement on the ministry of miraculous healing. While this declaration allowed for healing ministries in churches and celebrated God's healing power wherever it occurred, it placed these affirmations in a context that demanded restraints. The report emphasized Christian sensitivity to the constant signs of God's wonderful power in the seemingly ordinary events of life. It cautioned against putting central emphasis on spectacular healings in contemporary ministries and urged that those who heal should open their work to verification and report failures as well as successes. It also raised the question of whether the current emphasis on healing reflected the standards of the secular "culture of entitlement" and whether the occasional healings of a few physical ailments were not celebrated out of proportion to Christ's continual work in caring for the multitudes of starving and suffering throughout the world.

Most forcefully, the document stated that while genuine "signs and wonders" were to be welcomed in churches, they were not appropriate to the Fuller academic setting. The critical evaluation essential to the classroom seemed hardly compatible with the experiential intensity of spectacular healings. Moreover, the institution was deeply divided by the signs and wonders course. "Our consensus is of our essence," the document stated.

Fuller did deeply wish to cultivate its ministry to the pentecostal and charismatic wings of evangelicalism. One evidence of this was the establish-

30. See C. Peter Wagner, "Can Demons Harm Christians?" *Christian Life*, May 1985, 76.

Students praying in the Signs and Wonders class for the healing of a classmate

ment in 1958 of the David J. du Plessis Center for Christian Spirituality. The center, founded with the cooperation of du Plessis, the father of the mid-twentieth century charismatic renewal, is a research center especially for pentecostal studies and is headed by Russell P. Spittler, associate dean at the School of Theology and an Assemblies of God minister. Despite building such solid ties with charismatic evangelicalism, Fuller in 1987 stated that that would not be its dominant position. Rather, the community declared:

> Our evangelical commitment disposes us strongly to the theology
> of the Reformation; but we are neither cultic evangelical nor sectar-
> ian Reformed. We embrace within our faculty men and women
> who represent, among others, the Pentecostal, the Anabaptist, and
> the Anglican traditions, and we treasure the many incalculable ways
> they have enriched and sometimes corrected our classic evangelical
> ethos.[31]

NEW LIGHTS AND OLD LIGHTS AGAIN

The debate at Fuller over signs and wonders was a version of an old evangelical tension in America dating back to the Great Awakening. Ever since revivalism first began to shape American Protestantism, churches had been divided into "old light" traditionalists and "new light" prorevivalists. In the

---

31. *Ministry and the Miraculous: A Case Study at Fuller Theological Seminary*, ed. Lewis B. Smedes, with a foreword by David Allan Hubbard (Waco, Tex.: Word, 1987), 73, 80, and passim. Quote is from the draft of December 11, 1986. Grant Wacker provides a critical appraisal of the document in "Wimber and Wonders—What about Miracles Today?" *Reformed Journal* 37 (April 1987): 16-19.

nineteenth century this division recurred in the split between Old School and New School Presbyterians. As we have seen, Fuller grew mainly out of the New School prorevivalist heritage, though it contained Old School elements insofar as it had identified with old Princeton. One way to read the first thirty years of the seminary's history is as the triumph of the New School elements in the tradition over the Old School.

Nonetheless, one feature of American evangelicalism, which is largely a succession of "new light" groups, is that the "new light" of one era will be superseded by the "new light" of the next. In the signs and wonders controversy, Fuller faced this succession and the concomitant questions: To what extent should a pragmatic openness set the agenda? To what extent must that openness be bounded by a theological tradition? The prorevivalist New School party in nineteenth-century America had been divided on this very issue. Now, so was American evangelicalism of the 1980s.

Fuller Seminary, however, because of its history of struggle against fundamentalist divisiveness, was determined to remain genuinely open and to hold the two evangelical traditions, essentially the Reformed and the pentecostal, together. Whether this could be done over the long term was yet to be seen. That it had already been accomplished on the scale seen at Fuller was a remarkable achievement in evangelical ecumenicity.

THE UNANSWERED QUESTIONS

Some questions remained, one of which grew out of the recurring theme of the relationship of the theoretical to the practical. At Fuller, the accepted tradition included not only a theology but also a certain American evangelical pragmatism. As I suggested in the preceding chapter, the tension between theory and practice was central in debates about Fuller's educational mission. The heritage was both classically theological and also pragmatic. Each had claims to represent the true genius of Fuller. In this respect, the spirit of each of the cofounders, Harold Ockenga and Charles Fuller, lived on. That the two had gotten along together as well and as long as they had was always remarkable. That they would continue could not be taken for granted.

Closely related was the question of how Fuller was to determine what was central to the institution and what was peripheral. In practice, the working principle of the institution appeared to be theology: the core of the school was still its classic theological program. Whatever had been added had been intended to complement that core rather than to supplant it. Fuller was still a *theological* seminary, but one in which there was a remarkable mix of the intellectual and the practical. The School of Theology and those in classic theological studies within it clearly had influence disproportional to their numbers. But what was to guarantee that theology in the traditional sense would remain the core?

This question, in turn, was part of the larger one already alluded to: How solid were the moorings and to what ultimately were they tied? This was a version of the larger and legitimate point that Lindsell was raising, even if his way of connecting it to the inerrancy issue seemed far too simplistic to most people at Fuller. Surely the seminary was still anchored by the evangelical faith and by its commitment, strengthened by its fundamentalist and neo-evangelical heritages, to remain evangelical rather than turn theologically liberal. But evangelicalism could mean many things. Lacking major ties to the institutional church and so always liable to change on an ad hoc basis, what might keep Fuller on any particular course? In the future how would one determine the authentic Fuller tradition? As it continued to strengthen its ties to mainline denominations, might the seminary eventually change directions in order to accommodate such supporting communities? Or, conceivably, would the charismatic tradition eventually become dominant? Again, the questions were about what was central and what peripheral. Clearly the personality of its leadership had more to do with anwering those questions than it would for most institutions.

As long as the leadership, both administratively and intellectually, was predominantly second generation, remembering first hand the traditions and priorities of the early days, these questions were not difficult to answer. At the center was not only the School of Theology but also a commitment both to a moderately conservative though open-minded educational philosophy and, more importantly, to a moderate evangelical, mostly Reformed theological tradition defined by the current creed. The key administrators, board members, and faculty, while welcoming representatives of all sorts of compatible positions, remained deeply attached to these central commitments made by the school in the 1960s.

As we have seen, evangelical institutions are typically ad hoc operations founded and controlled by personalities, often as family enterprises. In Fuller's case, the power of personality remained immensely important. The seminary of the 1970s and 1980s reflected the personality of David Hubbard. One could not overestimate the importance of his masterful leadership in holding so many strands of the evangelical coalition and in distinguishing the essential from the nonessential.

The question of succession, then, is the crucial one. Because of the relative freedom from external restraints, individuals in such free-standing evangelical settings have unusal opportunities for leadership. For the same reason, however, the lack of easy means to resolve the problem of succession is especially troubling. Fuller had already undergone one major crisis of succession. It might undergo others. How much continuity with its past it would maintain in future transitions, no one can predict.

Since the founding of the school, its leadership had been trying to rid itself of the nonessentials of its heritages while conserving the essences. Such separation of the gold from the dross was often a dangerous process, since the fires of purging could easily ignite the firestorms of controversies. Nonetheless, this ongoing process was one of the continuities throughout Fuller's first forty years.

Perhaps what was most remarkable among the continuities was that amid these fires, and in spite of them, a generation of Fuller Seminary graduates throughout the world, sometimes as divided as their mentors, were agents through which a brighter light could shine.

SOLI DEO GLORIA

APPENDIX

How Evangelicalism Has Changed

Surveys of Fuller Alumni, Current Fuller Students, and
Students at Other Evangelical Seminaries

DURING its first three and a half decades Fuller went through several
transitions, often involving struggles with its fundamentalist heritage:
Fuller was changing because the movement of which it was a part was changing. There is no way to get an exact index of such change, and the indications
that follow are considerably more inexact than all the numbers would suggest.
Yet they do give us some index of what has changed and what has not and also
some sense of what has changed most.

These impressions are based on two surveys. The more reliable is that
conducted by James Davison Hunter in 1982 as "The Evangelical Academy
Project." Hunter has described his methodology and his results in *Evangelicalism: The Coming Generation* (Chicago: University of Chicago Press, 1987). He
also generously furnished me with valuable material relevant to gauging Fuller's position in the whole of evangelical education today. Although in Hunter's
own study of evangelical seminaries and colleges he agreed not to compare one
school with another, the administration of Fuller Seminary, in its characteristic display of openness, agreed to let him isolate the views of Fuller School of
Theology students so that they could be compared with the collective views of
students at the other evangelical seminaries surveyed. These seminaries were
Talbot Theological Seminary in Los Angeles, Conservative Baptist Seminary
in Denver, Wheaton Graduate School in Wheaton, Illinois, Asbury Theological Seminary in Wilmore, Kentucky, Westminster Theological Seminary in
Philadephia, and Gordon-Conwell Theological Seminary in Hamilton, Massachusetts. Hunter's survey's were conducted on campuses and so had very
high rates of participation and statistical reliablity.

With this interesting material made available to me, I developed a
survey of Fuller alumni to sketch in a less formal way changes that might have
taken place at Fuller. In the spring of 1985, with lists furnished from the Fuller
alumni office, I sent questionnaires to two-thirds of the alumni (randomly
selected) from each of three eras: 1950–52 (the first classes); 1957–59 (the
Carnell era); and 1965–67 (the early Hubbard era). (This last group includes a
scattering of those who attended the School of Psychology or the School of
World Mission.) As well as asking some questions for my own purposes, I
included about a dozen questions exactly from Hunter's much longer survey.

For these, I asked alumni to describe their attitudes "just before attending Fuller," "when leaving Fuller," and "at present."

In addition to the limitations of any survey, this one also has the shortcoming of being based partly on recollections. Nonetheless, the patterns of responses differentiating the alumni of the three eras are consistently close enough to what one might expect from other evidence to suggest that the participants' recollections are at least somewhat reliable. The response rate, I am told, is highly respectable, especially when dealing with homogeneous elites. Surveys went to a total of 348 alumni; 194 (55.8 percent) returned them (with little deviation in the percentages among the three groups). Fifty-three alumni from 1950–52 responded, 67 from 1957–59, and 74 from 1965–67. Seventy-three percent of these respondents said they were ordained. Forty percent described themselves as pastors, 9 percent as missionaries. I am most grateful to each of the alumni who helped with this project.

Here are the more interesting results.

CHARACTERIZATION OF FULLER STUDENTS AND STAFF

Theological Characterization

A number of the questions presented the following characterizations, allowing respondents to choose *just one* answer from the following: traditional/confessional, charismatic, liberal, neo-orthodox, fundamentalist, evangelical, other (please specify).

1. How would you characterize the theological stance of Fuller at the time you attended it?

2. Which of the above positions do you think *best* describes Fuller's theological position today?

3. Your own theological stance today?

4. Your own stance at the time just *before* you came to Fuller?

The answers to these questions were not startling.

Alumni overwhelmingly (87 percent) characterized Fuller at the time they attended it as evangelical. Graduates of the three eras varied little on this. The only notable variation is that about 9 percent of the 1950–52 group called it fundamentalist. Unfortunately, however, the meaning of *fundamentalism* has narrowed since 1950, and one cannot tell whether alumni were using today's usage or that of 1950.

Seventy percent of alumni still characterize *Fuller today* as evangelical. Only about 7 percent would call it neo-orthodox, and 4 percent call it traditional/confessional (other characterizations are scattered).

Almost the same number of alumni (69 percent) characterize *themselves* today as "evangelical," with the only other substantial figure being 11 percent who characterize themselves as traditional/confessional. Only one alumnus in 194 characterized himself as neo-orthodox. Only five classified themselves as charismatic. Seven said they were liberal.

   Alumni characterizations differ little from Fuller student evaluations of their own stances in James Hunter's 1982 survey (which offered the identical choices). The only notable difference is that 14 percent of the 1982 students characterized themselves as charismatic. (At the other evangelical seminaries only 7 percent chose charismatic.) About 7 percent of Fuller students said they were traditional/confessional. (Other responses were scattered.) Only 2 percent of them said they were neo-orthodox, suggesting again that this characterization, which one sometimes hears in regard to Fuller from conservatives today, has not been much perceived at Fuller itself.[1]
   None said he or she was liberal.
   The one notable evidence these questions yield of any shift at Fuller is in the alumni's characterizations of their own views *just before* attending Fuller. Forty percent of 1950–52 alumni said they were fundamentalist before attending Fuller compared to 24 percent of 1957–59 alumni and 16 percent of 1965–67 alumni who said the same. (Almost all the rest said they were evangelical.) Two percent of 1982 Fuller students said they were fundamentalists. (At other evangelical seminaries it was 5 percent.)

Would You Recommend Fuller to a Promising Student Today?

Another evidence of the change is that a significantly higher percentage (24 percent) of responding alumni from the 1950–52 period answered this question no than from the two later periods, for each of which the number answering no stayed around 13 percent.

Most Influential Professors

Alumni were asked, "While you were at Fuller, which professors had the greatest impact on you. (List no more than three, in order of influence, if possible.)"
   The top five finishers for the three eras were

1950-52	1957-59	1965-67
1. Carnell (decisively)	Carnell (decisively)	
		Carnell (barely)
2. Smith	Smith	Ladd
3. Harrison (close)	Harrison (still close)	Hubbard
4. Henry	Jewett	Jewett
5. La Sor	Ladd	Harrison

   1. One indication that neo-orthodox views are not dominant, although no doubt found among the Fuller faculty (and celebrated at a gala Karl Barth centennial at Fuller in May 1986), is an article by three professors at the School of Theology—Colin Brown, Richard Muller, and Richard Mouw—criticizing Barth for his departures from traditional Reformed orthodoxy. "Now that the Party's Over: Was Karl Barth that Good?" *Reformed Journal*, March 1987, 16-22.

One notable feature of these results that did not come through as clearly from interviews with alumni is Wilbur Smith's influence. About 40 percent of respondents from the first two eras (45 percent from the first era and 35 percent from the second) listed Smith as among the three most influential. Carnell's early popularity was impressive. He was listed by about 80 percent of the alumni from the first era and 75 percent from the second. The other notable feature is that, despite the numerous reports of Carnell's difficulties in his later years, he still retained a student following, though he was listed in the top three by only about 33 percent of the respondents from the latter period. One alumnus said that students in the sixties were either very pro-Carnell or quite negative about him. In any case, by the 1960s the faculty influence was spread about more evenly.

The remainder of the Appendix is based on responses to either or both surveys—my survey of Fuller alumni of the three periods and Hunter's survey of Fuller and other evangelical seminaries in 1982. A series of questions was put to the survey participants, and each person was asked to agree or disagree, or they were asked to choose from a range of supplied answers the *one* statement that was *closest* to their views. Unless otherwise noted, the percentages are of those who gave positive responses: those who answered the questions yes, or those who assented to the given statement. The answers in the alumni survey are further broken down into three categories, indicating the respondent's characterization of his or her views "just before attending Fuller Seminary," "when leaving Fuller Seminary," and "at present." These three different percentages are listed in this order from left to right. (The figures may not add up to exactly 100 percent because of rounding off.)

DOCTRINE

The Bible

Predictably, the biggest change at Fuller has been the decreasing adherence to the strict inerrancy of Scripture. Fuller students were presented with the following statements and asked to choose the one that best characterized their position.

1. The Bible is the inspired Word of God, not mistaken in its statements and teachings, and is to be taken literally, word for word.

1950-52	1957-59	1965-67	FTS 1982	Others 1982
75/61/48%	60/46/37%	43/25/22%	15%	51%

Note: Other evangelical seminary students were in 1982 about where Fuller students were in the 1950s. Many early Fuller alumni still affirm inerrancy.

2. The Bible is the inspired Word of God, not mistaken in its teachings, but is not always to be taken literally in its statements concerning matters of science, historical reporting, etc.

1950-52	1957-59	1965-67	FTS 1982	Others 1982
21/37/44%	40/52/57%	54/72/58%	82%	46%

3. The Bible becomes the Word of God for a person when he read[s] it in faith.

1950-52	1957-59	1965-67	FTS 1982	Others 1982
2/0/4%	0/2/5%	3/1/11%	3%	2%

Note: This is something like a neo-orthodox statement. There is virtually no evidence that Fuller ever successfully taught this position.

4. The Bible is an ancient book of legends, history, and moral precepts recorded by men.

1950-52	1957-59	1965-67	FTS 1982	Others 1982
0/0/4%	0/0/2%	0/0/6%	1%	0%

5. Don't Know. Negligible responses.

Life after Death

Alumni and students were asked: "Which *one* of these statements comes *closest* to describing your feelings about life after death?" The number of persons from any group selecting any of the first three answers was negligible except that 4 percent of the 1965–67 alumni choose number 1 and another 4 percent choose number 2 as the best description of their present position. This 8 percent of nonevangelicals among the alumni respondents from this era shows up in almost all the subsequent answers.

1. There is no life after death. See above; otherwise negligible responses.

2. There is life after death but what a person does in this life has no bearing on it. See above; otherwise negligible responses.

3. Heaven is a divine reward for those who earn it by their good life. Negligible responses.

4. The only hope of Heaven is through personal faith in Jesus Christ *except* for those who have not had the opportunity to hear of Jesus.

1950-52	1957-59	1965-67	FTS 1982	Others 1982
13/25/25%	21/27/29%	30/34/46%	43%	28%

Note: This question fairly effectively separates progressive evangelicals from conservative evangelicals. Presumably respondents choosing this answer would be less enthusiastic about missions than those choosing answer number 5.

5. The only hope for Heaven is through personal faith in Jesus Christ.

1950-52	1957-59	1965-67	FTS 1982	Others 1982
87/75/73%	79/71/65%	70/62/47%	56%	72%

Note: Even in the earliest decades about one quarter of the graduating students dissented from this, the strict evangelical view of this matter. This figure is similar to that at other evangelical seminaries in 1982. At Fuller the percentage of those who assent to the strict view has fallen (but little since the 1960s), though a majority still take that view. Apparently this is another doctrine on which the interdenominational evangelical leadership has been divided for some time.

Hell

Do you personally believe in a place of eternal torment for those who do not believe in Jesus Christ?

1950-52	1957-59	1965-67	FTS 1982	Others 1982
96/94/90%	92/88/78%	90/85/71%	86%	98%

Note: On this and most other questions, both doctrinal and ethical, Fuller students as of 1982 were overwhelmingly conservative. The difference between the Fuller student body and those at the other evangelical seminaries is little on most matters except for a more progressive element at Fuller (more or less 10 percent), which is evident here.

OTHER DOCTRINES: FULLER AND OTHER EVANGELICAL SEMINARIES, 1982

The following results are from questions on the Hunter survey but not on the alumni survey.

Jesus Christ

1. Jesus Christ was a man, but was divine in the sense that God worked through Him; He was the Son of God. FTS: 4% Others: 2%
2. Jesus Christ is both fully God and fully man. FTS: 96% Others: 98%
3. Jesus Christ is not God or the Son of God, but a great religious teacher. FTS: 1% Others: 0.2%
4. Don't Know. FTS: 0% Others: 0.2%

The Devil

1. The Devil is a personal *being* who directs evil forces and influences people to do wrong. FTS: 82% Others: 92%
2. The Devil is an impersonal *force* that influences people to do wrong. FTS: 8% Others: 3%
3. The Devil does not exist, either as a being or a force. FTS: 3% Others: 0.3%
4. Can't Say. FTS: 7% Others: 1%

Human Origins

1. God created Adam and Eve, which was the start of human life. FTS: 56% Others: 86%
2. God began an evolutionary cycle for all living things, including man, but personally intervened at a point in time and transformed man into a human being in His own image. FTS: 27% Others: 10%
3. God began an evolutionary cycle for all living things, including

man, but *did not* personally intervene at a point in time and transform man into a human being in His own image. FTS: 3% Others: 0%

    4. Man evolved from other animals. FTS: 1% Others: 0%

    5. Can't Say. FTS: 14% Others: 4%

Biblical Account of Origins

    1. The world was created in six twenty-four hour days. FTS: 15% Others: 34%

    2. The world was created in six days but each day was an age corresponding roughly to a geological age or period. FTS: 24% Others: 32%

    3. The Biblical account of the origin of the world is intended to be symbolic and not literal. FTS: 42% Others: 15%

    4. Can't say. FTS: 20% Others: 19%

Christ's Return

Jesus Christ Will Physically Return to Earth. FTS: 96% Others: 99%

Premillennial Views of Christ's Coming

(If Yes [to above]) Do you believe his coming will be to save the church, judge the world, and to establish a thousand-year reign? FTS: 75% Others: 83%

Charismatic Characterization

Do you consider yourself a pentecostal or charismatic Christian? FTS: 44% Others: 27%

Tongue Speaking

Have You Ever Spoken in Tongues? FTS: 43% Others: 32%

ETHICS: FULLER PAST AND PRESENT

Here again, the sets of three figures under 1950–52, etc., refer to the respondents' views "just before attending Fuller," "when leaving Fuller," and "at present."

God-Given Moral Code?

    1. God has given very clear, detailed rules that apply to everyone.

1950-52	1957-59	1965-67	FTS 1982	Others 1982
63/52/44%	63/48/47%	54/39/34%	28%	50%

    2. God has given us some general rules, but we have to decide how to apply them to our own situation.

1950-52	1957-59	1965-67	FTS 1982	Others 1982
36/46/48%	30/47/42%	38/48/49%	61%	47%

3. God gives rules, but the rules may be different for different people.

1950-52	1957-59	1965-67	FTS 1982	Others 1982
0/0/2%	3/5/8%	4/6/3%	6%	2%

4. I don't think that God has given us rules.

1950-52	1957-59	1965-67	FTS 1982	Others 1982
0/0/6%	0/0/2%	3/4/10%	3%	1%

5. I am really not sure.

1950-52	1957-59	1965-67	FTS 1982	Others 1982
0/2/0%	3/0/2%	1/3/4%	2%	0%

Note: In their responses to these five questions, early alumni's recollections of their views as students are almost identical to the views of students at other evangelical seminaries today. As usual the 1957–59 alumni are closer to those of the early 1950s than to those of the 1960s.

Drinking Alcohol Wrong?

	1950-52	1957-59	1965-67	FTS 1982	Others 1982
ALWAYS	60/44/25%	46/31/15%	21/14/6%	7%	13%
USUALLY	31/42/48%	43/51/46%	57/49/40%	27%	48%
RARELY	6/8/23%	8/12/29%	19/32/43%	48%	27%
NEVER	2/2/2%	2/3/6%	3/4/6%	3%	3%
?	2/4/2%	/3/3%	0/1/6%	15%	9%

Note: There has been a major change in views on drinking alcohol. Unlike on most other topics, early FTS alumni were, and still are, more conservative on this than other evangelical seminarians in 1982 are. Yet a fair number of the early alumni have changed. As other reports indicate, the most dramatic change at Fuller was between the students of the late 1950s and those of the 1960s.

Premarital Sexual Intercourse Wrong?

	1950-52	1957-59	1965-67	FTS 1982	Others 1982
ALWAYS	96/92/84%	88/85/75%	84/77/66%	79%	96%
USUALLY	4/8/12%	10/12/18%	12/19/19%	17%	4%
RARELY	0/0/2%	0/3/3%	3/3/10%	1%	0%
NEVER	0/0/0%	0/0/0%	1/1/3%*	0%	0%
?	0/0/2%	1/0/3%	0/0/3%	2%	0%

Note: There has not been as much change on this issue as on others over the years and hardly any change at Fuller since the 1960s.
      *Two truly hard-core liberals—or saboteurs of surveys—from the 1965–67 group show up here. These are the only two, among any of the groups surveyed, to say that premarital sexual intercourse is never wrong.

Homosexual Relations between Consenting Adults Wrong?

	1950-52	1957-59	1965-67	FTS 1982	Others 1982
ALWAYS	100/96/91%	96/91/81%	93/89/75%	92%	98%
USUALLY	0/4/8%	3/6/12%	3/7/12%	5%	2%
RARELY	0/0/1%	0/0/4%	1/1/5%	1%	0%
NEVER	0/0/0%	0/0/0%	3/3/6%	1%	0%
?	0/0/0%	1/3/3%	0/0/1%	2%	0%

Note: Relatively little has changed on this issue within the evangelical community. Alumni of all groups are somewhat more liberal in 1985 than were members of any group when they were students.

Extramarital Sexual Intercourse Wrong?

	1950-52	1957-59	1965-67	FTS 1982	Others 1982
ALWAYS	100/96/90%	96/93/85%	92/88/81%	92%	99%
USUALLY	0/4/8%	3/6/12%	7/11/15%	7%	1%

Note: The number of responses to the other choices was negligible. Only one of the 1965–67 group proved totally without scruples and responded that extramarital sexual intercourse is never wrong.

Abortion: Fuller and Other Evangelical Seminaries, 1982

1. Abortion is always acceptable. FTS: 0% Others: 0%
2. Abortion is acceptable under most circumstances. FTS: 2% Others: 1%
3. Abortion is acceptable only under certain extreme circumstances. FTS: 87% Others: 72%
4. Abortion is never acceptable. FTS: 9% Others: 27%
5. No opinion. FTS: 2% Others: 1%

Note: The above responses are from Hunter's 1982 survey. The following question, asking about abortion in another way (in a long list of questions on public issues), gets a much different sounding result.

[Should there be] a ban on all abortions?

	FTS	Others
MOSTLY FAVOR	46%	72%
MOSTLY OPPOSE	46%	22%
NO OPINION	8%	5%

VIEW OF WOMEN'S ROLE: FULLER AND OTHER EVANGELICAL SEMINARIES

Family and Career

A woman should put her husband and children ahead of her career.

	FTS	Others
STRONGLY AGREE	14%	31%
AGREE	42%	50%
NEITHER AGREE NOR DISAGREE	24%	14%
DISAGREE	14%	6%
STRONGLY DISAGREE	6%	1%

Husband the Spiritual Head

The husband is primarily responsible for the spiritual well-being of the family.

	FTS	Others
STRONGLY AGREE	10%	36%
AGREE	41%	46%
NEITHER AGREE NOR DISAGREE	17%	8%
DISAGREE	23%	8%
STRONGLY DISAGREE	9%	1%

Note: There is a substantial difference here between Fuller and the other seminaries, with the responses agree or strongly agree representing 51 percent of the students at Fuller but 82 percent of the students at other seminaries.

Husband Has Final Say

The husband has the "final say" in the family decision making.

	FTS	Others
STRONGLY AGREE	7%	21%
AGREE	25%	49%
NEITHER AGREE NOR DISAGREE	24%	14%
DISAGREE	29%	13%
STRONGLY DISAGREE	15%	3%

Note: A third of Fuller students agree or strongly agree; at other seminaries these categories were chosen by 60 percent of the student body.

The Ordination of Women to the Ministry

	FTS	Others
MOSTLY FAVOR	80%	42%
MOSTLY OPPOSE	15%	48%
NO OPINION	5%	10%

Note: Here, as might be expected, is an even larger area of difference between Fuller and the others.

POLITICS: FULLER AND OTHER EVANGELICAL SEMINARIES

Your Political Position

	1950-52	1957-59	1965-67	FTS 1982	Others 1982
VERY LIBERAL	2/2/2%	2/3/2%	1/1/3%	2%	1%
LIBERAL	4/4/11%	2/3/11%	11/11/13%	13%	7%
MODERATE	23/25/32%	27/32/40%	24/35/40%	56%	41%
CONSERVATIVE	63/64/47%	59/58/44%	53/49/42%	28%	49%
VERY CONS.	9/6/8%	11/5/3%	11/5/1%	1%	3%

Note: On the whole Fuller stays on the conservative side, though not as much as evangelicals generally. Taking each group as a whole, there seem to be remarkably close correlations between political, theological, and ethical conservatism. At Fuller, the strong conservative leaning of the constituency in the early years is confirmed (70-72 percent of the two earlier groups being either conservative or very conservative). The biggest shift appears to be from conservative to moderate from the 1960s to the 1980s. Very few identify themselves as liberal in any period.

Social Reform or Evangelism

Do you feel that the pursuit of social, economic, and political justice in the world is more important, just as important, almost as important, or less important than telling the world about the claims of Christ?

	1950-52	1957-59	1965-67	FTS 1982	Others 1982
MORE	0/0/4%	2/0/3%	1/1/4%	1%	1%
JUST AS	6/10/20%	3/8/17%	12/14/23%	37%	18%
ALMOST AS	10/16/16%	14/21/36%	15/33/30%	32%	32%
LESS	84/75/60%	82/71/44%	71/52/42%	30%	49%

Note: While evangelicals remained agreed that social justice is not more important than evangelism, there appears a significant shift, especially from the 1960s to the 1980s, from those who think it less important to those who think it at least almost as important. Just as important has risen dramatically at Fuller also. Unlike the trends on most other questions, the other seminarians in 1982 are considerably more ready to give a high priority to social issues than were the Fuller seminarians of the 1950s. This could reflect the influence of the resurgent conservative Christian politics in the 1980s. These results confirm the strong priority on evangelism at the early Fuller and in the original new evangelicalism.

Taking Part in Political Protests

	1950-52	1957-59	1965-67	FTS 1982	Others 1982
ALWAYS WRONG	4/2/0%	3/3/1%	7/1/0%	0%	1%
USUALLY WRONG	44/44/33%	41/36/24%	22/15/12%	10%	14%
RARELY WRONG	38/42/53%	36/42/53%	51/56/63%	69%	60%
NEVER WRONG	0/0/2%	9/8/12%	15/22/18%	15%	11%
CAN'T DECIDE	15/12/12%	11/11/11%	5/5/7%	7%	14%

Note: These results confirm that there was some very solid political conservatism at the early Fuller. Then, apparently, almost half the students were against protests. The lack of resemblance between the early Fuller and other evangelical seminaries today may again be explained by the rise of conservative political groups that champion protests.

Registering for the Draft

	1950-52	1957-59	1965-67	FTS 1982	Others 1982
ALWAYS WRONG	8/8/6%	2/2/0%	0/0/3%	5%	3%
USUALLY WRONG	6/6/10%	2/2/5%	7/7/4%	5%	4%
RARELY WRONG	27/29/38%	33/34/48%	27/30/34%	45%	39%
NEVER WRONG	60/58/46%	59/58/41%	62/58/54%	36%	46%
CAN'T DECIDE	0/0/0%	5/5/6%	4/6/6%	10%	9%

Note: The one surprise here is that in the 1950–52 group about 14 percent recall viewing registration for the draft as always or usually wrong. This is difficult to account for. Almost none of the students at the time came from anabaptist denominations.

OTHER POLITICAL VIEWS: FULLER AND OTHER EVANGELICAL SEMINARIES

Christianity as U.S. Official Religion?

Would you support a constitutional amendment to make Christianity the official religion of the United States?

	FTS 1982	Others 1982
YES	11%	13%
NO	89%	87%

Note: The percentages of positive responses show there is still a core support for this view after two hundred years of disestablishment of religion.

The Moral Majority

From as much as you know about the Moral Majority, would you say you

	FTS 1982	Others 1982
STRONGLY APPROVE	2%	6%
APPROVE	25%	42%
NEITHER APPROVE NOR DISAPPROVE	24%	27%
DISAPPROVE	36%	19%
STRONGLY DISAPPROVE	14%	5%

Need More Socialism?

The U.S. would be better off if it moved toward socialism.

	FTS 1982	Others 1982
STRONGLY AGREE	1%	1%
AGREE	13%	7%
NEITHER AGREE NOR DISAGREE	34%	23%
DISAGREE	41%	46%
STRONGLY DISAGREE	12%	23%

Note: As in their theological views, Fuller students remained overwhelmingly conservative to moderate in their politics, only slightly, although perceptibly, to the left of their evangelical counterparts.

Index